A STUDY OF SHAKESPEARE AND OF

ELIZABETHAN SPORT

He that will understand Shakespeare must not be content to study him in the closet, he must look for his meaning sometimes among the sports of the field—DR JOHNSON

THE DIARY OF MASTER WILLIAM SILENCE

A STUDY OF SHAKESPEARE & OF ELIZABETHAN SPORT

BY THE

RIGHT HON. D. H. MADDEN
VICE-CHANCELLOR OF THE UNIVERSITY OF DUBLIN

GREENWOOD PRESS, PUBLISHERS
NEW YORK

Originally published in 1897
by Longmans, Green & Co.

First Greenwood Reprinting 1969

Library of Congress Catalogue Card Number 78-89018

SBN 8371-2322-4

PRINTED IN UNITED STATES OF AMERICA

PREFACE

A GOOD many years ago accident brought to my knowledge the sport of hunting the wild red deer, which has been carried on in the Forest of Exmoor from time immemorial in accordance with ancient usage. The existence and nature of this pursuit had not as yet become matters of common knowledge. The Master at that time was Mr. Fenwick Bisset, an Irish gentleman settled in Somersetshire, to whom the sport owed its excellence and fame, if not its continued existence. Mr. Samuel Warren, of Dulverton, was secretary; the huntsman, Arthur Heal, was at the zenith of his fame; and the Rev. John Russell, although some seventy years had passed (so I learned from his lips) since he first hunted the wild red deer, had not as yet entered upon the duties of the parish in which he spent the last years of his life.

Beginning and ending with the long vacation, the wild sport of stag-hunting offered many attractions to one whose professional labours forbade him to yield to stronger temptations presented by Irish sport during the working months of the year. Again and again I revisited those happy hunting grounds, and in each succeeding autumn the thoroughly Shakespearian character of the sport and of its surroundings impressed me more and more. I began by collecting passages illustrating the scenes with which I became familiar. Then came the idea of a stag-hunt, after the manner of *The Noble Arte of Venerie* and of Exmoor, in which a description of the various incidents of the chase might serve to illustrate and to connect the scattered passages in which Shakespeare has recorded his recollections of the harbouring, the unharbouring, the hunting, the baying, and the breaking up of the hart.

The hounds were of necessity Master Robert Shallow's, and the tale was naturally told by Master William Silence, the lettered member of the family group.

Thus attracted to the study of Elizabethan sport, and gaining some knowledge of what Ben Jonson calls 'the hawking language,' I proceeded to conduct my Gloucestershire friends, with certain additions to their number, through a variety of scenes, in the company of William Silence, who records his experiences in a diary, and who finally collects certain notes, the loss of which I endeavour to supply in a chapter entitled *The Horse in Shakespeare*. Every lover of the horse who is a student of Shakespeare must have been struck by the number and appropriateness of his references to horses and to horsemanship ; and I found that some passages which once seemed obscure became clear, and that others gained a new significance, in the light of such knowledge of the old-world phraseology of the manage as may be acquired from the copious sources of information set forth in a note entitled *The Book of Sport*.

Thus, little by little, in successive vacations and spare moments of time, and in varying scenes, the book grew, and with it my amazement at Shakespeare's knowledge of the most intimate secrets of woodcraft and falconry, and, above all, of the nature and disposition of the horse. In his use of this knowledge for the illustration of human character, thought, and action, he stands alone. To understand the lessons which he would thus teach us, it is necessary to know the language in which they are conveyed, and to most readers the languages of ancient woodcraft, of the manage,

and of falconry are unknown tongues. I venture to hope
that these pages may in some degree aid the student
of Shakespeare in following the advice of Dr. Johnson
prefixed to this volume, and that he may succeed in finding
in the sports of the field a meaning which escaped him in
the study.

Whenever a knowledge of the incidents or of the terminology of Elizabethan sport suggested a departure from the
text of *The Globe Shakespeare*, which I have generally
adopted, I have noted the variance. The consequence has
uniformly been to restore the reading of the Folio of 1623.
This circumstance suggested an inquiry into the authority of
this edition, which I refer to as 'the Folio.' The result
is embodied in a note entitled *The Critical Significance of
Shakespeare's Allusions to Field Sports*, in which I venture to
present, for the consideration of Shakespearian critics, certain
matters of fact and certain suggestions which forced themselves on my attention during the progress of my studies.

I have to acknowledge with gratitude the assistance which
I received from Dr. INGRAM (Senior Fellow of Trinity College,
Dublin) and from Mr. PALMER (Fellow of Trinity College),
who have kindly read the proof-sheets of this volume as it
came through the press.

I believe that the book requiring least apology from
its author is one which adds to our understanding and
appreciation of the work or character of one of the great
men whom our race has produced. Whether these pages
have in this way justified their existence, it is for their
readers to determine.

D. H. MADDEN.

April 23, 1897.

CONTENTS

NOTES

CHAPTER I

THE DIARY

O, like a book of sport thou'lt read me o'er ;
But there's more in me than thou understand'st.
Troilus and Cressida.

ALTHOUGH the fact is not recorded in Camden's *Britannia*, you may rest assured that for many centuries the worshipful house of Shallow was of repute in Gloucestershire. The family is now extinct ; but the blood and quality of Shallow are so widely diffused throughout the three kingdoms that the fact need hardly be regretted.

The founder of this ancient house, one Robert de Châtelhault, is said to have flourished in the time of Henry II. Tradition asserts that he served as a butt for the rude witticisms of the Court, and that the King at the instigation of Thomas Becket conferred on him a grant of a large tract of land in the 'wilds of Gloucestershire,' in order (as the Chancellor suggested) that he might hold somewhat *in capite* in default of brains.

This practical joke endowed the courtier with possessions rather extensive than valuable, and the successive representatives of the house were never particularly successful in their efforts to increase them. They had an unhappy knack of attaching themselves to the losing side, not from any generous sympathy with the weaker, but from a firm belief in its prospects of success. They never happened to hit off the right answer to the question put to one of them on a noteworthy occasion,—'under which King, Besonian ? '

Partly from these causes, and partly by reason of some clever, but unlucky, dispositions of their money (among which was a sum of one thousand pounds advanced to one Sir John Falstaff, but not repaid) the estates and possessions of the house decreased rather than increased as years rolled by. It was probably due to inattention to spelling and to the niceties of pronunciation that the family name declined from the high-sounding Châtel-hault to the more homely Shallow:—causes which have sufficed to convert De la Pole into Poole, Bourchier into Butcher, Grenville into Greenfield, and De Vere into Weir. The losses, however, as well as the adventures of the family, were on a provincial scale. The head of the house was always a man of considerable position in his county; and, save in the cut of his beard and the fashion of his clothes, there was but little difference between the Robert de Châtel-hault of the Plantagenets and the Robert Shallow of the Tudors.

Now, whatever you may think of this account of the name and ancestry of Robert Shallow (and it is quite as trustworthy as many given by heralds) the man himself was, beyond all doubt, a fact. There was in the year of grace 1586 one Robert Shallow, Esquire, justice of the peace, if not also of the quorum, and custos rotulorum. The name by which he was known to the Gloucestershire folk of the day is a trifling matter of detail. It was quite as much a matter of course for this Robert Shallow and his ancestors to keep a kennel of hounds, as to write themselves 'armigero' in any bill, warrant, quittance, or obligation—for the Shallows could mostly write their names and additions. In his park, the dappled fallow deer yielded their lives to the crossbow of the woodman, and were coursed with greyhounds after the fashion of a long-forgotten sport, highly esteemed by our ancestors. His falcon, stooping from her pride of place, struck the mallard by the river banks, and when his tercel-gentle shook his bells, the partridge cowering in the stubble dared not stir a wing. His greyhounds contended for the silver-studded collar, the prize awarded at the games on Cotswold.

Trout were caught by tickling in the peculiar river of the Justice, and the young dace was a bait for the old pike in the sluggish Severn. To supply his larder, springes were set to catch woodcocks, birds were taken with lime-twigs, and bat-fowling was not despised, in the absence of better sport. Is it not as certain that Master Silence took part in his kins-man's sports, as that he sang snatches of song after supper in his hall?. What fitter name than Slender for the little man with cane-coloured beard—out of his element, and therefore very like a fool, in company with sweet Anne Page, but of whom a different account would be given by the sportsmen on Cotswold, by the warrener with whom he fought, or by the bear-ward when Sackerson was loose? Master Shallow, we may be sure, would never have troubled himself to push the fortunes of his kinsman Slender, if he had not been beholden to him for something beyond the occasional services of his man Simple. What could Master Slender do for the Justice, but look after his hounds and hawks? Such a hanger-on was a recognised part of the establishment of an old-fashioned country gentleman.

To join in the Justice's sports, the yeomen of the country and burgesses of the neighbouring towns were made heartily welcome, after the good old fashion which still survives in the custom of the English hunting field. The name of one only of the company thus assembled can be stated with absolute certainty, for he has recorded the incidents of each sport with an accuracy unattainable even to the highest genius save by actual experience. It is the name of William Shakespeare.

It so happens that by a curious train of circumstances I became possessed of a record of certain events in the history of this Robert Shallow and his fellows, which took place in the autumn of the year 1586. The story is as follows. In my boyhood I was a frequent visitor at an old-fashioned house in one of the southern counties of Ireland, the home of a family of English descent. The first of the race who settled in Ireland obtained a grant of a portion of the vast

estates forfeited by the Earl of Desmond. Sir William (so
he was known in the family) gave his name to a massive
square tower or keep, the oldest part of the rambling and
dilapidated residence of his descendants. A chronicle in stone,
the old house presented to the eye a sensible record of the
vicissitudes endured by the adopted country of Sir William.
The entrance hall had been the refectory of a Cistercian
abbey, founded by the piety of some forgotten Geraldine.
This portion of the ancient building had been incorporated
with the massive castle erected by Sir William, for the construction of which the remainder of the conventual buildings
served as a convenient quarry. The abbey church indeed was
spared, and mouldered hard at hand, scarcely concealed from
sight by thickly growing laurels. Of Sir William's castle,
one tower only remained. The rest of the building had been
demolished by one of Cromwell's lieutenants. The earth-
works on which his cannon were planted, known to this day
as Cromwell's Camp, are plainly traceable in an adjacent
field. For several generations, the descendants of Sir
William gloomily surveyed the desolation of his castle from
the tower which bore his name; but as times improved they
constructed out of the ruins a moderate-sized dwelling-house,
in the style of solemn hideousness which prevailed in the
early years of the Georges. The upper room in Sir William's
tower had always a strange fascination for my imagination.
It was used as a lumber-room, and contained a mixed assortment of broken furniture, old newspapers and account books,
oaken boxes, and worm-eaten books too unsightly for the
book-cases which lined the walls of the room beneath, dignified by the name of the library.

In course of time the old place passed into the possession
of a more distant relation ; and, my own employments leading
me into different paths, I had all but forgotten Sir William's
tower, when I chanced to meet its owner in a London street.
I dined with him at his hotel, and listened to his lamenta-
tions over the state of the country, by which I understood
him to mean the neglected condition of fox coverts and the

destruction of foxes. After dinner he produced a bundle of mouldy papers closely written over in an antique hand, which, he said, had been found among some title deeds in an oaken chest in Sir William's tower. He had brought them with him, thinking that some one might tell him what they were about. "I tried to make them out," said my worthy kinsman; "but I could not get very far. There is a lot of rubbish about lyme-hounds, vauntlays, hunting at force, and hawking, that I cannot make head or tail of. But the fellow is no sportsman, for he calls the hounds ' dogs,' and says a fox may be killed by gins, snares, as well as by hunting, so that you get rid of the vermin anyhow. When I came to that, I could read no more. But I thought that somebody might make something of it. However, I'm glad I met with you. You're welcome to it. It's of no use to me."

I took the papers home, and on examining them I found that they consisted of a journal, in which the writer (who was evidently Sir William, the founder of the family) had recorded with much minuteness the events of some days spent at his father's house in Gloucestershire in the autumn of 1586, shortly before he left England to adventure for Ireland. The journal was kept, the writer said, to preserve for old age a record of the happiest days of his life. The narrative begins with a memorable chase of a hart far into the Cotswold hills, and proceeds to tell of sport with the fallow deer in the park of some Gloucestershire Justice, apparently a kinsman of the writer. Various experiences in hawking are narrated, together with some matters of a personal nature, relating to the writer and one Mistress Anne whose father was a Cotswold man, and an old friend of the Justice.

My interest was excited no less by the date of the manuscript, than by its association with Sir William's tower, for I had long been a student of Elizabethan literature, and had taken pains to make myself acquainted with the manners and customs of the age of Shakespeare, Bacon, Marlowe, Ben Jonson, and Spenser. As I read and re-read the narrative, I became more and more conscious of living in the midst of scenes with which I had been long familiar The sensation was borne in· on me of having heard all this before, I knew not how or when. By degrees the figures, hazy and undefined at first, began to assume definite forms. There was no mistaking the Gloucestershire Justice for any other than Master Shallow, and this clue once obtained, it was easy to identify Abraham Slender, Justice Silence, Will Squele, and the rest. The writer was evidently a man of some education. He had been brought up at Oxford, and was a member of one of the Inns of Court. From his references to a sister named Ellen, and to Justice Shallow as his kinsman, I had no doubt whatever as to his identity. He was plainly William, the son of the Gloucestershire gentleman whom we know by the name of Silence.

Shal. And how doth my good cousin Silence?

Sil. Good morrow, good cousin Shallow.

Shal. And how doth my cousin, your bedfellow? and your fairest daughter and mine, my god-daughter Ellen?

Sil. Alas, a black ousel, cousin Shallow!

Shal. By yea and nay, sir, I dare say my cousin William is become a good scholar : he is at Oxford still, is he not?

Sil. Indeed, sir, to my cost.

Shal. A' must, then, to the inns o' court shortly.

2 Hen. IV. iii. 2. 3.

There were frequent references to some stranger from a neighbouring town, a visitor at the house of one whom I identified as Clement Perkes of the Hill—the honest yeoman for whose knavish antagonist William Visor of Woncot the countenance of the Justice was bespoken· by his serving-man Davy. This young man, carelessly mentioned at first, seemed to acquire a strong and unaccountable influence over the writer's mind. There was a time when I hoped to convince the world that the nameless stranger in Gloucestershire was none other than William Shakespeare. With this view I collected from time to time, and interwove with the narrative, the various passages in his works which led me to believe that he had been an actor in the scenes described by the diarist. But I have long since given up all idea of proving to the satisfaction of another mind this, or, indeed, any other proposition, except that the three angles of a triangle are equal to two right angles, or certain other truths similarly proved, and equally interesting. And now, when I read over the result of my labours, I have little hope that any one in this critical age will accept my explanation of the mysterious visitor to Cotswold, and I have some fears lest Sir William and his journal may have to be sacrificed to the doubts of an unbelieving generation.

After all, what a book contains is of more importance to the reader than the story of how it came to be written ; and the most sceptical reader of these pages cannot question the fact that Shakespeare tells you here, in his own words, his thoughts and memories of country life. The homely scenes and unintellectual pursuits on which his mind loved to dwell may not be unworthy the attention of yours. And it seems to me that his record of experiences in country life may in some sense be regarded as a fragment of an autobiography : in a limited sense only, and in relation to outward matters, but to facts which he thought of much, and which seriously affected the course of his life : one, moreover, which we may value in the utter hopelessness of any revelation, in his writings or elsewhere, of the inner life and real self of the man Shakespeare.

Vainly have succeeding generations beaten against the bars of the impenetrable reserve in which he has enclosed himself. In despair, some have fallen back on their inner consciousness, and have thereout developed theories, hypotheses, and transcendental criticisms. Others ransack archives and registers. These, at all events, discover truth, but mostly in the shape of parchments and entries in worm-eaten books in which the name of Shakespeare is written, with curious diversity of spelling.

Take any ' Life of Shakespeare : ' strip it of extracts from registers, copies of conveyances, exemplifications of fines, bonds, wills, pedigrees of Arden, suits for tithes, grants

of arms, records of Stratford ; these, and suchlike, are
nothing but legal evidence going to prove that he and
others were born and married; that they bought, sold, and
dealt with property, like their fellows; and finally died and
were buried.   What remains of the man or of his life?

We know that he lived in the country town of Stratford,
probably until his twenty-third year, and it is likely that he
exchanged this life for London, not of free choice, but under
some sort of compulsion. We know that he invested his earn-
ings in the purchase of property about Stratford, and finally in
building a house, whither he retired in the full splendour of
his fame as a poet, and (what he would seem to have valued
more) in the height of his fortune as a manager: that he never
troubled himself to collect or edit his plays : and that he
ceased to write for the stage some years before his death,
which took place somewhat suddenly (it is said) when he
was yet in middle life. We may, if we please, believe
certain traditions.   The most venerable of these was current
in Stratford in the seventeenth century, and can be traced
to several independent sources.   It is the well-known deer-
stealing story, thus recorded in its earliest and crudest form
by the Rev. Thomas Davies, a Gloucestershire clergyman,
who died in 1707 : 'Much given to all unluckinesse in
stealing venison and rabbits; particularly from Sir Lucy,
who had him oft whipt and sometimes imprisoned, and at
last made him fly his native country to his great advance-
ment.'   It was generally said at Stratford that his wife
and children remained there, and that when his fortunes
began to mend he spent each autumn with them.   There is
another story, traceable also to the seventeenth century,
according to which his skill in the matter of horses enabled
him to earn a livelihood on his arrival in London—distancing
all competitors in care of theatre-goers' horses, so that boys at
the theatre door (says the story) traded on his name, and
would say, "I am Shakespeare's boy, sir."

I care not to discuss which is more probable, the substantial truth of these stories, or their entire fabrication ; nor

yet the further question, how it came to pass that when people invented stories about Shakespeare (if they did invent them) they thought of deer and horses. Shakespeare's love of the country needs no illustration from the gossip of Stratford. It is a simple matter of fact that the life lived in Warwickshire had for him some charm sufficient to withdraw him from the full life of London, forsaking the wit-combats of the Mermaid tavern for a quiet game of shovel-board at the Falcon with John Combe. It is also a matter of fact that his mind was at all times so possessed with images and recollections of English rural life, that he refrained not from attributing a like possession to men of all sorts and conditions, regardless of time, place, or circumstance. Prospero sets on his spirits in hunter's language, by names well known in Gloucestershire kennels. Ulysses compares Achilles sulking in his tent to a hart keeping thicket. The fallen Cæsar suggests to Anthony a noble hart, whose forest was the world, bayed and slain by blood-stained hunters. Titus Andronicus proclaims a solemn hunting after the fashion of Gloucestershire. Egyptians, Athenians, and Romans are intimately acquainted with the coursing matches of Cotswold. Roderigo of Venice and Pandarus of Troy speak the language of English sportsmen. Theseus hunts the country round Athens with hounds as thoroughly English as was the horse of Adonis. The flowers of Warwickshire blossom in every clime, and we encounter in the most unlikely places the familiar characters of rural life—under a pent-house at Messina, in the cottage of a Bohemian shepherd, and in the hall of an Italian noble.

Shakespeare wrote no drama of country manners. The life of woods and fields was to him something more than a scene for the action of a play or two. It is the atmosphere in which the poet and the creatures of his fancy live, move, and have their being. His reminiscences are scattered throughout his works—here a little and there a little. And it seems to me that his scattered hints gain rather than lose in significance, when they are taken from a context with which they have often but slight connection, and are grouped with other passages inspired by a common idea.

Some sort of interpretation they need; for the pursuits and pastimes of the sixteenth century have, for the most part, disappeared with the physical aspect of the country, and without some explanation or illustration suggestions and hints of the past might not be understood. Of field sports, none are generally practised after the fashion of three centuries ago, with the exception of hare hunting in an unenclosed country; and even the hare is now pursued with other horses and other hounds. Woodlands have been felled. Vast tracts of arable land, then tilled by village commoners on the open field system, have been enclosed and allotted in severalty. What were once tracks across heather-clad or swampy wilds the home of red deer and native horses, are now macadamised highways, separated from richly cultivated fields by banks and hedge-rows. The natural landmarks of hill and river remain; but even they have suffered a change, and if Master Shallow were now to revisit his Gloucestershire manor, the only object which could satisfy him beyond doubt of its identity is the tower of the village church.

If we would realise in some degree the England of three centuries ago, we must seek it in the moorland districts of the west, where the general elevation of the surface has restricted the area of cultivation to the bottoms, and the lower slopes of the hills. Vast tracts of upland remain unenclosed, the haunt of red deer and moorland ponies. There also primitive manners linger, and ancient sport survives. The hart is hunted as he was hunted throughout England when Elizabeth was Queen. The *Noble Arte of Venerie* is still cited as an authority. The village fair; the wrestling green; the songs and catches of villagers in the inn kitchen; parson and yeoman discoursing by the covert side on the mysteries of woodcraft; the hare hunt on the unenclosed hillside; the 'assembly' on the opening day of the hunting season, the 'mort o' the deer' in the moorland stream ; the frank recognition of differences of rank ; the old-world games ; the harvest-home dinner ; are all stray wafts of the Elizabethan age.   No more than distant mutterings of the storms which have since then broken over England have reached the lonely moors of Exe and Barle, and merry England, like the setting sun, lovingly lingers on the hillsides of the west.

CHAPTER II

HOW THE HART WAS HARBOURED

> I with the morning's love have oft made sport,
> And like a forester, the groves may tread.
> *A Midsummer Night's Dream.*

THE Justice's deer park had been enclosed under a Royal license at a time when a man could no more take to himself without lawful title the right to empark animals *feræ naturæ*, than he might assume coat-armour, a barony, a manor, or the estate of esquire. These things were then clearly understood, and mistakes never occurred. The park was extensive and well stocked with fallow deer. Of red deer there were none, for an old prejudice of woodcraft, since exploded, forbad the keeping of deer of different species within the same pale.[1]

Outside the park, a valley, thickly wooded, extended upward to the higher level of Cotswold. Through this western valley a crystal trout stream hurried downward to join the Severn Sea. It was the 'peculiar river' of the Justice. But in defiance of his rights, youngsters from Dursley and Woncot would grope for trouts under the stones with which its bed was strewn, and catch them by tickling as they lay among the weeds in its sunny shallows.

But the horsemen who now follow its course are not thinking of the stream or of its inhabitants. As they slowly ascend the narrow path (or trench, as it was called in the language of woodcraft), they look around on every side for something which they evidently came forth to find in this seques-

[1] Shirley's *English Deer Parks.*

tered valley. The elder leads the way. His homely dress of russet brown, his keen eye and manly air, proclaim him an honest and independent yeoman. He is Clement Perkes of the Hill. The younger man's lofty cast of features and gentle bearing suggest a higher station. Those, however, who limited their observation to costume and outward matters would set him down as a scrivener or lawyer's clerk, or possibly a schoolmaster, from some neighbouring town. He is the nameless stranger of the journal.

"Here they be," says Clement Perkes to his companion, as they emerge from a tangled thicket. "Here be th' assembly. The Justice ha'n't come, but the serving-men ha' spread the cloths, and Davy and William Visor of Woncot be tasting the wines."

The scene which met the eyes of the younger horse-man as he joined his friend would to the eye of a modern looker-on suggest a picnic, but a sixteenth century sportsman would easily recognise the preparations for the ' assembly ' or outdoor dinner, with which our ancestors inaugurated the solemn hunting of the hart, when proclaimed on some noteworthy occasion, or in honour of a distinguished visitor.

A level spot of bright green turf met the eye, over-shadowed by many an oak, 'whose antique root peeps out Upon the brook, which brawls along this wood.' [1] Of such a spot the soldier-poet George Gascoigne wrote :

Who list by me to learne Assembly for to make
For Keysar, Kyng, or comely Queene, for Lord or Ladies' sake :
   Or where, and in what sort it should prepared be,
Marke well my wordes, and thanke me then, for thankes I craue
   in fee.
The place should first be pight on pleasant gladsome greene,
Yet under shade of stately trees, where little sunne is seene,
   And neare some fountaine spring whose chrystalle running
   streames
May helpe to coole the parching heate ycaught by Phœbus'
   beames.

.   .   .   .
.   .

[1] *As You L.* ii. 1. 31.

Where breath of westerne windes may calmely yield content,
Where casements neede not opened be, where ayre is never pent,
Where shade may serue for shryne and yet the sunne at
hande,
Where beautie neede not quake for cold, ne yet with sunne be
tande.[1]

The assembly is to be held at noon, and as the hour
approaches, gaunt serving-men, clad in their master's blue
coats and wearing his badge on their sleeves, appear on
the scene, leading heavily laden pack-horses, more hungry-
looking than themselves. First comes the butler, whose
jade carried baskets, packed with black-jacks of ale and
flagons of wine. Setting these to cool in the running brook,
the butler spreads on the levellest portion of the turf a large
linen cloth, on which he places some score of trenchers and
knives. Next come 'William cook,' and his men, and
as they unlade their pack-horses they afford appetising
glimpses of cold capons, loins of veal, neats' tongues powdered, sausages and other savoury knacks and kickshaws,
evidently provided for the entertainment of a numerous
company.

The explanation of the scene is soon given. Master
Petre, a man of note in these parts, had just brought home

[1] The book from which these lines are quoted is an important work,
referred to in these pages as the *Noble Arte*. It is entitled, 'The Noble Arte
of Venerie or Hunting, wherein is handled and set out the Vertues, Nature, and
Properties of fiuetene sundrie Chaces together, with the order and maner how
to Hunte and kill eueryone of them. Translated and collected for the pleasure
of all noblemen and gentlemen, out of the best approued authors, which haue
written anything concerning the same: and reduced into such order and proper
termes as are used here, in this noble Realme of England.' The *Noble Arte* was
published in 1575 by Christopher Barker, and is usually bound with Turbervile's
Booke of Faulconrie, published by Barker in the same year. The name of the
translator and collector is not given. I have in note on *The Book of Sport*
given some reasons for doubting the authorship of Turbervile, to whom it
has been ascribed. The volume contains many curious woodcuts, several of
which have been reproduced by Mr. Hedley Peek, in a series of articles in the
Badminton Magazine, entitled 'Old Sporting Prints.' It also contains a
number of poetical effusions contributed by George Gascoigne, the author of
the earliest English satire (*The Steel Glas*, 1576), to whom Hallam assigns ' a
respectable place among the Elizabethan versifiers.'

a fair and wealthy bride, the Lady Katherine, and the hunting was proclaimed in their honour. The Justice had insisted that none of the pomp and circumstance of the noble art of venery should be omitted. For Master Petre had travelled much, and Master Shallow would not have him say that a Gloucestershire Justice yielded to any in due observance of the ceremonies of the chase. On ordinary occasions no such formalities were observed. When the Justice rode a-hunting it was usually after dinner, but when Master Slender had his will, the welkin rang from early dawn with sound of horn and cry of hounds, and merry shouts of 'hunt's up' chased away the lingering shades of night.

Unwillingly, and with no expectation of a day's hunting after his mind, Abraham Slender proceeded to carry out his kinsman's behests, and to organise a solemn hunting, according to the use of princes and honourable persons. After all, the hounds were the Justice's, and he must be obeyed. He might have consoled himself with the reflections that in matters of the chase, if the master proposes he certainly does not dispose, and that the unexpected generally occurs. But Master Slender, as we know, had not sufficient philosophy to keep 'him from quarrelling at a bear-baiting, and his temper to-day is none of the sweetest.

The hour of noon drew near as Perkes and his companion reached the place of the assembly. The clatter of hoofs and sound of voices announced the approach of a large party from the direction of the Hall. The Justice led the way.

" Good morrow, good morrow, honest neighbour Perkes, thou art welcome, thou and thy friend. Nay, keep a good heart! for if judgment was given against thee at the sessions, 'twas no fault of thine, or of thy suit. Thou hast been always a good neighbour, and a true friend of the deer. Thy turn will——"

The rest of the sentence was lost. The Justice stopped short when his eye caught William Visor of Woncot, who stepped obsequiously forward, cap in hand, and with bended knee wished his worship good day, hoped his health was good, and received the Justice's welcome as it had been the benediction of a bishop.

By the time these greetings were over, the Justice and his companions had dismounted, and had handed their horses to the care of their attendants. Perkes and his friend, who were unattended, made their horses fast to neighbouring trees, and seated themselves on the turf by a cloth placed at a respectful distance from that which was spread for the Justice and his friends.

At Master Shallow's right sat Petre's bride, straight and slender as the hazel twig, ' as brown in hue As hazel nuts and sweeter than the kernels.'[1]   Opposite sat her husband.   We know him as Petruchio, masquerading in the thin disguise of a Veronese ; a disguise quickly thrown aside when he reaches his country house, and rates Nathaniel, Gregory, and Philip after the fashion of a Gloucestershire country gentleman.   There was an affected plainness in his attire, but a close observer would infer from his appearance and manner that he had seen somewhat of foreign countries and courts.

His next neighbour, Master Abraham Slender, was open to no such imputation.   Never, indeed, had he quitted Gloucestershire, save on one occasion some two years ago, of which we have heard somewhat, when he accompanied his uncle Master Shallow on a visit, certainly to Windsor, and for aught we know to London.   Never again will he be induced to leave his native county.   " London," he is wont to say, " may be a mighty fine place.   But Gloucestershire is the place for a gentleman.   Why, not a soul here but knows who I be, and doffs to me accordingly.   Whereas when I was in Windsor I might as well be a scholar or an ordinary man, for all the worship I had when I went abroad."

Old Justice Silence is there, of course, with his son

[1] *Tam. of Shrew*, ii. 1. 255.

William and his dark-eyed daughter Ellen, Master Shallow's god-daughter—'a black ousel'[1] her father would call her whenever her beauty was commended—but black or fair she would seem to find favour in the eyes of Master Petre's cousin Ferdinand. This Ferdinand Petre was a frequent visitor at Petre Manor.[2] He had been a fellow student with William Silence at Gray's Inn, of which he is now a member; 'to my cost,' his father always adds, when he announces the fact, and no doubt with truth; for while the fair Ellen, like Imogen, is simply attired in 'a riding suit, no costlier than would fit a franklin's housewife,'[3] her brother and his fellow student display all the bravery of the latest London fashion.

Will Squele and his fair daughter Anne had ridden many miles to take part in the Justice's solemn hunting. He and the Justice had been boon companions in the olden times—fifty-five years ago, as old Silence never fails to remind them—when they heard the chimes at midnight in all the inns of court.

Shal. I was once of Clement's Inn, where I think they will talk of mad Shallow yet.

Sil. You were called 'lusty Shallow' then, cousin.

Shal. By the mass, I was called anything; and I would have

---

[1] *2 Hen. IV.* iii. 2. 9. Both thrushes and blackbirds were included in the class 'ousel.' A black ousel simply means a blackbird. Brunettes were not admired in Tudor days. The 'woman coloured ill' (Sonnet cxliv.), 'as black as hell, as dark as night' (Sonnet cxlvii.), must have possessed strong counterbalancing charms to conquer the poet's objection to her colour. Her complexion is 'dun,' and 'black wires grow on her head' (Sonnet cxxx.). This prejudice survives in the use of the word 'fair' to denote light in colour, in conjunction with such words as hair and complexion. It is said of Beatrice :

> If fair-faced,
> She would swear the gentleman should be her sister;
> If black, why, Nature, drawing of an antique,
> Made a foul blot.   *Much Ado*, iii. 1. 61.

There was therefore no need for commentators to invent a saying, according to which a black ousel was equivalent to a black sheep; or to imagine a kind of bird, so called, which seldom mates.

[2] PET. Bid my cousin Ferdinand come hither. (*Tam. of Shrew*, iv. 1. 154.)

[3] *Cymb.* iii. 2. 78.

done any thing indeed too, and roundly too. There was I, and little John Doit of Staffordshire, and black George Barnes, and Francis Pickbone, and Will Squele, a Cotswold man; you had not four such swinge-bucklers in all the inns o' court again.

2 Hen. IV. iii. 2. 15.

Will Squele is old no doubt—he cannot choose but be old— yet he is hale and hearty, and his bright eye and russet cheek bespeak the healthiness of his Cotswold home.

"Much good may it do your good hearts, proface, pro-face," said the Justice as the company sat down to meat. Valiant trenchermen they were for the most part, and required little encouragement to do full justice to the repast. But there comes at length to Tudor sportsmen, as to Homeric heroes, a moment when the desire of eating and drinking has been expelled. Then comes business.

The arrival of this moment was marked by the approach of the huntsman to the Justice to make his report. You may see him on his knees in a woodcut in the *Noble Arte*, presenting on a dish the tokens from which the weight and age of the hart may be estimated, describing where he is harboured, and detailing the measurement of the impression of his slot, or forefoot :

> Lowe I crouche before the Lordings all.
> Out of my Horne the fewmets lette I fall ;
> And other signes and tokens do I tell
> To make them hope the Harte may like them well.
> Then they commande that I the wine should taste,
> So biddes mine Arte ; and so my throte I baste.[1]

Now it so happens that Master Silence, with another present at the assembly, had been out betimes with the huntsman and the forester. He tells in his diary the story of the hunting, beginning before the dawn of day ; for to harbour a stag, or to take a purse, you must 'go by the moon and the seven stars, and not by Phœbus.'[2]

Fal.   Marry then, sweet wag, when thou art king, let not us

---

[1] The Blazon pronounced by the Huntsman.—*Noble Arte.*
[2] *1 Hen. IV.* i. 2. 15.

that are squires of the night's body be called thieves of the day's
beauty ; let us be Diana's foresters, gentlemen of the shade,
minions of the moon : And let men say we be men of good government, being governed, as the sea is, by our noble and chaste mistress the moon, under whose countenance we steal.

1 Hen. IV. i. 2. 26.

Among the duties of the forester is to aid the huntsman
in harbouring the deer, finding out where he has made his
lair, and whether he may be yet found there when the time
has come for him to be hunted. And so Theseus, when he
would show Hippolyta sport with his hounds, bred out of
the Spartan kind, gave his orders to the forester betimes :

> Go, one of you, find out the forester ;
> For now our observation is perform'd ;
> And since we have the vaward of the day,
> My love shall hear the music of my hounds,
> Uncouple in the western valley : let them go :
> Despatch, I say, and find the forester.

Mids. N. Dr. iv. 1. 108.

On this occasion, as on many others, the skill of the
huntsman and of the forester was not unaided. That honest
yeoman, Clement Perkes of the Hill, had of late suffered
much of a great hart,[1] which had ravaged his fields, wasting

---

[1] The male red deer is now ordinarily called a stag, the female a hind, and
the young a calf. In the diarist's time the generic term for the male was
' hart.' But if you would speak in the strict language of woodcraft, you
would call him in the first year ' a Hind calfe, or a calfe, the second yeere you
shall call him a Broket ; the third yeere you shall call him a Spayad : the fourth
yeere you shall call him a Staggard ; the fift yeare you shall call him a Stag ; the
sixt yeere you shall call him a Hart. . . . . But if the king or queene doe hunt
or chace him, and he escape away aliue, then after such a hunting or chacing
he is called Hart Royall.' (Manwood, *The Forest Lawes*, 1598.) Thenceforth,
after proclamation, he was free to return to the forest from whence he came, and
no man might meddle with a hart royal proclaimed. Mr. Hunter (*Illustrations
of Shakespeare*) suggests that when Cæsar said of Cleopatra that she ' being
royal, Took her own way,' (*Ant. and Cleo.* v. 2. 339), the licence accorded to the
hart royal to go his own way was present to his mind ; and certainly instances may
be found in Shakespeare of similar conceits. The stag, or hart, at six years of
age should have acquired ' his rights,'—that is to say, the brow, bay, and trey
antlers—and two points on top of each horn. The modern use of the term
' royal' to denote a stag with all his rights and three on top, is altogether inaccurate, and without warranty of any writer of authority on woodcraft.

more than he destroyed, biting here and there an ear of corn, and for the sake of a single favourite morsel uprooting entire plants, after the manner of fastidious old males of the species red deer. He had seen him, in the evening twilight, browsing among his smaller cattle, and had noted the points which he bore on his wide and massy antlers. From long observation the yeoman knew well the haunts and habits of the deer, both in summer when they fed on his oats and turnips, and in winter when they were driven to eat strange food :

> Yea, like the stag, when snow the pasture sheets,
> The barks of trees thou browsed'st.
> *Ant. and Cleo.* i. 4. 65.

Now this hart was wont, having made a hearty meal at goodman Perkes's expense, to betake himself a little before dawn to a neighbouring wood, in the depth of whose shade he had often found refuge from the many terrors with which daylight is beset in the eyes of a hunted beast of the forest.[1] But on the night before the assembly his movements had been watched from an adjoining copse by eager eyes. In the uncertain light, dim shadows could be discerned flitting across the cornfields which lay between the Hill and the woods of Shallow Hall. They were deer beyond doubt, but was the great hart among them? As the light improved, Perkes and his companion descended to the field, and examined the place whence the deer had departed. The ground was too hard to preserve the slot, or impression of the foot of deer; but evidence of their presence was

---

[1] Manwood contrasts the beasts of the forest—the hart, the hind, the hare, the boar and the wolf—with the beasts of the chase, or of the field—the buck, the doe, the fox, the marten and the roe. The former feed by night, and 'make their abode all the daytime in the great couerts and secret places in the woods.' 'According, as the prophet Dauid saith in his 104th Psalme, *Thou makest darkness that it may bee night, wherein all the beasts of the forest doe mooue.*' Furthermore, 'it doth appeare by the prophet David in the 50th Psalme,' that there are also beasts of the field, which are the beasts of the chase ; for 'againe hee saith : *I know all the foules upon the mountaines, and the wilde beastes of the fields are mine.*'

not long wanting. Here some tender 'springs' or shoots had been cropped greedily. This was the work of a hind. Further off were stalks of oats with half the ear bitten off. This was more like the delicate feeding of a hart. Next they examine a patch of turnips which Perkes, a farmer of advanced views, had sown in the open. There they lie, some bitten in the ground, but others uprooted and tossed recklessly around. This is beyond doubt the work of the beast which they have come to seek. The heart of the honest yeoman leaps for joy; for what was the spoiling of his crops, weighed against the certainty of a glorious day's sport?

Now must the huntsman be sent for. Before he arrives the deer will have lain down in their lairs, and may be harboured without fear of disturbing them, due caution being observed.

> But, look, the morn, in russet mantle clad,
> Walks o'er the dew of yon high eastward hill.
>
> *Hamlet*, i. 1. 166.

As they await the huntsman, Perkes and his companion note the progress of the dawn, and mark

> what envious streaks
> Do lace the severing clouds in yonder east;
> Night's candles are burnt out, and jocund day
> Stands tiptoe on the misty mountain tops.
>
> *Rom. and Jul.* iii. 5. 7.

How is it that in Shakespeare we find the truest pictures of the glories of the sunrise? He tells us himself:

> I with the morning's love have oft made sport,
> And, like a forester, the groves may tread,
> Even till the eastern gate, all fiery-red,
> Opening on Neptune with fair blessed beams,
> Turns into yellow gold his salt green streams.
>
> *Mids. N. Dr.* iii. 2. 389.

Poets love to describe the evening twilight, and the splendours of the setting sun. They speak of that which they have seen. But the sportsman must be up betimes, and

watch the vagaries of the weather, on which his prospects
of sport depend, and if he should happen to turn poet, he may
tell us his experiences.[1]

> Full many a glorious morning have I seen
> Flatter the mountain-tops with sovereign eye,
> Kissing with golden face the meadows green,
> Gilding pale streams with heavenly alchemy;
> Anon permit the basest clouds to ride
> With ugly rack on his celestial face,
> And from the forlorn world his visage hide,
> Stealing unseen to west with this disgrace.
>
> *Sonnet* xxxiii.

The sun had risen over Cotswold before William Silence
and the huntsman joined Perkes and his friend in the
field. The huntsman brought with him his liam-hound.
This was a pure-bred blood-hound, used in those days for
finding and harbouring the deer. He was so called because
he was held in hand by means of a leather strap called a
liam; a Norman-French term of venery, derived from
ligamen. He was all nose and no cry, being used to hunt
absolutely mute. He was sometimes called slot-hound
(*Scottice* sleuth-hound), because he drew on the slot or
footmark of the deer; and sometimes a limer or lym, as in
Edgar's catalogue of dogs.

> Mastiff, greyhound, mongrel grim,
> Hound or spaniel, brach or lym,
> Or bobtail tike or trundle-tail;
> Tom will make them weep and wail:
> For, with throwing thus my head,
> Dogs leap the hatch, and all are fled.
>
> *K. Lear*, iii. 6. 71.

Holding his hound by the liam, the huntsman advanced
towards the place where the deer had been seen, after the
fashion described in George Gascoigne's verses in the *Noble
Arte*, entitled *The Blazon pronounced by the Huntsman.*

---

[1] For other descriptions of sunrise see, 1 *Hen. IV.* iii. 1. 221; 1 *Hen. IV.* v.
1. 1; *Ven. and Ad.* 855; *Rom. and Jul.* ii. 3. 1; *Jul. Cæs.* ii. 1. 101; 3 *Hen. VI.*
ii. 1. 21.

I am the Hunte, which rathe and earely ryse,
My bottell filde with wine in any wise;
Twoo draughts I drinke, to stay my steppes withall,
For eche foote one, bicause I would not fall.
Then take my Hownde in liam me behinde,
The stately Harte in fryth or fell to finde,
And whiles I seeke his slotte where he hath fedde
The sweete byrdes sing, to cheare my drowsie hedde.
And when my Hounde doth streyne upon good vent
I must confesse the same dothe me content.

It was not long before the blood-hound acknowledged
the line or 'trail'[1] of the hart, straining forwards and
feathering, but giving no tongue. In hunting language, he
had the hart in the wind. The huntsman then held him
short, pulling in the liam, and thus let him draw on the
line of the hart, until they reached a thickly-wooded part of
the valley, just outside the pale of the Justice's park. Here
was plainly marked the 'entry,' where the deer had displaced certain branches as he entered the thicket. To
mark the spot, the huntsman's companions formed a
'blemishing' by plashing down some twigs, so that the
place might be known again. Then the huntsman beat
round the wood with his hound twice or thrice, making
circuits or 'ring-walks,' one in the open where he could use
his eye to aid his hound, and another in the scent-carrying
thicket which surrounded the wood. He has thus ascer-
tained that the hart has not left the wood. In the soft
earth by the entry the print of the fore-foot or slot is clearly
visible. The huntsman takes the measurement. It is
plainly that of a great hart, showing the mettle of the rich
pastures of the western valley.[2]

Thus had the hart been harboured on the morning of the

---

[1] *Hamlet*, ii. 2. 47; iv. 5. 109; *Merry Wives*, iv. 2. 208.

[2] For 'harts beare their heads according to the pasture and feede of the
country where they are bred' (*Noble Arte*), as King Henry's soldiers knew when
he thus addressed them :

And you good yeomen,
Whose limbs were made in England, show us here
The mettle of your pasture.　*Hen. V.* iii. 1. 25.

assembly, and the day's sport arranged accordingly. The spot
for the assembly had been selected in the valley where the
deer was harboured, but about a mile lower down.   The hart
was to be unharboured in the presence of the company, and
forced by means of toils [1] or nets placed in the way which he
would naturally take, to run into the park at a spot where a
carefully constructed toil led up to an opening in the pale.
Once within the park escape was impossible.   The Justice
and his guests could follow the hounds if they pleased, or
better still betake themselves to the hill at the upper end of
the valley, and enjoy the music of the best tuned cry of
hounds in Gloucestershire as—the chorus swelled by relay
after relay—they pursued the unhappy hart from thicket to
thicket until exhausted by heat, fatigue, and his weight of
flesh, he could run no longer, but was forced to stand at
bay, and after a short struggle yield his life to the sword of
the huntsman.

This mode of pursuit was preferred by the Justice to
what was known as hunting at force, or pursuing the stag
whithersoever he might choose to go in the open country.[2]
It was fitter for the entertainment of guests, and it brought
out the qualities of cry for which his hounds had bred for
generations.   The Justice's hounds, like Theseus', were no
' common cry of curs ' as Coriolanus was wont to call the
populace,

> but match'd in mouth like bells,
> Each under each.   A cry more tuneable
> Was never holla'd to, nor cheer'd with horn.
>   *Mids. N. Dr.* iv. 1. 128.

---

[1] See *Love's L. L.* iv. 3. 2 ; *Jul. Cæs.* ii. 1. 206 ; *Hamlet*, iii. 2. 362 ; *Ant.
and Cleo.* v. 2. 351.

[2] This is the hunting of the buck or stag, ' if the bee not confyned within
the limits of a parke or pale, but haue libertie to chuse their waies according to
their own appetites, which of some Hunts-men is cald hunting at force.'—Markham, *Cavalarice.*   The disuse of the toil, or net, marks the emerging of a field
sport from the utilitarian epoch in which it had its birth.   So long as the final
cause of hunting was the destruction of beasts of prey or the acquisition of food,
the net was used to aid and expedite the labours of huntsmen and hounds.   When
love of sport became the motive power, the instinct of the hound and the craft of
the sportsman were left unaided.   Game, rabbits and fish are still taken in nets, but

This result was not attained without careful breeding. 'If you would have your kennell for sweetness of cry then you must compound it of some large dogs that have deep solemn mouths, and are swift in spending, which must, as it were, bear the base in the consort ; then a double number of roaring and loud ringing mouths, which must bear the counter tenor ; then some hollow plain sweet mouths, which must bear the mean or middle part ; and so with these three parts of musick you shall make your cry perfect ; and herein you shall observe that these hounds thus mixt, do run just and eaven together, and not hang off loose from one another, which is the vilest sight that may be; and you shall understand that this composition is best to be made of the swiftest and largest deep mouthed dog, the slowest middle siz'd dog, and the shortest legg'd slender dog; amongst these you may cast in a couple or two small single beagles, which as small trebles may warble amongst them : the cry will be a great deal the more sweet.' [1] What did it avail to have hounds bred for tenor, counter tenor, treble and bass, when the whole kennel run all but mute, hunting a hart at force over the Cotswold hills ? These were the sentiments of Shallow and many of his contemporaries, and so it is that in illustrations of the period you may see the huntsman and company furnished with poles and horns, pursuing the deer on foot, in a manner possible only when he is hunted, not at force, but within the confines of a pale.

not by sportsmen. Xenophon's harriers drove their hare into skilfully arranged nets. And Portia must have witnessed some such hunting, else she would not have said to Nerissa, ' The brain may devise laws for the blood, but a hot temper leaps o'er a cold decree : such a hare is madness the youth, to skip o'er the meshes of good counsel the cripple ' (*Merch. of Ven.* i. 2. 19). Good sport might be had even with the aid of nets, in the days of Shakespeare as in those of Horace,

> Manet sub Jove frigido
> Venator, teneræ conjugis immemor,
> Seu visa est catulis cerva fidelibus,
> Seu rupit teretes Marsus aper plagas.

But when the chase, not the death, of a beast of venery is solely in question, toils and nets are done away with. See an article in the *Quarterly Review*, Jan. 1895, entitled, *Our Sporting Ancestors*.
[1] G. Markham, *Country Contentments*.

CHAPTER III

HOW THE HART WAS UNHARBOURED

The poor frighted deer, that stands at gaze,
Wildly determining which way to fly.   *Lucrece.*

AND now, having learned how the hart was found, and how
it was intended to hunt him, let us go back to the assembly,
where we left the huntsman reporting to his master of the
size and whereabouts of the harboured deer.

" 'Tis well done, in faith, John Hunt," said the Justice,
" 'tis well done indeed too. A great hart, and in pride of
grease. Come Master Petre, we will lead the Lady Katherine to a vantage ground within the park, where she may
best hear the music of the cry. Come Cousin Silence, come
Master Squele, come on, come on. And my god-daughter
Ellen too, and the fair Ann Squele. By the mass, time was
when I would have found the deer myself, and harboured
him, and unharboured [1] him too."

[1] 'We herbor and unherbor a harte,' according to the *Noble Arte*, 'we lodge
and rowse a Bucke ; we forme and start a Hare ; we burrow and bolt a Conie ;
we kennell and unkennell a Fox.' The word 'rouse' seems to have been
generally used in the absence of special terms of venery. We find it applied to
the lion and the panther, and Gervase Markham in his edition of the *Boke of St.
Albans* (1595) sanctions its application to the hart. But it was in strictness a
term of art used in reference to the buck, and it is so used by Shakespeare. Thus,
even if other indications were wanting, we could have told that Belarius and the
sons of Cymbeline were engaged in the sport of shooting fallow deer with cross-
bow when he exclaimed, 'Hark, The game is roused'! (*Cymb.* iii. 3. 98), and
that Henry Bolingbroke had in his mind the chase of the buck, when he assured
the Duke of York that his son would have found in John of Gaunt a father 'to
rouse his wrongs and chase them to the bay' (*Rich. II.* ii. 3. 128). Neither ' harbour ' nor ' unharbour ' occur in Shakespeare in a sporting sense, unless indeed
the nightly refuges of the deer, both red and fallow, are suggested in the lines,

"Aye, and hunted and killed and powdered and eaten him, I warrant," said Petre.

" I' faith, I'd ha' done anything and roundly too.   But it may be, Master Petre, that you or your cousin Ferdinand would yourselves take part in the unharbouring of the game ? "

" Not I, in faith," said Ferdinand Petre, " the pleasure of the hunt for me, and the toil for those who like it, say I. 'Tis well that some are found to get out of their beds before cock-crow, and to tear their flesh in thorny brakes at mid-day, and all to see a liam-dog do what a Christian cannot. I'll hearken to the music of your organs, Master Shallow, and let those who love the task blow the bellows." [1]

> My thoughts do harbour with my Silvia nightly,
>   And slaves they are to me that send them flying :
> O, could their master come and go as lightly,
>   Himself would lodge where senseless they are lying !
> *Two Gent.* iii. 1. 140.

But the coney has his burrow (*Coriol.* iv. 5. 226) and the hare is started, ' O, the blood more stirs, To rouse a lion than to start a hare ! ' (1 *Hen. IV.* i. 3. 197).   When Sir Toby Belch drew his sword on Sebastian, Olivia took the offence as one offered to herself, saying to Sebastian, ' He started one poor heart of mine in thee ' (*Twelfth N.* iv. 1. 63).   Dr. Johnson writes : ' I know not whether here be not an ambiguity intended between heart and hart.'   The quibble is a favourite one, but assuredly it is not intended here.   Absolute certainty in Shakespearian criticism is attainable only in regard to matters of venery and horsemanship.   Shakespeare would as soon write of rousing a fox as of starting a deer.   ' I'll warrant we'll unkennel the fox,' said Master Ford (*Merry Wives*, iii. 3. 174), an operation present to the mind of Hamlet when he tells Horatio to observe his uncle at the play,

> If his occulted guilt,
> Do not itself unkennel in one speech,
> It is a damned ghost that we have seen.—*Hamlet*, iii. 2. 85.

[1] The references in the diary to Ferdinand Petre are not without significance. Scanty though they be, they suggest him as a disciple of the then fashionable school of Lyly, the author of Euphues.   He would be therefore, of necessity, hateful to one of the temperament of the Lady Katherine.   With this knowledge, we can understand what Petre meant when, in the course of taming his shrew, he said to his servant,

> Sirrah, get you hence,
> And bid my cousin Ferdinand come hither ;
> One, Kate, that you must kiss, and be acquainted with.
> *Tam. of Shrew*, iv. 1. 153.

It did not become necessary to resort to this extremest discipline, and we hear

From this conversation I infer that Master Ferdinand Petre belonged to the modern school of fashionable and cultured Englishmen, who affected to despise the sports of their fathers, except as leading up to a social event, such as a solemn hunting or hawking party, capable of scenic effect, and affording refined enjoyment to eye and ear. ' At these dayes ' (1575), writes the author of the *Noble Arte*, ' there are many men which beare hornes and bewgles, and yet cannot tell how to use them, neyther how to encourage and helpe theyr hounds therewith, but rather do hinder than furder them, hauing neyther skill nor delight to use true measure in blowyng : and therewithal seyng that Princes and Noble men take no delight in hūtyng, having their eyes muffled with the scarfe of worldly wealth, and thinking thereby to make theyr names immortall, which in deede doth often leade them to destruction bothe of bodie and soule, and oftener is cause of the shortening of theyr lyfe (which is their principall treasure here on earth), since a man shall hardly see any of them reygne or liue so long as they did in those dayes that every Forest rong with houndes and hornes, and when plentie of flagon bottels were caried in every quarter to refresh them temperately.'

A generation earlier, the most cultured man of his day, Master Thomas More, afterwards Lord Chancellor of England and Martyr, devised certain pageants for a painted cloth, representing the stages of the life of man, and over the pageant representing manhood was written :

> Manhod I am, therefore I me delyght
> To hunt and hawke, to nourishe up and fede
> The grayhounde to the course, the hawke to th' flyght,
> And to bestryde a good and lusty stede ;
> These thynges become a very man in dede.

In the age of euphuism, as in the days of dandyism and æstheticism, there must have been many who would have

no more of Ferdinand. Indeed, but for our diarist, he, with William and Ellen Silence, and Will Squele the Cotswold man, would have for ever remained names and nothing more.

gently shuddered at the robust sentiments of Sir Thomas More.[1] And indeed some of the choicest spirits of the age, dazzled by the light of the new learning, were blind to the beauty and significance of the facts which nature reveals to her faithful followers, in pursuit of science or of sport; the falcon 'waiting on' beneath the cloud; the mallard on the wing; the subtlety of the hare; the mysteries of scent; the patient labour of the hounds; the music of their cry; the tragedy of the hart at bay; the wariness of the many-summered trout; the inexhaustible wonder of the horse; and the infinite variety of that world of animal instinct, the study and development of which constitute the essence of all that deserves the name of sport. To many the country was, in the words of Bacon,[2]

a den
Of savage men ;

and the lover of country sports

a loose unruly swayne
Who had more ioy to raunge the forrest wyde
And chase the salvage beast with busie payne
Than serve his Ladies' love, and waste in pleasures vayne.
Fairie Queen.

But no such ideas were current in Gloucestershire, nor indeed do we find any trace of them in the pages of the diarist, who simply records that as the Justice led his party

---

[1] See Note, *Sir Thomas More on Field Sports.*

[2] In attributing to Bacon the poem from which these lines are taken, I follow Archbishop Trench and Mr. Palgrave, who include it in their collections on the authority of the evidence collected by Mr. Spedding in his edition of Bacon's Works. It is described by Mr. Palgrave (notes to the *Golden Treasury*) as ' a fine example of a peculiar class of poetry—that written by thoughtful men, who practised this art but little.' Verses of this kind may be attributed to Bacon without violent improbability, though he has been at pains to prove his incapacity of the higher flights of poetry by printing in the year 1625 a *Translation of certain Psalms into English Verse*, with a dedication to his very good friend Mr. George Herbert, in which he has transmuted fine oriental imagery into poor rhyming prose. *Si sic omnia dixisset,* Aristotle might yet reign in the schools. It would, however, be unreasonable, and contrary to experience, to look for poetry of the highest order at the hands of a great philosopher, statesman, and lawyer.

to the hill-top, the rest of the company made ready to assist at the unharbouring of the hart.

William Silence seemed especially keen. For turning to Abraham Slender, who with the huntsman was employed in setting apart four or five couples of hounds, he said, " Cousin Abraham, if it so be that you send a vauntelay or a relay [1] into the park, I will, if it so please you, accompany them, and thus help in the hunting."

Abraham Slender's mind worked slowly. He could not understand such a proposal coming from William Silence, who, though fond of sport after a fashion, seldom troubled himself about details, and was not at all likely to volunteer to act as a pricker in setting a relay. As he turned round to answer William, he caught sight of the Justice and his guests making their way towards the park. Master Shallow led the way, entertaining the Lady Katherine and her husband with his very best conversation. Then followed old Silence and his daughter Ellen, and last of all came the fair Anne Squele, casting, as it seemed to Abraham Slender, a longing, lingering look behind, which was not directed towards him.

" No," said Slender, " I will set no relay to-day."

" Nay, but Master Slender," said the huntsman, " if the master be not content with the cry, and the worshipful lady——"

" I'll warrant ye," said Slender, " take up the hounds, and bring them to the western valley."

" Now for the hart ! " said William Silence, " what hart could withstand you, Cousin Abraham, when furnished like a hunter you go forth to kill it ? "

Abraham Slender mounted his horse with an uneasy

[1] ' When they set houndes in a readynesse whereas they thinke a chase will passe, and cast them off before the rest of the kennell come in, it is called a *Vaunte laye.* When they tarrie till the rest of the kennell come in, and then cast off, it is called an *Allay.* But when they hold until the kennell be past them, then it is called a *Relay.*' (*Noble Arte.*) The relay, the liam-hound, and many other ancient observances of the chase, seem to be still in use in French stag-hunting.

feeling that William was laughing at him, and that the by-standers enjoyed it.

This apparently trivial incident was recorded by the diarist because it determined not only the issue of the day's sport, but the course of his life.

William and Anne Squele had been playmates in child-hood. In early youth they had together followed the Justice's hounds, and flown their hawks on the breezy uplands of Cotswold.

> How should love,
> Whom the cross lightnings of four chance-met eyes
> Flash into fiery life from nothing, follow
> Such dear familiarities of dawn?
> Seldom, but when he does, Master of all.

So it fared with William Silence and Anne Squele, though, like Leolin Averill and Edith Aylmer, they were not

> by plight on broken ring
> Bound, but an immemorial intimacy.

Abraham Slender had been with them always. They had looked upon him as a necessary instrument of sport, like horse, hound, or hawk. Considered as a human being he served rather as a butt than as a companion, and it certainly never occurred to Silence to regard his kinsman as a possible rival. At the assembly, however, the Justice had somewhat markedly placed his nephew next to Anne, while Silence's knife and trencher had been laid at a distance. Moreover, there was something in the manner of his old friend Will Squele which he did not quite understand. And Abraham Slender must have had some pretty strong motive for keeping Silence from joining the party in the park, when he risked the ruin of the day's sport, and the just wrath of the Justice, by departing from the usual course of sending forward relays of hounds to be laid on at the various points where the chase was expected to pass, so as to strengthen the cry and enhance the excitement of the sport. William Silence's mind worked rapidly, and led him to a conclusion not very far removed from the truth. It was shortly this:

Abraham Slender was a suitor for the hand of Anne, approved by her father, and supported by the powerful influence of Master Shallow, who had sworn a great oath that he would not be baulked a second time in his designs for the settlement in life of his nephew.

The immediate result of Abraham Slender's refusal to send forward relays of hounds to the park was that the huntsman had with him the whole kennel of hounds when he arrived at the thicket in the western valley, where the hart had been harboured.

The covert was a small one, and so Slender and the huntsman decided on drawing it with the entire cry. It was in those days usual to single [1] the harboured deer, and unharbour, or force him to break covert, by means of the liam-hound, held in hand by the huntsman, and laid on the trail at the 'blemishing' which marked the place where the hart had entered the covert. In modern stag-hunting the work of segregating the warrantable stag and compelling him to break cover is performed by the huntsman with the aid of three or four couples of the steadiest hounds, called, when so employed, tufters; a course absolutely necessary to be followed in the case of large woodlands when many deer of various kinds are certain to be on foot, and to divide the pack. This process, however, whether conducted by liam-hound or by tufters, may be dispensed with when the

---

[1] ' When he (the hart) is hunted and doth first leave the hearde, we say that he is *syngled* or empryned.' (*Noble Arte*.) Thus Aaron, saying ' Single you thither then this dainty doe ' (*Tit. Andr.* ii. 1. 117), uses a term of art. So do Richard, when he says to Warwick, ' Single out some other chase, for I myself will hunt this wolf to death ' (3 *Hen. VI.* ii. 4. 13) ; and Armado, when he says to Holofernes, ' Arts-man preambulate, we will be singled from the barbarous ' (*Love's L. L.* v. 1. 85). Thus the Folio. The first quarto, pirated doubtless by some one ignorant of the language of the chase, reads ' singuled,' and is followed by the *Globe Shakespeare* and by the Cambridge editor, who writes, ' The Folio edition is a reprint of this Quarto, differing only in its being divided into Acts, and as usual, inferior in accuracy,' this passage being possibly one of those upon which the charge of inaccuracy is founded. The term ' single ' was also applied to picking out the scent of the hunted beast, ' till they have singled With much ado the cold fault cleanly out ' (*Ven. and Ad.* 693).

deer has been harboured within the narrow limits of a small thicket, whence he can be expelled by the entire pack.

The 'prickers' or mounted huntsmen were disposed around the wood, on the opposite side to the toils, so that the hart might have them in the wind.[1] If, notwithstanding, he should break covert in their direction, the prickers were to 'blench'[2] or head him, so as to force him into the toils.

No sooner had the hounds been uncoupled and put into cover, than a triumphant note from Belman, followed by a jubilant chorus, announced that the hart had been found.

'The game is up,' whispers Clement Perkes, in words which long afterwards fell naturally from the lips of the banished Belarius.[3] He and his friend eagerly scan the corner of a wood extending upwards from the western valley to the common which stretches up the hillside, unenclosed and covered with bracken and rough grass. Beyond the summit of the hill lie many miles of dreary moorland and

---

[1] 'When he (the hart) smelleth or venteth anye thing, then we saye he *hath* (*this or that*) in the winde.' (*Noble Arte.*) 'I sent to her,' said Bertram, of Rousillon,

> By this same coxcomb that we have i' the wind,
> Tokens and letters which she did re-send.
>
> *All's Well*, iii. 6. 121.

In order to drive a deer into the toils it was needful to get to windward of him, so that, having you in the wind, he might break in the opposite direction; a stratagem of woodcraft well known to Hamlet, when he said of his hunters, Rosencrantz and Guildenstern, 'Why do you go about to recover the wind of me, as if you would drive me into a toil?' (*Hamlet*, iii. 2. 361.) If, notwithstanding, the hart should break in the wrong direction, he must be 'blenched,' or headed, so as to drive him into the toil. This word is used in Shakespeare in the sense of to start aside, or fly off: a sense akin to its meaning in woodcraft, and possibly derived from it. (See *Sonnet* cx.; *Measure for M.* iv. 5. 5; *Wint. Tale*, i. 2. 333; *Troil. and Cres.* i. 1. 28; ii. 2. 68; *Hamlet*, ii. 2. 626.)

[2] The following passages are cited in the great historical dictionary of the English language now in course of publication, under the word 'blench.' 'Blawnsherrs to kepe the deere within the wood' (R. Langton in *Ellis Orig.*), 'Saw you not the deare come this way? . . . I beleeve you have blancht him.' (Lyly, *Galathea.*)

[3] *Cymb.* iii. 3. 107.

barren waste—the 'wilds in Gloucestershire.'[1]   They have
not long to wait. A magpie, chattering volubly, has risen
startled from the thicket; and a moment afterwards, thrust-
ing aside the brushwood, the monarch of the forest stands
at gaze before them.

For an instant his kingliness is forgotten. He is

> the poor frighted deer, that stands at gaze,
> Wildly determining which way to fly.   *Lucrece*, 1149.

But only for an instant. The first amazemenc over, his
majesty returns. He scorns to run like ' coward hares,'[2] or
to slink away like the 'fox in stealth.'[3] As one who takes
part in some royal pageant, he moves with grave dignity
through the field, disdaining to notice the lookers on. He
turns upwards from the corner of the wood, and, slanting
along the side of the open valley, ascends to the upland
level, shows for an instant his crowned head over the sky
line, and then is lost to sight.

Clement Perkes's companion knew too much of hunting
to intermeddle in matters demanding an intimate acquaintance with the mystery of woodcraft. Such intermeddling is
as pernicious as was the interference of the ignorant in matters
of state in the eyes of Menenius, when he thus addressed
the rabble of Rome as they cried out against Coriolanus,

> Do not cry havoc, where you should but hunt
> With modest warrant.   *Coriol*. iii. 1. 274.

And so he kept silence.

Clement Perkes was also silent for a moment, but owing
to another reason. This was not the hart he harboured in the
thicket. A glance informed his practised eye that it was a
somewhat younger deer—a conclusion confirmed by further
examination. His body was not so heavy; his colour was
darker; his antlers smaller, and of fewer points; and his
tread more elastic. He was, however, a warrantable deer;
a hart of ten, carrying all his rights, with two points on

---

[1] *Rich. II*. ii. 3 (stage direction).   [3] *K. Lear*, iii. 4. 96.
[2] *Cymb*. iv. 4. 37.

either side. He might have entered the thicket after the
great hart had been harboured in the early morning. He
had doubtless been roused by the older deer, then quietly
lying concealed in the harbour whence he had ejected his
younger and weaker brother on the approach of the hounds.
This is one of the many devices, which it were tedious here
to relate, practised by an aged and experienced hart when
he would avoid breaking covert, or thicket as it was sometimes termed. And so, when the Grecian leaders fail to
induce Achilles to quit his tent, the similitude is suggested
of a noble hart whom no device may drive from his chosen
covert, and Ulysses says :

> There is no tarrying here ; the hart Achilles
> Keeps thicket.   *Troil. and Cres.* ii. 3. 269.

Abraham Slender likewise saw the deer break covert,
and ascend the hill. He, too, was silent for a moment. Then,
as with a sudden impulse, he shouted, "the hunt is up, the
hunt is up."

"Nay, nay, Master Slender," cried the huntsman, emerging from the thicket with the leading hounds ; "whip off the
hounds. 'Tis not the hart."

"It is the hart," said Slender ; "collect the hounds, and
lay them on."

"Nay, but Master Slender, the great hart keeps thicket,
and a' may yet be driven into the toils ; but as for this
other, a'll be half over Cotsall or ever the hounds be out of
covert."

"I say it is the hart," said Slender, and added in a lower
tone, "I'll warrant you with the Justice, John Hunt. I be
not so big a fool as I look. An' you hunt not this hart,
you and William Visor may look for my countenance when
you lack it."

John Hunt was never so puzzled in his life. Abraham
Slender never made a mistake in a matter of woodcraft. He
had a full view of the deer. What could it mean ? This,
however, was certain, that neither he nor his friend William

Visor of Woncot could risk the displeasure of Abraham Slender; he knew by far too much; and so he, too, joins in the cry of "the hunt is up."

"The hunt is up, the hunt is up," the tally-ho of our ancestors—the heart-stirring signal that the game has gone away—the chorus of many a Tudor hunting-song—now echoes from the western valley to the mountain top.

> The hunt is up, the morn is bright and grey,
> The fields are fragrant and the woods are green.
>
> *Tit. Andr.* ii. 2. 1.

The prickers hurry to the spot from all sides of the covert, while footmen join in loudest chorus.

The hart catches a distant echo of the cry, and hastens with redoubled speed across the wilds of Cotswold. Of such a startling note thought Juliet when she said:

> It is the lark that sings so out of tune,
> Straining harsh discords and unpleasing sharps.
> Some say the lark makes sweet division;
> This doth not so, for she divideth us;
> Some say the lark and loathed toad change eyes;
> O, now I would they had changed voices too!
> Since arm from arm that voice doth us affray,
> Hunting thee hence with hunt's-up to the day.
>
> *Rom. and Jul.* iii. 5. 26.

Meanwhile the hounds are being collected. A couple, Brabbler and Fury, have followed the line of the hart half way up the hillside. They must be stopped. "Turn head, and stop pursuit," cries the huntsman, and as Perkes gallops forward at the words his companion reflects that a chase may be too hotly followed; that the truest man is not he who flashes wildly ahead of his fellows at the outset of the chase; and that there are bawlers, babblers and overtoppers among men as among hounds. 'You see this chase is hotly follow'd, friends,' said the French king of the English advance on Agincourt. Whereupon the Dauphin exclaims, in words well known in the English hunting field, 'Turn head, and stop pursuit.' He thus explains his meaning, delivering himself of a maxim of woodcraft, excellent in itself, but somewhat out of place, as events soon proved ;

For coward dogs
Most spend their mouths when what they seem to threaten
Runs far before them. *Hen. V.* ii. 4. 68.

" 'Hang, cur, hang,' " cried John Hunt, as Brabbler returned crestfallen and in disgrace ; surely the very hound present to Thersites' mind when he said of Diomed, ' He will spend his mouth, and promise, like Brabbler the hound, but when he performs, astronomers foretell it.' [1]

" Ay, marry, hang him," said Abraham Slender, " and if Fury be not trashed a'll overtop and destroy the cry."

" I'll warrant ye," said John Hunt, producing some long straps from a bag which he carried at his side, " I han't ben hunt for forty year to Master Shallow without knowing well ' who to trash for overtopping.' [2] I'ld ha' trashed Fury and Tyrant before a' left kennel if a'd only known what was i' the wind ; but," he added in a low growl, " as for this day's hunting, it fairly passes, and the great hart a-waitin, as one might say, to be driven into the toil."

It is certain that the scene now presented to the eye, and the sounds which reached the ear, often recurred to the memory of one who loved to dwell upon all incidents of the chase. If he deemed them worthy of his thoughts, we may well spare a few moments, while the hounds are being collected and (when needful) trashed, in order to learn the lessons of the bawling, the babbling, and the overtopping hound. They are to be met with elsewhere than by the covert side, but nowhere do their qualities meet with quicker recognition or surer retribution. ' If they be to busie before they finde the Sent good, we say *they Bawle*,' says the author of the *Noble Arte*; ' If they be to busie after they finde good Sent, we say *they Bable*.'

The bawler who cries upon no scent is a degree worse than the babbler. If he be a hound, he is straightway hanged.

---

[1] *Troil. and Cres.* v. 1. 98   [2] *Tempest*, i. 2. 81.

'Hang, cur! hang,' says Antonio to the boatswain, needlessly busy, as he thinks, with his nautical outcry. We know why he was to hang, for Sebastian had just denounced him as a 'bawling, blasphemous, incharitable dog.' [1] If the bawler be a man, no one heeds him, and he is lost to use, and name, and fame, as if he were hanged. Master Ford of Windsor was a bawler, giving tongue and busy before he found the scent to be good. 'I'll warrant we'll unkennel the fox.' [2] Thus, he cried out, thinking that Jack Falstaff had been run to ground in his chamber. 'I cannot find him,' was the confession of the convicted bawler; but he was ready next moment, with the fatuity of his kind, to spend his mouth and promise; 'Will you follow, gentlemen? I beseech you, follow; see but the issue of my jealousy; if I cry out thus upon no trail, never trust me when I open again.' [3]

The babbler, or brabbler, has more to say for himself than Master Ford. There is no mistake about the scent, but the babbler in his fussy impatience is in danger of misleading others, and of over-running the line. We remember how busily Buckingham cried out and spent his mouth, when Wolsey passing by in state fixed on him his eye, full of disdain. The cardinal was a venom-mouthed butcher's cur, an Ipswich fellow, who should be forthwith cried down to the king; brave words, but babble. 'Be advised,' said Norfolk, in whose experienced eyes Buckingham was a babbling puppy, too busy, though the scent was good :

we may outrun,
By violent swiftness, that which we run at,
And lose by over-running.   *Hen. VIII.* i. 1. 139.

The overtopping hound is not necessarily a bawler, or even a babbler. His fault is that his hunting is too quick for the rest of the pack. Nowadays he would probably be drafted. In the days of the diarist, ready means of communication between masters of hounds not being in existence,

[1] *Tempest*, i. 1. 43.   [2] *Merry Wives*, iii. 3. 173.
[3] *Ibid*. iv. 2. 206

the huntsman would level him down to the body of his companions by a process known as trashing.[1] There is no connection, etymological or otherwise, between the trashed and the trashy hound. When Iago associates the words, he does so in obedience to an instinct always strong, but specially powerful in regard to terms of venery. Embarrassed by the impatience of Roderigo, he compares the too eager lover to an overtopping hound;

> If this poor trash of Venice, whom I trash
> For his quick hunting, stand the putting on,
> I'll have our Michael Cassio on the hip.
>
> *Othello*, ii. 1. 312.

---

[1] The use of the word 'trash' among terms of venery, both as a verb and as a substantive, is now clearly established (see the note on the word in *Nares' Glossary*, and the examples collected in *Johnson's Dictionary*, by Todd). It is used as a substantive by Gervase Markham in his *Country Contentments*. He mentions trashes, with couples, liams, collars, etc., among articles commonly kept in a huntsman's lodgings. Curiously enough the verb has not been found in books of sport, but there is some evidence of its use by hunters up to the beginning of the present century. (See the notes to *Othello*, ii. 1, in the *Variorum* of 1821.) But of the nature and use of the trash there can be no doubt. They are clearly shown in the following note to Beckford's *Thoughts on Hunting* (Letter X.) ; a book of the highest authority, the work of a scholar, a sportsman, a keen observer, and an entertaining writer. ' A hound that runs too fast for the rest ought not to be kept. Some huntsmen load them with heavy collars ; some tie a long strap round their necks ; a better way would be to part with them. Whether they go too slow or too fast, they ought equally to be drafted.' However the trash may have been applied, it clearly appears, from Beckford's words, to have consisted of a long strap, kept by the huntsman (according to Markham) with collars, liams, and other articles of the same kind. When the hound was running this long strap, dragged along the ground, handicapped the overtopping hound. I have been so fortunate as to see an accurate representation of Prospero's trash in a painting in the possession of the Right Hon. Arthur Smith Barry, M.P., in which one of his ancestors—master of the Cheshire foxhounds about the middle of last century—is depicted hunting with his pack. One of the hounds has attached to his collar a long strap, which trails on the ground. This hound, Bluecap, the winner of a match mentioned in Daniel's *Rural Sports*, was considered worthy of a separate portrait, also in the possession of Mr. Smith Barry. He was thus an exceptionally fast hound, and would certainly have been trashed by Prospero or his brother by means of the long strap which Beckford mentions as in use about the time when this picture was painted. It is quite possible that this strap may have been used, not only to restrain a hound from overtopping, but, held in hand by the huntsman, to prevent a hound that was 'embossed' owing to overwork, from adding to his fatigue by running about at large. (See note at p. 78.)

None knew better than Prospero that the best of hounds
need trashing, if you would have your pack run together, and
so he tells us that his usurping brother,

> Being once perfected how to grant suits,
> How to deny them, who to advance and who
> To trash for overtopping, new created
> The creatures that were mine, I say, or changed 'em,
> Or else new form'd 'em.   *Tempest*, i. 2. 79.

Ben Jonson was not afraid to suggest the application of
some such process to Shakespeare himself,[1] in whom he notes
'excellent phantasy, brave notions, and gentle expressions,
wherein he flowed with that facility that sometimes it was
necessary he should be stopped.' Shakespeare would have
called it 'trashed for overtopping;' but the learned Jonson,
borrowing words spoken by Augustus of Haterius, writes
Sufflaminandus erat. And if poets, like hounds, must needs
be levelled down lest one should overtop the rest of the cry,
a trash of no ordinary dimensions would have been needed
to bring Shakespeare to the level of even rare Ben himself.
Let us therefore rejoice that Shakespeare was allowed to hunt
the trail of his fancy unrestrained by trash—such, for example, as would have been supplied by the dramatic unities
of time, place, and action.

[1] *Discoveries, De Shakespeare nostrat.*

CHAPTER IV

HOW THE HART WAS HUNTED

I have horse will follow where the game
Makes way, and run like swallows o'er the plain.
Titus Andronicus.

MASTER SHALLOW and his friends from their vantage
ground in the park, like Theseus and Hippolyta on the
mountain top, could with their ears 'mark the musical confusion Of hounds and echo in conjunction;'[1] and with their
eyes they might follow the hart until, ascending the hillside,
he had reached the upper stretches of the wold.

When it became apparent that the hounds were about to be
laid on the trail of this deer, three members of the company,
impelled by different motives, left the park and approached
the hounds.

Master Ferdinand Petre, though he despised hunting,
affected the riding of the great horse, as did most of his
school. He was now mounted upon a grey Flanders mare,
well trained in the manage, and bought at a great price
from Petre's neighbour, one Sir Smile. A modern critic,
had the mare appeared by the covert side, would call her a
cart-horse. But Ferdinand was proud of her shapes and
dimensions, which he rather ostentatiously contrasted with
those of the homebred hunting jades—uncomely curtals
he would call them — to the obvious discontent of the
Gloucestershire Justices, and the no small amusement of

[1] *Mids. N. Dr.* iv. 1. 115.

Petre, who never lost a chance of making sport at the expense of his cousin.

"Come," said Petre, as his cousin Ferdinand was parading his prancing bean-fed steed before the admiring eyes of Ellen Silence, "if thou art a man, and thy grey mare be ought but 'a hollow pampered jade,' match thyself and her against one of these uncomely curtals, and take thy choice."

Old Silence said nothing, but there was meaning in his grunt, and Ferdinand Petre, slowly, and with a bad grace, joined the party by the covert side.

It was surely by a feeling akin to instinct that Will Squele, when the hart made for the hills, was impelled to quit the Justice's party, and to turn the head of his stout bay curtal towards his Cotswold home. But was it instinct, or filial affection, or some other motive power, that impelled the fair Anne, turning a deaf ear to all entreaties, and saying "I must needs follow my father," to canter down the hillside, cross the western valley, and join Will Squele in his homeward ride? Time, and the sequel of the chase, can alone make their motives clear. Suffice it to note here the fact that the party in the park was thus reduced to Justice Shallow, his god-daughter Ellen, Petre and his bride, with old Master Silence. There we may leave them for the present—for they will hear or see no more of the chase to-day—and return to Abraham Slender and the hounds.

The early moments of a great moorland run differ widely from the quick find and eager rush by which, in modern times, a brilliant burst with fox-hounds is inaugurated. There is plenty of time and no lack of space. These metaphysical conditions being satisfactory, a quiet air of pleasurable anticipation pervades the assembly during the interval —sometimes a long one—between the unharbouring of the deer and the laying on of the pack. None of our Gloucestershire friends would have been guilty of the unsportsmanlike malpractice of pursuing the hart, instead of riding to the hounds; and accordingly they are collected in a group by the thicket near the spot where the deer broke covert.

Here comes John Hunt with the hounds, old but wiry and hard bitten, 'furnished like a hunter,' [1] with sword by his side and twisted horn slung over his shoulder, mounted on a compact home-bred gelding, somewhat under fifteen 'handfuls' (as he would tell you) in height. Abraham Slender is close at hand. I need not here describe in detail his horse, for you shall in due time see his picture, drawn as 'when a painter would surpass the life In limning out a well-proportion'd steed.' [2]

But I would ask you to note that William Silence has discarded the little ambling nag on which some days before he had ridden from London, for a great horse or horse of service of the High Almain breed, borrowed for the occasion from his friend Petre, by his management of which within the pale he had hoped to commend himself to the eyes of Mistress Anne, and like Henry the Fifth ' bound his horse for her favours.' Now the discarded ambler was of a breed which took kindly to this artificial pace, but could, if need be, gallop as well. It was known as the Irish hobby, a light but wiry horse, swift, pleasant to ride, and of great endurance. It had not the imposing presence of Petre's horse of service, nor had it been so perfectly broken to the manage. Hence Silence's choice, to which we owe much ; for thus it came about that he lent his Irish hobby to Clement Perkes for the use of a visitor, who otherwise must needs follow on foot as best he could, inasmuch as with gentle persistence he had refused the kindly yeoman's offer of a stout galloway, the only hunting nag which the modest stable of the Hill could provide. When we have added William Visor of Woncot, the number of prickers is complete. He had hired a half-starved jade in the village of Woncot, where Marian Hacket kept a plain ale-house, without welt or gard of any ivy-bush, and sold beer and cheese by pint and by pound to all that came, over her door being a legend, 'vilely painted, and in such great letters as they write, *Here is good horse to hire.*' [3]

Meanwhile, the collected cry were laid on the line of the hart. The western valley re-echoed with loud shouts of

---

[1] *As You L.* iii. 2. 258.   [2] *Ven. and Ad.* 289.   [3] *Much Ado*, i. 1. 267.

"there boy, there, to him, to him," [1] and with the music of the hounds, as opening on the trail, and acknowledging the burning scent, they raced along the hillside, flashing through the rough and tangled grass.

" Ten miles, as the crow flieth, to the water where the Cotsall harts mostly soil, and if so be that we set him not up there, and a' runneth straight, a'll make for the brook in the long wood seven miles further across the wold. But 'tis my galloway nag to a packhorse that a'll turn towards Hog-shearing, for there goeth yonder Master Squele to bid him welcome home, and not a hart on Cotsall knoweth his own run as well as Master Squele. I' faith, he's a ' Cotsall man,' true bred."

Thus Clement Perkes, as the hounds, now in full cry, began the steep ascent towards the point where we lost sight of the hart. His companion understood that his horse must be carefully nursed, if he would see the finish of this glo-rious chase. Steep is the ascent from the western valley to the upper ranges of the wolds. Now must be practised the wholesome self-restraint which Norfolk inculcated on Buckingham when, incensed by the insolence of Wolsey, he spent his tongue, and incurred reproof as a babbling hound. The experience of to-day approves Norfolk's horsemanship, no less than his woodcraft :

> Stay, my lord,
> And let your reason with your choler question
> What 'tis you go about: to climb steep hills
> Requires slow pace at first: anger is like
> A full-hot horse, who being allow'd his way,
> Self-mettle tires him.   *Hen. VIII.* i. 1. 129.

It is quicker no doubt to ascend the hill after the fashion

---

[1] Pistol's words ' As many devils entertain ; ' and ' To her, boy, say I ' (*Merry Wives*, i. 3. 61) ; and Lucio's aside to Isabella, ' to him, to him, wench,' when she addressed the deputy Angelo on behalf of her brother (*Measure for M.* ii. 2. 124), suggest a reminiscence of this exclamation. That it was in strict accord-ance with the usage of hunters is vouched by the author of the *Noble Arte*, who enjoins the huntsmen when the hart prepareth to flee to ' blowe for the houndes, and crye to them, that's he ; that's he, to him, to him ; ' an echo of Xenophon's ἀναβοᾶν δ' ἐκεῖνον μέν, αὐτῷ παῖς, αὐτῷ παῖς, παῖ δή, παῖ δή (*Cynegeticus*, vi. 18).

of ' that sprightly Scot of Scots, Douglas, that runs o' horseback up a hill perpendicular.' [1]

> *Prin.* Was that the king, that spurred his horse so hard
> Against the steep uprising of the hill?
> *Boyet.* I know not ; but I think it was not he.
> *Prin.* Whoe'er a' was, a' show'd a mounting mind.
>
> *Love's L. L.* iv. 1. 1.

On this occasion it was Master Ferdinand Petre who
showed a mounting mind.   He and his steed had more experience of the sudden and swift career of the manage than
of the art of riding to hounds.   Not only did he allow his
full hot horse his way, but he spurred him forward after the
fashion of the career, as though he would ' outrun By violent swiftness that which we run at.' [2]   The result showed
the truth of the old saying quoted by Fitzwalter, ' How
fondly dost thou spur a forward horse ! ' [3]   He flashed past the
remainder of the field, and was the first to reach the summit
of the ascent, whence a long gradual slope led to a small
stream struggling through a marshy bottom.   No sooner
did his bean-fed horse scent the keen upland breeze, and
see before him the long descent with the hounds ascending
the opposite side of the valley, than he took the bit in his
teeth, and aided by the downward sloping hill defied his
rider's control ; for

> What rein can hold licentious wickedness
> When down the hill he holds his fierce career?
>
> *Hen. V.* iii. 3. 22.

Not Ferdinand Petre's, certainly, although he was not ' wanting the manage of unruly jades.' [4]   Clement Perkes and his
companion reached the summit of the ascent just in
time to see him disappear among the rushes of the marsh,
into which his horse wildly plunged.   But his fate points a
moral.   Surely some such experience suggested these words :

> *Biron.* You must not be so quick.
> *Ros.* 'Tis 'long of you that spur me with such questions.

[1] 1 *Hen. IV.* ii. 4. 376.   [2] *Hen. VIII.* i. 1. 141.
[3] *Rich. II.* iv. 1. 72.   [4] *Rich. II.* iii. 3. 179.

Biron. Your wit's too hot, it speeds too fast, 'twill tire.
Ros. Not till it leave the rider in the mire.

Love's L. L. ii. 1. 118.

The path along which Will Squele and Anne were cantering homewards had not diverged too far from the line of the chase to allow them to witness the catastrophe. It did not surprise them, for Will Squele was experienced in horsemanship and in woodcraft, as was John of Gaunt in statecraft when he foretold of Richard II:

> Methinks I am a prophet new inspired
> And thus expiring do foretell of him :
> His rash fierce blaze of riot cannot last,
> For violent fires soon burn out themselves ;
> Small showers last long, but sudden storms are short ;
> He tires betimes that spurs too fast betimes.

Rich. II. ii. 1. 31.

Master Ferdinand's disappearance did not lose him much of the run, for his horse was all but pumped out. William Silence fared better for a time. He knew too much of hunting and of Cotswold to press his horse, or even to give him his head, at the beginning of a run across the wilds of Gloucestershire. And so he kept with Clement Perkes, who was husbanding the resources of his hardy galloway, so far as was consistent with retaining command of the hounds. Too generous to accept the proffered return of his Irish hobby, William Silence soon became conscious that the exchange was a disastrous one, as events had turned out. The stately paces of the High Almain might have charmed Anne Squele as they chased the hart from thicket to thicket within the pale; but before the summit of the second hill had been gained, his great unwieldy carcass showed unmistakable symptoms of distress,[1] and in a few minutes more he was ridden to a standstill, while the Irish

---

[1] There is a reminiscence of a pumped-out and labouring horse in Philostrate's description of Bottom and his company as having ' toiled their unbreathed memories ' with the lamentable comedy of Pyramus and Thisbe (*Mids. N. Dr.* v. 1. 74).

hobby was as fresh as at the start. The reason is not far
to seek. The speed of the great horse and of the hobby
had been absolutely the same, but relatively very different.
Pace, like age, is a relative term. What is slow for the
hare is fast for the tortoise, and the hobby could maintain
with ease for half a day a speed that would tire out the
High Almain in a couple of miles.

When the summit of the second ascent had been reached,
a wide and swelling expanse of upland afforded better galloping. It was rough enough here and there, and the horses,
like the unbacked colts following Ariel's tabor, had to make
their way through ' tooth'd briers, sharp furzes, pricking goss
and thorns, Which enter'd their frail shins.' [1]

There was many an ' acre of barren ground, long heath,
brown furze,' for which nevertheless Gonzalo in *The
Tempest* would gladly have exchanged ' a thousand
furlongs of sea.' [2] Here and there, where water had
accumulated and could find no escape (as on certain
level places at the summits of hills) there were soft
spots, whose dangerously green hue warned the galloping
rider to have ' good judgement in horsemanship,' for, as
the Dauphin of France added, with a vivid recollection of
past disaster, ' they that ride so and ride not warily, fall
into foul bogs.' [3] But, on the whole, the going was sound
enough, and the discreet and careful rider found no difficulty in fulfilling Venus' injunction to Adonis, ' on thy well
breath'd horse keep with thy hounds.' [4]

As for the hounds, I must on their behalf crave indulgence at the hands of some reader who may perchance
treasure amongst his brightest memories a glorious run
over Exmoor ; recalling, as he summons up remembrance
of things past, how hard was the task to keep within
measurable distance of Arthur Heal and his hounds, racing
with a burning scent across the sedgy uplands of the North
Forest and the treacherous bogs around Exe Head, until

---

[1] *Tempest*, iv. 1. 180.   [2] *Tempest*, i. 1. 68.
[3] *Hen. V.* iii. 7. 59.   [4] *Ven. and Ad.* 678.

the welcome slopes of Brendon were reached ; how the horse-hoofs, dashing through the sweet honey-scented heather now in the full glory of its autumn colouring, scattered light wreaths of delicate bloom as they descended to the classic water of Badgeworthy; how, when the line was hit off again after a short and welcome check, his little thorough-bred mare ascended the hill towards Farley Combe, fresh as when she left Yard Down ; and how, when the stag turned to bay in the valley of Watersmeet, he called to mind the scene where the deer was set up after the moorland run recorded in the pages of Katerfelto.[1] Master Shallow's hounds could not compete in dash or speed with these huge twenty-five inch fox-hounds, overdrafts from the best kennels in England. If the truth must be told, the fastest of his pack was not much superior in speed to an average harrier of the present day. The speed of the old-fashioned running hound may be estimated from the sentiment of an old-world sportsman, recorded by Peter Beckford, who was wont to say that a fox shows no sport unless he stands up for four hours before hounds. Theseus' hounds were 'slow in pursuit.'[2] But though slow, the hounds were sure, and it must be remembered that they were seldom uncoupled save at a mature and obese hart, such as could not stand up in the open for many minutes before the Exmoor stag-hounds of to-day. And due proportion being maintained between horse, hound, hart, and hunter's expectations, good sport is the result.

For all that, the cry soon began to present but a sorry appearance. The couple or two of small hounds cast in for treble were soon left behind, and the rest, tho' 'matched in mouth like bells, each under each,' were unequal in speed and endurance. A compact body when first laid on, they have become a straggling line. Although they do not run so mute as the modern fox-hound when hunting deer, yet they give but little tongue.

This did not escape the notice of the hare-hunter from

---

[1] Wednesday, Sept. 7, 1881.   [2] *Mids. N. Dr.* iv. 1. 128.

Stratford, and an observation which he put long afterwards into the mouth of one Roderigo, suggests the reason of the difference between the hunting of the same hounds in pursuit of the hart, and of the hare or the fox. When that sportsman, nominally of Venice (whom Iago had just compared to an overtopping hound), began to discover that he was getting very little in return for his expenditure of time and money, he reflected: ' I do follow here in the chase, not like a hound that hunts, but one that fills up the cry. My money is almost spent; I have been to-night exceedingly well cudgelled; and, I think, the issue will be, I shall have so much experience for my pains, and so, with no money at all and a little more wit, return to Venice.' [1]

The scent of deer is much more powerful to canine perception than that of fox or of hare. Each hound may receive his share and enjoy the treat in decorous silence, without noisy expression of either exultation or envy, unlike those who compete for the possession of a more precarious joy. In hunting the hare, there must be many a Roderigo, clamorously demanding his share of the fun; while the scent of the stag suffices to supply every hound with his quantum of enjoyment, each in his turn.

After some miles of galloping the line crossed a stream, and the leading hounds threw up their heads. As often happens in the chase of the hare, so now in hunting the hart, ' the hot scent-snuffing hounds are driven to doubt.' [2] The hounds are at fault, and the result is a ' let,' [3] or, as it would now be called, a check.

Drawing rein, and dismounting to ease his panting nag, Clement Perkes's companion watches with keen interest the working of the hounds, as they try to single ' with much ado the cold fault cleanly out.' Many a time did the scene recur to his mind; notably when he pictured Malvolio trying to puzzle out a meaning from the scattered symbols and obscure hints in Maria's letter:

---

[1] *Othello*, ii. 3. 369.   [2] *Ven. and Ad.* 692.
[3] *Two Noble Kinsmen*, iii. 5. 156.

Mal. What should that alphabetical position portend? If I could make that resemble something in me,—Softly! M, O, A, I—
Sir To. O, ay, make up that: he is now at a cold scent.
Fab. Sowter will cry upon't, for all this, though it be as rank as a fox.[1]   *Twelfth Night*, ii. 5. 130.

And, again, in *The Tempest* we may catch an echo of cries overheard by the side of a Cotswold stream.

A noise of hunters heard. Enter divers spirits in shape of dogs and hounds, and hunt them about, PROSPERO *and* ARIEL *setting them on.*
Pros. Hey, Mountain, hey!
Ari. Silver! there it goes, Silver!
Pros. Fury, Fury! there, Tyrant, there! hark! hark!
                   Tempest, iv. 1. 256.

The huntsman, now that scent is lost for a time, at all events, jeopards [2] with his horn, an ancient usage that places the prospects of the chase indeed in jeopardy. The jeopard; the 'recheat' (which Benedick, jesting after the fashion of his day, would have winded upon a horn elsewhere than in his own forehead [3]) ; and the mort, are mentioned among the measures of blowing in general use by Gascoigne, in the *Wofull Wordes of the Hart to the Hunter* printed in the *Noble Arte*:

---

[1] This passage has puzzled those who approach it with the idea that the fox was the object of Sowter's pursuit, and Hanmer suggests 'be n't.' The word ' rank ' was generally used in a bad sense, never (so far as I know) to denote a burning scent. The idea seems to be that the line of the hunted hare or deer was cleverly picked out, though foiled by some scent as rank as a fox, which was known as a beast of stinking flight, and detested, as the cause of ' riot,' by hare-hunters, pure and simple, from Xenophon to Shakespeare; ἴχνη . . . ταραχώδη δὲ ὅταν ἀλώπεκες προδιεξέλθωσι γίγνεται (*Cynegeticus*).

[2] I have sought in vain for any explanation of this term of art, which is plainly akin to the word in common use—jeopardy. An old legal term, derived like many terms of venery from Norman-French, suggests a possible etymology. There are certain ancient Acts of Parliament known as Statutes of Jeofails, by which error in legal process might be amended, when the pleader acknowledged his mistake, and which derived their name from his admission—*J'ai faillé*. The word ' jeopard,' as a term of woodcraft, may be similarly derived from *J'ai perdu*, signifying the loss of the trail pursued by the hounds.

[3] *Much Ado*, i. 1. 242.

So now he blowes his horne, even at the kennell dore,
Alas, alas, he blowes a seeke, alas yet blowes he more ;
He jeopardes and rechates ; alas he blowes the Fall,
And soundes that deadly dolefull Mote, which I must die withall.

At length a hound gave tongue, and several of the pack
followed him, as he noisily pursued a line in the direction
whence we have just come. Not so Belman, Silver, or Echo,
who treated the incident with the contempt it deserved. He
was merely hunting counter (or heel, as it is now called),
that is to say, pursuing backwards the line of the hunted
hart. A halter will probably be the fate of the hound who
persists in thus misleading his fellows. ' If thou gettest any
leave of me, hang me, hang me ; if thou takest leave,
thou wert better be hanged. You hunt-counter : [1] hence !
avaunt ! ' [2] said Falstaff to the servant of the Lord Chief
Justice ; meaning thereby that he was on a wrong scent.

How readily the mob, like the puppies of the pack, follow
the misleading cry ; ' the rabble call him lord,' reports a certain gentleman to the King and Queen of Denmark.

They cry, ' Choose we ; Laertes shall be king ; '
Caps, hands, and tongues, applaud it to the clouds ;
' Laertes shall be king, Laertes king ! '
Queen. How cheerfully on the false trail they cry !
O, this is counter, you false Danish dogs !
Hamlet, iv. 5. 106.

Abraham Slender and the huntsman leave the hounds
to themselves, and Perkes's friend looks on, while they cast in
quest of the missing scent. He has noted them well as
they swing around, and, opening like a fan, sweep over the
neighbouring ground. He has told us their very names.
There go Mountain, Fury and Tyrant.[3] There goes Ringwood,[4] *clarum et venerabile nomen.* Here is Sowter, truest
hound,[5] who will carry the line of a hunted deer, even
though it be foiled by scents as rank as that of a fox was

---

[1] The words thus united, and so forming a term of venery, in the Folio are
separated in the Quarto.
[2] *2 Hen. IV.* i. 2. 100.
[3] *Tempest,* iv. 1. 256.
[4] *Merry Wives,* ii. 1. 122.
[5] *Twelfth N.* ii. 5. 135.

supposed to be.   Yonder is Lady the brach, known both
to Harry Hotspur [1] and to King Lear's fool ; [2] and there go
the pick of the kennel—Merriman ; Clowder ; the deep-
mouthed brach whose name we know not ; Echo, slow but
sure ; Silver and Belman, whose comparative merits have
given rise to many a long discussion between Silence and
John Hunt ; [3] and lastly, there is ' Brabbler the hound ;' [4] of
whom, from to-day's performance, there are hopes that he
may, after all, escape a halter.   Six couples in all, or about
one-half of the entire cry. [5]

"Hark to Belman."   These few words completely change
the aspect of affairs.   The trusty hound has—in the words
of the huntsman's report to his master, which found its way
into the Induction to *The Taming of the Shrew*—' cried
upon it at the merest loss, And twice to-day picked out
the dullest scent.'   Aware from his lengthened experience

---

[1] 1 *Hen. IV.* iii. 1. 240.   [2] *K. Lear*, i. 4. 125.
[3] *Tam. of Shrew*, Ind. i. 17–26.   [4] *Troil and Cres.* v. 1. 99.
[5] The man who can tell by their names the hounds with which he is used
to hunt, if he is not the huntsman, generally knows quite as much about hunting—sometimes more—and Shakespeare has given proof that he is no exception
to this rule.   Mr. Beckford, in his *Thoughts on Hunting* (1781), includes among
the names of hounds in common use, Fury, Tyrant, Ringwood, Merryman,
Belman, Echo, Mounter, and Saunter.   For the last two, Shakespeare's Mountain and Sowter may be misprints.   All the other names have some meaning
applied to hounds ; but Mountain and Sowter (cobbler) absolutely none.   Mr.
Beckford, who lived in a county adjoining Gloucestershire, must have got hold
somehow of Master Shallow's nomenclature.   For the names which they employ
in common were by no means then in general use.   They are not among the
fifteen familiar names of hounds mentioned in verses on fox hunting printed by
Mr. Beckford, and in an earlier list, in Cox's *Gentleman's Recreation* (1674), I
find none of them, with the single exception of Ringwood.   But Ringwood was
the typical name of a running hound, from the time of Xenophon, whose catalogue of forty-seven names for hounds, each possessing some significance, includes °Υλεύς.   The word ' brach,' which occurs also in *Troil. and Cres.* ii. 1. 126,
and *K. Lear*, iii. 6. 72 (Fr. *brac* or *braque*), originally meant a hound hunting by
scent, but in time was exclusively appropriated to females of that class ; ' a brach
is a mannerly name for all hound bitches ' (*Gentleman's Recreation*).   There is
some difficulty in fixing, even approximately, the number of hounds in the
Justice's cry.   It was certainly less than that of the modern pack.   For Somerville, writing in 1735 (*The Chase*), feels bound to

> Censure that numerous pack, that crowd of state
> With which the vain profusion of the great
> Covers the lawn.

that scent travels downstream, he has been anticipating the Baconian philosophy by a systematic interrogation of nature in an upstream direction, and has at last hit on a scent-holding tuft of rushes at the point where the stag left the stream (or broke soil as it was termed) to ascend the slope of the opposite hill. No sooner had the hound acknowledged the scent than his whole nature seemed to change. From being lethargic, mute, dull, and 'at a fault,' he at once became 'sprightly walking, audible, and full of vent,' as different from his former self as war from peace. Could Dr. Johnson have practised as he preached, and looked for Shakespeare's meaning among the sports of the field, he surely would not have mutilated the words put into the mouth of a certain serving-man of the Volscian general, Tullus Aufidius, (his huntsman for aught I know), which was thus printed in the Folio :

Let me have war, say I; it exceeds peace as far as day does night; it's spritely walking, audible, and full of vent.[1] Peace is a very apoplexy, lethargy ; mulled, deaf, sleepy, insensible.

Coriol. iv. 5. 236.

[1] Pope, re-writing *Shakespeare* after his fashion, read 'sprightly, waking, audible, and full of vent,' and Dr. Johnson, adopting this reading, explained the last term as meaning 'full of rumour, full of materials for discourse.' Dr. Baynes, in an Article in the *Edinburgh Review* (Oct. 1872), afterwards printed in *Shakespeare Studies* (1894), first pointed out that 'vent' was a term of art in woodcraft, signifying 'scent.' In the lines of Gascoigne quoted from the *Noble Arte*, the hound is described as straining 'upon good vent,' and the word is used in the same sense in other passages of the same work. The word 'vent' occurs as a verb, in the sense of 'to scent' in Spenser (*Shepheard's Calendar*) and Drayton (*Polyolbion*). It is the Norman-French equivalent for the Anglo-Saxon 'wind,' used frequently in the sense of scent by Shakespeare, both as a verb and as a substantive ; *Tit. Andr.* iv. 1. 97; *ibid.* iv. 2. 133 ; *All's Well*, iii. 6. 122 ;. *ibid.* v. 2. 10; 3 *Hen. VI.* iii. 2. 14 ; *Hamlet*, iii. 2. 362. In *The Shepheard's Calendar*, the bullock 'venteth into the winde.' This term of art must have been somewhat unusual in poetry, for Spenser thinks it needful to explain it in his *Glosse* thus, '*venteth*, snuffeth in the winde.' It is strange that the restoration of the folio thus suggested has not been generally adopted. Dr. Schmidt (*Shakespeare Lexicon*) accepts it conditionally upon its being shown that the word 'vent' bore the meaning attributed to it ; a condition surely amply fulfilled. The comparison of war (*K. John*, iv. 3. 149), to an eager hound, is a favourite one with Shakespeare, as in *Hen. V.* iii. 1. 31, and *Jul. Cæs.* iii. 1. 273. The Globe and Cambridge editions read 'spritely, waking,' with Pope.

Now may be seen the advantage of a good character, honestly won. The words " Hark to Belman " are scarcely out of the huntsman's lips before the pack have flown to his summons, and in another moment they are carrying the line along the side of the opposite hill.

No one heeds the bawler or the babbler. But there is no mistake about Belman. In hunting language, he is 'true-bred,'[1] and of ' such as can hold in,'[2] and ' will ne'er out.'[3] There can be no reasonable doubt that he is the very hound present to the mind of his master when he thus enlarged on his serving-man Davy's powers of sticking to his quarry. ' The knave will stick by thee, I can assure thee that. A' will not out, he is true bred.'[4]

The line taken by the hart after he had broken soil was that which had suggested itself to the mind of Will Squele, when he turned his horse's head homewards. Doubt-ful of his power to stand up before hounds until the long wood was reached, the hunted deer turned sharply to the left after crossing the stream, with the evident intention of reaching the well-known wood and water near Master Squele's abode.

The hounds settled down on the line of the straining hart,[5] and his fate was sealed. He had as little chance of

---

[1] *Twelfth N.* ii. 3. 195.   [2] 1 *Hen. IV.* ii. 1. 85.   [3] *Ant. and Cleo.* ii. 7. 35.

[4] 2 *Hen. IV.* v. 3. 69.   When you uncouple your young hounds from the old and experienced hounds, ' you must,' says the author of the *Noble Arte*, ' have good prickers and huntesmen on horsebacke in the tayle of them to make them holde in close.'   To ' hold in chase ' was a phrase in common use : *K. John*, i. 1. 223 ; *Coriol.* i. 6. 19 ; *Lucrece*, 1736 ; *Sonnet* cxliii.

[5] ' When he (the hart) runneth verie fast, then he streyneth ' (*Noble Arte*). If Mr. Collier had known of this meaning of the word, he need not have con-jectured ' strayed ' in the passage where Hermione, forced to appear in a Court of Justice, thus addresses Leontes :

> I appeal
> To your own conscience, sir, before Polixenes
> Came to your Court, how I was in your grace,
> How merited to be so ; since he came
> With what encounter so uncurrent I
> Have strain'd to appear thus.   *Wint. Tale*, iii. 2. 46.

Nor need Dr. Johnson have conjectured ' have I been stain'd ' for the reading of the Folio.

escape from his fell and cruel pursuers as the Duke of
Illyria from the love of the fair Olivia :

Cur. Will you go hunt, my lord ?
Duke. What, Curio ?
Cur. The hart.
Duke. Why, so I do, the noblest that I have :
O, when mine eyes did see Olivia first,
Methought she purged the air of pestilence !
That instant was I turn'd into a hart ;
And my desires, like fell and cruel hounds,
E'er since pursue me.   *Twelfth Night*, i. 1. 16.

" ' We have almost embossed him,' " [1] said Slender to the
huntsman, in words familiar to the lords at the French
Court, " ' you shall see his fall to-night.' " [2]   The practical
question is how to keep on terms with the hounds until
the woodland stream is reached, some seven miles distant,
where the stag is almost certain to turn to bay.   Now can
the happy possessor of a good continuer (as a stayer was then
called by horsemen) realise the force of the ditty, ' As true as
truest horse, that yet would never tire.' [3]   And if to continu-
ing power he adds a fair turn of speed, he is all that can be
desired.   So thought Benedick, when with such a chase as
this present to his mind he said to Beatrice :

I would my horse had the speed of your tongue, and so good
a continuer, but keep your way i' God's name ; I have done.
Beat. You always end with a jade's trick : I know you of old.
     Much Ado, i. 1. 139.

---

[1] ' When he (the hart) is foamy at the mouth, we saye that he is *embost*
(*Noble Arte*). An ' embossed rascal ' is a sporting term of contempt playfully
applied by Prince Harry to Falstaff (1 *Hen. IV.* iii. 3. 177), whom it was very
gracious fooling to liken to a rascal or lean deer, as Doll Tearsheet, when she
thus addressed him, ' come you thin thing, come you rascal ' (2 *Hen. IV.* v. 4.
34).   Dr. Johnson's note on the former passage is ' to emboss a deer is to enclose
him in a wood,' and on the latter ' embossed, is swollen, puffy.'   Dr. Schmidt
(*Shakespeare Lexicon*) thus interprets the word ; ' to ambuscade (French *em-
busquer*, Ital. *imboscare*).'   The word is used in each of these three meanings
in Chaucer.   Applied to Falstaff, it was probably intended to suggest a play on
the word in the sense of ' swollen, puffy.'   Compare *Tam. of Shrew*, Ind. i. 17 ;
Ant. and Cleo. iv. 13. 3 ; *Tim. of Ath.* v. 1. 220.
[2] *All's Well*, iii. 6. 107.   [3] *Mids. N. Dr.* iii. 1. 105.

Long afterwards, the idea was suggested to the mind of
the Stratford sportsman of a continuer who had settled down
to his stride, who had, as it were, got his second wind in the
pursuit of virtue ; and he made the merchant describe Timon
of Athens as

> A most incomparable man ; breathed, as it were,
> To an untirable and continuate goodness.
>
> *Tim. of Ath.* i. 1. 10.

Master Slender is with John Hunt and the main body of
the pack. He could say with Titus Andronicus,

> I have horse will follow where the game
> Makes way, and run like swallows o'er the plain.
>
> *Tit. And.* ii. 2. 23.

William Visor of Woncot has long since taken the last
groatsworth out of his hired jade, but Perkes and his companion hold good places. 'Know we not galloway nags?'[1]
asked Ancient Pistol, irrelevantly after his fashion, but not
without significance. If we know them, we can have no
difficulty in recognising the hardy little animal on which
the yeoman is mounted. If we do not, Gervase Markham
tells us of the character which they bore, 'There is a certain
race of little horses in Scotland, called Galway Nagges,
which I have seene hunt the Buck and stagge exceeding
well, and indure the chase with good courage.'[2] As to the
Irish hobby, and Master Slender's English horse, their
powers of endurance are attested by the same authority,
for he tells us of 'the best Barbarys that ever were in their
prime I saw them overrun by a black hobby at Salisbury ;
yet that hobby was more overrun by a horse called Valentine,
which Valentine neither in hunting nor running was ever
equalled, yet was a plain-bred English horse both by sire
and dam.'

As for the hounds, they have again become an ever
lengthening line, and three couples only carry the trail of the
hunted deer to the bottom of the valley, near the woods of

[1] 2 *Hen. IV.* ii. 4. 204.   [2] *Cavalarice.*

Hogshearing. There they check. There is a stream at the bottom, and the hill beyond is steep, covered with rough bracken and gorse.

" He ha'nt taken soil," said Perkes to Slender. " No ! but a' will soon," he added, eagerly scanning the opposite bank, " for there a' goeth, straight up hill."

To the yeoman's practised eye this unwonted mode of ascending a hill betokened a last reckless effort on the part of the deer doomed to failure.

The hounds saw him too, and opened in louder chorus as they dashed forward to the view. Heavily labouring; his antlers thrown back; his head hanging down; his mouth embossed no longer, but black, dry, and open ; his fur bedrabbled and torn ; the poor hunted beast, after a few vain attempts to climb the hill, turned back. His strength, unequal to the labour of ascent, carried him quickly downwards, and dashing into the thick woodlands he was lost to view.

The hounds, driven again to their noses, carried a burning scent, until they arrived at the bed of the stream. The scent of the deer, unlike that of the hare, improves as the animal sinks. A track, or ' trench,' led along the side of the stream, so narrow as to admit but a single horseman. Along this trench the riders followed in single file until they reached the extremity of the woodland, where was a long deep pool, formed by damming the stream in order to flood Master Squele's water meadows. Again the hart is viewed. He is swimming, keeping in the middle of the stream so as to avoid touching any scent-holding bough. The hounds dash in, but, as he knew well, they could only approach him by swimming. Up and down this pool, now swimming, now running, sweep hart and hounds, while the narrow valley resounds with the music of the hounds and the shouting of the hunters, and all knew well that the end was nigh at hand.

CHAPTER V

HOW THE HART WAS BAYED AND BROKEN UP

> Here wast thou bay'd, brave hart;
> Here did'st thou fall; and here thy hunters stand
> Sign'd in thy spoil and crimson'd in thy lethe.
>
> *Julius Cæsar.*

THERE are those to whom the sequel of the day, when the run is over, is mere shambles work, fit for butchers, not for sportsmen. To some, the notes which tell that all is over with a noble beast of venery summon up sad associations, for Leonatus, among the tokens of woman's frailty, includes

> to sigh, as 'twere
> The mort o' the deer.   *Wint. Tale*, i. 2. 117.

This feeling was certainly not generally shared by sportsmen, and these pages would forfeit all claim to strict veracity if they did not reflect the interest which the writer of the journal, in common with most of our ancestors, took in the obsequies of the hunted hart. The gentle reader is warned off the following pages. Deer must be killed, but in the quibbling words of the thane of Ross—for even in telling to Macduff the sad story of the slaughter of his dear ones, he could not forego a familiar pun—

> To relate the manner
> Were, on the quarry of these murder'd deer,
> To add the death of you.   *Macbeth*, iv. 3. 206.

The hart was no sooner strengthened by the cooling

stream than he bethought him of the traditions of his kingly
race. ' If we be English deer,' said the gallant Talbot, liken-
ing his host to the Cotswold hart, fighting stoutly to the last
in face of overwhelming numbers,

> be then in blood ;
> Not rascal-like, to fall down with a pinch,
> But rather, moody-mad and desperate stags,
> Turn on the bloody hounds with heads of steel
> And make the cowards stand aloof at bay ;
> Sell every man his life as dear as mine,
> And they shall find dear deer of us, my friends.
>> 1 *Hen. VI.* iv. 2. 48.

In deep water, beneath a great rock, he makes his final
stand. His enemies can approach him only in front, and
swimming. Calmly he awaits their attack, while the leading hounds, reinforced by a few stragglers, bay in a semi-
circle around their foe.

The familiar and welcome sound of the bay serves to
guide Clement Perkes and his companion to the spot where
the hart was set up. Although not actually with Abraham
Slender and the huntsman at the end of the run, they are
nigh at hand, and the ' timorous yelping of the hounds '[1]
informs their experienced ears that ' the hounds are at a bay.' [2]

The hopes of the hunters were raised by the same
sounds that caused alarm in the breast of Venus, fearful for
the safety of her beloved Adonis,

> Because the cry remaineth in one place,
> Where fearfully the dogs exclaim aloud ;
>> Finding their enemy to be so curst,
>> They all strain courtesy who shall cope him first.
>> *Ven. and Ad.* 885.

Who goes first ? Young Fury, trashed though he was, rushed
on the foe, and received a wound from the formidable brow
antlers of the hart. He retired howling. Who goes next ?
The courtesy of the cry became more strained, and the
chorus waxed louder and louder, as the gallant hart gave

---

[1] *Ven. and Ad.* 881.   [2] *Ibid.* 877.

proof that he was no ' dull and muddy-mettled rascal,' [1] but ' in blood ' not alone to run, but to fight too, and sell his life right dearly.

He to whose lot it has fallen from time to time to view the hart in his native wild—not the dishorned and carted deer in some potato garden—' hold at a bay ' his foes ' the fell and cruel hounds,' will not be surprised to find the image recurring again and again to one present at the death of the Cotswold hart, although he may well marvel at the truthfulness with which every feature of the familiar scene is reflected in the poet's mirror.   If any words could convey to the imagination an adequate idea of the effect produced upon the senses, they are surely those put into the mouth of Hippolyta.   She tells us that she

> was with Hercules and Cadmus once,
> When in a wood of Crete [2] they bay'd the bear
> With hounds of Sparta : never did I hear
> Such gallant chiding ; for, besides the groves,
> The skies, the fountains, every region near
> Seem'd all one mutual cry : I never heard
> So musical a discord, such sweet thunder.
>
> *Mids. N. Dr.* iv. 1. 117.

The effect of echo in enhancing the cry of hounds—' the musical confusion of hounds and echo in conjunction ' [3]

---

[1] *Hamlet*, ii. 2. 594.   A rascal was a lean and worthless deer (Anglo-Saxon = a lean beast).   ' Come, you thin thing ; come you rascal,' Mistress Dorothy Tearsheet says pleasantly to Falstaff (2 *Hen. IV.* v. 4. 34 ; cf. 1 *Hen. VI.* i. 2 35).   ' Muddy,' or ' muddy-mettled ' rascal, would seem from the passage quoted from *Hamlet*, and from another exclamation of Mistress Tearsheet's (2 *Hen. IV.* ii. 4. 43) to have been phrases in use among woodmen.   ' Thou rascal that art worst in blood to run ' (*Coriol.* i. 1. 163, cf. *Love's L. L.* iv. 2. 3, and 1 *Hen. VI.* iv. 2. 48).   In the sense in which it is now used as a term of reproach, it was in the first instance spoken by the ' figure *Metaphore* . . . . as one should in reproch say to a poore man thou rascale knaue, when *rascall* is properly the hunter's terme giuen to young deere, leane and out of season, and not to people.' (Puttenham, *Arte of English Poesie*, 1589.)   Shakespeare was better versed in woodcraft than Puttenham, and he tells us that an old deer may yet be a rascal, as we shall see later on.

[2] It is evident that the Spartan hounds and Cretan bears behave after the fashion of the Southern hound and English hart.

[3] *Mids. N. Dr.* iv. 1. 115.

was often noted. 'Wilt thou hunt?' asks the Lord of Christopher Sly:

> Thy hounds shall make the welkin answer them
> And fetch shrill echoes from the hollow earth.
>
> *Tam. of Shrew*, Ind. 2. 46.

And Tamora, the Gothic Queen, thus addressed her beloved Moor:

> Whilst the babbling echo mocks the hounds,
> Replying shrilly to the well-tun'd horns,
> As if a double hunt were heard at once,
> Let us sit down and mark their yelping noise.
>
> *Tit. Andr.* ii. 3. 17.

In the chase of the hare, when the pack gives tongue and 'spend their mouths: Echo replies As if another chase were in the skies.' [1] But it is at the baying of the hart, when hounds are pent within the confines of the narrow valley where he mostly soils, and when the music of the cry is turned to the thunder of the bay—as by some mighty organ-stop—that the truthfulness of Hippolyta's description is borne in on the mind. Then we feel certain that she speaks the words of one who had often stood by woodland stream, and marked how, by re-echoing the sweet thunder, the groves, the skies, the fountains, and every region near seem'd all one mutual cry, as if all nature took part in the tragedy of the hart at bay.

How long this scene would have lasted, had not man interposed, cannot be told. Certain it is that many a gallant hound must have fallen a victim to the fury of the hart, and that the cry would have told a tale of disaster such as that which met the eyes of Venus. Led onwards by the sound of the bay,

> Here kennell'd in a brake she finds a hound,
> And asks the weary caitiff for his master,
> And there another licking of his wound,
> 'Gainst venom'd sores the only sovereign plaster:
> And here she meets another sadly scowling,
> To whom she speaks, and he replies with howling.

[1] *Ven. and Ad.* 695.

When he hath ceased his ill-resounding noise,
Another flap-mouth'd mourner, black and grim,
Against the welkin volleys out his voice ;
Another and another answer him,
   Clapping their proud tails to the ground below,
   Shaking their scratch'd ears, bleeding as they go.
                          Ven. and Ad. 913.

As soon as the deer began to hold the hounds at a bay, Slender and the huntsman dismounted. As they approached the stream, a clear voice beside them said :

" Give me your horses to hold. I knew well that he must needs take soil in this water when I noted what point he made after breaking thicket."

It was the voice of Will Squele. A Cotswold man, he knew every inch of the country ; an old sportsman, he could tell the run of the deer to a nicety ; and while we have been galloping up and down hill with the hounds, he and Anne have taken the shortest road from point to point.

" Ecod," says Abraham Slender, " go as I may, Will Squele on Bay Curtal is ever there before me."

Clement Perkes and his companion, warily approaching the hart from behind, cast around his antlers a rope carried by the huntsman for that purpose. His head having been thus pulled back, the huntsman cut his throat with his sword, and crying " Ware hound ! " to keep the hounds from breaking into the deer, blooded the puppies, ' that they may the better love a deer, and learn to leap at his throat,' as Mr. Cox quaintly explains in his *Gentleman's Recreation.*

' The mort o' the deer ' having been duly blown by such of the company as carried horns,' there next came the solemnity of taking assay, and breaking up the deer.

The assay should be taken by the best person of the company that hath not taken assay before. ' Oure order is,' says the author of the *Noble Arte,* ' that the prince or chiefe (if so please them) doe auger and take assaye of the deare with a sharpe knyfe, the whiche is done in this manner.

The deare being layd upon his backe, the prince, chiefe, or such as they shall appoint, comes to it ; And the chiefe hunts-man (kneeling, if it be to a prince) doth holde the deare by the forefoote, whiles the prince or chief cut a slyt drawn alongst the brysket of the deare, somewhat lower than the brysket towards the belly. This is done to see the goodnesse of the flesh, and how thicke it is.'

On this occasion the honour of taking assay fell to Mistress Anne Squele. You may realise the scene if you look at an interesting woodcut in the *Noble Arte*, depicting the chiefest huntsman, on bended knee, handing the knife to a noble lady, while an attendant holds her richly caparisoned horse.

But it were long to tell of the cutting and cabbaging of the head, and of the ceremony to be used in taking out the shoulder, and selecting the ' deintie morsels,' and ' the caule, the tong, the eares, the doulcets,[1] the tenderlings (if his head be tender), and the sweet gut, which some call the Inchpinne, in a faire handkercher together, for the prince or chiefe ; ' how a little gristle upon the spoon of the brisket is cast to the crows or ravens which attend hunters ; how there has been seen ' a raven so wont and accustomed to it that she would never fayle to croake and crye for it all the while you were in breaking up of the deare, and would not depart untill she had it ; ' how the numbles or umbles are wound up, to serve in the making of umble-pie.

These weighty matters of the art of venery were, indeed, foolishness in the eyes of the learned and satirical Erasmus. ' When they have run down their game,' he says of the sportsmen of his day, among whom he held his own when in England,[2] ' what strange pleasure they take in cutting it up. Cows and sheep may be slaughtered by common butchers, but what is killed in hunting must be broke up by none under a gentleman, who shall throw down his hat, fall devoutly on his knees, and drawing out a slashing hanger

---

[1] *Two Noble Kinsmen*, iii. 5. 154.
[2] See Note, *Sir Thomas More on Field Sports*.

(for a common knife is not good enough) after several ceremonies shall dissect all the parts as artificially as the best
skilled anatomist, while all that stand round shall look very
intently, and seem to be mightily surprised with the novelty,
though they have seen the same a hundred times before,
and he that can but dip his finger and taste of the blood,
shall think his own bettered thereby.'[1]

If these daring words had come to the knowledge of
our Gloucestershire friends, they would simply have said
that much learning had made the writer mad, so firm an
article of faith it was that the carcase of the hart should
not be thrown rudely to the hounds, as the fox, the marten,
or the gray, but should be reverently disposed of. 'Let's kill
him boldly, but not wrathfully;' said Brutus of Julius
Cæsar;

> Let's carve him as a dish fit for the gods,
> Not hew him as a carcase fit for hounds.
>
> *Jul. Cæs.* ii. 1. 172.

Cæsar fell, having been given less law by his pursuers
than the Cotswold hart. And as we read Mark Antony's
words, we could almost believe that he too had stood with
Abraham Slender by the waterside; 'stained with the
variation of each soil' betwixt find and finish, as was 'Sir
Walter Blunt new lighted from his horse;'[2] and 'bloody as
the hunter,'[3] signed and crimsoned with the blood of the
deer, after the somewhat barbarous fashion of the chase.

> Here wast thou bay'd, brave hart;
> Here didst thou fall; and here thy hunters stand
> Sign'd in thy spoil, and crimson'd in thy lethe.[4]
> O world, thou wast the forest to this hart;

---

[1] Erasmus, *Moriæ Encomium.*   [2] 1 *Hen. IV.* i. 1. 64.

[3] *Twelfth N.* iii. 4. 243. Compare the English herald's description of his
troops;

> Like a jolly troop of huntsmen, come
> Our lusty English, all with purpled hands,
> Dyed in the dying slaughter of their foes.
>
> *K. John*, ii. 1. 321.

[4] Lethe (for which Theobald and Collier read 'death') according to Capell
(*Glossary*) is 'a term used by hunters to signify the blood shed by a deer at

And this, indeed, O world, the heart of thee.
How like a deer, strucken by many princes,
Dost thou here lie!   *Jul. Cæs.* iii. 1. 204.

As time went on, the observances at the death of the
deer grew into a burden too heavy to be borne. Life
became fuller of action and incident, and was felt to be
too short for such old-world ceremonies. They were more
solemn and elaborate in 1486 [1] than in 1575, and a hundred
years later they seem to have resolved themselves into the
summary process of handing a knife to the prince, or lady
of quality, with which to cut the deer's throat, leaving the
rest to inferiors : a form in which the ceremony was observed
in the forest of Exmoor on a notable occasion in the month
of August 1879. [2]

The ceremonial of assay and breaking up having ended,
the paunch is given to the hounds as their quarry or
reward. The blood-hound, or limer, would have been entitled
to the first share, according to the usage of the chase, [3] had
he been there to claim his rights. But this day's chase
exceeded his limited powers of hunting. Keen-scented, but
unaccustomed to hunt at large, he has not the trained
sagacity which would enable him to run down the scent
which he is the first to detect. He is at this moment hunting counter, pursuing the trail backwards, with keen enjoyment, across the hills towards Shallow Hall. He is, in the
words applied by Dromio of Syracuse to the catchpole,

its fall, with which it is still a custom to mark those who come in at the
death.'

[1] *Boke of St. Albans.*

[2] This custom was generally observed in the last century. Pope contributed
to the *Guardian* a paper on cruelty to animals (No. 61). He dares not attack
hunting, 'a diversion which has such authority and custom to support it. . . .
But,' he adds, ' I must animadvert upon a certain custom yet in use with us, and
barbarous enough to be derived from the Goths, or even the Scythians ; I mean
that savage compliment our huntsmen pass upon ladies of quality, who are
present at the death of a stag, when they put the knife in their hands to cut the
throat of a helpless, trembling, and weeping creature,

> questuque cruentus
> Atque imploranti similis.'

[3] *Noble Arte.*

A hound that runs counter and yet draws dry-foot well.[1]

Com. of Err. iv. 2. 39.

The deer having been thus disembowelled *secundum artem*, the venison is reserved for the powdering tub, and we know on the best authority that his 'skin's a keeper's fee.'[2] Jack Falstaff had not seen a deer killed for many a year, but he knew well of what the prince was thinking when he said,

What, old acquaintance! could not all this flesh
Keep in a little life? Poor Jack, farewell!
I could have better spared a better man :
O, I should have a heavy miss of thee,
If I were much in love with vanity!
Death hath not struck so fat a deer to-day,
Though many dearer, in this bloody fray.
Embowell'd will I see thee by and by:
Till then, in blood, by noble Percy lie.   (*Exit.*)
    Fal. (*Rising up*) Embowelled! If thou embowel me to-day,
I'll give you leave to powder me and eat me too, to-morrow.

1 *Hen. IV.* v. 4. 102.

The day's sport over, the hounds were recoupled, and a strake of nine, to call the company home, was wound by the huntsman. This had the effect of bringing another figure on the scene.

----

[1] There is a quibble in these words, as in many of Shakespeare's allusions to woodcraft. The counter or compter, according to Dr. Johnson, was the name of a London prison, served by the catchpole, who thus was humorously said to 'run counter' though keen of scent. 'To draw dry-foot' was a phrase in constant use. Thus Gervase Markham gives instructions by which a horse may be taught to draw dry-foot, like a hound (*Cavalarice*). It is used, in contradistinction to tracking footsteps in wet or moist ground, to signify hunting with nothing to guide the hound but the scent where the object of pursuit has passed along dry-foot. Mr. Monck Mason points out that the phrase occurs in an Irish Statute, 10 William III. c. 8, sec. 10, under which the training of a hound 'to hunt on dry foot' is attached as a condition to obtaining a licence to use a setting dog. The jest would have no prosperity save in the ears of those who knew the defects, as well as the virtues, of the liam-hound, who indeed is often represented in old engravings as held in hand during the chase. Otherwise he would probably be found running counter. The fool in Fletcher's *Mad Lover* quibbles on the word 'counter' (i. 1), but his thoughts turn, not to the chase, but to false coin

[2] 3 *Hen. VI.* iii. 1. 22.

CHAPTER VI

AFTER THE CHASE

Where is the horse that doth untread again
His tedious measures with the unbated fire
That he did pace them first ? All things that are,
Are with more spirit chased than enjoy'd.
Merchant of Venice.

WHEN William Silence had been passed by Slender on the hillside, all idea of taking part in the chase was at an end. His first thought was of his over-ridden horse. Satisfied that no permanent harm has been done, he applied his mind to the inquiry—which way have the hounds gone?

In the wilds of Gloucestershire, as on Exmoor, this question must be asked of nature, not of man. There is this advantage, that nature never lies. But you must know her language. William Silence had not forgotten at Oxford or at Gray's Inn the early teaching of Cotswold. He gains the summit of the hill, and looks around him. In a pool to the right, a heron calmly resting on one leg plainly says—neither horse nor hound has passed my way. In another direction sheep huddled in masses, and wild horses disturbed and excited as plainly tell the story of the chase which has swept over the hills in their sight.

The deer has most probably made for the wooded valley near Hogshearing. If so, Squele and Anne will be up before he is taken. This was certain. What was to be done? Should he return home and leave Master Slender in undisputed possession? Or should he follow as best he

could, trusting to his ready wit to regain the advantage
which he had lost? This would, at all events, insure an
early meeting with Anne Squele. And if this accursed hart
would only go elsewhere, and take Abraham Slender with
him, no invidious comparisons could be drawn, and he
would be sure of a hearty welcome as a victim of one of the
numberless mishaps to which hunters are subject. So he
makes his way as best he can towards Hogshearing. If the
deer has gone in that direction, the riders must have crossed
the morass in the bottom of the next valley. There is but
one sound crossing, and as Silence reaches it his conjecture
is converted into certainty by the sight of fresh prints of
horse-hoofs in the soft earth. Still he follows on. At
last the sound of the mort reaches his ear, borne thither
amidst the intense stillness of the waste. The hart has
been killed. No doubt Anne and Slender are making merry
over his discomfiture. Still he follows on. He is making
his way through the tangled woodland by the stream when
a strake of nine, close at hand, reveals the whereabouts of
the company. A few more steps bring him face to face
with Master Squele, who, with his daughter, was leading
the way to the house.

"Welcome, Master William," said the cheery franklin.
"Turn back with us. The company will eat and drink
under my roof before they turn homewards. 'Tis a good
head, a hart of ten. 'Tis a pity you missed the sport when
he held the hounds at a bay. But Master Slender says that
you had enough of it by the time you were half way up the
long hill. Well, I rode not the chase myself to-day. But
when I was your age——"

"My horse had enough of it, not I. But 'tis all one. I
missed the chase."

"Nay," said Anne, "how can it all be one, for

> by Saint Jamy,
> I hold you a penny,
> A horse and a man
> Is more than one,
> And yet not many.   *Tam. of Shrew*, iii. 2. 84.

What, that great and serviceable horse, whose 'tender hide'[1] shone so brightly? Why, when next you and your fellow hunt in these parts, you must condescend to one of those uncomely country curtals which you derided at the assembly. And pr'ythee, Master Silence, has Master Ferdinand Petre yet regained his great and serviceable mare?"

"I know not," said Silence gloomily.

"Be of good heart," said Anne, "you know the country saying, 'Jack shall have Jill; Nought shall go ill. The man shall have his mare again, and all shall be well.'[2] As for you, Master Slender, you and your beast are too fit company ever to part."

"Oh la, Mistress Anne." Repartee never was Slender's strong point, much as he had studied the *Book of Riddles*, and even the *Hundred Merrie Tales*.

The party now emerged from the wood, and found themselves in front of the old house at Hogshearing—so intimately associated with Squele.

It was a long, low, two-storied house, built of grey stone, with mullioned windows, pointed gables, and high chimneys. Many such residences of the franklin, or country gentleman of moderate means, have escaped destruction on the one hand, and on the other reconstruction and modernisation, by becoming the residences of substantial farmers. It was surrounded by a moat. This appendage of a country house had ceased to be necessary for purposes of defence, and was condemned by the sanitary reformers of the day as unwholesome. Reformers, however, made but slow progress in those days. Mariana, as we know, lived in the moated grange, and all men could understand when England was compared to a

> precious stone set in the silver sea,
> Which serves it in the office of a wall
> Or as a moat defensive to a house,
> Against the envy of less happier lands.
>
> *Rich. II*. ii. 1. 46.

---

[1] *Ven. and Ad.* 298. [2] *Mids. N. Dr.* iii. 2. 461.

Besides, the moat had its uses. In the absence of a regularly constructed fish-pond, it served as a convenient stew, in which fish might be kept and fattened for the master's table. For our ancestors loved fish, even the coarser sorts, especially when cooked with poignant sauce. But whether they loved them or not, they must needs eat them in time of Lent. For even after the Reformation, stringent laws were passed ' against eating of flesh upon days forbidden,' and ' for restraint of eating flesh in Lent, and on fish dayes ; ' and Justice Shallow, when giving the charge at quarter sessions,[1] would commend it to the jury to inquire ' if any person (other than by reason of age, sickness, childing, or licence) have within this year eaten flesh in Lent, or upon any fish day observed by the custom of this realm ; ' and further, ' If any innholder, taverner, alehouse-keeper, common victualler, common cook, or common table-keeper, hath uttered or put to sale any kind of flesh victual upon any day in the time of Lent, or upon any Friday, Saturday, or other day appointed by former law to be fish day (not being Christmas day), except it be to such person as (resorting to such house) had lawful licence to eat the same according to the statute thereof made.'[2] With these statutes did Sir John Falstaff seek to frighten Mistress Quickly, when he told her,

Marry, there is another indictment upon thee, for suffering flesh to be eaten in thy house, contrary to the law ; for the which, I think, thou wilt howl.

Host. All victuallers do so : What's a joint of mutton or two in a whole Lent ?   2 *Hen. IV.* ii. 4. 371.

We must not therefore hastily credit our ancestors with

[1] See Lambarde's *Eirenarcha, or of the Office of Justices of Peace* (1581).

[2] 5 *Eliz.* c. 5 ; 27 *Eliz.* c. 11. In the 39th section of the former statute it is carefully explained that this legislation is politically meant for the increase of fishermen and mariners, and not for any superstition in the choice of meats ; and under the 40th section, any one publicly preaching or teaching that this statutory eating of fish or forbearing of flesh is ' of any necessity for the saving of the soul of man ' is punishable ' as spreaders of false news are and ought to be.'

depraved taste when we find them preserving and fattening
for the table such abominations as tench and bream, but we
should rather regard their fishponds, stews, and moats as
part of the general policy of the realm, and very conducive
to the due observance of the law, especially as administered
by justices of the peace.

Beside the moat was a mound, crowned with a summer-
house, in which you could sit, and angle from the water a
carp, or perch, or other dainty fish. For many held with
Ursula, that

> The pleasant'st angling is to see the fish
> Cut with her golden oars the silver stream,
> And greedily devour the treacherous bait.
> > *Much Ado*, iii. 1. 26.

Beyond were a fair orchard and garden. Squele, like
most country gentlemen of the day, was a practical gardener,
with special skill in the art of graffing.[1] By this art, he
would explain,

> we marry
> A gentler scion to the wildest stock,
> And make conceive a bark of baser kind
> By bud of nobler race : this is an art
> Which does mend nature, change it rather, but
> The art itself is nature.   *Wint. Tale*, iv. 4. 92.

He would point with pride to certain box trees, cut into
the shapes of beagles, pursuing a flying hare. The training
of these hounds he would call an old man's hunting,
delighting the eyes while it tired not the legs, and wasting
neither corn nor coin.

It was a ' curious-knotted garden,' [2] where walks and beds
were arranged in quaint devices. The air was heavy with
the perfume of autumn flowers ;

---

[1] The *Plant-lore and Garden-craft of Shakespeare*, by the Rev. Henry N.
Ellacombe, M.A., will be read with pleasure by every student of Shakespeare
who shares his master's love of the garden
[2] *Love's L. L.* i. 1. 249.

Hot lavender, mints, savory, marjoram;
The marigold, that goes to bed wi' the sun
And with him rises weeping: these are flowers
Of middle summer, and I think they are given
To men of middle age.   *Wint. Tale,* iv. 4. 104.

On the sunny walls of the house hang

dangling apricocks,
Which, like unruly children, make their sire
Stoop with oppression of their prodigal weight.
                                         Rich. II. iii. 4. 29.

Around the porch

Doth the woodbine, the sweet honeysuckle
Gently entwist,   *Mids. N. D.* iv. 1. 47.

and sweet eglantine and rosemary are planted under the windows. It was a bright spot amidst the waste, pleasant to the eye and sweet scented, where generation after generation of English gentlemen had passed their uneventful lives. They wished for no happier lot. Many a time had Squele spoken words which one who knew him well put into the mouth of Alexander Iden, a gentleman of Kent:

Lord, who would live turmoiled in the court,
And may enjoy such quiet walks as these?
This small inheritance my father left me
Contenteth me, and worth a monarchy.
I seek not to wax great by others' waning,
Or gather wealth, I care not, with what envy:
Sufficeth that I have maintains my state
And sends the poor well pleased from my gate.
                                         2 Hen. VI. iv. 10. 18.

You may believe the Idens and Squeles when they so protest, for they knew no other life. But as for your banished dukes and courtiers, in Arden or in the frontiers of Mantua, put no faith in them. They will sing you sweetly ' of the green holly,' and try to persuade themselves that ' this life is most jolly.'[1] They will protest that they ' better brook than flourishing peopled towns. . . . . This shadowy

    [1] *As You L.* ii. 7. 183.

desert, unfrequented woods.'[1]   But believe them not.   For towards the end of the fifth act (as soon, in fact, as opportunity offers) they hasten to return to the life they despise; a fact much marked by the melancholy Jacques, who alone is faithful to Arden :

> What you would have
> I'll stay to know at your abandon'd cave.
> *As You L.* v. 4, 201.

Over the doorway were emblazoned on sculptured stone the arms of the Squeles of Hogshearing ; in a field, *vert*, a hog, *squelant, proper*, charged with a pair of shears, *gules* ; motto, *Great Squele, little wool* ; a supposed allusion to the barrenness of the family acres, compared with the pretensions of their owners.   Like many other examples of the canting heraldry so lightly esteemed by the Baron of Bradwardine, it was founded on false etymology.   For we, who live in an age that is nothing if not critical, know that Hogshearing—or Ugs-wearing as it appears in old documents—has nothing to do with either swine or wool.   The former part of the compound—ugs or usk—is plainly British, and suggests the water in which the hart was killed.   As to the latter, it would be rash to express an opinion, inasmuch as it has been the subject of learned disquisitions before various archæological societies, and opinions differ as to whether it is traceable to a British, Saxon, or Norman-French root ; or (as the more learned opine) is an interesting fragment of a Turanian tongue, spoken in Cotswold before the advent of the British Celt.

However this may be, the Squeles were gentlemen, not only of coat-armour, but of blood and ancestry, and had held the lands and advowson of Hogshearing for centuries. These were, in fact, an outlying portion of the Shallow estates, granted by a Châtelhault to a follower of gentle blood, to hold of the manor of Châtelhault, at a time when such subinfeudation was legal.   Somewhat of the old relationship survived, and although they had been companions

[1] *Two Gent.* v. 4. 2.

as boys and men, neither old Silence nor Will Squele ever quite forgot that, while they held of the manor of Shallow, Robert Shallow held *in capite* of the Queen. He was their lord, and they were his men. It was hard to withstand him, even when he would dispose of their children in marriage. If their lands were to descend to an infant heir, the lord, as guardian in chivalry, could dispose of his ward in marriage by way of sale, for his own profit, subject only to exception for disparagement. This was of the nature of things, an incident of land. What, then, did William Silence mean when he called Justice Shallow an old meddling fool?

"And now, my masters," said Squele, as the company arrived at his garden gate, "come in and refresh yourselves before you turn homewards. 'Tis a long and weary ride across the wold."

"By your leave," said Slender, "if John Hunt and I may have some barley-water for our horses, I have no stomach for victual, and I am loth to leave the hounds."

"If that be your will," said Squele, "come into the stables, and while you look to your nags, my Gregory will bring you out some cakes and ale, if ye will have no better victual. Why, Master William, your horse is sorely tired."

"In truth he is, and I fear much he will never carry me home," said Silence, who foresaw the possibility of an invitation to man and horse to pass the night at Hogshearing.

"Leave him here for this night," said Squele hastily, "you may ride home on 'my horse Grey Capilet . . . he will bear you easily and reins well.' [1] My man, when he brings the venison to the Justice in the morning, shall lead over your horse and bring my nag back with him."

It was impossible to refuse so friendly an offer. But William could not help reflecting that the occasion must have been urgent which lent him Grey Capilet, for Will

[1] *Twelfth N.* iii. 4. 314.

Squele was never known before to share with another the bonny beast he loved so well.'[1]

"Saddle Grey Capilet," shouted Squele to his stable varlet. "Here, take the furniture from off Master Silence's horse. The saddle fits him well enough. But stay, Master William, his mouth has never been used to such a new-fangled bit We country folk ride our horses to make them go, not to throw them on their haunches, to play the dancing horse, like Bankes's curtal."[2]

"I will fetch Grey Capilet's bridle," said Silence eagerly ; "I know of old where it hangs."

He had long been seeking for an excuse to follow Anne into the house, but found none hitherto ; for, as we have seen, Slender and Squele had managed to keep the company in the stables.

Silence left the yard, and going round to the front door, passed into the hall. It was a low dark room, flagged, and scantily strewn with rushes. In one corner an oaken book-case contained a few classical authors, Ovid, Virgil, Horace, and Tully's philosophical writings ; the *Grammar of Henry VIII.* well marked, *The Dictionary of Syr Thomas Elliot, declaring Latin by English, as greatly improved and enriched by Thomas Coope in 1552 ;* and *The Schoolmaster, a Plaine and Perfite way of teaching children to understand, write,*

---

[1] 2 *Hen. VI.* v. 2. 12.

[2] When Moth said to Armado, ' the dancing horse will tell you ' (*Love's L. L.* i. 2. 56), he had in his mind Bankes's celebrated performing horse Morocco, alluded to in many contemporary plays, and even in such grave treatises as Sir Walter Raleigh's *History of the World* and Sir Kenelm Digby's *Treatise on Bodies.* (See the Notes to *Love's L. L.* in the *Variorum* edition of 1821, and a note to *The Parson's Wedding* in Dodsley's *Old Plays.*) It is said that poor Bankes and his unhappy curtal were burned as magicians in Italy. G. Markham, moved perhaps by his love of the horse, defends Bankes against the opinion main-tained by ' euen some of good wisdome . . . that it was not possible to bee done by a Horse that which that curtal did, but by the assistance of the Deuill ; ' holding not only that ' the man was exceeding honest,' but that any horse could be brought in less than a month to do the same ; such is ' the excellency of a Horse's aptnesse and understanding ' (*Cavalarice*). Morocco must have lived to an extraordinary age, unless (as would appear more probable) the allusion in the diary is to an earlier curtal trained by Bankes, who is not likely to have attained at once the absolute perfection displayed in his training of Morocco.

and speak the Latin Tong, by Roger Ascham, 1571. For Will Squele had gone to Oxford from an ancient school at Shrewsbury, and had brought thence a strong love for a few Latin masters, and for a poor Welsh lad, Hugh Evans, who had received a free education at Shrewsbury, and afterwards as servitor at Oxford, and whom he had made happy for life by presenting him to the vicarage of Hogshearing, the tithes of which were worth full sixteen marks a year. It was from Evans that William Silence learned the elements of Latin, and it was the conversation of the parson and his patron that early instilled into his mind a love of learning. For Will Squele (whose exploits at Clement's Inn were grossly exaggerated by Master Shallow) was

> certainly a gentleman, thereto
> Clerk-like experienced, which no less adorns
> Our gentry than our parents' noble names,
> In whose success we are gentle.
>
> *Wint. Tale*, i. 2. 391.

At the other side of the hall a door led into a small closet, which served as a harness-room, amongst other offices of a varied character. Here hung Grey Capilet's bridle. Silence paused for a moment, then opening the door of the adjoining parlour, he passed through it, and knocked gently at a door.

" Come in," said a voice he knew well. He opened the door, and found himself in the small withdrawing room, which Anne Squele had appropriated as her own. Through the open window came in the sweet scent of gilliflowers and honeysuckle. A few books lay on the table, Lyly's *Euphues*, the *Eclogues* of Virgil (for Anne read Latin with her father and Sir Hugh), and a huge manuscript book of recipes, which had grown under the hands of the successive generations of feminine Squeles. You will find many of those secrets disclosed by the industrious Gervase Markham in his ' *English Housewife*, containing the inward and outward Vertues which ought to be in a compleat woman ; as her skill in Physick, Surgery, Cookery, extraction of oyls, Banqueting stuff, ordering of great Feasts, Preserving of all sorts of wines, conceited Secrets, Distillations, Perfumes, ordering of Wool, Hemp, Flax, making Cloth and Dying : the knowledge of Dayries ; Office of Malting ; of Oats their excellent use in a family ; of Brewing, Baking, and all other things belonging to a household.' There you may learn how to make a kickshaw, or quelquechose, and the same authority tells you elsewhere that ' spermaceti is . . . excellent for inward bruises, and to be bought at the apothecaries.' [1] The virginal was a gift from her godfather, Master Shallow. The room was adorned with needlework of various kinds, cut works, spinning, bone-lace, and many pretty devices, with which the cushions, carpets, chairs, and stools were covered.

"I came to seek Grey Capilet's bridle," said William ; and his manner had lost the assurance which had marked it at the assembly.

"And have you so forgotten the ways of the place, Master William, that you need to be shown where the bridle hangs ? "

"I have forgotten nothing, nor am I like to. It is not because I have forgotten, but because I cannot forget that —that——"

"That you want Grey Capilet's bridle," said Anne hastily, running into the hall. "Nay, here it is, but you must take it and begone, or we shall have Master Slender looking for the bridle too. Stay a moment. Did my father tell you that the Lady Katherine had bidden us to ride a hawking with her on Monday? Now farewell, for I hear father's voice, and he will want the bridle."

Grey Capilet was saddled, bridled, and mounted at last. The company took leave of Master Squele, and proceeded homewards across the waste.

Master Silence's feelings were somewhat mingled. He had intended to say something to Anne—much conveyed in few words—and he had only asked for a bridle. But then

---

[1] *Cheap and Good Husbandry.*

she had told him that they were bidden to Master Petre's.
Did not this imply, be thou bidden also?

Master Slender and the huntsman were occupied with
the hounds. Young Fury's wound was not serious, and he
had treated his case after the manner of Adonis' hound
by

> licking of his wound,
> 'Gainst venom'd sores the only sovereign plaster. [1]

> *Ven. and Ad.* 915.

Merriman is sorely fatigued, or (in the language of venery)
embossed. He must be tended. It may be (as Mr. Dyce
suggests) that he is to be trashed; that is to say, restrained
from running about and thus adding to his fatigue, by using
for this purpose the long strap known as a trash, buckled to
his couple and held by the huntsman. [2] The other hounds
are coupled, in the fashion in which they were brought to
the assembly, and so they journey homeward. On the way
Abraham Slender and the huntsman discuss the performances of the hounds. Not one event during the long day
escapes their recollection. There can be no doubt as to the
converse held by them, for their very words have been recorded by one who heard them.

> *Lord.* Huntsman, I charge thee, tender well my hounds:
> † Brach Merriman, the poor cur is emboss'd;
> And couple Clowder with the deep-mouth'd brach.
> Saw'st thou not, boy, how Silver made it good
> At the hedge corner, in the coldest fault?
> I would not lose the dog for twenty pound.
> *First Hun.* Why, Belman is as good as he, my lord;
> He cried upon it at the merest loss

[1] 'The tongue of the dog in most cases is his best surgeon; when he can
apply that, he seldom needs any other remedy." (Beckford, *Thoughts on
Hunting*.)

[2] The text is certainly corrupt, for Merriman was not a brach, or female
hound. Mr. Dyce reads: 'Trash Merriman,' an emendation which has not
found favour with critics who, regarding the trash as a weight or clog,
naturally remark that Merriman's fatigue would be rather aggravated than
lightened by such an appendage. It appears, however, that the trash sometimes, at all events, took the form of a long strap attached to the couple of an
over-topping hound (see note, *ante*, p. 39).

And twice to-day pick'd out the dullest scent :
Trust me, I take him for the better dog.
　　Lord. Thou art a fool ; if Echo were as fleet,
I would esteem him worth a dozen such.
　　　　　　　　　　　　Tam. of Shrew, Ind. i. 16.

Thus their critical discourse ' distinguishes the swift, the
slow, the subtle ; ' for hound differs from hound, as man from
man,　　　　　　　　　　　　　every one
　　　According to the gift which bounteous nature
　　　Hath in him closed.　　　　　*Macbeth*, iii. 1. 96.

I cannot answer with the same certainty for William
Silence and his companion. But I have never thought that
doubt was cast on the authenticity of the diary, or on the
identity of the nameless stranger, by the fact that its author
is silent, just when we should wish him to speak. A day
spent with Shakespeare is in our eyes something so wonderful that we can scarcely understand its passing without note
or comment. And yet many days were so spent by many
scores of people, not one of whom has thought fit to record
its events. Why should the diarist differ from his fellows?
Besides, I see no proof that Shakespeare possessed at any
time of his life those personal qualities which afford, or seem
to afford to the casual looker on, assurance of greatness. To
those who knew him in the flesh he was ' gentle ' Shakespeare. This word is without counterpart in our speech of
to-day, but it certainly excludes the idea of an overpowering
or self-asserting personality. Indeed, had not William
Silence been possessed of education and discernment above
his Gloucestershire neighbours, he would scarcely have
admitted to companionship one so far below him in condition.

But although there may have been some discourse of
weightier matters, which we would have gladly shared, the
hounds and their doings were not forgotten. Had it been
otherwise, one of the company would not have known their
very names, nor could he have drawn with pen and ink a

portrait so lifelike, that the author of the *Chase of the Wild Red Deer*, when he would describe the hounds [1] with which the stag was hunted on Exmoor in his youth—lineal descendants of Master Shallow's kennel—finds that he can do so most aptly in the words of Theseus:

> My hounds are bred out of the Spartan kind,
> So flew'd, so sanded, and their heads are hung
> With ears that sweep away the morning dew:
> Crook-knee'd and dew-lapp'd like Thessalian bulls;
> Slow in pursuit, but match'd in mouth like bells,
> Each under each. A cry more tuneable
> Was never holla'd to, nor cheer'd with horn.'
>
> *Mids. N. Dr.* iv. 1. 124.

In Shakespeare's time hounds hunting by scent were roughly divided into three classes. There was the bloodhound, or limer, whose acquaintance we have already made, used for the most part in finding and harbouring the game; there was the 'beagle pure-bred,' about which we shall hear something by-and-by; and, lastly, there were the ordinary running hounds.

Your pack of beagles hunted the hare, as their proper quarry; but your kennel of hounds 'will indeed hunt any chase exceeding well, especially the hare, stag, buck, roe, or other.' Adonis was wont to add the fox to the category set forth in the *Noble Arte*, for he was thus bidden by Venus:

---

[1] The old Exmoor stag-hounds, the last survivors of the southern hound, were sold in 1825 to a German baron, and their place was taken by a pack composed of large drafts of fox-hounds. These hounds are superior in dash and speed to their predecessors, but among the defects of their qualities must be noted an absence of that tuneable cry, musical discord, and sweet thunder, which were characteristic of the older breed. ' A nobler pack of hounds no man ever saw. . . . . In height the hounds were about twenty-six to twenty-eight inches, colour generally hare-pied, yellow, yellow and white, or badger pied, with long ears, deep muzzles, large throats, and deep chests. In tongue they were perfect, and when hunting in the water, or on half scent, or baying a deer, they might be heard at an immense distance.' (*Chase of the Wild Red Deer.*) In the composition of this interesting work, the late Dr. Collyns of Dulverton was assisted (to what extent is a matter of dispute) by a friend, referred to in the preface as ' a dear lover of the sport,' who is known to have been Sir John Karslake, some time Attorney-General for England.

Uncouple at the timorous flying hare,
Or at the fox which lives by subtlety,
Or at the roe which no encounter dare :
    Pursue these fearful creatures o'er the downs,
    And on thy well-breath'd horse keep with thy hounds.
                                    Ven. and Ad. 673.

The running hounds differed widely as regards size and
speed, according to the nature of the country in which they
were bred and hunted.   You may read much in the old books
of sport about northern, west country, and southern hounds,
and about their several qualities ; and also of the complexion
and nature of the fallow, the dun, and the white hound, and of
the ' blacke hounds anciently come from Sainct Hubert Abbey
in Ardene.' You may also learn from the *Noble Arte* how their
breeding is affected by the ' starre Arcture, and sygnes of
Gemini and Aquarius, for the dogges which shall be engendered under those signes shall not be subject to madnesse,
and shall commonly be more dogges than bytches.'

The common stock from which these several varieties
sprang was the blood-hound. The characteristics of this
species are more apparent the further back we go in the
history of the hound. They may be plainly traced in the
old Exmoor stag-hounds, and in the kennel of Theseus.
They become less evident, as, generation after generation, the
modern fox-hound was developed from the old southern hound
by careful breeding and judicious crossing.   In the course of
this development some rare qualities of nose and cry have
certainly been lost.   But the philosophic stag-hunter, dismounting after a twenty-mile gallop across Exmoor from
Yard's Down, may reflect that Theseus' hounds, tuneable as
was their cry, could no more have accounted for the four-year-
old galloper set up at Watersmeet, than a pack of beagles
could kill a fox in Leicestershire ; and that neither to hounds
nor to men has the grace of absolute perfection been vouchsafed.

But however ' sweet and delectable ' the way over the
' high wild hills and rough uneven ways ' of Cotswold was

made by such 'fair discourse,' [1] neither riders nor horses
retraced their steps with the keen enjoyment which they
felt in the early day.

>   Who riseth from a feast
> With that keen appetite that he sits down?
> Where is the horse that doth untread again
> His tedious measures with the unbated fire
> That he did pace them first?   *Merch. of Ven.* ii. 6. 8.

Each participated in the weariness of the other with that
subtle sympathy and inter-communication of feeling which
exists between man and a brute companion.   'Imitari is
nothing : so doth the hound his master, the ape his keeper,
the tired horse his rider.' [2]

[1] *Rich. II.* ii. 3. 4.

[2] *Love's L. L.* iv. 2. 129.   This passage is explained by commentators
as referring to 'the dancing horse,' Bankes's famous curtal, said to have
been attired with ribbons ; and Mr. Grant White goes so far as to print the
words ' 'tired horse.'   I believe it to express in condensed and elliptical
language, characteristic of Shakespeare, the same idea which is fully developed in the Sonnet quoted above ;—the sympathy of the horse with his rider,
the mysterious 'instinct' by which 'the beast that bears me, tired with
my woe,' becomes a partaker of my feelings, as the hound shares thoughts
of his master, and the ape of his keeper.   As it has been elsewhere
expressed 'that horse his mettle from his rider takes' (*A Lover's Complaint*,
107).   The passage, thus interpreted, expresses a favourite thought of the author's ;
but I cannot understand how a riderless horse going through a barebacked performance can be said to imitate a rider, because its master chooses to adorn it
with ribbons.   The sense of the passage would have been more apparent if the
meaning had been noted which was formerly borne in the language of farriers
by the word 'tired' as applied to the horse.   It was a term of art, and as such
is fully explained in the chapter of Markham's *Maister-peece* entitled 'Of Tyred
Horses' (Book I, ch. 62).   'In our common and vulgar speech we say every
horse that giveth over his labour is tyred.'   This may proceed 'from the most
extreme Labour and Travail which is true tyredness indeed,' or from some fault
of the horse's, among others, 'from dulness of spirit,' for which an excellent
remedy is to take 'three or four round pebble stones, and put them into one of
his ears, and then tye the ear that the stones fall not out, and the noise of those
stones will make the Horse go after he is utterly tyred.'   Shakespeare (as we
shall see more fully by-and-by) put into the mouths of his characters, irre-
spective of nationality or condition in life, the common and vulgar speech of
English farriers—according to Markham, for the most part very simple smiths,
to suit whose capacity he writes in his *Maister-peece* so as to be understood by
the weakest brain.   Blundevill, whose readers were more enlightened, and who
translated largely from foreign authors, in his chapter 'Of Tired Horses' uses

Some such experience, one of the company afterwards developed in the form of a sonnet :

How heavy do I journey on the way,
   When what I seek, my weary travel's end,
Doth teach that ease and that repose to say
   ' Thus far the miles are measured from thy friend ! '
The beast that bears me, tired with my woe,
   Plods dully on, to bear that weight in me,
As if by some instinct the wretch did know
   His rider loved not speed, being made from thee :
The bloody spur cannot provoke him on
   That sometimes anger thrusts into his hide ;
Which heavily he answers with a groan,
   More sharp to me than spurring to his side ;
For that same gròan doth put this in my mind ;
   My grief lies onward, and my joy behind.   *Sonnet* L.

Master Silence's feelings agree so perfectly with the temper of his horse that he forbears to rail at his sluggish pace, as he would have done at other times ;—for he was sufficiently energetic to sympathise with Harry Hotspur, who says of mincing poetry, ' 'Tis like the forced gait of a shuffling nag ; '[1] and of the mystic Owen Glendower,

O, he is as tedious
As a tired horse, a railing wife ;
Worse than a smoky house.
                1 *Hen. IV.* iii. 1. 159.

the word in its correct sense, as ' tired with over much labour.' (*Four Chiefest Offices of Horsemanship*, 1580.) It is, I think, certain that the beast of Sonnet L., plodding dully on tired with his rider's woe, was affected with the kind of tiring that ' proceedeth from dulness of spirit,' otherwise Shakespeare would never have said, in the person of the rider,

The bloody spur cannot provoke him on,
That sometimes anger thrusts into his hide.

Had he suffered from ' true tyredness,' his treatment at his hands would have been very different ;
               sodden water
  A drench for sur-reined jades, their barley-broth.   *Hen. V.* iii. 5. 1.

If Shakespeare had translated into ordinary English the ' common and vulgar speech ' of the farrier, and told us that the dull-spirited horse imitates his rider, no one, however tired, could have misunderstood his meaning.
  [1] 1 *Hen. IV.* iii. 1. 135.

'All things that are,' Gratiano tells us, 'are with more spirit chased than enjoyed.' This is the secret of the fascination which the sports of the field exercise over mankind. Their very essence is pursuit and endeavour, not possession; and in these lies the chief enjoyment of life. The objects of the sportsman's pursuit are often 'past reason hunted,' and though (unlike other objects) they contain no poison so as to be 'past reason hated,' yet they are indeed 'before, a joy proposed; behind, a dream.'[1] Happy is he whose slumbers are visited by no worse dreams than the harbouring and hunting of the Cotswold hart.

[1] Sonnet cxxix.

CHAPTER VII

SUPPER AT SHALLOW HALL

Some pigeons, Davy, a couple of short-legged hens, a joint of mutton, and any pretty tiny kickshaws, tell William cook.

Second Part of King Henry IV.

IF you visit the western slope of Cotswold in search of the ancient dwelling of the Shallows, which we are now approaching in the company of the diarist, you need not be disappointed.

I do not promise that you will succeed in tracing the foundations of the Hall, or in fixing to your satisfaction the site of the dovecot, or of the arbour in which the Justice was wont to regale his guests with a dish of caraways and a last year's pippin of his own graffing.[1] But although these matters may be left in doubt, evidence will not be wanting that you have come to the right place. You have only to bear in mind the local indications given by Davy, the Justice's factotum :

Davy. I beseech you, sir, to countenance William Visor of Woncot against Clement Perkes of the hill.

Shal. There is many complaints, Davy, against that Visor; that Visor is an arrant knave, on my knowledge.

Davy. I grant your worship that he is a knave, sir; but yet, God forbid, sir, but a knave should have some countenance at his

---

[1] 'Pepyns with carawey in confite' are prescribed for dessert by John Russell, of the household of Humphrey, the good Duke of Gloucester, in the *Boke of Nurture* (circ. 1430), and in Wynkyn de Worde's *Boke of Keruinge* (1513). These curious treatises on the household management of the day were annotated and reprinted (with Hugh Rhodes's *Boke of Nurture*, 1577) by Mr. Frederick Furnival in 1866.

friend's request. An honest man, sir, is able to speak for himself,
when a knave is not. I have served your worship truly, sir, this
eight years; and if I cannot once or twice in a quarter bear out a
knave against an honest man, I have but a very little credit with
your worship. The knave is mine honest friend, sir; therefore I
beseech your worship, let him be countenanced.

Shal. Go to; I say he shall have no wrong. *2 Hen. IV.* v. 1. 41.

If you seek for proof that you are in the neighbourhood
of these worthies, you need but look around you.

Looking northward, you may see how the Cotswold uplands send forth in the direction of the estuary of the Severn
a detached portion, or spur, which, standing forth from the
mass in well-defined outline, has received from the country
folk the distinctive name of the Hill. Here local tradition,
oblivious of the worshipful Shallows, long pointed out the
site of a modest homestead, once the dwelling-place of a
family of yeoman race, named Perkis or Perkes, of whom
one has been discovered by searchers in parish registers,
born in 1568, and bearing the name of Clement. The home
of his antagonist, William Visor, is not far distant, but is
hidden from sight by intervening uplands. It is Woodmancote, or Woncot, a suburb of Dursley, which has
retained to the present century its connection with the
family of Visor, or Vizard. For in the list of wardens of
St. Mark's Chapel of Ease at Woodmancote, the name of
Vizard occurs in 1847, 1848, and 1861, and in a pedigree of
the family, printed in *Dursley and its Neighbourhood* (by
the Rev. John Henry Blunt, Rector of Beverston), we read
that William Vizard died February 14, 1807, and the descent
of this nineteenth-century William Visor of Woncot is
traced from Arthur Vizard, bailiff of Dursley in 1612, whose
tomb is in Dursley churchyard.

If you ascend the Hill, and look towards the setting sun
and the far distant mountains of Wales, the thought is still
borne in on you, *quocunque ingredimur in aliquam historiam
vestigia ponimus.* For as the eye travels over the rich and
smiling landscape stretching westward to the estuary of the

Severn, and rests for a moment on a spot near the town of
Berkeley, you are startled to find yourself exclaiming in the
words of Hotspur, ' There stands the castle, by yon tuft of
trees.' [1]

' 'Fore God, you have here a goodly dwelling and a rich,'
exclaimed Sir John Falstaff, as he surveyed this very
prospect from the Justice's orchard ; ' Barren, barren,
barren ; beggars all, beggars all, Sir John,' his host thought
it polite to protest, but truth compelled him to add, ' Marry,
good air.' Good air and comparative barrenness were
indeed the main characteristics of the swelling uplands,
extending eastward from the Justice's Hall to the ancient
city of Cirencester, and northward as far as the borders of
Warwickshire. A region of bare hills and billowy downs,
famed for a breed of white-fleeced sheep, and for its
Whitsun games, whose fame might have perished but for
their restoration by Robert Dover, and their celebration by
the poets of the day.

Shallow and his surroundings are distinctly of Gloucestershire. There never was any reason for transferring them
to Warwickshire and the neighbourhood of Stratford, even
if there did not exist at the farthest side of Gloucestershire
Woncot with its Visor; the Hill with its Perkes ; Berkeley
Castle standing by its tuft of trees; an ancient tradition of
Shakespeare's sojourn; and a family of the name claiming
kinship with the poet.[2]

[1] *Rich. II.* ii. 3. 53.
[2] In the autumn of the year 1887 (and here I speak in my proper person),
finding myself in the neighbourhood, I visited Dursley. Leaving the railway
station, I met an aged countryman, of whom I asked the way to Woncot. He
at once pointed out the road to Woodmancote. I then asked him the shortest
way to the Hill. Without further question he directed me to Stinchcombe
Hill, one of several surrounding eminences, of which the Rev. R. Webster
Huntley, in his *Glossary of the Cotswold Dialect*, writes, ' On Stinchcombe
Hill there is the site of a house wherein a family named Purchase or Perkis
once lived.' On the level table land, which forms the summit of the hill,
I met a groom exercising a horse in training for some local race, of whom I
inquired, as a stranger in Gloucestershire, " How far is it to Berkeley ? " and
he made answer thus (I wrote down his words), " Ye can see a tower of the
castle. It lays along of the clump of trees." Unfortunately the day was too

It is strange that this combination of circumstances has not attracted more of the attention which has been lavished on the surroundings of Shakespeare's Warwickshire life ; for the belief current in Dursley from time immemorial that Shakespeare passed some part of his early life in or near that town, holds a distinct position among the many traditions that have clustered around the name of Shakespeare.   The mere fact of the existence of such a tradition bespeaks careful consideration, for the notoriety of Shakespeare's connection with Stratford-on-Avon has warned off all other rivals, and the claim of Dursley to be associated with his name is unique.   If the story is unfounded it is difficult to suggest how it came to be thought of.   For the tradition is certainly older than any knowledge of the facts discovered by modern register-hunters ; and Dursley—a small country town, lying at the south-western extremity of Cotswold, distant a few miles from the estuary of the Severn, and separated from Warwickshire by almost the entire length of Gloucestershire—is not in any way connected with Stratford-on-Avon, or with any patent fact in the life of Shakespeare.

The truth is that Shakespeare completely foiled his pursuers and led them on a false trail, when it one day occurred to him, in a wicked mood, to take a fling at the Lucys of Charlecote by identifying with some member of the Lucy family a character which had already taken hold

misty to allow me to verify his statement, but I am quite prepared to accept its truth, for it does not rest on his testimony alone :—

> *North.* I am a stranger here in Gloucestershire :
> These high wild hills and rough uneven ways
> Draw out our miles. . . .
> How far is it to Berkeley ? . . .
> *Percy.* There stands the castle by yon tuft of trees.
> > *Richard II.* ii. 3. 3. 51.

' This is an exact description of the Castle as seen from the Hill, the Castle having been from time immemorial shut in on one side, as viewed therefrom, by an ancient cluster of thick lofty trees.'   Thus Mr. Huntley, in a note to his *Glossary*, in which he collects some further evidence of the connection of the family of Shakespeare with the neighbourhood of Dursley.   See Note, *Shakespeare and Gloucestershire*.

of the public, and was accepted as a type. Thenceforth
Shallow was Lucy, and his local habitation was Charlecote,
not the 'wilds of Gloucestershire.' I have elsewhere stated
in detail my reasons for believing that the Gloucestershire
Justice of Henry IV. is not a study of Sir Thomas Lucy, and
that the touches which have connected him with the family
of Lucy appear for the first time in the second edition of
the *Merry Wives*. At present I simply ask the reader to
take Shakespeare at his word, and to believe that when he
wrote of Gloucestershire, of Woncot, and of the Hill he meant
what he said.

Of the original dwelling of the Shallows little remained
in the time of the diarist save a strong vaulted chamber
used as a kitchen, and some adjoining rooms which served
as buttery, pantry, and for other domestic purposes. The
part of the house surrounding the Court where we first
made the acquaintance of the Gloucestershire Justices, was
built in the early years of the Queen's reign. The security
of the times, with advancing civilisation and increased means
of enjoyment, had led to a wonderful development of
domestic architecture; and Shallow Hall, though it could
not, in point of dimensions, beauty, and associations, compete with Haddon, Penshurst, or Knole, or even with
Charlecote, presented nevertheless an interesting example of
an ancient manor-house, rebuilt and enlarged in the Tudor
period. How is it that in certain ages of the world the
meanest man cannot do ill that which at other times the
noblest fails to do well, save by way of imitation? Was
ever parish church designed amiss in the thirteenth century,
or dwelling-house in the sixteenth? Was ever tolerable
church or house built in the nineteenth, unless by repro-
ducing the work of an earlier age? We are so boastful of
our enlightenment and progress that it is well to be reminded of the depths of our incapacity. The last decade of
this century may perhaps—for it has yet some years to run
—give to the world a great dramatist, poet, or writer of
romance. It will not, I think, produce a building of original

nineteenth century design upon which the eye can be content to rest with the pleasure imparted by the harmonious
combination of mullioned windows, pointed gables, and
clustering chimneys, which constitute the charm of Tudor
architecture.

Long and wearisome as were the miles across the high
wild hills and rough uneven ways of Cotswold, they came to
an end at last, and our party, having seen to the comfort of
their horses, crossed the court-yard and entered the hall.
A long oaken table ran from top to bottom of the hall, which
was spacious, and flagged with stone. It had an open oaken
roof, with massive beams and rafters. Great bay windows,
diamond-paned and mullioned, extended in height the entire
way from the floor to the roof. The floor had been newly
strewn with rushes, the ' cobwebs swept; the serving men
in their new fustian, their white stockings, and every officer
his wedding garment on ' [1] in honour of Petre and his bride.
The walls were hung, not indeed with the arras of which we
read in lordly mansions, but with the more homely painted
cloth, ' wherein,' says Harrison,[2] ' either diverse histories, or
hearbes, beasts, knots, and suchlike are stained.'

There were moral and religious stories, like ' Lazarus in
the painted cloth, where the glutton's dogs licked his sores.' [3]
There were pretty poesies too, such as were engraven by
goldsmiths on rings. ' Set this in your painted cloths,' [4] said
Pandarus, when he had instanced his experience in verse.
These legends and pictures suggested many smart questions
and pretty answers, and if the merry Beatrice had her
' good wit out of the *Hundred Merry Tales*,' [5] the melancholy
Jaques was accused of indebtedness for his matter to the
painted cloth. ' You are full of pretty answers,' said he to
Orlando. ' Have you not been acquainted with goldsmiths'
wives, and conned them out of rings ? '

---

[1] *Tam. of Shrew*, iv. 1. 48.
[2] *Description of England* (1577), prefixed to Holinshed's *Chronicle*.
[3] 1 *Hen. IV.* iv. 2. 27.　　　　　　[4] *Troil. and Cres.* v. 10. 46.
[5] *Much Ado*, ii. 1. 135.

Orl. Not so, but I answer you right painted cloth,[1] from whence you have studied your questions.

As You L. iii. 2. 287.

The great oaken screen, separating the hall from the passage by which you entered, was hung with corslets, helmets, bucklers, pikes, halberts, and spears. On it there hung, a prey to rust and decay, the coat of mail in which Robert de Châtelhault was clad when he rode with his patron, Henry II., into the city of Dublin to receive the homage of Irish chieftains. To one who looked upon this venerable relic, it suggested a fine simile, of which Ulysses made good use when he would impress upon Achilles the folly of virtue seeking 'remuneration for the thing it was.' For ' good deeds past,' he tells him,

> are devour'd
> As fast as they are made, forgot as soon
> As done : perseverance, dear my lord,
> Keeps honour bright : to have done is to hang
> Quite out of fashion, like a rusty mail
> In monumental mockery.' *Troil. and Cres.* iii. 3. 148.

But most of the surroundings of the hall were suggestive of less gloomy reflections. In the deep embrasures of one window cross-bows, arrows, hunting and hawking poles were piled in confusion. Upon an oaken board in another lay the Justice's library. It was scanty, even for those times, for the Shallows never affected literary tastes. But the book-hunter would hail it with delight could he chance on it in some forgotten cupboard, for it contained a well-worn copy of the *Boke of St. Albans*, Nicholas Malbie's *Remedies for the Dyseases in Horses*, Fitzherbert's *Boke of Husbandrie*, Lambarde's *Eirenarcha ; or, Office of Justices of Peace* (presented by William Silence), and Turbervile's *Boke of Falconrie*, bound with the *Noble Arte of Venerie*. These were for serious use. For books of sport were used by the Shallows and Silences for practical purposes, and not as manuals of etiquette and guides to polite conversation ; as was the custom of the

---

[1] *Lucrece,* 245.

upstart gentlemen of the day, who bought them by the
score, but who rarely understood their inner meaning.
Of such a reading public, the genuine sportsman would say,
with Hector :

> O, like a book of sport [1] thou'lt read me o'er ;
> But there's more in me than thou understand'st.
>
> *Troil. and Cres.* iv. 5. 239.

Light literature was represented by *Sir Guy of War-
wicke*, the *Foure Sonnes of Amon*, the *Ship of Fooles*, the
Budget of Demaundes, and the *Hundred Merrie Tales ;*
and I gather from the conversation at supper that, but for
Abraham Slender, it should have been furnished with the
Booke of Riddles, in which the Justice specially delighted.

In the deep recess of another window stood a small table,
with a double desk, on one side of which lay Foxe's *Book
of Martyrs*, and on another a large Church Bible, from
which (as we know) the Justice now and then borrowed a
quotation, and, I am sorry to add, but little else.   There
were a few small tables, useful in foul weather when the
Justice would play at dice or cards, calling in his honest
neighbours, yeomen of the country, such as Clement Perkes
of the Hill ; for in those days distinctions of class were so
clearly marked and rigidly observed, that associations such
as this led to no misunderstanding or confusion.   Those
who were thus bidden took their places below the great
silver Salt, separating guests who supped on terms of
equality with the Justice from the 'lower messes,' [2] a
phrase which came to have a meaning (as in the mouth of
Leontes) somewhat akin to that of the masses, whom some
are used to contrast with the classes who sit above the
Salt.

The walls above the painted cloths were adorned with
antlers of harts and other trophies of the chase, the Justice's
devotion to which was attested by other visible signs.
Benches were littered with hawks' hoods and jesses, hawking

---

[1] See Note, *The Book of Sport.*   [2] *Wint. Tale*, i. 2. 227.

gloves, and collars, liams, and trashes for hounds. A few dogs lay on the rushes; but of the running hounds, Lady the brach alone was admitted to the hall. She was not half so good and true a hound as Belman, but because she happened to please the Justice, everything was permitted to her; for in hounds as with men, in Gloucestershire as in Rome, under Tudors as under Cæsars, *probitas laudatur et alget*. ' Truth's a dog must to kennel;' said Lear's most material fool, ' he must be whipped out, when Lady the brach may stand by the fire and '—do as she pleases.[1]

Although Silence and his companions had returned to Shallow Hall by the shortest route, it was dark when they arrived, and the Justice had already led his guests to supper in the hall. It was expected that those who took part in the chase should sup with the Justice, and accordingly the whole party, gentle and simple, came together into the hall. The head of the deer was borne aloft before the huntsman, who blew a strake on his horn as he entered. The Justice sat at the head of the long oaken table. At his right hand sat the Lady Katherine; at his left her husband, with old Silence. His daughter Ellen with Ferdinand Petre (who seems to have found his way back to the park at an early hour) were nigh at hand. They were joined by William Silence and Abraham Slender, while Perkes and his companion, with John Hunt, took their places below the Salt.

" Ho, ho !" cried the Justice, when he saw the deer's head, " how's this? This cannot be the hart whose tokens and measurements were reported to me at noon. How's this? This must be answered, John Hunt. How came you not to hunt the hart which was harboured for the delectation of my guests? You, goodman Perkes, 'twas you harboured the hart, and you saw him break thicket. How's this, how's this? Have you forgotten your woodcraft? This must be answered."

This was too bad;—to have his woodcraft put to shame before the company, and the great hart ravaging his corn-

<hr />

[1] *K. Lear*, i. 4. 124.

field at this very moment. Clement Perkes could not lie to save his life, not to say his character for woodcraft. He gasped, grew red, and looked doubtingly at Slender, who was not prepared for this emergency.

"The great hart, an't please your worship," said the huntsman promptly, " did break thicket; but they changed to another deer in the round wood. I said I thought it, Master Slender."

"Aye, aye, good lack," said Slender, in amazement at such dexterity.

" But a' was not right certain till we viewed him in the Hogshearing valley, and then 'twas too late. I met a varlet as saw the great hart leave the round wood after sunset."

"I knew well how it was," said Shallow triumphantly. " I knew it well, and I said it throughout. I said they had changed somewhere. But I am sorry, Master Petre, I am sorry. I had wished you better sport."

" Nay, Master Shallow," said Petre, " vex not yourself for me, we have had a right merry day, have we not, Kate? For my part I care not for hunting at force, though I love well enough the music of a well-chosen cry of hounds, or a pack of merry beagles, bred for music, not for murder. Live and let live, for me."

When the hunting party had taken their places at the table, the Justice resumed his conversation with Master Petre, and we are in time to hear a few of his comments on topics of the day.

"And now that you have brought home your bride, Master Petre, you will, I doubt not, follow the use and ancient custom of your worshipful ancestors, dwelling in the country alway, and resorting neither to courts nor to foreign countries. Your father, Sir Anthony, was of that mind. He spent his whole rent and revenue (scot and lot only excepted) in hospitality and good house-keeping. His house was no Mock-beggar Hall. It was ever open to all comers——"

" Yea, that it was, and sometimes closed to its master.

Many a time hath he been driven out of his own bed to lie at a tenant's house for a night or two, so haunted was his house by unbidden guests, resorting thither with man and horse, hawk and hound. Give me the house-keeping of cities and towns, where a man may make choice of his own guests, and where he need not fill his hall with great tall hulking, useless fellows, but may keep such serving-men only as are required for necessary uses. Our fathers needed them to sustain their quarrels. But we need them not."

"Nay, there thou speakest foolishly, for what profiteth it a man to be better than his neighbours if he have no greater worship? If a gentleman be not largely resorted to, what worship can he have in the shire, or what authority on the bench at quarter sessions, when he giveth the charge? If I walk in the town at assize time but slenderly attended how shall it be known that I am a better man than my kinsman Silence here, or my cousin Slender, who keeps but three men and a boy yet, until his mother be dead?"

"How, indeed," said old Silence; "for if one who is not only of the peace but of the quorum and cust——"

"Cousin Silence, it is as I have said: need more be said?"

"In truth, Master Shallow, you have asked me a hard question," said Master Petre, "and I cannot answer it; you are too clever for me."

"Now that is spoken like a worthy son of your father, and I doubt not but that after further converse with me, you and all your brethren will dwell at home, and be no longer scattered abroad thoughout the world."

"To my mind," said Petre, "it is a good wind that scatters young men over the world, to seek their fortunes further than at home, where small experience grows. For myself, my substance is such that I could live at home, as did my father. But what should my younger brethren do at home?"

"It is true," said Master Shallow, "the old saying now holds not good that service is the younger son's inheritance.

The more's the pity. I mind the time when the younger son of an esquire would be proud to serve a knight, and the younger son of a gentleman an esquire, as the younger son of a duke would serve his prince. But now, goodman Tomkins' Jack is thrust into a blue coat, and Peter Patchpanel taken from the carpenter's bench to the parlour, to the great detriment of those of gentle blood. And yet even at this very day I know gentlemen's younger brothers that wear their elder brother's blue coat and badge, attending him with reverent regard and dutiful obedience, as if he were their prince sovereign. This is as it should be."

"A beggarly profession, say I. As the old saying hath it, 'A young serving-man, an old beggar.' Unless, indeed, he turn tapster, as another saying hath it : 'An old cloak makes a new jerkin ; a withered serving-man a fresh tapster.'[1] I allow, indeed, that if a younger son profiteth by his learning at the University or at the Inns of Court, he may proceed in the study of the common law, divinity, or physic. But besides your kinsman William, how many of your blood or acquaintance have so profited ? And for the rest I say, better seek their fortunes abroad, than turn ploughman at home, or even wear the blue coat of their eldest brother. Indeed, if their eldest brother were of my mind, he would not be in the country for them to serve, but would lead a civil life in cities and great towns, as do the nobility of foreign countries."

"But if you live not at home, tilling your demesne land, how shall your house be kept, and your neighbours love you?"

"My father," said Petre, "had six or seven hundred acres of demesne land, whereon grew the provision for his household. This I let out to husbandmen, and there is scarcely an acre but yields me a crown. And so both fare best. I can live where I please, and need not to play the ploughman myself, and the ploughmen can live on the land, as their calling is. Believe me, the husbandman loves.

[1] *Merry Wives*, i. 3. 18.

his landlord best, when he lives like a gentleman in the
city, though for fear or flattery, when he dineth at your
board, he may say he is sorry your worship should dwell
away. As for your country sports and pastimes, I allow,
indeed, that a gentleman may exercise himself in hunting,
and especially in hawking, but these pastimes may be followed
in the neighbourhood of courts and cities. But his great
delight should be in arms, in the riding of great and serviceable horses, and also in study of books."

"As to books," said Master Shallow, "we have good
store of them, and we lack not pleasant mad-headed knaves
that be properly learned, and will read for us in diverse
pleasant books, as *Sir Guy of Warwick*, the *Four Sons of
Amon*, the *Ship of Fools*, the *Budget of Demands*, the
Hundred Merrie Tales, the *Book of Songs and Sonnets*, the
Book of Riddles, and many other pithy and excellent authors.
The *Book of Riddles*, indeed, cousin Slender, has not been
found since Allhallowmas last, when thou borrowedst it, for
thy mother as thou sayedst. I pray thee, see to it."

"Your learning is, indeed, most seemly and suitable,"
said Petre. "How sayest thou, Master Silence, would not
learning like this amaze and delight thy fellow at Gray's
Inn, Master Francis Bacon?"

"Why, that is spoken like a most grave and reverend
young man," said the Justice, "and, Master Petre, persuade
me not, but rest well assured that Robert Shallow, Esquire,
will dwell continually at home among his neighbours, as he
hath done any time these three hundred years, for all your
brave words."

"'All his successors gone before him hath done't,'"
said Slender, "'and all his ancestors that come after him
may; they—'"[1]

---

[1] The conversation at the Justice's table closely resembles a dialogue between
Vincent and Valentine, contained in a curious old tract entitled '*Cyuile and
Vncyuile Life*. A discourse very profitable, pleasant, and fit to be read of all
Nobilitie and Gentlemen, where in the forme of a dialogue is disputed what
order of lyfe best beseemeth a gentleman in all ages and times' (1579. Reprinted
by the Roxburghe Society in a volume entitled *Inedited Tracts*). So close

The remainder of Slender's speech has been lost to the
world, for supper being ended, the company rose from their
seats while the ladies sought the withdrawing room, where
Ellen Silence did the honours of her godfather's house.
It was the custom at the Justice's to sit long after supper.
Sometimes the company would adjourn to the orchard,
sometimes (as now) they would make merry in the hall.

" And now," said the Justice, " is there no merry wag
who will give us a song? "

" I know one who can give you a hunter's song," said
William Silence, " for I heard him singing snatches of it as
we rode homewards together—the song must speak for itself,
but I can answer for the voice of the singer."

And here, not for the first or the last time, the hope that I
might find somewhere in the diary some words which fell from
the lips of the nameless stranger was doomed to disappointment.   There was, indeed, a song enclosed in the pages of the
diary.   But it was written on a separate piece of paper, and
appeared from internal evidence to have been written at a much
later period by the diarist, who would seem to have occupied
himself in embodying his recollections of the older song in
words borrowed from the writings of the singer.   To enable
the reader to form his own opinion upon this matter, I here
print the song exactly as I found it, adding references to the

---

is the resemblance, that did the dates admit of it, it might be supposed that the
writer of the tractate had sat at Master Shallow's board.   There are also certain
suggestions of two other tracts reprinted in the same volume, *The Seruing-
man's Comfort* (1598), and *The Courtier and the Countryman*, by Nicholas
Breton (1618).   It seemed worth while preserving from authentic sources some
hints of a conflict which raged whenever Petres and Shallows met together,
the course of which may be clearly traced in the literature of the day—for instance, in the popular songs of the Old and the New English Gentleman.   Victory
rested with those whom, no doubt, the Petres and Valentines regarded as the
stupid party—the Shallows, the Silences, and the Vincents.   This result was
due to solid immobility, rather than to any success in dialectics.   And thus
England escaped the disasters which were brought upon France by estrangement
of the landed aristocracy from local interests and affairs, resulting from their
devotion to the *Cyuile Life* ; and if the old order must needs change in time and
give place to new, Master Shallow and his fellows have had no small share in
bringing it to pass that the revolution shall be a gradual and a bloodless one.

passages of which—whatever be the value of my theory—it
is undoubtedly compounded.

THE HUNTE, HIS SONG.

My houndes are bred of Southern kinde,[1]
    So flew'd, so sanded they ;
With crooked knees and dew-laps depe,
With eares the morning dew that sweepe
      Slowly they chase their praye ;
Their mouths, as tunable as belles
Each under each in concert swells.
[*The reste shall bear this burden* [2]
The hunte is up, the morne is bright and gray,[3]
Hunting us hence with hunte's up to the day.[4]

My horse eache common one excels [5]
    In shape, in courage, pace,
In colour, bone, and symmetry ;
Of fire compacte, and pure ayre he,[6]
    The minion of his race ; [7]
Pryde in his braided mane, his tayle
Aloft, or falling like a vaile.[8]
The hunte is up, &c.

His hooves are round, his joints are short,[9]
    His fetlocks shagge and longe ;
His breaste is broad, and full his eye,
His head is small, his crest is highe,
    His legs are straight and stronge,
His ears are shorte, his buttockes wide
Swelling beneath his tender hyde.
The hunte is up, &c.

The foxe that lives by subtilty [10]
    We kill as best we can,
By gynnes or snares,[11] but in the chase
We'll have some sporte before we case [12]
    This enemy of man ;

---

[1] *Mids. N. Dr.* iv. 1. 124.
[2] *As You L.* iv. 2. 14.
[3] *Tit. Andr.* ii. 2. 1.
[4] *Rom. and Jul.* iii. 5. 34.
[5] *Ven. and Ad.* 293.
[6] *Hen. V.* iii. 7. 22.
[7] *Macbeth,* ii. 4. 15.
[8] *Ven. and Ad.* 314.
[9] *Ven. and Ad.* 295.
[10] *Cymb.* iii. 3. 40.
[11] *2 Hen. VI.* iii. 1. 257.
[12] *All's Well,* iii. 6. 110.

And if he stowes his bush away [1]
He lives to runne another daye.
The hunte is up, &c.

The harte unharboured, stands at gaze [2]
One moment, then awaye
He trippes with light and aery boundes,
Until the fell and cruel houndes [3]
He holdeth at a bay ; [4]
No rascall he—his head of stele
The bloody houndes shall surely feele.[5]
The hunte is up, &c.

Beyond all beastys poor tim'rous Wat [6]
The hunter's skille doth trye,
See how the hounds, with many a doubte
The cold fault cleanly single out !
Hark to their merrie crie !
They spende their mouthes, echoe replies,
Another chase is in the skies.
The hunte is up, &c.

Their quarry or their hallowe wonne [7]
I tender well my houndes,[8]
I wind my horne to call the lost,
I care them when they are emboss'd,
And binde their bleeding woundes.
'Tis merrie hunting, but in hall
'Tis merrier yet, when beards wagge all
The hunte is up, &c.

The hunting song, whatever may have been its words,
was right well received by the company. When the
applause had ended the Justice thus addressed William
Silence. "Now, cousin William, your father had you at

---

[1] 'The tayle of a foxe is called his bush, or (as some used to say) his holly water sprinkle.'—*Noble Arte.*

[2] *Lucrece*, 1149.   [3] *Twelfth N.* i. 1. 22.

[4] *Tam. of Shrew*, v. 2. 56.   [5] *1 Hen. VI.* iv. 2. 49.

[6] The hare, see *Ven. and Ad.* 673-708.

[7] ' The rewarde of death of any beast of Venerie is called the quarry or reward ; of all other chases it is to be called the hallowe.'—*Noble Arte.*

[8] *Tam. of Shrew.* Ind. 1. 16.   [9] *2 Hen. IV.* v. 3. 37.

Oxford, to his cost, and have you learned there no merry song, strange tale, or pleasant riddle, wherewith to divert the company? "

" I cannot sing, Master Shallow," said William Silence; " one singer is enough in a family, and you will hear my father anon. But I will, with your leave, repeat you a certain ancient drinking-song writ by one Quintus Horatius Flaccus, which I have made bold to do into English :

> Persian-like pomp, boy, is not to my mind :
> Hateful are chaplets with linden entwined :
> Spare, then, to search through the gardens to find
> The latest blown rose.
>
> Naught to plain myrtle add—rack not thy brain—
> Master nor man need the myrtle disdain ;
> Bowered in vines, whilst thou serv'st, and I drain
> This cup in repose.

" At all events," continued young Silence, " it is good philosophy, if so be that a man be accommodated thereto."

"Accommodated ! " said the Justice, "' it is good : yea, indeed, is it : good phrases are surely, and ever were, very commendable. Accommodated ! it comes of *accommodo*, very good : a good phrase.' [1] But for the matter of the song, 'tis no philosophy. Quintus Horatius was a poet, he was no philosopher. Have I not construed him myself ? When I was a boy, I tell thee Master William, I'ld ha' been soundly breeched for calling a poet a philosopher. A poet's a poet, though he write the Latin tongue. The song is a good song. But you should sing it to the tune of *Green Sleeves*, or *Light o' Love*, and 'twill sound merrier far ; and if you put to it a refrain, as the ' hunt is up ' or ' down, derry down,' the rest of the company may bear the burden, for a song without a burden is, I take it, no better than ' a curtal dog,' or a fox that hath lost his bush."

The conversational powers of the Justice could not long be maintained at this high level. As the evening wore on, Petre, William Silence, and Master Ferdinand formed a group

[1] 2 *Hen. IV.* iii. 2. 74.

by themselves, while Justice Shallow and old Silence fell into their wonted groove of discourse. The serving-men were appealed to, and joined freely in conversation. For a good serving-man was expected to make himself not only generally useful, but agreeable to boot. He was not only to wear his garments decently (especially his livery coat, sword and buckler), to carve well—knowing how to unlace a cony, raise a capon, and trump a crane—but he should have skill in wrestling, leaping, running, and dancing. In the words of an old writer 'there are also of those that can shoote in long Bowes, crosse Bowes, or handgunne ; yea there wanteth not some that are both so wise and of so good audacitie as they can & doo (for lacke of better company) entertain their Maister with table talke, bee it his pleasure to speake either of Hawkes or houndes, fishinge or fowling, sowing or graffinge, ditchinge or hedginge, the dearth or cheapenes of grayne, or any such matters wherof Gentlemen commonly speake in the Country, bee it either of pleasure or profit, these good fellowes know sumwhat in all.'[1]

We know well the matters of which Shallow and old Silence would discourse before supper. Then it was 'How a good yoke of bullocks at Stamford fair ? How a score of ewes now ?' ; and as to Davy, he would entertain his master with talk of the serving of precepts ; of sowing the headland with wheat ; of 'the smith's note, for shoeing, and plough-irons ; ' of how 'a new link to the bucket must needs be had ; ' and of the stopping 'of William's wages, about the sack he lost the other day at Hinckley fair.'[2]

But why not, when we may, exchange the dull notes of the diarist for a lively record of the very words spoken ? It needs only to read Master Petre and Ferdinand for Falstaff and Bardolph as the visitors at the Hall, and the story is complete. This change matters little, for though at Shallow Hall men might come and men might go, yet the after-dinner talk ever flowed in the self-same stream. And if you observe a change in Master Ferdinand Petre after supper,

---

[1] *The Cyuile and Vncyuile Life*, 1579.   [2] *2 Hen. IV.* v. 1. 14.

and seek for an explanation, you must study the operations
of ' good sherris-sack ' upon the brain, and upon ' the foolish and dull and crudy vapours which environ it,' noting the
no less wonderful change wrought thereby in the deportment
of old Silence.

     Petr. [*Fal.*] This Davy serves you for good uses ; he is your
serving-man and your husbandman.

     Shal. A good varlet, a good varlet, a very good varlet. . . .
By the mass, I have drunk too much sack at supper ; a good
varlet. Now sit down, now sit down : come, cousin.

     Sil. Ah, sirrah ! quoth-a,—we shall

> Do nothing but eat, and make good cheer.
> > [*Singing.*

> And praise God for the merry year ;
> When flesh is cheap and females dear,
> And lusty lads roam here and there
> > So merrily,
> And ever among so merrily.

     Petr. [*Fal.*] There's a merry heart ! Good Master Silence, I'll
give you a health for that anon.

     Shal. Give Master Ferdinand [Bardolph] some wine, Davy.

     Davy. Sweet sir, sit. . . . Proface ! What you want in meat,
we'll have in drink. But you must bear : the heart's all. (*Exit.*)

     Shal. Be merry, Master Ferdinand [Bardolph], . . . be merry.

     Sil. Be merry, be merry, my wife has all.
> > [*Singing.*

> For women are shrews, both short and tall :
> 'Tis merry in hall, when beards wag all,[1]
> > And welcome merry Shrove-tide.
> Be merry, be merry.

     Petr. [*Fal.*] I did not think Master Silence had been a man of
this mettle.

     Sil. Who, I ? I have been merry twice and once ere now.

Re-enter DAVY.

     Davy. There is a dish of leather-coats for you.
> > (*To Ferdinand* [*Bardolph*].)

     Shal. Davy !

---

[1] A song with this line as a burden is mentioned in *The Serving-man's
Comfort* (1598), as commonly sung after supper in hall.

Davy. Your worship ! I'll be with you straight. (*To Ferdinand* [*Bardolph*])—A cup of wine, sir ?

    Sil. A cup of wine, that's brisk and fine,
                (*Singing.*)
    And drink unto the leman mine :
    And a merry heart lives long-a.

Petr. [*Fal.*] Well said, Master Silence.

Sil. An we shall be merry, now comes in the sweet o' the night.

    Petr. [*Fal.*] Health and long life to you, Master Silence.

    Sil. Fill the cup and let it come ;   (*Singing.*)
    I'll pledge you a mile to the bottom.

Shal. Master Ferdinand [Honest Bardolph] welcome : If thou wantest any thing, and wilt not call, beshrew thy heart . . . welcome, indeed, too. I'll drink to Master Ferdinand [Bardolph] and to all the cavaleros about London.

Davy. I hope to see London once ere I die.

Ferd. [*Bard.*] An I might see you there, Davy,——

Shal. By the mass, you'll crack a quart together, ha ! will you not, master ?

Ferd. [*Bard.*] Yes, sir, in a pottle-pot.

Shal. By God's liggens I thank thee : the knave will stick by thee, I can assure thee that ; A' will not out : he is true bred.

Ferd. [*Bard.*] And I'll stick by him, sir.

Shal. Why, there spoke a king. Lack nothing ; be merry.

Petr. [*Fal.*] Why, now you have done me right.

      (*To Silence, seeing him take off a bumper.*)

    Sil. Do me right,   (*Singing.*)
    And dub me knight :
    Samingo.

Is't not so ?

Petr. [*Fal.*] 'Tis so.

Sil. Is't so ? Why, then say, an old man can do somewhat.
                           2 *Hen. IV.* v. 3. 10.

So they talked, and so old Silence sang, until the word was given ' carry Master Silence to bed ; ' while one that sat at the board thought thus with himself of Master Shallow and his men.

' It is a wonderful thing to see the semblable coherence

of his men's spirits and his : they, by observing of him, do bear themselves like foolish justices ; he, by conversing with them, is turned into a justice-like serving-man : their spirits are so married in conjunction with the participation of society that they flock together in consent, like so many wild-geese.   If I had a suit to Master Shallow, I would humour his men with the imputation of being near their master : if to his men I would curry with Master Shallow that no man could better command his servants.   It is certain, that either wise bearing or ignorant carriage is caught, as men take diseases, one of another : therefore, let men take heed of their company.

'I will devise matter enough out of this Shallow to keep in continual laughter' [1] . . . not Prince Harry, but the world; and that beyond the wearing out of many fashions, even so long as the English tongue shall be spoken.

And he kept his word.

[1] *2 Hen. IV.* **v.** 1. 72.

CHAPTER VIII

THE GLOUCESTERSHIRE JUSTICES

I will fetch off these Justices : I do see the bottom of Justice Shallow.
Second Part of King Henry IV.

IT has been already observed that the original outlines of
Master Robert Shallow of Gloucestershire ; of his fellows
Slender and Silence ; and of Davy, Clement Perkes, William
Visor, with their local surroundings, were somewhat obscured
by the subsequent identification of the Justice with Sir
Thomas Lucy of Charlecot, in Warwickshire. That Shakespeare at some time of his life intended this identification is
beyond doubt. But I am convinced that no such design
formed part of his original conception. In some notes to
these pages I have collected various local indications which
seem to show that the Gloucestershire of Shakespeare was
no mere geographical expression, but a real place trodden
by his feet, and inhabited by real men and women with
whom he had held converse. We have spent so much time
in their company, that it may be worth while to pursue
the subject somewhat further, and to devote a few pages to
the inquiries : was Master Robert Shallow originally intended
as a caricature of Sir Thomas Lucy ? And if not, how
happened it that the characters came to be generally identified ? [1]

---

[1] Many of the facts referred to in this chapter are collected in Malone's *Life
of Shakespeare*, and in an interesting and suggestive article which appeared in
Fraser's Magazine (April 1877), entitled *Master Robert Shallow*, signed, C.

The Lucys of Charlecot were among the foremost knightly families of England. Their associations were courtly, as well as literary. Sir Thomas Lucy was born in 1532, and was educated by Fox the martyrologist, no mean scholar, and the author of several comedies in Latin, who found a refuge at Charlecot after his expulsion from Magdalen College, and before he became tutor in the family of the Duke of Norfolk. At the early age of fifteen, or thereabout, Thomas Lucy married a rich heiress, and four years afterwards succeeded to the family estates, on the death of his father, Sir William Lucy, Knight. A few years later he rebuilt the ancient hall at Charlecot, constructing it in the form of the letter E by way of delicate compliment to his sovereign, who recognised his loyal devotion by visiting him in the year 1572. He was elected knight of the shire in 1571, and again in 1584. The *Commons Journal* bears witness to his attention to public business. In 1571 we find him serving on a committee appointed upon a motion for uniformity of religion, and for redress of certain defections ; the object of the motion being (as appears from the speech of the mover) to ' purge the common prayer book, and free it from certain superstitious ceremonies, as using the sign of the cross in baptism, &c.' He took part in a conference with members of the House of Lords, ' touching the bill against priests disguising themselves in servingmen's apparel.' In 1584 he presented a petition touching the liberty of godly preachers, ' and also for the speedy supply of able and sufficient men into divers places now destitute, and void of the ordinary means of salvation.' In the same year we find him associated with Sir Philip Sydney, the Lord Russell, Sir Walter Raleigh, and Sir Thomas Cecil on a committee to consider ' in what measure and manner they should supply Her Majesty by subsidy.' His latest parliamentary appearance was as member of a committee, to whom was referred a bill for the preservation

Elliot Browne. I have not thought it necessary to verify Malone's dates, or his extracts from the *Commons Journal* and other sources of information.

of grain and game. This bill never became law; it ma
have been to the same effect as 7 James I. c. 11, entitled ' A
Act to prevent the spoil of corn and grain by untimel
hawking, and for the better preservation of pheasants an
partridges.'

He served twice as sheriff, in 1569 and in 1578. H
appears to have been chosen as arbitrator in dispute
between burgesses of Stratford. Clarenceux king-at-arms
in the person of Camden the antiquarian, with Windso
and Lancaster heralds, attended the knight's funeral (so h
certifies) and bore 'the cote of arms' of which we have
heard, probably (for it was then autumn) flaunting the white
luces (*hauriant, arg.*) in the sight of one who was just
then re-writing his first hasty rough sketch of a comedy
entitled *The Merry Wives of Windsor*. His son Sir Thomas
appears to have been possessed of a collection of French and
Italian books. Of his grandson, also Sir Thomas, a contemporary poetaster writes :

> The all beloved and highly-prized gem,
>   That in the Court's brow like a diamond,
> Or Hesperus in heaven doth lighten them
>   For men to see their way in glory's ground.

Another grandson of Sir Thomas Lucy was Bishop of St.
David's, and I have read that a third was to have been a
member of James I.'s ' Academe Royal.'

Altogether, the family of Lucy had many points of contact
with the great world of the day, and life and conversation
at Charlecot must have been affected by various currents
of contemporary thought and action—religious, political,
courtly, and literary.

Essentially shallow the old Puritan knight may have
been, but his associations and surroundings, and (so far as
we can judge) his characteristics were widely different from
those of the Gloucestershire Justice whom the world knows
by the name of Robert Shallow. Socially, morally, and
intellectually they breathed atmospheres as different as is
the air which clings to the warm meadows, scented pastures,

nd stately woodlands of Charlecot, from the thin and eager
breezes of a Cotswold hillside.

The Robert Shallow of the second part of *Henry IV.*
had in early life enjoyed one glimpse of the larger and fuller
life of the metropolis. That golden time was now fifty-five
years distant. He had been in truth but an outsider, a
spectator of scenes enacted by others. But to his sight the
very ordinary adventures of his youth assumed gigantic
proportions, as he looked back to them across the dead
level of his Gloucestershire existence. The advent of Sir
John Falstaff 'about soldiers' revived ancient recollections
of Clement's Inn, 'where, I think, they will talk of mad
Shallow yet.' Those were the days when he 'would have
done anything, indeed, and roundly too,' when he and old
Silence heard the chimes of midnight, with the famous
swinge-bucklers, little John Doit of Staffordshire, black
George Bare, Francis Pickbone, and our friend Will
Squele a Cotswold man. These memories mingled strangely
with the prosaic realities of everyday life.

Shal. The mad days that I have spent! and to see how many
of mine old acquaintance are dead!

Sil. We shall all follow, cousin.

Shal. Certain, 'tis certain; very sure, very sure: death, as the
Psalmist saith, is certain to all; all shall die. How a good yoke
of bullocks at Stamford fair?

Sil. By my troth, I was not there.

Shal. Death is certain. Is old Double of your town living
yet?

Sil. Dead, sir.

Shal. Jesu, Jesu, dead! A' drew a good bow! And dead! a'
shot a fine shoot: John a Gaunt loved him well, and betted much
money on his head. Dead! a' would have clapp'd i' the clout at
twelve score; and carried you a forehand shaft a fourteen and
fourteen and a half, that it would have done a man's heart good to
see. How a score of ewes now?

Sil. Thereafter as they be: a score of good ewes may be worth
ten pounds.

Shal. And is old Double dead?   2 *Hen. IV.* iii. 2. 36.

Sir John arrives, and is greeted as an old acquaintance,

but with the deference due to a visitor from the great
world.   He affects to recognise Shallow's companion :

Fal. Master Surecard, as I think ?

Shal. No, Sir John ; it is my cousin Silence, in commissio
with me.

Fal. Good Master Silence, it well befits you should be of th
peace.

Sil. Your good worship is welcome.   *Ibid.* 95.

Shallow proceeds to call the roll of recruits, with his wonte
fussy iteration :

.Where's the roll? where's the roll? where's the roll ?   Let m
see, let me see, let me see.   So, so, so, so, so, so, so ; Yea, marr
sir !   Ralph Mouldy !   Let them appear as I call ; let them do so
let them do so.   Let me see.   *Ibid.* 106.

Business concluded, the Justice talks of old times.   He doe
not get much response at first from the knight, who probabl
never exchanged a word with him in their youth :

Shal. O Sir John, do you remember since we lay all night i
the windmill in Saint George's field ?

Fal. No more of that, good Master Shallow, no more of that.

Shal. Ha ! it was a merry night.   And is Jane Nightworl
alive ?

Fal. She lives, Master Shallow.

Shal. She never could away with me.

Fal. Never, never : she would always say, she could not abide
Master Shallow.

Shal. By the mass, I could anger her to the heart.   She was
then a bona-roba.   Doth she hold her own well ?

Fal. Old, old, Master Shallow.   *Ibid.* 206.

The knight, all this time, has been turning over in his mind
and considering to what profitable use he may turn the proffered friendship of the Justice :

As I return, I will fetch off these justices : I do see the bottom
of Justice Shallow.   Lord, lord, how subject we old men are to
this vice of lying !   This same starved justice hath done nothing
but prate to me of the wildness of his youth, and the feats he hath
done about Turnbull-street, and every third word a lie, duer paid
to the hearer than the Turk's tribute.   I do remember him at

Clement's Inn like a man made after supper of a cheese-paring:
when a' was naked, he was, for all the world, like a forked radish,
with a head fantastically carved upon it with a knife: a' was so
forlorn, that his dimensions to any thick sight were invincible; a'
was the very genius of famine.   *Ibid.* 323.

In those bygone days Jack Falstaff, page to Thomas Mowbray Duke of Norfolk, would not have been conscious of the
existence of the Gloucestershire squireling.   But times have
changed, the knight's purse needs replenishing, 'and now
has he land and beefs.   Well, I'll be acquainted with
him, if I return : and it shall go hard but I will make him a
philosopher's two stones to me ; if the young dace be a bait
for the old pike, I see no reason in the law of nature but I
may snap at him.   Let time shape, and there an end.' [1]
He does return.   And sorely are the resources of the
Shallow establishment taxed to provide a suitable entertainment for him and his followers.

Shal. Some pigeons, Davy, a couple of short-legged hens, a
joint of mutton, and any pretty little tiny kickshaws, tell William
cook.
Davy. Doth the man of war stay all night, sir ?
Shal. Yes, Davy.   I will use him well: A friend i' the Court
is better than a penny in purse.   *Ibid.* v. 1 27.

Such is the Shallow of the second part of *Henry IV*.   If
he is intended as the counterfeit presentment of Sir Thomas
Lucy, the satire is certainly veiled, and it was not necessary
to conceal it further by locating the whole group of characters at the further extremity of an adjoining county.   In
outward circumstances there is nothing in common between
the head of the household in which Davy served so many
good uses, and the wealthy entertainer of royalty at Charlecot.
It is not possible that the old precisian; married at fifteen ;
full of prayer-book revision, priest's apparel, parliamentary
committees, preservation of game and grain, domestic architecture, affairs of court and state, and varied activities continued throughout life, could have discoursed, like Robert

[1] *Ibid.* 353.

Shallow, of nothing beyond the homely surroundings, the trivial occurrences, and petty economies of rustic life, with occasional reminiscences of a half-mythical youth in which he saw afar off the doings of a great world of which he formed no part.   There would have been no point in representing Sir Thomas Lucy, the host of the Queen, as having a distant view of royalty but once in the tilt-yard, and then getting his head broken for crowding among the marshal's men.   Indeed, from what we know of the master of Charlecot, his history, position, tastes, pursuits, and surroundings, he might fairly be selected as a type of country gentleman contrasting in every particular with the immortal Justice of *Henry IV.*

The second part of *Henry IV.* was produced about the year 1597.   The Gloucestershire justices attained immediate popularity, and were recognised as types.   Ben Jonson in *Every Man out of his Humour,* first acted in 1599, thus alludes to Master Shallow :

Savi. What's he, gentle Mons. Brisk?   Not that gentleman?
Fast. No, lady : this is a kinsman to Justice Shallow.

In Decker's *Satiromastix* (1602) we read of 'spangle babies, these true heirs of Master Justice Shallow.'   And a letter has been preserved from one Sir Charles Percy, a member of the Northumberland family, settled at Dumbleton in Gloucestershire, addressed to a friend in London, probably in the year 1600, in which this passage occurs : ' I am here so pestred with cuntrie businesse that I shall not bee able as yet to come to London.   If I stay heere long in this fashion I think you will find mee so dull that I shall be taken for Justice Silence or Justice Shallow.'

We now come to Robert Shallow of the *Merry Wives of Windsor.*   According to a tradition of respectable antiquity the *Merry Wives* was written in fourteen days, by command of the Queen, who wished to enjoy the spectacle of Falstaff making love.   The existence of the quarto—an early edition of the first sketch as performed ' both before her Maiestie and elsewhere '—affords some confirmation of

a story which is more likely to be true than fabricated for no
reason that can be readily imagined. The quarto differs
from the folio as a rough draft from a completed work, not
as an imperfect copy from an original document. Scenes are
re-arranged and entire passages transposed. Nor is this all.
In the quarto, Shallow plays a very subordinate part. Now
Shallow was one of the best known and most popular of
Shakespeare's creations. If the first scene of the comedy
had originally stood as we have it now, it is unlikely that
the most hasty or careless of surreptitious copyists could
have missed all about the Justice's new-born dignities, his
dozen white luces in his coat, with their suggestions, to his
apprehension so apt and sensible. In the quarto, Shallow,
so far from bragging of his county offices and ancient coat-
armour, keeps up his old deferential bearing towards Falstaff.
' Tho' he be a knight, he shall not thinke to carrie it so
away.' He is, in short, the Gloucestershire Robert Shallow
of *Henry IV.* without any suggestion of Sir Thomas Lucy
as yet superadded. He is, no doubt, owner of a deer-park,
for he has deer and a keeper. But this would never suggest
Sir Thomas Lucy, who had no park, though he probably
had deer. Parks were numerous in Gloucestershire, and
Robert Shallow, simple though he stood, was of sufficient substance to lay his hands forthwith on one thousand pounds, and
may well have possessed a deer-park.

Shallow takes but little part in the action of the early
sketch. His chief business is to introduce his nephew Slender,
and to identify him with the Gloucestershire group. This
inimitable character assumes his full proportions in the folio,
but is fairly developed in the quarto. It has been well said
that he represents the young Gloucestershire of the day. He
may have been endowed by nature with a fair share of intelligence, but it has all been devoted to the study of the habits
of the lower animals for purposes of sport. He can detect the
presence of bears in Windsor by the peculiar barking of the
town curs. He knows the performance of every greyhound
on Cotswold.

To him Master Page is the master of the celebrated fallow greyhound, rather than the father of sweet Anne Page. He had fought with a warrener, and had thus taken the first degree in that school of fashion, of which the masters have ' full often struck a doe, And borne her cleanly by the keeper's nose ? ' [1] His serving-man boasts that ' he is as tall a man of his hands as any is between this and his head.' He measures the relative proportions of men and things by the standard of Gloucestershire. He is interested in the blazonry of arms—very necessary to be understood of gentlemen, and a part of every manual of etiquette, from the *Boke of St. Albans* to the *Compleat Gentleman*.

> *Slen.* I may quarter, coz.
> *Shal.* You may, by marrying.[2]

His uncle, though he came to Windsor unattended, is a person of consequence in his own county, for ' a justice of the peace sometime may be beholden to his friend for a man. I keep but three men and a boy yet, till my mother be dead : But what though ? yet I live like a poor gentleman born.' [3]

But still he can make a hundred and fifty pounds jointure (no mean sum in those days), and Page chooses him for his money and position, among the suitors for his daughter's hand. He is a degree above the burgesses of Windsor, ' O, I should remember him,' says Mrs. Quickly ; ' does not he hold up his head, as it were, and strut in his gait ? '

It was rare humour to exhibit this specimen of young Gloucestershire in sharp contrast with the civil burgesses of Windsor, and with the gilded youth of London represented by Fenton the companion of ' the wild prince and Poins,' of whom it is said, he ' capers, he dances, he has eyes of youth, he writes verses, he speaks holyday, he smells April and May.' In this company Slender was accounted a fool. Awkward in address, unaccustomed to the give and take of civil society, and not having at hand his *Book of Songs and Sonnets* or his *Book of Riddles*, he was unhappy alike in

---

[1] *Tit. Andr.* ii. 1. 93.   [2] *Merry Wives*, i. 1. 24.   [3] *Ibid.* 281.

earnest and in jest. He makes love to Anne Page by
talking to her of bear-baiting. He offends Master Page by
insisting on the defeat of his dog on Cotsall. Conversa-
tionally at his wits' end, he appeals to his uncle to come to
his rescue with the marvellous family joke of how his father
stole two geese out of a pen.

By the addition of Slender, the group of Gloucestershire
worthies was complete. As types of English country life
they stand unrivalled. It is strangest of Shakespearian
paradoxes that the limner of these portraits never professed
to sketch a contemporary Englishman.

Years passed by. The *Merry Wives* was re-written, we
know not when, and in the completed edition the identity
of Robert Shallow was destroyed, we know not why. In
the opening lines of the first scene the old Gloucestershire
Justice tells the audience that he is now a great county
magnate, of the quorum, and no less than *custos rotulorum*,
and that his name is Lucy, for this is meant by the heraldic
device by which his coat was charged with luces. It was a
pity. Critics have deplored the degradation of Jack Falstaff
into another and a lesser man in obedience to the Queen's
commands, and we may regret the sacrifice of old Robert
Shallow to the promptings of resentment against some
member of the Lucy family. What the provocation was can
never be known. The least probable of all theories is that
Shallow was identified with Lucy to avenge an old quarrel
about deer-stealing, raked up after twenty years, and when
old Sir Thomas was dead. It is more probable that the
deer-stealing legend had its origin in the first scene of the
re-written *Merry Wives*, and colour is given to this suppo-
sition by the earliest version of the story, as it appears in
the diary of Mr. Davies. But Falstaff steals Shallow's deer
in the early sketch, before the county dignities and white
luces come on the scene. So far from receiving any confirmation from the opening scene of the *Merry Wives*,
the story is distinctly discredited by the discovery of its
probable origin. The tradition, however, should not be

wholly disregarded, for the fact that it was accepted in Stratford at an early date is evidence that Shakespeare's tastes and habits made it seem likely to the townsfolk that he might have got into trouble by loving sport, not wisely, but too well.

To fit him for his new-born dignities, and probably to heighten the satire as regards Sir Thomas Lucy, Shallow undergoes a perceptible change. The old Gloucestershire Justice is fussy, important in his way, and self-complacent; but deferential rather than self-asserting. Shallow, the *custos rotulorum*, is decidedly pompous. He dwells on his dignities, and poses as a personage. 'Robert Shallow, Esquire, saith he is wronged.' He patronises 'honest Master Page,' on whom he had bestowed a gift of venison, ('you know, sir, one says honest to one's inferiors,' remarked Fag to Captain Absolute).

Page. I am glad to see your worships well. I thank you for my venison, Master Shallow.
Shal. Master Page, I am glad to see you : much good do it your good heart ! I wished your venison better ; it was ill killed. How doth good Mistress Page ?—and I love you always with my heart, la ! with my heart.[1]

He has a way of summing up a discussion with an expression of his opinion, as if all further question were idle, as in the matter of Page's dog : 'Sir, he's a good dog, and a fair dog : can there be more said ? he is good, and fair.'[2] This may have been a trick of Sir Thomas's. We have one composition undoubtedly from his pen, 'set down by him that best did know what hath been written to be true, Thomas Lucy'—it is the epitaph on his wife the Lady Joyce Lucy, which may be read upon her monument in Charlecot church. After enumerating her many virtues, amongst others the negative one that she was 'never convicted of any vice or crime,' the knight sums up : 'when all is spoken that can be said, a woman so furnished and

---

[1] *Merry Wives*, i. 1. 80.   [2] *Ibid.* 98.

garnished with virtue as not to be bettered and hardly to be equalled by any.'

But whatever may have induced Shakespeare to transmute Shallow into Lucy, we who are not in the quarrel may disport ourselves with the old Justice in his Gloucestershire manor in the hundred of Berkeley. What took Shakespeare to the abode of the Perkeses and Visors can never be known ; from which is derived this advantage that it is impossible to disprove the story told in these pages. A yeoman's guest in a remote country neighbourhood, he would have many opportunities of mixing on familiar terms with the country esquires, and thus seeing the bottom of Master Shallow and his fellows. It was the custom of the cultured and civilised Lucys to sneer at the old-fashioned Shallows, who, for want of better company, filled their halls with yeoman neighbours. This we may learn from the following fragment of a dialogue between Vincent, the country gentleman, and Vallentine, the courtier, taken from the *Cyuile and Vncyuile Life*, already referred to and published in the year 1579.

Vincent. In fowle weather, we send for some honest neighbours, if happely we bee with our wiues alone at home (as seldome we are), and with them we play at Dice and Cardes, sorting our selues accordinge to the number of Players, and their skill, some to Ticktacke, some Lurche, some to Irish game, or Dublets : other sit close to the Cardes at Post & Paire, at Ruffe, or Colchester Trumpe, at Mack or Maw : yea, there are some euer so fresh gamesters, as wil bare you cōpany at Nouem Quinque, at Faring, Trey trip, or one & thirty, for I warrant you we haue right good fellowes in the countrey, sumtimes also (for shift of sports, you know, is delectable) we fall to slide thrifte, to Penny prick, & in winter nights we use certaine Christmas games very propper & of much agilitie. . . . Or if we haue cōtinually dwelt at home & bin Justices of Peace, we accōpt what graue Judges & gentlemen we haue seene sit on our Bench, & with what eloquence we haue (when it was our turne) geuen the charge.

Vallentine. Certainly, Syr, you haue told me of many proper pleasures, and honest exercises. But with all let me aske you what Neighboures these companions bee, of whom you have told me.

Vincent. They are our honest neighbours, Yeomen of the Countrey, and good honest fellowes, dwellers there about : as Grasiers, Butchers, Farmers, Drovers, Carpenters, Carriers, Taylors, & suchlike men, very honest and good companions.

Vallentine. And so I thinke, but not for you beeing a Gentleman. For as their resort vnto your house shall give them occasion to learne some point of ciuility, and curtesie, so your conuersinge with them will make you taste of their bluntnes and rusticitie, which wil very euill become a man of your calling.

Vincent. What, would you then haue me liue alone and solitary ? That were worse then to be dead.

Master Shallow and this Vincent had much in common. They were both justices of the peace, who dwelt continually at home.   Shallow, like Vincent, had his views on the subject of the education of youth.   Having sent them 'to the Universitie where may become so learned as they gaine by learning their owne living,' he would have them brought up 'in ye Innes of Court where if they profite, wee suffer them to proceede ;   if not, speedily revoke them from thence, least they acquaint themselves to much with the licentious customes of the Cittie ;' reasons which may have induced the elder Shallow to revoke Master Robert from the company of the swashbucklers of Clement's Inn, where after fifty-five years they talked of mad Shallow yet. Shallow, like Vincent, expected his serving-man to discourse of 'sowing or graffing, ditchinge or hedginge, the dearth or cheapnes of grayne, or any such matters.'   And Shallow, like Vincent, was wont to bid to Shallow Hall not only the Slenders and Squeles, but old Double of the next town,[1] with the Perkeses, the Visors, and I make no doubt the Shakespeares and their kindred.

Shakespeare's selection of the rustic Vincents, rather than

---

[1] Dursley was the 'town' to dwellers in the neighbourhood of Woncot and the Hill.   In old times, says De Foe, it was 'noted for sharp over-reaching people, from whence arose a saying of a tricking man, "He is a man of Dursley,"' a saying equivalent, according to Fuller, to *fides Punica* (quoted in *Dursley and its Neighbourhood*, by the Rev. John H. Blunt, 1877).   Shakespeare's country Justice is Shallow, and his kinsman Slender.   Was it without design that the dweller in the neighbouring town of Dursley was old Double ?

the civil Vallentines, for immortalisation in his plays, was no doubt influenced by the consideration that they lent themselves more readily to caricature. It may also be due, in part, to the fact that their mode of life afforded him better opportunities of studying their special characteristics. Thus it came to pass that the silent youth who in Master Shallow's hall noted 'the semblable coherence of his men's spirits and his,' could 'see the bottom of Justice Shallow,' and thereby attained such excellent matter as without the same opportunities it might have been, even for him, impossible to devise.

CHAPTER IX

THE HOLY ALE

Were I in England now . . . there would this monster make a man ; any strange beast there makes a man ; when they will not give a doit to relieve a lame beggar.
The Tempest.

IT was from no Sabbatarian feeling that Abraham Slender rested from hunting on the day following the chase of the Cotswold hart.

It was all very well for parson Savage of Dursley to denounce the country customs of church-ales, and morris-dances in the churchyard, with Robin Hood, Maid Marian, and such-like abominations. For Master George Savage was, as all the countryside knew, a puritan. To the Slenders and Aguecheeks of the day, a puritan was simply the arch enemy of human enjoyment. 'O, if I thought that, I'ld beat him like a dog!' [1] Such would have been Slender's short method with the puritans, if he had thought of the subject at all.

As for the Justice, he had (as we all know) a leaning towards puritanism ; but even ⸻ ·ould never have gone so far as to hold that Sunday was an unfit day for sport. He would often ride over on Sundays to Dursley, where he was used to put up his horse with his kinsman, old Silence. "Master George Savage," he would say, "is a godly and painful preacher ; moreover, the church is fair and lightsome, the windows having been glassed with clear white glass, and

[1] *Twelfth N.* ii. 3. 153.

all Popish abominations having been throughly removed.
I mind well when Dursley church was whitelimed throughout. Old Double did it. Aye, that he did, and throughly
too. I mind well when he bought twenty-five sacks of lime
of the lime burner of Sudbury.[1] Truly your quicklime is
a marvellous great purger of your false doctrine. Whatsoever is expended on my own church at Shallow must needs
be laid out of my own charge, and the cost of glassing and
of lime is great, or else you would see no idle images or lying
histories in the windows, or on the walls."

The Perkeses and Bullcalfs of the next century made short
work of windows, wall paintings, and images, with but little
thought of the cost of replacing them. The whirligig of time
has brought in his revenges. Their descendants of to-day
have raised quite a large sum, notwithstanding agricultural
depression, for the purpose of replacing the stained glass in
accordance with ancient fragments, and of restoring the wall
paintings, traces of which were discovered beneath the seven-
teenth-century plaster.

But Master Shallow was not in earnest like these men,
or even as his thirteenth century ancestor, who built the
church at his proper cost to avoid the consequences in the
next world of having in the present life forcibly deprived his
neighbour of his wife. Little practical result of Master
Savage's teaching was discernible beyond an occasional pious
ejaculation, or doubtful quotation from psalmist or apostle,
and the substitution of the approved ' by cock and pie,'
' by yea and nay,' for the racier expletives of Clement's Inn.

As for his tenants at Shallow, Sir Topaz and the un-
cleansed church, with ' Pharaoh's soldiers in the reechy
painting,' and ' god Bel's priests '[2] in its idolatrous windows,
were good enough for them. The advowson, part of the
estates of Shallow, was, of course, turned to as profitable use
as might be. The Justice was one of those of whom Burton
writes :[3] ' Patrons they are by right of inheritance, and put

---

[1] See Note, *Shakespeare and Gloucestershire.*
[2] *Much Ado,* iii. 3. 142.   [3] *Anatomy of Melancholy.*

in trust freely to dispose of such livings to the church's good : but (hard taskmasters they prove) they take away their straw and compel them to make their number of bricks ; commodity is the straw of all their actions ; and him they present in conclusions, as a man of greatest gifts that will give most ; no penny, no Paternoster, as the saying is . . . a clerk may offer himself, approve his worth, honesty, religion, zeal, they will commend him for it, but *probitas laudatur et alget*. If he be a man of extraordinary parts, they will flock afar off to hear him. . . . But if some poor scholar, some parson chaff, will offer himself, some trencher chaplain that will take it to the halves, thirds, or accept of what he will give, he is welcome.' On these terms it was that Sir Topaz was made welcome to the advowson of Shallow —a dull man, learned, however, in the nature of spirits, and with some skill in the matter of exorcism.

But the Justice had no intention of deserting Shallow church and Sir Topaz on the Sunday which followed the chase of the Cotswold hart. A memorable and significant event had taken place in the parish, which was to be the occasion of a function of unusual solemnity.

A few days previously Mistress Slender's brindled cow had brought into the world a calf, in other respects ordinary enough, but possessing two heads instead of the customary allowance of one.

A reader unacquainted with the habits of thought prevalent in the Elizabethan age may be pardoned for inquiring what relation such an event could bear to a religious celebration in the village of Shallow, and his curiosity is so reasonable that I proceed to gratify it ; the more readily because the events of the day as detailed by the diarist may afford some idea of the manner in which a Sunday festival was held in a Gloucestershire village three hundred years ago.

Old Mistress Slender was sitting in her parlour, concocting a cordial mixture for which her family had long been famous, when Simple rushed in, followed by the entire household and exclaiming, "For the Lord's sake, mistress, the devil is born to the brindled cow, and Sir Topaz is out hunting with Master Abraham. I fear we be all undone."

Now, at this very moment, the sound of Master Slender's horn announced that he and Sir Topaz were returning from hunting; a fact that the excellent lady accounts among the fortunate circumstances of her life, as often as she recounts a story which took its place among the family narratives, second only to the famous tale of how her late lamented husband stole two geese out of a pen. "For what," she would say, "might a poor lorn widow do with the devil in her byre, and she not a papist, and not having so much as an agnus in the house, which, indeed, the Justice calls idolatry, and he must needs be right; but I mind well that my mother never was without an agnus, though kept under lock and key, and in those days never a calf had more than one head. But the saying is you cannot eat your cake and have your cake, and it may be that the agnus is not worth the fine, especially with Sir Topaz nigh at hand, for all the county knows that he is mighty powerful with the foul fiend."

Scarcely had these thoughts passed through the mind of the worthy lady when Sir Topaz and Abraham Slender entered the parlour.

"For heaven's sake, Sir Topaz," exclaimed Mistress Slender, "may mercy preserve us, the foul fiend is in the byre, and hath been seen of Simple. For the love of heaven cast him forth, Sir Topaz, or we are undone."

A clergyman of the Church of England requested by a parishioner to cast out a devil would in these days probably manifest some surprise. Sir Topaz showed none. He accepted the appeal as a call to the discharge of occasional duty, of a kind rare, perhaps, but quite within the scope of his clerical office.

Turning to Simple he asked, "How hath the foul fiend manifested himself?"

"With two heads, an't please your worship," said Simple,

" and four hoofs, and that smell of brimstone as is not to be believed."

"This must be looked to forthwith," said Sir Topaz, " for the safety of the family, and for the credit of the parish, in the which there hath been known no manifestation of the powers of evil since Nan Kettle was burned for witchcraft. You, Simple, show me the *locus in quo*."

"Aye, forsooth, if that be the name o't. But a' be within the byre. It be the door beyond the stable, your worship knows it well. I'll tarry with my mistress to protect her, an't it please your worship, lest the foul fiend may perchance assault her when cast out by your worship."

"Follow me, Mistress Slender," said Sir Topaz, "and thou, cowardly hind. Be not afraid of the fiends of darkness. They may not withstand the powers of light."

Opening the door of the out-house, Sir Topaz looked in, saw the brindled cow quietly standing by her unhappy offspring, now no more, and thus addressed Mistress Slender :

" Fear not, madam, and thou Peter Simple hide not behind thy mistress ; this is no manifestation of the powers of evil. This is a portent of the same order of things as comets, eclipses, falling stars, or the commoner marvel of the rainbow, which obey no natural law but are set forth for the admonition and guidance of peoples. It may be that this sign is vouchsafed for the rising and fall of many in this parish, or even in this county. Let the creature be placed with all care in the church porch, so that it may be reverently viewed by all. It is my design to discourse thereon next Sunday."

The news of the monstrous birth spread far and wide. Squires and yeomen from neighbouring parishes, burgesses from Dursley, and even the parson from Berkeley came to see the marvellous portent.[1] Opinions were much divided

---

[1] The dramatists take many sly hits at the love of the British public for such spectacles as monsters. ' Were I in England now,' said Trinculo, when he discovered Caliban lying on the ground, ' as once I was, and had but this fish

as to its significance. The most popular theory connected its appearance in some way with designs of the papists. Clement Perkes hoped it boded no ill to the Queen. William Visor asked what could men expect when commons were enclosed and rents raised?

There was, indeed, an opposition party. It was said that parson Savage of Dursley talked of foolish superstition. But this was generally attributed to envy on his part, inasmuch as the marvel had not been vouchsafed to his parish, and the announcement of his intention to discourse on the subject of idle beliefs attracted but little attention when it became known that the portent would be visible for the last time in the porch of Shallow church on Sunday.

The quiet little hamlet presented an unusually gay appearance on this memorable occasion. The village green was covered with booths. There were attractions of various kinds. The churchwardens had taken advantage of the unusual concourse of strangers as the occasion of a church-ale. Great barrels of ale, the product of malt contributed by the parishioners according to their several abilities, were set abroach in the north aisle of the church, and their contents sold to the public. This was an ordinary way of providing for church expenses, against which earnest reformers inveighed, but as yet in vain so far as Shallow was concerned.

The church stood conveniently near the village green, and the brisk trade which was carried on all day was not interrupted by the progress of divine service. Sir Topaz's discourse suffered serious interruption by reason of the numbers who crowded into the aisles to gaze on the portent,

---

painted, not a holiday fool there but would give a piece of silver : then would this monster make a man ; any strange beast makes a man ' (*Temp.* ii. 2. 29). ' I beseech you, heartily,' said Ford to the company, ' some of you go home with me to dinner : besides your cheer, you shall have sport ; I will show you a monster. . . . *All.* Have with you to see this monster.' (*Merry Wives*, iii. 2. 80.) ' We'll have thee,' says Macduff to Macbeth, as he calls on him to yield, ' as our rarer monsters are, Painted upon a pole, and underwrit " Here you may see the tyrant " ' (*Macbeth*, v. 8. 25).

or to patronise the church-ale. A few from time to time made their way to the chancel, so as to catch portions of the discourse, and joined in. the hum of approval by which the regular listeners testified their appreciation of each telling point. The majority of the congregation stood, a few only being accommodated with seats. Amongst these were the Justice, Abraham Slender and his mother, William Silence, with Squire Petre and the Lady Katherine, who had ridden over from Petre Manor for the interesting occasion.

The discourse was indeed worth riding many miles to hear. The preacher chose as his text the words *Being dead, yet speaketh*. After a learned exordium, in the course of which he referred to Aristotle *de Historiâ Animalium*, lib. vii. cap. 9, he approached the topic of the day. The word ' monster ' he derived ' *a monstrando, quia monstrantur,* as this portent is now displayed before your eyes. But I would also add *ut monstrent*. They are showed that they may show the special handiwork of Providence, and though peradventure dead, yet speak.' Why should not this portent be as instructive as the appearance of a comet? ' Each comet (as experience hath taught men) is in its kind doctrinal, and blazeth forth something or other worthy our observation. *Nec in vanum toties arsere cometæ :* seldom are those super-terrestrial blazes kindled in vain. Men do commonly count them *prænuncios belli et calamitatum,* forerunners of some imminent calamities.' Then followed the practical application. At this point, however, the notes of the diarist become somewhat defective.[1] The preacher had asked *Quis peccavit ?* and was replying.*Neque hic neque*

---

[1] The learning displayed in this discourse raised doubts in my mind as to whether it was the original composition of Sir Topaz, or something in the nature of a homily, proper to be used on occasions of the kind. The latter theory is borne out by the fact that the selfsame discourse was delivered at Plymouth in the year 1635, and printed in a pamphlet entitled ' A True and Certaine Relation of a Strange-Birth which was borne at Stonehouse in the Parish of Plimmouth on the 20th of October, 1635, together with the Notes of a Sermon preached October 23, 1635, in the Church of Plimmouth at the interring of the sayd Birth.' (Reprinted in Arber's *Old Book Collectors' Miscellany*).

parentes, when he found the attention of his audience
suddenly distracted. ' Have patience, good people,' he exclaimed again and again with increasing warmth ; for he
was not so meek as that 'most gentle pulpiter' of whom
Rosalind asks ; ' what tedious homily of love have you wearied
your parishioners withal, and never cried, "Have patience,
good people " ? ' [1] His efforts were in vain, and the cause of
the disturbance soon became apparent. It was due to
the arrival in the church porch of a pedlar, who proceeded
to advertise his wares at the top of his voice, somewhat as
follows :

> Lawn as white as driven snow ;
> Cyprus black as e'er was crow ;
> Gloves as sweet as damask roses ;
> Masks for faces and for noses ;
> Bugle bracelet, necklace amber,
> Perfume for a lady's chamber ;
> Golden quoifs and stomachers,
> For my lads to give their dears.
> Pins and poking sticks of steel,
> What maids lack from head to heel :
> Come buy of me, come : come buy, come buy ;
> Buy, lads, or else your lasses cry :
> Come buy.[2]   *Wint. Tale*, iv. 4. 220.

The attraction was evidently great, for Sir Topaz was
speedily deserted by the female portion of his congregation,
and by not a few of the other sex. He soon brought his discourse to a somewhat inglorious conclusion, in the presence
of few beyond the ' ring of country gentles ' seated in the
chancel.

"Come home with us to dinner, Master Silence," said
Petre to William, as they left the church together ; " we
will discourse of Oxford days after the fashion of your

[1] *As You L.* iii. 2. 165.

[2] Some such experience, we may be sure, prompted Bishop Grindal's injunction to the laity at York : ' The churchwardens shall not suffer any pedlar, or
others whatsoever, to set out any wares to sale, either in the porches of churches
or in the churchyard, nor anywhere else on holy days or Sundays while any
part of divine service is in doing or while any sermon is in preaching.' (1571-2.)

father and Master Shallow, when they touch on Clement's Inn."

" I cannot withstand the temptation of such excellent discourse," said William Silence, " and with the leave of the fair Lady Katherine, I gladly accept your proffered hospitality."

As they left the church together, they found the pedlar the centre of an eager crowd, before whom he was displaying a broadsheet on which was printed a marvellous ballad. This was a true and certain history of the portent, in doggerel verse, illustrated with a rude woodcut, and attested by the hands of Sir Topaz and the churchwardens of the parish, Abraham Slender witnessing it as a marksman. 'Why should I carry lies abroad ? ' said the pedlar, whom we know as Autolycus.

This was not the only ballad in his wallet, and Petre and his companion pause to listen for a moment as Simple and his sweetheart Mopsa, with their friend Dorcas, cheapen his wares.

Simple. [*Clown.*] What hast here ? ballads ?

Mop. Pray now, buy some : I love a ballad in print o' life, for then we are sure they are true.

Ped. [*Autolycus.*] Here's one to a very doleful tune, how a usurer's wife was brought to bed of twenty money bags at a burden, and how she longed to eat adders' heads and toads carbonadoed.

Mop. Is it true, think you ?

Ped. Very true, and but a month old.

Dor. Bless me from marrying a usurer !

Ped. Here's the midwife's name to 't, one Mistress Tale-porter, and five or six honest wives that were present. Why should I carry lies abroad ?

Mop. Pray you now, buy it.

Sim. Come on, lay it by : and let's first see moe ballads ; we'll buy the other things anon.

Ped. Here's another ballad of a fish that appeared upon the coast on Wednesday the four-score of April, forty thousand fathom above water, and sung this ballad against the hard hearts of maids : it was thought she was a woman and was turned into a cold fish,

for she would not exchange flesh with one that loved her. The
ballad is very pitiful and as true.

Dor. Is it true too, think you ?

Ped. Five justices' hands at it, and witnesses more than my
pack will hold.

Sim. Lay it by too : another.

Ped. This is a merry ballad, but a very pretty one.

Mop. Let's have some merry ones.

Ped. Why, this is a passing merry one and goes to the tune of
' Two maids wooing a man ; ' there's scarce a maid westward but
she sings it ; 'tis in request, I can tell you.[1]

Wint. Tale, iv. 4. 262.

This is the self-same roguish pedlar whom we have met
in foreign parts travelling under the name of Autolycus, but
who is in truth when at home in Gloucestershire none other
than the elder Sly the pedlar of Burton-heath, whose son
Christopher, ' by education a card-maker, by transmutation
a bear-herd, and now by present profession a tinker,' was
(he tells us) ' by birth a pedlar.' [2]

Standing in the church porch, the pedlar is quickly
surrounded by an admiring crowd. There are matrons who
listen with sympathetic ears to the gruesome tales told by
his well authenticated ballads and broadsides ; simple
village maidens gazing with rapture on his glittering gew-
gaws ; and simpler rustic swains ensnared into cheapening
his wares. Well may he exclaim when his day's work is

---

[1] Ballads and broadsides on the popular subject of monsters were numerous
in the days of the diarist. No fewer than ten are included in a collection of
seventy-nine black letter ballads and broadsides printed between the years 1559
and 1597 (London, J. Lilly, 1870). Autolycus may have had some of them in
his pack, for one is entitled, ' The true discription of this marueilous straunge
Fishe which was taken on Thursday was Sennight the xvi. day of June this
present month in the yeare of our Lord God, MD. lxix.' Some of these curious
productions were evidently composed with a view to some religious function like
that celebrated in Shallow Church, concluding with pious doggerel of which
the following is a fair specimen :

> All ye that dothe beholde and see this monstrous sight so strange,
> Let it to you a preachyng be from synfull lyfe to chaunge
> For in these latter dayes trulye the Lord straunge syghts doth showe,
> By tokens in the heauens hye and on the yearth belowe. (Ballad 1564.)

[2] *Tam. of Shrew*, Ind. ii. 20.

done, and his trumpery all sold : ' Ha, ha! what a fool
Honesty is ! and Trust, his sworn brother, a very simple
gentleman ! ' [1]

The crowd made way for the Petres and Silence as they
leave the church and, passing through the churchyard, reach
the village green.

With them let us pause for a moment and note the
scene which presented itself to their eyes. The entire space
between the churchyard and Abraham Slender's house was
studded with booths and alive with preparations for the
merry-making which was to follow the church service of the
morning. Hither had flocked, as vultures to a carcass, the
rogues and vagabonds of the county. In the years which
preceded the establishment of a poor-law England was
flooded with a mass of vagrancy and pauperism constituting
a real social danger of the age. This feature of rural life
will be found faithfully reflected in the mirror held up to it
by Shakespeare.

These are the ' vagrom men ' whom Dogberry bid the
watch to comprehend, and if one would not stand, to
' take no note of him, but let him go ; and presently call
the rest of the watch together, and thank God you are
rid of a knave.' [2] They are the ' vagabonds, rascals and
runaways . . . famish'd beggars, weary of their lives,' with
whom, according to Richard, his army had to cope.[3]

These rogues and vagabonds were of certain recognised orders, clearly defined as the estates of the realm.
The Abraham man according to Awdelay [4] ' is he that
walketh bare armed, and bare legged, and fayneth hym selfe
mad, and caryeth a packe of wool, or a stycke with baken
on it, or such lyke toy, and nameth himself poore Tom.'
And so when Edgar came on the stage in *King Lear*
' disguised as a madman,' and naming himself poor Tom,
the audience at the Globe at once recognised a familiar
figure.

[1] *Wint. Tale*, iv. 4. 606. [2] *Much Ado*, ii. 3. 25.
[3] *Rich. III.* v. 3. 316. [4] *Fraternitie of Vacabondes*, 1565.

Edg. Who gives anything to poor Tom? whom the foul fiend hath led through fire and through flame, and through ford and whirlpool, o'er bog and quagmire. . . . Bless thy fine wits! Tom's a-cold—O do de, do de, do de. Bless thee from whirlwinds, star-blasting and taking! Do poor Tom some charity, whom the foul fiend vexes. *K. Lear*, iii. 4. 51.

Then there was the prygman [1] or prygger; 'for to prigge signifieth in their language to steal.' [2] 'What manner of fellow was he that robbed you?' asked the clown of Autolycus who had just picked his pocket.

Aut. A fellow, sir, that I have known to go about with troll-my dames [3] . . . having flown over many knavish professions, he settled only in rogue; some call him Autolycus.
Clo. Out upon him! prig, for my life, prig; he haunts wakes, fairs, and bear-baitings. *Wint. Tale*, iv. 3. 89.

The pedlars were comparatively respectable, for Harman says of them that 'they bee not all euill, but of an indifferent behauiour.' In this particular they were not very unlike to him whom we have just left vending his wares in the church porch.

Akin to the prigs are the 'dronken tynckers,' of whom Harman says that they 'be beastly people,' an opinion shared, I doubt not, by 'Marian Hacket, the fat ale-wife of Wincot,' in regard to a certain member of the fraternity of vagabonds, by birth as well as by profession; namely, Christopher Sly, 'by present profession a tinker,' who was on his own showing 'fourteen pence on the score for sheer ale.' [4]

A troublesome knave was he who was known as choplogic. According to Awdelay the choplogyke is 'he that when his mayte rebuketh him of hys fault he wyll geue hym XX wordes for one, els byd the deuils Pater noster in silence. This proude prating knave wyll maintaine his naughtines when he is rebuked for them.' 'How now, how now, chop-

---

[1] Awdelay. [2] Harman, *Caveat for Cursitors*, 1567.
[3] The ladies with whom these gentry consorted were known as trolls, or doxies; 'with heigh! the doxy over the dale,' sings Autolycus.
[4] *Tam. of Shrew*, Ind. 2. 21.

logic ! ' said Capulet to Juliet, when she would maintain her
naughtiness though rebuked by her father; ' what is this ? '

> ' Proud,' and ' I thank you,' and ' I thank you not,'
> And yet ' not proud ; ' mistress minion, you,
> Thank me no thankings, nor proud me no prouds.
>
> *Rom. and Jul.* iii. 5. 150.

Then there is the ruffler, placed by Harman first among
the vagabonds, ' because he is first in degre of this odious
order, and is so called in a Statute made for the punishment
of Vacabonds, in the XXVII yeare of Kyng Henry the eight,
late of most famous memory.' And when Saturninus spoke
reproachful words to Andronicus, he offered him a valiant
son-in-law :

> One fit to bandy with thy lawless sons,
> To ruffle in the commonwealth of Rome.
>
> *Tit. Andr.* i. 1. 312.

The rogue, properly so-called, was a vagabond of low
degree, herding with the beasts of the field, and ' their end
is eyther hanginge, wnich they call trininge in their language,
or die miserably of some loathsome disease.' ' Mine enemy's
dog,' says Cordelia,

> Though he had bit me, should have stood that night
> Against my fire ; and wast thou fain, poor father,
> To hovel thee with swine, and rogues forlorn,
> In short and musty straw?   *K. Lear*, iv. 7. 36.

It is said by Harrison [1] that Henry VIII. ' did hang up
threescore and twelve thousand in his time.' But in spite
of hanging, starvation, misery, and diseases, the country
swarmed with these ' roguing thieves.' [2] Their number is
estimated by Harrison as not less than ten thousand; and
we may be certain that the rest of the fraternity, with
Autolycus, were always to be found at wakes, fairs, bear-
baitings, and (not least of all) on such occasions as the holy-
ale at Shallow.[3]

William Silence little thought as he stood with the

---

[1] *Description of England.*   [2] *Pericles*, iv. 1. 97.
[3] See Note, *Rogues and Vagabonds.*

Petres on the village green, amused spectators of the humours of the church-ale, that his fate and that of Anne Squele trembled in the balance. And yet such was the fact. Master Shallow was at that moment walking with his sister Mistress Slender across the green, arranging the preliminaries of the projected marriage between Abraham Slender and Anne Squele. He had opened the matter to old Will Squele the day before at the hunting, and had found as little difficulty with him as with Master Page of Windsor when he went to him on a similar errand about a year before. It was the old story. William Silence was the younger son of a small country gentleman. He had to make his way in the world by his wits, not being (as was Hamlet's waterfly Osric) 'spacious in the possession of dirt.' [1] Now the wit of man is a commodity that cannot be surveyed, walked over, and appraised by your Squeles and your Shallows, in the same manner as the soil by which the crust of the earth is now for the most part covered. No doubt Abraham Slender kept but three men and a boy; but this was only until his mother be dead, and he could make a jointure of one hundred and fifty pounds a year. The land was there. It could be seen, and the assurances could be kept under lock and key in a strong chest. And so Will Squele's choice fell on Abraham Slender.

As for Anne, she said, with her predecessor in the Justice's favour:

This is my father's choice.
O, what a world of vile ill-favour'd faults
Looks handsome in three hundred pounds a-year!
Merry Wives, iii. 4. 31.

But let us not despair of William Silence's suit, but rather let us wish him victory over his 'foolish rival, that her father likes Only for his possessions are so huge,' [2] and let us say with mine host of the Garter: 'he will carry 't, he will carry 't; 'tis in his buttons; he will carry 't.' [3]

[1] *Hamlet*, v. 2. 90.   [2] *Two Gent.* ii. 4. 174.
[3] *Merry Wives*, iii. 2. 70.

"William Silence doth affect the wench," said Shallow to his sister; "this much I learned from Will Squele, and it may be that she favoureth his suit. These wenches be but silly fools. The lad hath a ready wit and a high spirit, and it may be that these vanities overcloud her vision, so that she discerneth not the land. It must be remembered, good sister, that though she be a Shallow, 'tis but on her great grandmother's side; thou didst not say yea to Abraham Slender's father for his wit or his learning, I warrant thee, good sister."

"I hope I knew my duties better than so to demean myself, and yet my goodman had a pleasant and a ready wit. I've ofttimes heard thee tell the tale of how a' stole——"

"Aye, marry, it is a good jest. It is an old jest. It is both good and old. Can there be more said? Abraham Slender shall wed the wench. Robert Shallow shall not be withstood in his own county of Gloucester, and by the younger son of cousin Silence, save the mark! It was not so in Windsor. A justice of the peace should not essay to command a wife but in his own county. Master Squele and cousin Silence will have a care that I am answered in this matter. As for William Silence, I fear that much learning hath undone him."

"The which can never be laid to the charge of my son, brother Robert. When a' doth speak, a's an absolute Shallow, though I say it that should not glory in my infirmities. But in feature a' somewhat favoureth his father, which is indeed as it should be, for what's bred in the bone will come out in the face."

"Well, well," said the Justice, "he's well enough. I have broken the matter to Master Will Squele. He will give his daughter three hundred pounds. Abraham can make her a jointure of one hundred and fifty. The man of law is drawing the specialties, and Sir Hugh Evans will marry them when it shall please me to fix the day."

"And hast opened the matter to my son Abraham?"

"Aye, marry," said the Justice, "and he hath dealt with

it in a becoming fashion. He said he would marry her upon any reasonable demands. He would do a greater thing than that, upon my request, in any reason. A' meant well, ay, that a' did. Ay, I think my cousin meant well."

Thus disposing of the fate of William Silence and Anne Squele, Master Robert Shallow and his sister arrived at the home of the latter. All that remains of the old dwelling of the Slenders, long since converted into a farmhouse, may be seen standing at the further end of the village green from the ancient church. The passing stranger pauses to admire the fine old Tudor archway, now built up into the farmyard wall, through which Shallow and his sister entered the courtyard where the Petres and William Silence were mounting their horses to ride across the wold to dinner at Petre Manor.

Taking leave courteously of old Mistress Slender and of the Justice, and bestowing a groat on Peter Simple who held his horse's head, Petre mustered his small party for their homeward ride. Following a track defined by ruts of passing wagons, which would not now be dignified by the name of a road, the riders arrived at the pale enclosing the park in which Petre had expected to meet 'these rascal knaves' his serving men, when he brought home his bride to his old-fashioned manor-house among the Cotswold Hills.

There were strange doings then in Petre Manor, and the tale lost nothing by telling in the taverns and alehouses of Gloucestershire. Clement Perkes, we may be sure, had told the story to his Stratford visitor over their ale. But William Silence was a late arrival from London, and had not time to pick up the gossip of the neighbourhood. His head just now was full of other matters, and his only information on the subject was that conveyed to him by his senses;— that his old Oxford friend had wedded a lady of spirit and beauty, who made him to all appearance a most loving and charming wife.

The place wore a neglected and deserted air, as of one whose master cared more for wandering abroad than for looking after domestic matters at home. Crossing the half-choked and neglected moat, Silence and his friends dismounted in a grass-grown courtyard, surrounded by the ancient and mouldering manor-house, half stonework, half timber, which had sheltered many generations of Petres. There had been indeed some improvement in the condition of the serving men who rushed out to meet their master, since it was said of them :

> Nathaniel's coat, sir, was not fully made,
> And Gabriel's pumps were all unpink'd i' the heel ;
> There was no link to colour Peter's hat,
> And Walter's dagger was not come from sheathing :
> There were none fine but Adam, Ralph, and Gregory :
> The rest were ragged, old, and beggarly ;
> Yet, as they are, here are they come to meet you.
>
> *Tam. of Shrew*, iv. 1. 135.

For the orders of old Groome (he was as much Grumio, as Petre was Petruchio) had in some sort been attended to. 'Let their heads be sleekly combed, their blue coats brushed and their garters of an indifferent knit : let them curtsy with their left legs and not presume to touch a hair of my master's horse-tail till they kiss their hands.' [1]

As William Silence looked round the court-yard his attention was diverted from the mouldering house and ancient retainers by the cordial and unmistakable welcome accorded to its master by another class of occupants. In one corner a badger peered cautiously from a butt or barrel which, lying on the ground, served it as an earth. In another, a fine old dog-fox of the greyhound kind rattled the chain by which he was fastened, to attract the attention of his master ; a handsome but a treacherous pet. The tale of his misdeeds in after life suggested a simile :

> For treason is but trusted like the fox,
> Who, ne'er so tame, so cherish'd and lock'd up,
> Will have a wild trick of his ancestors.
>
> *1 Hen. IV.* v. 2. 9.

[1] *Tam. of Shrew*, iv. 1. 93.

Along one side of the court-yard ran a long low shed in which were hawks of every kind, from the proud falcon to the humble eyess-musket. They recognised the presence of their master after the fashion of the 'royal bird' of Jupiter, the 'holy eagle,' who 'prunes [1] the immortal wing and cloys his beak, As when his god is pleased.' [2]

A raven of glossiest plumage hopped eagerly across the pavement, and, eyeing Silence with curious glance, greeted Master Petre by directing against his jack-boots vigorous but ineffective charges of his long and sharp beak. When the door of the hall was opened by Curtis, a chorus of sporting dogs headed by Troilus the spaniel greeted their master, while 'the little dogs and all, Tray, Blanch, and Sweetheart,' [3] barked joyously around their mistress.

"I perceive, Master Petre," said Silence, "that you have not lost your love for the brute creation, which gave you as your companion at Oxford yonder brock that is now daring the assaults of the dog so that he may welcome your approach."

"These," said Petre, " are friendships which I have laid in store against evil days. If it should be my lot to fall out with fortune, I would have around me some eyes besides thine, my bonnie Kate, into which I may look without reading therein the story of my decline.[4] But come, Master

---

[1] To 'prune' is a technical term in falconry, 'one of the kyndeli termis that belong to hawkis,' according to the *Boke of St. Albans*. When a hawk prunes, or picks her feathers, 'she is lyking and lusty, and whanne she hathe doone she will rowse hire myghtyly.' '*Cloys* is doubtless a misprint for *cleys*, that is, *claws*. Those who have kept hawks must often have observed the habit which they have of raising one foot, and whetting the beak against it. This is the action to which Shakespeare refers ' (Harting, *Ornithology of Shakespeare*).

[2] *Cymb.* v. 4. 118.   [3] *K. Lear*, iii. 6. 65.

[4] Homer, like Shakespeare, has many bad words and few good to throw at a dog. But they both bear testimony to his fidelity and unchanging love of his master. Sir Henry Holland (*Recollections of Past Life*) relates that Lord Nugent (whom he calls the greatest Shakespearian scholar of his day) bet him a guinea that no passage could be found in Shakespeare commending directly or indirectly the moral qualities of the dog. Sir Henry paid, after a year's careful search—this was before the days of Mrs. Cowden Clarke, Dr. Schmidt, or the monumental *Lexicon*, which Shakespearian students owe to the industry of

Silence, I hope Sir Topaz and the ride have bestowed on you as good an appetite as they have on me."

As William Silence sat down with his host to the plain but substantial dinner set forth in the long dark oaken hall, he observed that foreign travel and experience had wrought but little change in the Petre whom he knew so well at Oxford. While he recalled his 'odd humours' which had prompted him ofttimes to go but 'mean apparelled,' and sometimes led him into more serious adventures, he reflected on the substratum of good sense, pluck, and mother-wit which always stood him in stead. And after the Lady Katherine had withdrawn, when his heart was warmed by Petre's generous wine he determined to act on an impulse which had been gradually gaining strength during the day, and, opening to his friend the state of affairs between him and Anne Squele, he resolved to appeal to him for advice and assistance. Although he had not the knowledge which we possess of Petre's matrimonial views and experiences, he knew enough of his character to divine that his advice would not be hampered by the local prejudices

Mr. Bartlett. It was money paid under a mistake of fact, for Timon, turned misanthrope, thus contrasted the faithfulness of the dog with the faithlessness of mankind :

Tim. Who, without those means thou talkest of, didst thou ever know beloved ?

Apem. Myself.

Tim. I understand thee ; thou hadst some means to keep a dog.

Tim. of Athens, iv. 3. 314.

The useful qualities of the dog are fully recognised, 'every one According to the gift which bounteous nature Hath in him closed' (*Macbeth*, iii. 1. 97), and especially the qualities which are valuable in the running hound. But the horse, not the dog, was the chosen friend and companion of Shakespeare. Scott, on the other hand, loved the dog as a friend, but traduced him as a hound hunting by scent. Scott, as we know from his early letters, had been an enthusiastic courser. But he did not possess Shakespeare's knowledge of running hounds and of their methods of pursuit when they can no longer hunt by sight but are driven to their noses. Had it been otherwise he could not have described the hounds with which Fitz-James hunted the stag (blood-hounds of black St. Hubert's breed) as baffled and unable to account for their stag, simply because he dashed down a darksome glen and was lost to hound and hunter's ken, in a sinking condition, when (as we have seen) scent becomes more and more burning. The word 'ken' tells its own tale. The hounds were then coursing the deer.

and conventional views which William Silence had never
regarded with respect, and towards which he now found himself in an attitude of hopeless antagonism.

Petre listened to his friend's story with evident interest.
When Silence had concluded, he thought for a moment.
Then, rising from his seat, and striking the table so violently
that the parrot dropped from his perch in fright, he said:
"If I mistake not, I can help you in this matter with somewhat better than good advice. I have of late received letters
from my kinsman, Sir John Perrott, now Lord Deputy of
Ireland, in which he bids me tell him if I know of any
young gentleman of parts, who is willing to adventure for
that country—but stay, I will fetch the letter itself."

Opening a worm-eaten cabinet of the blackest oak, Petre
pulled out a miscellaneous assortment of articles—jesses
for hawks, couples, leashes, capes, collars and trashes for
hounds ; with tavern bills, and other such-like unconsidered
trifles.

"As you know of old, Master Silence, my coffers are not
of the well-ordered sort, but all will come right at last—nay,
here is the letter ; my kinsman writes : ' And now of the
happy and blessed turn the Queen's affaires have taken in
this Ilande.   The Irishrie, being by continual warres so
wasted that scarce anie of them—' nay, this concerns the
wars, but you are a man of peace ; stay, here it is :

Moreover, the lande of this islande is for the most part held by no
tenure of lawful origin, but by a certain lewde custom to which the
barbarous inhabitants give the name of Tanistry, wherein is much
that is contrary to the lawes both of God and man, and to the
nature and eternall fitness of things in regard to the tenure of
lande.   And I am informed by those of my council who are
skilled in such matters that the rightful title of the Queen Her
most excellent Majestie to good store of the lande of this islande
might be peaceably established by the labours of cunninge and
paynful lawyers, whereby it might be purged of the unlawful
usages & salvage customs by which it is now overlayd and defiled,
to the dishonour of God, and the great losse of the Queen Her
Majesty.   Wherefore if you can send to me any younge man of

gentyl birth and good repute, learned in the lawe & with special skille in the matter of tenures, escheats, and forfeiture, I will ensure him profitable employement herein, and such a degree of favour and countenance as may gain for him faire recompense in this worlde, as well as the assurance of partaking in such good workes as may tend to his eternall welfare.

" Now, Master Silence, what say you to the prospect thus held out to you ? "

" I like it well, Master Petre, and I heartily thank you. What especially moves me is the hope thereby held out to me of being forthwith enabled to maintain a wife. For being but of late admitted to the degree of an utter barrister——"

" I take you," said Petre, " you have learned already to set more store on the bird in the hand than on two in the bush. But come, let us join the Lady Katherine in her bower. If I mistake not she will further your suit, and if I help you to a living, why, she may help' you to a wife."

When the matter was opened to Katherine, she entered into the project with all the energy of her nature. The plan of campaign was soon arranged. It was, as might have been expected from its authors, short, sharp, and decisive. There were to be no tedious long-drawn wooings, no parleyings with old Will Squele, no negotiations with Master Shallow. William Silence was to ask Anne, fair and straight, to marry him forthwith and go with him to Ireland, to seek their fortune under the patronage of the Lord Deputy bespoken on their behalf by Master Petre.

The sports which had been arranged for the following days lent themselves readily to the development of the plan.

On Monday, Petre flew his hawks on Cotswold, and Will Squele with his daughter Anne were to be of the company, and on the following day all had been bidden to hunt the deer with greyhound and cross-bow in the Justice's park. This hunt had been in fact designed by the Justice so that Abraham Slender might have an opportunity of advancing his suit to Anne Squele in the seclusion of the stand or ambush from which they would shoot the driven deer. This much was shrewdly suspected by Silence, and he imparted his suspicions to his friend.

"'Twere rare sport," said Petre, "to upset their schemes. You know the old saw, 'there's no such sport as sport by sport o'erthrown.'[1] Can you prevail with John Hunt that he may put Mistress Anne in some sequestered stand of which Abraham Slender wots not, and so carry it off with the Justice that it may be believed that he did it in error?"

"I know not whether I may prevail with John Hunt," said Silence, "but I know of somewhat that will."

"Then," said Petre, "put money in thy purse, use it and spare not. It may be that in lieu of a buck you slay a hart. And now, my Kate, let's to the court and view the hawks. Here, take thy hood like a noble falcon as thou art. None but an eyess may weather unhooded. Come, let's to the hawks. They are of the best, though I say it that should not."

[1] *Love's L. L.* v. 2. 153.

CHAPTER X

THE TAMING OF THE SHREW

I know her spirits are as coy and wild
As haggards of the rock. *Much Ado about Nothing.*

MASTER PETRE'S hawks were, in truth, worthy of his commendation, and since our diarist has thought it worth while to bestow upon them a large share of his tediousness, we of the nineteenth century who cannot hope to see them in the flesh may find a few minutes spent in his company to be not altogether wasted, if we are enabled thereby to realise in some degree the favourite sport of our ancestors and to apprehend allusions which might otherwise have escaped us.

When Silence had passed with his host from the hall into the courtyard they found there an arrival. This was a young man mounted on a stout Galloway nag and bearing with him a newly taken and untrained hawk. Petre immediately recognised the stranger who had accompanied Clement Perkes to yesterday's assembly, by whose gentle bearing and superiority to his surroundings Petre had been more strongly impressed than were the untravelled and unsophisticated natives of Gloucestershire. His errand was soon explained. Clement Perkes had captured a fine young hawk, and he begged Master Petre to accept it at his hands. It would seem that the worthy yeoman conceived himself to be under some obligation to his powerful neighbour. It may be that Petre in his blunt honest way had counteracted the influence bespoken by Davy on behalf of that arrant knave, William Visor of Woncot. This, however, is mere conjecture. The diary contains no notice of the suit of Visor against Perkes. I wish it were otherwise. A day would have been well spent at quarter sessions in hearing Justice Shallow give the charge,[1] and in enjoying the humours of constables and third-boroughs, as the head-boroughs were commonly called,—'third, or fourth or fifth borough'[2] as Christopher Sly has it—Dogberry, Verges, Elbow, or Dull; all would have afforded matter for the diarist's pen. But we must take things as we find them. I only know that Petre graciously accepted Clement Perkes's gift, and courteously invited the stranger, when he had committed the hawk to the falconer's care, to accompany the party on their visit to the hawks.

To such chance encounters the world owes more than it suspects.

The afternoon was fine, and the hawks had been taken from the hawk-house or mews where they were confined at night and during the moulting season.[3] They stood 'weathering' in the open courtyard, attached by long leathern thongs to upright cylindrical pieces of wood, known as blocks. Around the legs of each bird there constantly remained fastened 'jesses';[4] narrow strips of soft leather, with small flat silver rings called 'varvels,' through which passed the leash or line by which the hawk was held in hand by the falconer in the field or attached to perch or block.

---

[1] 'Common forms' of charges to be delivered at quarter sessions, very useful to Justices lacking in knowledge or invention, are given in Lambarde's *Eirenarcha, a Treatise on the Office of Justices of Peace*, already referred to, and published in 1581. Dogberry's charge to the watch was a reminiscence of what he had heard with admiration from the lips of the Justices at quarter sessions. [2] *Tam. of Shrew*, Ind. i. 13.

[3] Hence the expression 'mew up' or 'mew' in the sense of 'confine.' *Tam. of Shrew*, i. 1. 87. 188 ; *K. John*, iv. 2. 57 ; *Mids. N. Dr.* i. 1. 71 ; *Rich. III.* i. 1. 38. 132 ; *Ibid.* 3. 139 ; *Rom. and Jul.* iii. 4. 11.

[4] *Othello*, iii. 3. 261.

There stood ' old Joan,' her master's delight and pride.
She was a true falcon, a female of the species properly
called 'peregrine,' [1] but sometimes, by way of special
honour, 'gentle;' a noble bird, with full dark eye, hooked
and azure beak, the rich brown of her plumage on back and
head contrasting with the sober colours of the plain but
useful goshawk standing by her side.

' The female of all byrdes of praye and ravyne is ever
more huge than the male, more ventrous, hardie, and
watchful,' and the female peregrine has given her name to
the gentle art of falconry, 'because,' says Turbervile, ' the
falcon doth pass all other hawkes in boldness and curtesie,
and is most familiar to man of all other byrdes of praye.'

But those who, like Shakespeare, were careful to use
terms of art aright, distinguished the 'falconer,' who pursued his quarry with the long-winged hawk or falcon, from
the 'astringer.' The latter was so called from the goshawk
or estridge (Fr. *austour* or *autour*; Lat. *astur*), the repre-
sentative of the race of short-winged hawks.[2]

For you must know that every hawk is not a falcon,
although every falcon is included under the generic term of
hawk. Amidst all the confused nomenclature of the older
books on falconry, the distinction between the long-winged
falcon and the short-winged hawk is never lost sight of.
The 'falcon, towering in her pride of place,' [3] is a different

---

[1] The 'peregrine' falcons, though of an indigenous species, were mostly
imported from abroad. Great numbers were taken at Valkenswaard in Holland,
during the annual migration of birds. A description of the mode of capture will
be found in Mr. Harting's *Essays on Sport and Natural History*. An account of
last year's capture is given in the *Field* of December 12, 1896, from which it
appears that the haggard falcon still deserves the character given her by the
old writers. One of the hawks taken was a fine haggard falcon, described as
having become very tame and gentle, notwithstanding her recent capture.

[2] Bert, in his *Treatise of Hawks and Hawking* (1619), gives directions
' worthy to be had in good estimation both of the falconer and austringer,' but
specially addressed to the latter; and the *Perfect booke of keeping sparkawkes
and goshawkes* (reprinted by Mr. Harting from a MS. of about the year 1575) is
intended to correct errors of ' unskilful ostringers.' 'They be called ostringers
which are the keepers of Goshawkes or Tercelles ' (*Gentleman's Academie*).

[3] *Macbeth*, ii. 4. 12.

creature from Master Ford's 'fine hawk for the bush,' [1] with
which he invited his friends to go a-birding after breakfast.
The reader will be in no danger of confounding these different
species after he has witnessed their performances in the
company of the diarist and his friends.   In the meantime,
suffice it to say that the long-winged hawks—such as the
gerfalcon, peregrine falcon, merlin, and hobby—differ not only
in structure of wing and beak, but in their mode of flying
and seizing their quarry, from the short-winged kinds, of
which the goshawk and sparrow-hawk alone were used in
falconry.

The former are the true falcons, 'fine-tempered, generous
birds, whose home is in the open country, and whose dashing
style of flight is only adapted to wild plains and hills.' [2]   They
are hawks of the tower and of the lure, towering aloft in
their pride of place, thence descending on their prey with
a downward stoop or swoop, and finally coming to the lure.

The short-winged goshawk and sparrow-hawk, on the
other hand, are the true 'hawks,' as distinguished from
the nobler race of 'falcons.'   They are birds of the fist,
flying after their prey from their master's hand and returning to it when the flight is over ; using it, in fact, in lieu
of the bush whence in a state of nature they pursue bird
or rabbit.   They are 'shifty, lurching fliers, deadly enough
in their own country, which is the close woodland, through
which they can thread their way like a woodcock or owl, and
that with extreme rapidity for a short distance.' [2]

And so we can understand how the art of an astringer
differed from that of a falconer as widely as the hunting of a
pack of beagles from that of fox-hounds.   Each had its own
professors and treatises, and the stage direction in *All's Well
that Ends Well*,[3] 'enter a gentle astringer,' would not have
puzzled an Elizabethan sportsman as it has perplexed learned
editors, who now for the most part omit this term of art,
thereby missing a distinct and characteristic point.

[1] *Merry Wives*, iii. 3. 247.   [2] *Falconry*, Badminton Library.
[3] *All's Well*, v. 1. 7.

It was the fashion of our ancestors to sneer at the French as falconers. They did not regard the rigour of the game, but condescended to any quarry that came in their way ; as their descendants are accused by British sportsmen of including in their gamebags the blackbird and the lark. ' We'll e'en to it like French falconers,' said Hamlet, ' fly at any thing we see.' [1] But of their skill in the art of an astringer there was no doubt. When Turbervile comes to treat of the short-winged hawks he puts the opinion of his French masters in the forefront. He writes ' of the goshawke, after the opinion of William Tardiff, a Frenchman,' and ' of the sparowhawke out of the French authors,' both being included in the ' genrall division of goshawkes, whom the Frenchmen call *autour*.' There was thus a special fitness in attaching to the Court of France a gentle astringer,[2] and there may have been good grounds for Helena's confidence in

---

[1] *Hamlet*, ii. 2. 450.

[2] The short-winged hawk, especially the goshawk, appears to have been from an early period held in high estimation by the French. For Cavendish in his *Life of Wolsey* (1557) describes a visit to the house of a great French noble, in the hall of which stood a hawk's perch whereon stood three or four fair goshawks. In England the place of honour would certainly have been occupied by peregrine falcon or tercel-gentle. According to the *Boke of St. Albans*, the peregrine was the hawk of an earl, the goshawk of a yeoman. We learn from Mr. Harting's *Bibliotheca Accipitraria* that French falconers to this day apply the term *fauconnerie* to flights with long-winged hawks only, giving to flights with the short-winged kinds the ' expressive and very convenient term *autourserie*,' and that two treatises on *Autourserie* were published in Paris so lately as 1887. For ' a gentle astringer ' Stevens conjectured ' a gentle stranger,' but subsequently discovered his error, which, he says, ' should teach diffidence to those who conceive the words which they do not understand to be corruptions ; ' a lesson, alas, easily forgotten. Mr. Grant White, retaining the words of the Folio, and quoting from the *Boke of St. Albans*, ' they ben called Ostrigeres that keep goshawkes or tercels,' adds ' the tercel was the aristocrat among hawks ; Juliet calls Romeo " tercel-gentle." ' Mr. Hunter (*Illustrations of Shakespeare*), rightly conceiving that ' a word or two more than commentators have given us is necessary for the just apprehension of the kind of person intended,' supplies the want by pointing out that the astringer in question had the care of ' a species of hawk called gentles.' It is a pity to spoil so excellent a point, but an astringer had no more to do with a tercel-gentle than a M.F.H. with beagles. The tercel-gentle was the male of the peregrine ; the tercel of the goshawk. The word ' gentle ' indicates that this particular astringer was, as we should expect from his associates, a gentleman.

the power of the king's astringer whom she remembered
to have seen in the Court.

> This man may help me to his majesty's ear,
> If he would spend his power.   *All's Well*, v. 1. 7.

But let us return to old Joan, before whose block we left
the company assembled.

" I perceive," said Silence, " that your favourite falcon is
hooded when she weathers, from which I conclude you hold
with Master Turbervile that pains are but lost with an eyess,
and that you rather labour to man and reclaim the wild
haggard of the rock."

" Aye, my Kate," said Petre, " hath he not well said ?
He knoweth thee for a haggard by thy hood. Nay, frown not,
Kate, for what falconer would choose an eyess if he had
skill to man a haggard ? "

These words, I confess, as I read them in the diary,
although they awakened some slumbering recollections, conveyed no very clear idea to my mind, and as the reader may
be in the same mental condition, I willingly impart to him
the knowledge which enabled me to understand allusions,
the point of which would otherwise have been lost.

You may train your falcon in either of two ways. You
may take from the eyrie the nestling or eyess (Fr. *niais*),
rearing and making it to your use from its earliest days.
Or you may capture a full-grown wild hawk, after she has
been taught to fare for herself by the sternest of taskmasters
for man or bird,—hunger :

> Quis expedivit psittaco suum χαῖρε,
> Picasque docuit verba nostra conari ?
> Magister artis ingenique largitor
> Venter.

The lessons learned in this school will not be forgotten,
and the wild hawk or haggard, reclaimed and manned, has
learned somewhat to which the eyess can never attain.
' Eyasses,' says Master Turbervile, ' are tedious, and do use
to cry very much in their feedings, they are troublesome

and paynfull to be entered.' To the experienced falconer they seemed as useful and promising as a company of children in the eyes of an astute stage manager. 'An aery of children, little eyases, that cry out on the top of question, and are most tyrannically clapped for't,' [1] may be the fashion of the hour and berattle the common stages, but they afford scant hope of mature excellence. 'He that meddleth with an eyess,' says Master Bert, 'will spend his time to no purpose, except a long expectation of good will give him satisfaction.'

And so, if you would have a hawk at once high-spirited, loving and tractable, you must man and train a haggard; that is to say, a wild hawk which has lived and fared at liberty until she has moulted for the first time and has assumed her adult plumage. On this point all the masters of falconry are of one mind. 'She has been forced often to praye for herself,' says Turbervile, and so her flight and stooping are more deadly, for in her old life, if she missed her bird, she had to go supperless to bed.

But though the wild falcon makes the best hawk when manned and trained, the haggard unreclaimed is the type of worthlessness and inconstancy.

> If I do prove her haggard,
> Though that her jesses were my dear heart-strings,
> I'ld whistle her off and let her down the wind,
> To prey at fortune.   *Othello*, iii. 3. 260.

The haggard falcon that has never learned constancy to her legitimate pursuit will 'check,' or change the quarry at which she is flown for any magpie or crow that fortune may throw in her way. 'The peregrine seems often to strike down birds for his amusement,' says Mr. St. John, writing of the male haggard; 'I have seen one knock down and kill two rooks who were unlucky enough to cross his flight without taking the trouble to look at them after they fell.' [2] Inconstant and profitless ever, the untrained haggard is like the random jester. Clever he may be: for

---

[1] *Hamlet*, ii. 2. 354.   [2] *Wild Sports of the Highlands.*

> to do that well craves a kind of wit:
> He must observe their mood on whom he jests,
> The quality of persons, and the time,
> And, like the haggard, check at every feather
> That comes before his eye.[1] This is a practice
> As full of labour as a wise man's art.
>
> > *Twelfth N.* iii. 1. 68.

And many a man has built on no more solid foundation a reputation for wisdom, which a lifetime of fruitless flights has failed to destroy.

It is no easy task to reclaim the 'proud disdainful haggard.'[2] ' She hath lived long at liberty,' says Bert, ' having many things at her command, and she is therefore the harder to be brought to subjection and obedience.' You cannot begin with kindness. The wild hawk must be half starved and watched all night so as to tire her out, and tame her by hunger and sleeplessness.[3] ' You must be watched ere you be made tame, must you ? ' said Pandarus to Cressida.[4] ' My lord shall never rest,' Desdemona promised :

> I'll watch him tame and talk him out of patience;
> His bed shall seem a school, his board a shrift;
> I'll intermingle everything he does
> With Cassio's suit. *Othello,* iii. 3. 22.

When discipline has done its work, then, but not till then, 'there cannot be too much familiarity between the man and hawke.' Then may her wild heart be tamed to regard her keeper's hand with loving apprehension. ' My inducements to carry her thus in the evening and night would make her love me as her perch, and by taking her up so early in the morning I would persuade her that there had

---

[1] See note, *The Language of Falconry.*

[2] *Tam. of Shrew,* iv. 2. 39.

[3] It may be that Master Page spoke the language of falconry when he said to Falstaff, tamed and subdued, ' Nay, do not fly; I think we have watch'd you now.' (*Merry Wives,* v. 5. 107.) Adonis is compared to ' a wild bird, being tamed by too much handling ' (*Ven. and Ad.* 560).

[4] *Troil. and Cres.* iii. 2. 45.

beene her pearch all night.' What Bert teaches in prose Beatrice has said in poetry. Hero had said of her :

> I know her spirits are as coy and wild
> As haggards of the rock. *Much Ado*, iii. 1. 35.

Hear her profession when manned and reclaimed :

> Contempt, farewell ! and maiden pride, adieu !
> No glory lives behind the back of such.
> And, Benedick, love on, I will requite thee,
> Taming my wild heart to thy loving hand.
>
> *Ibid.* 109.

All the masters of falconry, ancient and modern, would bid Benedick be of good cheer. Mark their testimony ; ' onely I say and so conclude,' says Bert, ' that your haggard is very loving and kinde to her keeper, after he hath brought her by his sweet and kind familiarity to understand him.' ' Moreover,' says Mr. Lascelles, ' though we cannot definitely account for this, the temper of the wild-caught hawk is, as a rule, far gentler and more amiable when once she is tamed than is that of a hawk taken from the nest.' [1] To the same effect says Master Symon Latham : ' but leaving to speak any more of these kinde of scratching hawkes that I did never love should come too neere my fingers [eyesses], and to returne unto the curteous and faire conditioned haggard falcon, whose gallant disposition I know not how to extoll or praise so sufficiently as she deserves.' [2]

But there will ever remain somewhat of the wild bird about your reclaimed haggard, noble and loving though she be, and I am certain that neither Benedick nor our friend whom they call Petruchio would have it otherwise. And so she must be hooded when she comes abroad on the fist or on the block, else she would bate (Fr. *se battre*) and flutter, with an eagerness to which the placid eyess is a stranger. The eyess may be set abroad to weather unhooded at any time of day, but a haggard should always be hooded, to prevent her

[1] *Falconry*, Badminton Series.
[2] Symon Latham, *The Faulcon's Lure and Cure*, 1615.

from 'bating' and continually striving to be gone, whereby her training would be greatly hindered. 'Come, civil night,' says Juliet, 'Hood my unmann'd blood, bating in my cheeks,'[1] thus combining pun and poetry after a fashion possible only to Shakespeare, who indeed, at times gives us pun without poetry, when visited by recollections of horse, hound, or hawk. The Constable of France, when he would belittle the Dauphin's valour, called it a hidden virtue, never seen by any but his lackey; ''tis a hooded valour, and when it appears it will bate' (abate).[2]

And this was what Master Petre meant when he would say that William Silence knew the Lady Katherine for a haggard by her hood.

"Come, keep on thy hood, my lady Kate," said Petre, laughing; "be the haggard never so reclaimed, she must needs wear her hood when she weathers, else she will bate. Or if thou bate not weathering hoodless, thou wilt take a rheum, and fare worse. Nay, I did but praise thee, sweet Kate, when I called thee a haggard. God forbid that I should have wedded an eyess. In regard to all manner of creatures," he continued, "I have ever observed that they which be wildest of nature are often the easiest tamed, and when tamed, are the most loving. What can be wilder than the raven or the haggard of the rock? Think you that a barn-door fowl with all its seeming gentleness would ever be so loving to mankind as these creatures of the wild? My parrot loves me better than his daily food, for he is ever ready to forsake it if I but offer to stroke his head. And yet the sailor from whom I had him told me that there is no bird more wild when he liveth at liberty. The wild goose is of all wild-fowl the most fearful, and shunneth most the abode of man, and yet I have myself taken one from the nest and kept him pinioned with his sober kith and kin, marvelling much how familiar he would be with man, and how he would follow and come at my call, while his sleek, home-bred fellows heeded me not. I have read that the

---

[1] *Rom. and Jul.* iii. 2. 10.   [2] *Hen. V.* iii. 7. 121.

Numidian lion can requite a kindness and be loving to man, if only you approach him not at feeding time. I have heard moreover that the Arab steeds of late brought into this land, although children of the desert, are more faithful and loving to their masters than the gentler-seeming grey mare of Flanders. If you seek to have, with obedience, love and not liking only, take a wild thing and tame it."

"Then," said Silence, " he did not amiss who took a shrew to wife to tame her. You know the merry conceited jest of *The Shrewd Wife lapped in Morel's Skin?* " [1]

" He might do worse than tame a shrew," said Petre, " but if he would reclaim a haggard, let him be assured that she came forth out of the eyrie of a peregrine, and let him ' avoid a puttock.' " [2]

"I fear that your good man preaches as he did not practise," said Silence to the Lady Katherine politely.

"Be not too assured of that, Master Silence," said the lady, smiling; " 'tis a good falconer can tell an eyess from a haggard when he sees her manned and hooded on her master's fist."

" An' your ladyship were a falcon," pursued Silence, led by ignorance and desire to please into dangerous ground, " I must needs confess that you was sometime a haggard, since it were but scant courtesy to call you an eyess. But being so fair and gentle a lady, I may not believe that you needed ever to be reclaimed from ill conditions, even though it were by so skilled and painful a falconer as Master Petre."

It was not until some time afterwards that Silence understood the significance of the shout of laughter with which this carefully prepared speech of his was received by Petre ; laughter in which the Lady Katherine, although at first she seemed disposed to bite her lip and frown, heartily joined.

" 'Tis an excellent conceited jest, i' faith it is," said Petre, " to tame a shrew as you would man a haggard, by the

---

[1] Reprinted by the Shakespeare Society, 1853.   [2] *Cymb.* i. 1. 140.

book of sports. Come Kate, sit down on this bench, and do
you hearken, my masters. I will make known unto you the
first heir of my invention—perchance indeed it may be the
last—and you may name it *The Taming of the Shrew*, or
The Manning of the Haggard, as you please. It may serve
your turn, Master Silence, sooner than you wot of, as it has
served mine."

So saying, Petre drew from his pocket a bundle of manuscript notes.   These were written, he explained to Silence,
by the desire of Master Edmund Bert, a gentleman of Essex,
who had been their fellow-student at Oxford.   They had all
been enthusiastic falconers, but Bert had devoted special attention to training and flying the short-winged hawk, and as a
'gentle astringer' was second to none, even in France.
Petre loved flying at the brook with falcon or tercel-gentle,
and above all things, when occasion served, the flight at the
heron with a cast of well-trained haggard falcons.   When
they had parted, Petre on his travels and Bert for Essex,
vowing life-long friendship, it had been arranged that each
should commit to writing his experiences in the practice of
his favourite art, in the hope that they might sometime
meet and compare notes together.   Long afterwards, when
Master Edmund Bert was advanced in years and in failing
health, he gave to the world *An Approved Treatise of Hawkes
and Hawking*.[1] In his preface addressed to the friendly
readers, he says, ' I did never purpose to publish in common
these my labours, but to have given them privately to whom
they are dedicated, and to whom I stand devoted [a clear
reference to Master Petre] ; but being discovered to some of
my friends, and by them made knowne to many of the rest,
their importunities and earnest perswasions have made mee
put it to the presse.'

Master Petre's notes on the art of reclaiming a haggard
have been lost to mankind. They appear to have been
somewhat resented by the diarist, inasmuch as Petre in-

[1] London, 1619 ; reprinted with an introduction by Mr J. T. Harting.
London, Quaritch, 1891.

sisted on reading them out in the disguise of a free translation, and offering them to his friend as personal experiences which might prove useful in his future relations with Anne Squele. ' A jest's prosperity lies in the ear of him that hears it.' Curiously enough, the Lady Katherine seemed rather to enjoy what might be supposed to reflect on herself, while the effect on William Silence was altogether different. Petre's rough jokes and blunt allusions jarred on his feelings, and he half repented that he had exposed his tender feelings to this coarse handling. However, when he called to mind the practical sympathy and ready help extended to him by Petre, he reflected,

> Though he be blunt, I know him passing wise;
> Though he be merry, yet withal he's honest.
>
> *Tam. of Shrew*, iii. 2. 24.

So he was content to dismiss the incident without comment as an example of the 'odd humours' which occasionally led his friend into extravagance. Indeed the only remark of Petre's noted by him is one described as 'an excellent conceipted jeste.' I should have deemed it a poor pun, did I not find it reproduced in three several sonnets included in a collection comprising some of the finest poetry in the English language. " Aye, Master William, tame her as thou mayest, I warrant thee thy wife will yet have her Will."

But Master Petre's practical application of the maxims of falconry has not been lost to the world through the reticence of the diarist. So well did the jest prosper in the ears of one who heard it, that we need not the services of the diarist to reproduce the speech.

> *Pet.* Thus have I politicly begun my reign,
> And 'tis my hope to end successfully.
> My falcon now is sharp and passing empty ;
> And till she stoop she must not be full-gorged,
> For then she never looks upon her lure.
> Another way I have to man my haggard,
> To make her come and know her keeper's call,
> That is, to watch her, as we watch these kites
> That bate and beat and will not be obedient.

She ate no meat to-day, nor none shall eat ;
Last night she slept not, nor to-night she shall not ;
As with the meat, some undeserved fault
I'll find about the making of the bed ;
And here I'll fling the pillow, there the bolster,
This way the coverlet, another way the sheets :
Ay, and amid this hurly I intend
That all is done in reverend care of her :
And in conclusion she shall watch all night :
And if she chance to nod I'll rail and brawl
And with the clamour keep her still awake.
This is a way to kill a wife with kindness ;
And thus I'll curb her mad and headstrong humour.
He that knows better how to tame a shrew,
Now let him speak ; 'tis charity to show.[1]

Tam. of Shrew, iv. 1. 191.

I cannot say to what this scene might have led, had not
the Lady Katherine brought it to a close by rising from her
seat and proposing to go round the hawks with Master
Silence and the stranger who had brought with him the
latest addition to their number.

You will find in Shakespeare the names of the hawks in
common use : the falcon and her tercel-gentle ; the estridge,[2]

[1] Mr. Lascelles (*Falconry*, Badminton Library) notes ten words in this passage as technical terms in falconry, and adds, ' Had Petruchio been a falconer describing exactly the management of a real falcon of unruly temper, he could not have done it in more accurate language.' That the central idea of Petruchio's method of training was thoroughly understood in the age of falconry, appears from Fletcher's sequel to the *Taming of the Shrew*, entitled, *The Woman's Prize; or, the Tamer Tamed.* See note, *The Language of Falconry.*

[2] Mr Douce (*Illustrations of Shakespeare*, 1807) was the first to point out that Shakespeare wrote of the estridge or goshawk, not of the ostrich, when he made Enobarbus say of Antony :

Now he'll outstare the lightning. To be furious,
Is to be frighted out of fear ; and in that mood
The dove will peck the estridge ; and I see still,
A diminution in our captain's brain
Restores his heart.   *Ant. and Cleo.* iii. 13. 195.

The same idea was present to the mind of Clifford when he thus taunted Richard
Duke of York :

So cowards fight when they can fly no further ;
So doves do peck the falcon's piercing talons.

3 *Hen. VI.* i. 4. 40.

A dove pecking an ostrich is not a lively image, and I doubt that the idea would

or goshawk, and her tercel ; and the musket. These were the names oftenest in the mouths of practical falconers, but other kinds were used for special purposes. In the *Boke of St. Albans*, the eagle is for an emperor, the gerfalcon for a king, the peregrine for an earl, and the merlin for a lady. The goshawk, so highly placed in the great . houses of France, was in England assigned to a yeoman, the sparrow-hawk to a priest, and the musket to ' an holiwater clerke.' These subtle distinctions of rank had become somewhat out of date in what our diarist regarded as the democratic age in which he lived. Master Petre aspired neither to imperial eagle nor kingly gerfalcon, nor did he possess the exotics of the race, the lanner, sacre, or Barbary falcon. The eagle was never of practical account. The great northern falcons—known as ger-falcons—nearly twice the size of the peregrine, were indeed incomparable in regard to flight and stoop, especially for the flight at the heron, but they were costly, hard to reclaim, and liable to disease in the damp climate of these rainy isles.

The peregrines were represented not only by the falcon

ever have occurred to a commentator, had he been aware that a kind of hawk in common use was known as an estridge.

When Hotspur inquired of Sir Richard Vernon as to the nimble-footed mad-cap Prince of Wales and his comrades, that daff'd the world aside and bid it pass, they were described as

> all furnish'd, all in arms ;
> All plumed like estridges that with the wind
> Bated, like eagles having lately bathed.
>
> 1 *Hen. IV.* iv. 1. 97.

Thus Shakespeare wrote, and thus the Folio reads. But critics, with the ostrich still in their thoughts, could not understand the allusion, and chose to read

> All plumed like estridges [ostriches] that wing the wind,
> Bated like eagles having lately bathed. .

This emendation labours under the disadvantage that it reduces to nonsense what is at all events intelligible. The only objection to what Shakespeare wrote is that the feathers of a goshawk, bating and fluttering with the wind, do not afford so striking a simile as the plumes of an ostrich. But if this objection did not occur to Shakespeare we need not trouble ourselves about it. The Cambridge editors obelise the passage. But I have followed Dr. Schmidt (*Shakespeare Lexicon*) in accepting the text of the Folio, which is clear enough when the meaning of the technical terms of falconry is understood.

proper, but by a cast of tercel-gentles. The males of the hawks principally used in falconry—the peregrine and goshawk—were called 'tiercels,' or 'tercels,' because (it is said) they are smaller than the females by one third; the male of the nobler species—the peregrine—being distinguished by the addition of the word 'gentle.' There was thus a subtle tribute paid by Juliet to her lover's nobility of nature when she would call him back as a falconer lures the 'tassel-gentle.' Smallest, and of least reputation, on the other hand, was the musket or male sparrow-hawk, especially when an eyess. 'Here comes little Robin,' says Mrs. Page, as Falstaff's tiny page enters, and is thus accosted by Mrs. Ford: 'How now, my eyas-musket! What news with you?'[1] Between Romeo and Robin there was fixed a gulf as wide as that which parted the tercel-gentle from the eyess-musket in the estimation of the falconer.

Of the long-winged hawks, besides the peregrine, the merlin and the hobby were in constant use. The former were bold, active, and tractable, and in appearance, miniature falcons. They were flown at the lesser birds, but Petre showed with pride a cast of females, which had proved themselves capable of coping with the pigeon. The hobby, a beautiful bird and a high-flyer, was also easily tamed. It was not so bold as the merlin, and was chiefly used in the daring of larks. The lark was 'dared' or terrified by the approach of the hobby, and thus fell an easy prey to the fowler, lying still until it found itself enclosed in his net. 'The dogs range the field to spring the fowl,' says Nicholas Cox,[2] 'and the hobbies soar over them in the air, and the silly birds, fearing a conspiracy between the hawks and the dogs to their utter destruction, dare not commit themselves to their wings, but think it safer to lie close to the ground, and so are taken in the nets.' In default of a hobby the larks were dared by other means; by a mirror or by a piece of scarlet cloth. Thus Wolsey, with his Cardinal's scarlet, cowed the barons

[1] *Merry Wives*, iii. 3. 21.   [2] *Gentleman's Recreation*.

of England. 'If we live thus tamely,' says the Earl of Surrey,

> To be thus jaded by a piece of scarlet,
> Farewell nobility ; let his grace go forward,
> And dare us with his cap like larks.
>
> *Hen. VIII.* iii. 2. 279.

Of the short-winged kind, the goshawk, by her name of estridge, attained the honour, as we have seen, of giving its name to a distinct branch of the art of hawking. Strong, useful, and capable, though not so handsome as the falcon, from which she differed widely (as we shall see) in her mode of flight, the goshawk held an honourable place in the order of hawks. Less efficient was the tercel or male of the goshawk, and lower still the sparrow-hawk of either sex ; though in the eyes of some ' the quicke handling of them in his flying pleaseth more than the goshawke.' But as Master Bert adds : ' They may be fitly compared unto a large gelding and a smaller, the first having a large and long stroke goeth faster than he seemeth, the other that gathereth short and thick seemeth to goe much faster than he doth ; the larger shall inforce the lesser and strike thrise for the ground that he will almost at twice performe ; my opinion is he that riddeth most ground, with most ease, shall longest endure. Judge your selve the difference betweene the gos-hawke, Tarsell, and spar-hawke.' [1]

These are the aristocracy of the race ; each had its own

[1] Irish goshawks were of high repute. Derricke has some verses in their praise (*Image of Ireland*, 1581), and Nathaniel Cox (*Gentleman's Recreation*) tells us that ' there are none better than those which are bred in the North parts of Ireland, as in the province of Ulster, but more especially in the county of Tyrone.' Large tracts of Ireland now unhappily denuded of trees were in the days of falconry thickly wooded, and a happy hunting ground for the short-winged hawk. ' Tyrone among the bushes ' is a saying current in that county, and Master Ford's 'fine hawk for the bush ' may have been a native of Tyrone, of the breed so highly commended by the author of the *Gentleman's Recreation.* Fynes Moryson, in his *Description of Ireland*, says that Irish goshawks were much esteemed in England and ' sought out by many and all means to be transported thither.' King John, Mr. Harting tells us (*Essays on Sport and Natural History*) used to send to Ireland, amongst other places to Carrickfergus, Co. Antrim, for hawks.

merits, and was flown at its proper quarry. As for the
canaille of the tribe *raptores*—kites, kestrels, buzzards, hen-
harriers, and such like—they found no place in the hawk-
house, and were regarded by the falconer as next of kin to
barndoor owl, of whom a portent was recorded :

> A falcon towering in her pride of place,
> Was by a mousing owl hawk'd at and kill'd.
> *Macbeth*, ii. 4. 12.

These were what Turbervile calls 'base bastardly refuse
hawks, which are somewhat in name, and nothing in deed.'
Their names were often on the lips of the falconer, but only
as terms of reproach. To 'play the kite,' or to use 'vile
buzardly parts' bespeaks a worthless hawk (according to
Turbervile), and Shakespeare had a true falconer's contempt
for 'kites That bate and beat and will not be obedient,' [1]
and also for the worthless kestrel, or staniel. This hawk
was sometimes trained. But it was lacking in courage, and
was allotted by the old writers to the knave or servant. 'He's
a coward and a coystril that will not drink to my niece till
his brains turn o' the toe like a parish top,'[2] says Sir Toby
Belch. 'With what wing the staniel checks at it,'[3] he
exclaims, as Malvolio, with the fatuity of this ignoble hawk,
catches at the sham letter laid in his way.

As the eagle is the noblest, so the kite or puttock is the
basest of his tribe. 'I chose an eagle,' says Imogen, 'and
did avoid a puttock.'[4] And Hastings says of Clarence, sent
to the Tower, while Richard is at large :

> More pity that the eagle should be mew'd,
> While kites and buzzards prey at liberty.
> *Rich. III.* i. 1. 132.

The hawks having been visited and their points dis-

[1] *Tam. of Shrew*, iv. 1. 198.
[2] *Twelfth N.* i. 3. 42. Mr. Freeman (*How I became a Falconer*) tells of early
experiences with a kestrel which he mistook for a sparrowhawk. 'The kestrel
disappointed me very much, for he was frightened out of his wits at a live
starling, and would not always kill a sparrow.' Perhaps some such experience
suggested the words 'a coward and a kestrel.'
[3] *Ibid.* ii. 5. 124. [4] *Cymb.* i. 1. 139.

cussed, the company bethought them of Clement Perkes's
newly-taken hawk, which had been delivered by his messenger
into the falconer's hands. They passed from the court-yard
to the hawk-house. This was a long covered shed where
the hawks were sheltered at night. Here, too, they were
set down to mew, or moult, when the season came round,
from which use buildings of this kind derived their name of
'mews.' The Royal mews by St. Martin's Lane became
the Royal stables, and the name was borrowed by humbler
localities, with no clear appreciation of the original meaning
or history of the word.

In a room at the end of the mews the falconer was hard
at work, surrounded by the implements of his art. 'Every
good falconer,' says Turbervile, 'should have his imping
needles at hand.' The loss of a principal feather from a
falcon's wing seriously interfered with her high-flying powers.
And as the falconer would have his falcon fly the highest
pitch, it was part of his art to repair occasional mishaps by
the process known as 'imping.' The stump of the broken
feather was joined either to the separated fragment, or to a
similar feather, of which the falconer was careful to have
good store. This was commonly effected by inserting into
the pith of both feathers a slender piece of iron, called an
'imping needle,' steeped in brine, which forthwith rusted,
and incorporated both parts into a single feather. To effect
this neatly was one of the triumphs of the falconer's art ;

What finer feate than so to ympe a feather as in vew
A man should sweare it were the olde, and not set on anew ? [1]

Thus would the falconer restore his hawk's injured wing,
and when the statesman would redeem the broken fortunes
of his country, he urged his hearers to

Imp out our drooping country's broken wing,
Redeem from broking pawn the blemish'd crown,
Wipe off the dust that hides our sceptre's gilt
And make high majesty look like itself.

Rich. II. ii. 1. 292.

[1] Turbervile.

The falconer and the statesman would level up. But it
is ever the desire of the envious to level down to their own
standard those whom natural advantages and training have
enabled to fly a higher pitch. Thus, when the tribunes
Flavius and Marullus forbade that images should be decked
with Cæsar's trophies, and drove from the streets the crowds
who assembled to rejoice in his triumph, they reasoned
thus :

> These growing feathers pluck'd from Cæsar's wing [1]
> Will make him fly an ordinary pitch,
> Who else would soar above the view of men
> And keep us all in servile fearfulness. *Jul. Cæs.* i. 1. 77.

The company found the falconer busily engaged in seeling
the eyes of the new arrival. It was then the custom to close
the eyes of a newly-taken hawk until she had become accustomed to the hood, by drawing through the eyelids a fine
silken thread. Desdemona, said Iago,

> could give out such a seeming,
> To seel her father's eyes up close as oak.
> *Othello*, iii. 3. 210.[2]

The poor bird was completely blindfolded. I am sorry to
say that the company laughed merrily at her confusion as
she staggered and strutted along the floor, unable to find her
perch, or to save herself from destruction without her keeper's
helping hand ; and as I read of the scene, I understood what
Antony meant when he said :

> The wise gods seel our eyes ;
> In our own filth drop our clear judgements ; make us
> Adore our errors ; laugh at's, while we strut
> To our confusion. *Ant. and Cleo.* iii. 13. 112.

And yet, did the bird but know it, this seeling and these
blind endeavours were but steps in the course of training
which was to convert the profitless haggard into the noble
falcon, reclaimed from ill conditions, and fitted for her
master's use.

---

[1] Cf. Sonnet lxxviii. 6. [2] Cf. *Othello*, i. 3. 270.

The hawks having been visited, their achievements re-
counted, and their points discussed, the party returned to the
house.   Petre courteously invited his visitors to stay for
supper.   But Silence must needs return to his father's house,
whither some company had been bidden, and the stranger
begged to be excused.   So they mounted their horses and
rode together homewards across the wolds.

CHAPTER XI

A RIDE ON COTSWOLD

In Gloucestershire :
These high wild hills and rough uneven ways
Draw out our miles, and make them wearisome ;
And yet your fair discourse hath been as sugar,
Making the hard way sweet and delectable. *King Richard II.*

'AND after some converse concerning matters of grave moment touching our several affairs (whereof more anon), we fell to speak of Cotswold and of Arden, and of the sports and pastimes which may be there enjoyed in their seasons, and so merrily homewards.'

Thus the diarist begins the story of his ride across Cotswold. The convenient time for writing of graver matters seems never to have come, and what they were is left to conjecture.

You may, therefore, not hold it proven that a ride homeward with William Silence was the occasion of the resolve that robbed Stratford-on-Avon of a sporting attorney to give Shakespeare to the world. This resolve, however, must have been made at some time, and under some circumstances ; and what is more likely to have caused it than chance association with a visitor from the great world, whose conversation unfolded to the eyes of home-bred youth visions of the boundless possibilities offered by London to genius and daring ? The humours of the town ; the newsmongers and diners with good Duke Humphrey at Paul's ; the playhouse

at Blackfriars ; the wit-combats in the taverns ; the bravery
of fair ladies and gallants, and far-off visions of the splendid
Court of great Elizabeth, appealed to his imagination.
But most of all he was moved by the immediate prospect of
a sufficient livelihood, and by the remoter possibility of
such wealth as might enable him to walk the quiet paths at
home with surer footing, partaking of the real enjoyments of
life.

And as years advanced, his knowledge of what he had
gained, and what he had escaped, with observation of the
consequences of the fateful resolve which each man must,
once for all, make for himself, found expression in words.

It was when Shakespeare had arrived at middle age that
he wrote what Professor Dowden calls his reflective dramas.
Looking back from the serene table-land of the Delectable
Mountains on the way which he had trodden, he could mark
where Bypath meadow led astray, and could discern certain
who had taken the wrong path, wandering blindfold among
the tombs, victims of Giant Despair.

The selfsame thought which the tinker of Elstow, turned
preacher, was impelled by the necessity of his genius to
embody in action, gave the dramatist pause, and with him
action for a moment gave place to teaching.

For he tells us by the mouth of Cassius that ' men at
some time are masters of their fates.' [1]   That is to say, each
man born into the world may expect that to him will come,
sooner or later, his golden opportunity. If he seize it, he
may become that for which he is best fitted by nature, be
it dramatist, soldier, handicraftsman, lawyer, statesman, or
divine ; for all men have not the same gifts. But if he let
it slip, he has no right to expect that it will recur. It may
be right that he should let it pass. But it remains true all
the same that

> Who seeks, and will not take when once 'tis offer'd,
> Shall never find it more.   *Ant. and Cleo.* ii. **7**. 88.

[1] *Jul. Cæs.* i. 2. 139.

It was while this thought was present to his mind that he thus taught us by the mouth of Brutus,

> There is a tide in the affairs of men,
> Which, taken at the flood, leads on to fortune :
> Omitted, all the voyage of their life
> Is bound in shallows and in miseries.
>
> *Jul. Cæs.* iv. 3. 218.

And as he pondered still further on such matters, he thought over the riddle of success and failure in life.

> O heavens, what some men do,
> While some men leave to do !
> How some men creep in skittish fortune's hall,
> Whiles others play the idiots in her eyes !
>
> *Troil. and Cres.* iii. 3. 132.

The task of rounding off the lesson of life is fitly entrusted to him who was to the Greek πολύμητις; a word aptly rendered by an English sportsman—'that same dog-fox Ulysses.' [1]

He contrives that Achilles shall see himself treated by the Greeks as if he were forgotten. The 'general' pass strangely by, and the princes lay negligent and loose regard on him. He cannot understand the change. He has not fallen out with fortune ; why should he have fallen out with men ?

Ulysses suggests the reason. The Greeks look upon Ajax as the coming man, and they have turned to worship him.

> *Achil.* I do believe it ; for they pass'd by me
> As misers do by beggars, neither gave to me
> Good word nor look ; what, are my deeds forgot ?
>
> *Ibid.* 142.

Then Ulysses takes up his parable, and in words so familiar that I need not quote them, explains that forgetfulness of good deeds past is simply obedience to the laws of

---

[1] *Troil. and Cres.* v. 4. 12.

nature, one touch of which makes the whole world kin, adding that

> beauty, wit,
> High birth, vigour of bone, desert in service,
> Love, friendship, charity, are subjects all
> To envious and calumniating time.

This, therefore, is the conclusion of the whole matter : choose the right path and continue to walk therein, for

> perseverance, dear my lord,
> Keeps honour bright : to have done is to hang
> Quite out of fashion, like a rusty mail
> In monumental mockery.   Take the instant way ;
> For honour travels in a strait so narrow,
> Where one but goes abreast : keep then the path ;
> For emulation hath a thousand sons
> That one by one pursue ; if you give way,
> Or hedge aside from the direct forthright,
> Like to an enter'd tide, they all rush by
> And leave you hindmost.   *Ibid.* 150.

And yet Mr. Ruskin writes : ' At this time of being and speaking, among active and purposeful Englishmen I know not one who shows a trace of ever having felt a passion of Shakespeare's, or learnt a lesson from him.' [1]

But though the diarist's notes of his homeward ride may bring us no nearer to a knowledge of what Shakespeare was, we may be helped towards a better understanding of what he wrote by a more familiar acquaintance with the scenes and occupations amidst which a great part of his life was spent.   In the pursuit of this knowledge no aid is to be despised, and something may be learned from the discourse chronicled by the diarist, even though it related to no higher topics than the sporting capabilities of Stratford-on-Avon and Cotswold.

In truth, if you would enjoy the sports of the field in their seasons, no better spot on earth need have been desired three centuries ago than the neighbourhood of Stratford-on-Avon.

---

[1] *Præterita* (1886).

There every variety of sporting country was to be found :
'frith,' or woodland; 'fell,' or open field ; and 'wold,' or
open, forest-like land.   On one side of Avon lay the frith, or
woodlands of Arden, and on the other a richly cultivated fell,
or open champaign country. 'Warwickshire,' writes Camden,
'is divided into two parts, the Felden and the woodland, *i.e.*
the Champain and woody country, severed in some sort by
the river Avon, running obliquely from north-east to south-
west through the middle of the county.   On the south side
of the Avon lies Felden, a champain country whose fertile
fields of corn and verdant pastures yield a most delightful
prospect from the top of Edgehill.'

To one who had long dwelt between Felden and Arden,
the physical characteristics of these several districts seemed
to illustrate the difference between an open and a furtive
disposition, and so he wrote of woman :

> Their smoothness, like a goodly champaign plain,
> Lays open all the little worms that creep ;
> In men, as in a rough-grown grove, remain
> Cave-keeping evils that obscurely sleep :
> Through crystal walls each little mote will peep :
>   Though men can cover crimes with bold stern looks,
>   Poor women's faces are their own faults' books.
> *Lucrece*, 1247.

Let us then, with Camden, take a view of the woodland
which (he tells us) lay north of the Avon, occupying a larger
extent, being for the most part covered with woods, though not
without pastures, cornfields, and iron-mines.   Arden was in
Shakespeare's time a district throughout which were scattered survivals of the primeval forest which once clothed
the English midlands.   The Britons retreating before the
advancing Saxon found shelter in its fastnesses, and the
names by which the physical features of the country are still
known bear witness to their presence.   In their tongue, the
river which separated their retreat from the open country is
Avon, and the forest fastness is Arden.   The forest of
Ardennes owes its name to a kindred word in the language

of the Gaulish Celt. The British woodland gave its name
to a family of gentle birth, of which some branches were
rich and powerful, while others approached in condition to
the yeomen, with whom they intermarried; for the wife of
John Shakespeare of Stratford was Mary Arden, daughter
of Robert Arden of Wilmecote.

Arden was never a forest in the legal sense of the term.
Nor was it in the sixteenth century a tract of continuous
woodland. Towns and villages had come into existence,
whose names still tell the tale of their woodland origin:
Henley in Arden; Hampton in Arden; Weston in Arden.
Towards Stratford the country had been generally cleared.
Leland, who travelled from Warwick to Stratford about the
year 1533, describes the country through which he passed
as for the most part under cultivation. Had he held a
northward course, he would have emerged from Arden only
to reach the open moorland which is now the Black Country,
and guiding his course by the fires of the iron-workers, he
would have come upon a town not long afterwards described
as 'Bremicham, swarming with inhabitants, and echoing
with the noise of anvils.' [1]

It is a pleasing illusion to imagine that Shakespeare chose
as the scene of his most poetical comedy the woodlands of
his native Warwickshire, linked with the memories of his
early youth, and associated with his mother's name. It is
an illusion, for we know that the scene and plot of *As You
Like It* were borrowed from Thomas Lodge's novel *Rosalynd*
published in 1590, the Arden of which is the Luxemburg
Ardennes. Shakespeare's Arden is peopled with inhabitants
of English birth. But the fact that William and Audrey
are of Warwickshire does not prove that they inhabit an
English forest; for was not Anthony Dull, constable, of
Navarre; Autolycus of Bohemia; Dogberry of Messina
and Nicholas Bottom of Greece?

But it really matters little whether Shakespeare thought
of the Warwickshire Arden when by the alchemy of his

[1] Camden's *Britannia*.

mighty genius he transmuted into an immortal drama
Lodge's perishable tale; pretty and full of quaint conceits,
but writ in water, and only remembered, or worth remem-
bering, as the quarry of Pentelicus is regarded because of the
glory of the Parthenon.   Shakespeare did unto Lodge's
Arden as he would have done unto the desert of Sahara if
the exiles of the novel had happened to wander thither; he
filled it with the creatures of his native midlands.

Michael Drayton, a Warwickshire man, takes Arden as
the subject of the thirteenth song of his *Polyolbion*.

> This song our shire of Warwick sounds,
> Revives old Arden's ancient bounds.
> Through many shapes the Muse here roves,
> Now sporting in these shady groves
> The tunes of birds oft stays to hear,
> Then finding herds of lusty deer,
> She huntress-like the hart pursues.

To his imagination, Arden, though fallen from the ancient
greatness of 'her one hand touching Trent, the other
Severn's side,' was still a vast region of dim mysterious
woodland, the haunt of song-birds of every note, and of

> both sorts of seasoned deer,
> Here walk the stately red, the freckled fallow there.

And so Drayton lays the scene of his stag-hunt in this woodland district.   'To express that wondrous sport . . . to our
old Arden here most fitly it belongs.'
In its groves

> Hunt's up, to the morn the feathered sylvans sing . . .
> The mirthful quires with their clear open throats
> Unto the joyful morn so strain their warbling notes
> That hills and valleys ring, and even the echoing air
> Seems all composed of sounds about them everywhere.

Such was the country around Stratford, a region like to
that with which Lear endowed Goneril,

> With shadowy forests and with champains rich'd:
> With plenteous rivers and wide-skirted meads.
>   *K. Lear*, i. 1. 65.

The river afforded quarry for the falconer, who loved
' flying at the brook,' at

> The duck and mallard first, the falconer's only sport
> (Of river flights the chief, so that all other sort
> They only green fowl term).[1]

It supplied also fish for the angler—coarse fish for the most
part, the pursuit of which was not likely to inspire that love
of the subtler mysteries of the gentle art, of which no
trace can be found in Shakespeare. For strict observance
of truth, the constant feature of these pages, compels an
admission. I find in the diary little mention of the angler's
art, and that little of a disappointing kind; such sentiments, for example, as one that was long afterwards put into
the mouth of Ursula, when she would catch Beatrice with a
feigned story of Benedick's devotion:

> The pleasant'st angling is to see the fish
> Cut with her golden oars the silver stream,
> And greedily devour the treacherous bait;
> So angle we for Beatrice.   *Much Ado*, iii. 1. 26.

I wish it were otherwise, but I cannot say that I am
surprised. In those dark pre-Waltonian ages the ordinary
experiences of the angler included neither the mystery of
trout-fishing with fly, nor the heart-stirring rush of the
salmon in the pool, that crowded hour of glorious life com-
pensating in enjoyment for an age without a rise.

Wipe away from the table of the angler's memory all
experiences with salmon and trout, and what remains?
Boyish recollections of the gregarious ' fool gudgeon ' swarming around worm on crooked pin, rushing in shoals on
their destruction—apt image of the ' opinion ' of the crowd,
mostly fools, caught by the ' melancholy bait ' of assumed
gravity.[2] In riper years, having attained an age when ' no
fisher but the ungrown fry forbears,' [3] he marks how the
' carp of truth ' may be taken by ' bait of falsehood,' [4] and ' if
the young dace be bait for the old pike ' he sees ' no reason

---

[1] *Polyolbion.*
[2] *Merch. of Ven.* i. 1. 101.
[3] *Ven. and Ad.* 526.
[4] *Hamlet*, ii. 1. 63.

in the law of nature' [1] why he should not catch him, any more than why the pike should not snap at his natural prey. But all this is poor sport at best, and I am not surprised to find that it engaged but a small share of the thoughts of the diarist and his companion. [2]

Such were the resources of the country by which Stratford was immediately surrounded. But at no great distance were the vast wolds, stretching from the border of Warwickshire to the south-western extremity of Gloucestershire, then, as now, known as Cotswold. So famed was this district for sports of various kinds, that a Cotswold country became a common expression of the day. ' The best soyl,' says Burton—a Leicestershire man—' commonly yields the worst ayr; a dry sandy plat is fittest to build upon, and such as is rather hilly than plain, full of downes, a Cotswold country, as being most commodious for hawking hunting wood waters and all manner of pleasures.' Cotswold; its sports and pastimes; its Whitsun week games, at which sturdy shepherds contended for the mastery before the assembled ' ring of country gentiles ' [3] in leaping, throwing the bar, running at quintain, and other manly exercises, were household words among the Warwick folk dwelling near the Gloucestershire border. The ancient Cotswold games seem to have declined somewhat, and to have been revived by one Robert Dover, an attorney of Barton-on-the-heath in Warwickshire, to whom were addressed a number of odes by Ben Jonson, Drayton, and other poets of the day, which were collected and published in 1636, under the title of *Annalia Dubrensia*. The programme comprised field sports as well as athletic exercises.

> The swallow-footed greyhound hath the prize,
> A silver studded collar.

Dover is celebrated in this volume as the restorer, not the founder of these games, and we may be sure that the per-

---

[1] 2 *Hen. IV.* iii. 2. 355   [2] See Note, *Shakespeare and Angling.*
[3] *Annalia Dubrensia.* Of Dover it is recorded in this volume, ' He was bred an attorney, who never try'd but two causes, always made up the difference.'

formances of their greyhounds on Cotswold supplied a frequent topic of conversation to the burgesses of Stratford in the days of Shakespeare's youth.   And even if the diary were silent on the subject, we should have been certain that this topic must have been suggested by a ride across Cotswold.

For Cotswold was then to coursing what Newmarket is to horse-racing, and St. Andrews to golf; the recognised home and centre of the sport.   Abraham Slender knew by heart the performance of every dog that had ever contended for the silver collar at the Cotswold games, a knowledge which he at times let appear when there was no need of such vanity.   For we all remember how it was needful for Master Shallow, when he would pay court to Master Page of Windsor, to smooth his feathers which had been somewhat ruffled by an unhappy suggestion of Slender's.

Slen. How does your fallow greyhound, sir?   I heard say he was outrun on Cotsall.

Page. It could not be judged, sir.

Slen. You'll not confess, you'll not confess.

Shal. That he will not.   'Tis your fault, 'tis your fault, 'tis a good dog.

Page. A cur, sir.

Shal. Sir, he's a good dog, and a fair dog; can there be more said?   He is good and fair.   *Merry Wives,* i. 1. 91.

Eagerly did the riders discuss the incidents and humours of the sport.   First comes the hare-finder, most venerable of institutions.   For Arrian, writing some fourteen centuries before our diarist, tells us that in his day it was the custom to send out hare-finders (τοὺς κατοπτεύσοντας) early in the mornings of coursing days.[1]

To detect a hare in brown fallow or russet bracken needs sharp and practised eyes.   And so it was as good a jest for Benedick to say of the blind god of love that ' Cupid is a good hare-finder,' [2] as to call Vulcan ' a rare carpenter.'

---

[1] The *Cynegeticus* of Arrian (sometimes called the younger Xenophon) was intended to supplement the work of his master, by treating of the sport of coursing with greyhounds.

[2] *Much Ado,* i. 1. 186.

"As soone as he espieth her, he must cry So how."
Thus writes the author of the *Noble Arte* of the hare-finder.
And so when Mercutio cried ' So ho,' Romeo, recognising the
familiar hunting language, asks 'What hast thou found?'

Mer. No hare, sir, unless a hare, sir, in a lenten pie, that is
somewhat stale and hoar ere it be spent.   (*Sings.*)

> An old hare hoar,
> And an old hare hoar,
> Is very good meat in lent;
> But a hare that is hoar
> Is too much for a score,
> When it hoars ere it be spent.' [1]
>
> > *Rom. and Jul.* ii. 4. 136.

The greyhound, fawning upon his master, is an image
familiar of old:—ὑποπτήξασα λιπαρεῖ Arrian writes:
'What a canny deal of courtesy,' says Hotspur of Henry
Bolingbroke, 'This fawning greyhound then did proffer
me.' [2] Caius Marcius describes Titus Lartius as

> Holding Corioli in the name of Rome,
> Even like a fawning greyhound in the leash,
> To let him slip at will.   *Coriol.* i. 6. 37.

A livelier image is suggested by the chorus in the prologue to *Henry V.*, picturing the 'swelling scene' when

> should the warlike Harry, like himself,
> Assume the port of Mars ; and at his heels,
> Leash'd in like hounds, should famine, sword and fire
> Crouch for employment.

But as the sport advances, fawning gives place to excitement, and the careful slipper must beware lest he spoil sport
by too much eagerness ; like Harry Hotspur, to whom
Northumberland thus complained : ' Before the game is afoot,
thou still let'st slip.' [3] He must keep back his hound, well
knowing that by so doing he whets rather than disedges his

---

[1] These lines are fairly described by Dr. Johnson as a ' series of quibbles
unworthy of explanation, which he who does not understand, needs not lament
his ignorance.' A hare is still called a bawd in some parts of Scotland (Jamie-
son's *Scottish Dictionary*).

[2] 1 *Hen. IV.* i. 3. 251.   [3] 1 *Hen. IV.* i. 3. 278.

appetite for the chase. ' I am sorry but not afeard ; delayed but not altered,' said Florizel, when thwarted and opposed in his love for Perdita :

> what I was, I am ;
> More straining on for plucking back, not following
> My leash unwillingly.   *Wint. Tale*, iv. 4. 475.

When the game's afoot, though not before, you may cry havoc, and unslip the dogs of war. ' There is none of you so mean and base,' said King Harry to his yeomen soldiers before the breach at Harfleur,

> That hath not noble lustre in your eyes.
> I see you stand like greyhounds in the slips,
> Straining upon the start.   *Hen. V.* iii. 1. 30.

' The game's afoot,' he adds, ' follow your spirit.' When this word has been given, you may enjoy the humours of the course, and admire the speed and dexterity of your greyhound, ' which runs himself and catches for his master.'[1]

Thus spoke Tranio, when he complained that Lucentio slipped him like his greyhound, and used him for his own ends, and his words were commended as ' a good swift simile, but something currish.'[2]

And if you chance to witness the kill, you may call to mind Benedick's commendation of Margaret's jest, ' Thy wit is as quick as the greyhound's mouth ; it catches.'[3]

'It could not be judged,' according to Master Page, whether or not his fallow greyhound was ' outrun on Cotsall.' How this came to pass you may learn from a study of the laws of the leash, or coursing, as they were commanded, allowed, and subscribed by Thomas Duke of Norfolk in the reign of Queen Elizabeth. There we read of the judge of the leash, who, in Drayton's words,

> Runs his horse with fixed eyes, and notes
> Which dog first turns the hare, which first the other coats.[4]

In these laws it is prescribed that the judges shall give their

---

[1] *Tam. of Shrew*, v. 2. 52.   [2] See also 3 *Hen. VI.* ii. 5, 129.
[3] *Much Ado*, v. 2. 11.   [4] *Polyolbion*.

judgments presently before they depart from the field; but if the course be equal, and the hare be not borne, then the course must be adjudged equal. Thus it was that Master Page's fallow greyhound, although not outrun on Cotsall, failed to win the course.

The comparative merits of the dogs, then as now, were determined by a variety of performances, or points of the course, such as the turn, go by, wrench, cote, and the bearing, or taking of the hare. Those who are interested in this ancient sport (among whom I cannot be included), and who desire to compare these laws with the rules of the National Coursing Club, will find both codes printed in Mr. Harding Cox's contribution to the Badminton Library. They will note the disappearance from the modern rules of a term denoting one of the most important points of the course according to ancient authorities; that, namely, which was known as the cote. This was when a greyhound turned the hare, having first outstripped, or coted, his competitor; ' we coted them on the way, and hither they are coming,' [1] said Rosencrantz of the players, using a term of art, perfectly intelligible to Hamlet, but which has been generally interpreted as meaning ' to overtake.' It is plain, however, from Rosencrantz's words ' hither they are coming,' that he had not only overtaken, but outstripped, or ' coted them on the way.'

' On Cotswoldian ground,' sings Master William Denny.[2]

> The swallow footed greyhound hath the prize
> A silver studded coller; who outflies
> The rest in lightnings speed, who first comes by
> His strayning copes-mate, with celerity
> Turns his affrighted game, then coates againe
> His forward Rivall on the senselesse plaine
> And after Laborinthian turnes surprise
> The game, whilst he doth pant her obsequies.

[1] *Hamlet*, ii. 2. 330.

[2] *Annalia Dubrensia*. The folio of 1623 reads (*Love's Labour's Lost*, iv. 3. 87): ' Her amber hair for foul hath amber coted.' The last word is now usually spelt ' quoted,' and probably rightly; for although amber hair might well be said to outstrip or excel amber, yet it is not easy with this interpretation to assign any intelligible meaning to the words ' for foul.'

If I am compelled to admit that Shakespeare preferred coursing to angling, the balance is in some degree redressed by his love for the hunting of the hare with running hounds.

It is easy to understand why, in common with the sportsmen of his age, he preferred the pursuit of the hare to that of the fox. For fox-hunting, as we now understand it, did not exist in his day. There was then no systematic keeping of country, or stopping of earths. Coverts were left entirely to nature. If cubs were hunted, it was merely for the purpose of exterminating vermin. The ordinary kennel of running hounds, uncoupled at every chase, was master of none ; and even the best of the breed, if reserved exclusively for fox-hunting, would have been wanting in the speed and drive needful to enable them to account for a straight-necked fox in Meath or Leicestershire. The riders would have fared even worse, for the modern hunter is still further in advance of the hunting and hawking nag of our ancestors.

The author of *Noble Arte* writes of the chase of the ' foxe and badgerd and such like vermine.' But he says of the fox, ' I account small pastime of hunting them, especially within the ground.' There was, in truth, but little sport in bolting the fox with terriers from earth to earth, and destroying the vermin anyhow, somewhat after the fashion of the Scottish fox-hunter, described by Scott in *Guy Mannering*, and by Mr. St. John in his charming *Wild Sports of the Highlands*.

But there may be discerned in the works of Shakespeare the germs of modern fox-hunting. Adonis is advised by Venus, in lieu of hunting the savage and dangerous boar, to uncouple at the hare, roe, or ' the fox which lives by subtlety ; '

> Pursue these fearful creatures o'er the downs,
> And on thy well-breath'd horse keep with thy hounds.
> *Ven. and Ad.* 677.

This was the chase of the fox above ground or in the open, for which you may find directions in the *Noble Arte*, and

in other books of sport of the Elizabethan age. When you
have marked a fox to ground and stopped the neighbouring
earths or 'kennels,' you may uncouple your running hounds,
unkennel your fox, and say with the lord in *All's Well*,[1]
' We'll make you some sport with the fox ere we case him.'[2]

Master Ford understood hunting as well as birding.
When he had, as he thought, safely marked to ground that
old dog-fox, Jack Falstaff, he thus addressed the company
assembled at the earth :

Here, here, here be my keys; ascend my chambers; search,
seek, find out; I'll warrant we'll unkennel the fox. Let me
stop this way first. [*Locking the door.*] So, now uncape.[3]

Merry Wives, iii. 3. 172.

---

[1] iii. 6. 110.

[2] The fox's skin was, in hunting language, his case. ' O thou dissembling
cub ! ' says the Duke to Viola,

what wilt thou be
When time hath sow'd a grizzle on thy case ?
Or will not else thy craft so quickly grow,
That thine own trip shall be thine overthrow ?

Twelfth N. v. 1. 167.

This meaning of the word ' case ' was present to the framer of the following
pun : ' Though my case be a pitiful one, I hope I shall not be flayed out of it '
(*Wint. Tale*, iv. 4. 844).

[3] The Right Hon. John Monck Mason was an Irish sportsman as well as a
Shakespearian critic, and his early experiences in county Galway stood him in
stead when seeking for the poet's meaning in the sports of the field. He detected the absurdity of explanation given by Warburton and Stevens of the word
' uncape ' as signifying the letting out of a bagged fox. ' Ford,' he writes,
' like a good sportsman, first stops the earths and then uncouples the hounds.'
It is not necessary, however, to read with him ' uncouple ' for ' uncape.'
Professor Baynes, in an article in the *Edinburgh Review* (Oct. 1872 ; reprinted
with other essays, 1894), points out that ' though no example of its technical
use has yet been found, there can be little doubt that " uncape " was a sporting
term locally or colloquially employed instead of " uncouple." ' He then proceeds to show that the word ' cape ' had in Shakespeare's day the meaning of
a narrow band encircling the neck, and that it might fairly be used as a synonym
for what was in the case of a greyhound called his collar, and in the case of a
running hound his couple. In *Tam. of Shrew*, iv. 3. 140, the ' small compassed
cape ' attached to Katherine's ' loose-bodied gown ' was a small circular collar
around her throat. In support of Professor Baynes's suggestion that various
kinds of collars, couples, or capes for hounds were certainly in use, I may add
that in an inventory of furniture in the palace of King Henry VIII. (reprinted
in the *Retrospective Review*, 1827) we find with ' hawkes whoddes embraw-

But although some sport might thus be had with the fox
ere you case him, the final cause of fox-hunting was the
destruction of noxious vermin.   No word is too bad for 'the
fox that lives by subtlety.'   He is 'a crafty murderer,'[1] and
'subtle as the fox for prey'[2] is the miscreant who may be
likened to the 'fox in stealth.'[3]   This custom of giving the
fox a bad name survived among sportsmen to the days of
Somerville and Beckford, in poetry as well as in prose.   For
in the classic pages of *The Chase* the fox is denounced as
the wily fox, the felon vile, the conscious villain, and the
subtle pilfering fox.   And even in the early years of the
present century, there were districts where the church bell
was rung when a fox had been marked to ground, to summon
'every man who possessed a pick-axe, a gun or a terrier
to hasten to the sport and lend a hand in destroying the
noxious animal.'[4]

No law was given to a fox.   'Do not stand on quillets
how to slay him,' says Suffolk of Duke Humphrey of
Gloucester—whose appointment as protector to the king
he had compared to making the fox surveyor of the fold,—

> Who being accused a crafty murderer,
> His guilt should be but idly posted over,
> Because his purpose is not executed.
> No ; let him die, in that he is a fox,
> By nature proved an enemy to the flock,
> Before his chaps be stain'd with crimson blood,
> As Humphrey, proved by reasons, to my liege.
> And do not stand on quillets how to slay him :
> Be it by gins, by snares, by subtlety,
> Sleeping or waking, 'tis no matter how,
> So he be dead.   *2 Hen. VI.* iii. 1. 254.

'It was true we give laws to hares and deer, because

dered, hawkes belles, Irishe arrowes,' and other sporting appliances, ' Itm,
lxv lyams and collors of dyvers sortes.'   Furthermore, it appears from the
word ' copesmate,' in the lines of William Denny, quoted at p. 175, that the collar
of the greyhound was sometimes called his cope, or cape ; a term which would
appear to be equally applicable to the couple of the running hound.

[1] *2 Hen. VI.* iii. 1. 254.   [2] *Cymb.* iii. 3. 40.
[3] *K. Lear*, iii. 4. 96.   [4] *Memoir of the Rev. John Russell.*

they are beasts of chace, but it was never accounted either cruelty or foul play to knock foxes or wolves on the head as they can be found, because they are beasts of prey.' Thus Oliver Saint John met the plea of law put forward on behalf of Strafford. 'This illustration would be by no means a happy one, if addressed to country gentlemen of our time; but in Saint John's day there were not seldom great massacres of foxes, to which the peasantry thronged with all the dogs that could be mustered; traps were set; nets were spread, no quarter was given, and to shoot a female with cub was considered as a feat which merited the warmest gratitude of the neighbourhood.' [1] Some such massacre Lear had in his mind when, clasping Cordelia in his arms, he exclaimed:

> He that parts us shall bring a brand from heaven,
> And fire us hence like foxes.   *K. Lear*, v. 3. 22.

Far different was the language used in regard to the hare. 'He is the mervellest beest that is in any londe,' wrote Dame Juliana Barnes—a sentiment which she thus expands:

> That beest kyng shall be calde of all Venery
> For all the fayre spekyng and blawing lest fere
> Commyth of sechyng and fyndyng of the hare.

'Of all chases,' says the author of the *Noble Arte*, 'the hare makes the greatest pastime and pleasure;' and Gervase Markham declares [2] that 'the hunting of the hare is every honest man's and good man's chase,' ranking far above the hunting of the fox or badger, which are 'not so much desired as the rest, because there is not so much art and cunning.'

The days spent by the diarist under his father's roof were occupied with other pursuits than the chase of the hare. I cannot, therefore, say for certain that the Justice kept, in addition to his kennel of running hounds suitable for every chase, a pack of beagles devoted exclusively to the hunting of the hare. I know, however, that they were in high

---

[1] Macaulay, *History of England*.   [2] *Country Contentments*.

favour with Gloucestershire sportsmen. The sordid pot-hunter, when he uncouples at his game, may care only to 'score their backs, And snatch 'em up, as we take hares behind.' [1] But the true sportsman took delight in the music of a pack composed of 'the little beagle which may be carried in a man's glove, and bred in many countries for delight onely, being of curious scents, and passing cunning in their hunting ; for the most part tyring (but seldom killing) the prey except at some strange advantage.' [2] Thus when Sir Toby Belch said of Maria, 'she is a beagle true-bred,' [3] he meant to compliment her keenness and sagacity.

The performances of such a pack divided with Master Page's fallow greyhound the attention of the Gloucester-shire folk assembled at the Cotswold games, where

> greyhound is for coller tride
> More than for death of harmelesse Hare
> And kennells pack't, that how they cry'd
> Not what they kill'd, men may declare
> For hunters most heroyick are they
> That seeke the prise and shun the prey. [4]

But we have in truth lost little by the diarist's omission to chronicle the incidents of the chase of the hare. For this pastime, as it is at present pursued, approaches more closely to the use of our forefathers than any other field sport of the present day. It has, indeed, suffered but little change since the days of Xenophon. I have known a master of harriers, of rare skill, listen with respect to the precepts and observations on hare-hunting contained in the *Noble Arte* ; but I should

---

[1] *Ant. and Cleo.* iv. 7. 12.

[2] Gervase Markham, *Country Contentments.*   [3] *Twelfth N.* ii. 3. 195.

[4] Poem by William Basse on the Cotswold games (*Annalia Dubrensia*). His motto—*Dulcia sunt quæ rarius eveniunt solatia*—has been well rendered by a frequenter of the games, with a lively recollection of his annual holiday on Cotsall :

> If all the year were playing holidays,
> To sport would be as tedious as to work ;
> But when they seldom come, they wish'd for come,
> And nothing pleaseth but rare accidents. 1 *Hen. IV.* i. 2. 228.

not like to try the experiment of reading to an enthusiastic
fox-hunter the opinions of the author in regard to the fox.
Moreover, I am quite certain that all that could be said by the
diarist or by his companion in regard to the hare-hunt is to be
found in a poem entitled *Venus and Adonis*, published in
the year 1592, the ' first heir ' of the author's ' invention,'
and written, in all probability, about the time of the ride on
Cotswold.

And when thou hast on foot the purblind hare,
    Mark the poor wretch, to overshoot his troubles
How he outruns the wind and with what care
    He cranks and crosses with a thousand doubles : [1]
The many musets through the which he goes
Are like a labyrinth to amaze his foes.

Sometime he runs among a flock of sheep,
    To make the cunning hounds mistake their smell,
And sometime where earth-delving conies keep,
    To stop the loud pursuers in their yell,
And sometime sorteth with a herd of deer :
Danger deviseth shifts ; wit waits on fear :

For there his smell with others being mingled,
    The hot scent-snuffing hounds are driven to doubt,
Ceasing their clamourous cry till they have singled
    With much ado the cold fault cleanly out ;
Then do they spend their mouths : Echo replies,
As if another chase were in the skies.

By this, poor Wat, far off upon a hill,
    Stands on his hinder legs with listening ear,
To hearken if his foes pursue him still ; [2]
    Anon their loud alarums he doth hear ;
And now his grief may be compared well
To one sore sick that hears the passing-bell.

---

[1] Cf. 2 *Hen. VI.* ii. 3. 94.

[2] These lines read like a poetical version of Xenophon's words: προλαμ-
βάνοντες δὲ τὰς κύνας ἐφίστανται καὶ ἀνακαθίζοντες ἐπαίρουσιν αὐτοὺς καὶ ἐπακούουσιν,
εἴ που πλησίον κλαγγὴ ἤ ψόφος τῶν κυνῶν (*Cynegeticus*).

> Then shalt thou see the dew-bedabbled wretch
>   Turn and return, indenting with the way;
> Each envious briar his weary legs doth scratch,
>   Each shadow makes him stop, each murmur stay:
> For misery is trodden on by many,.
> And being low never relieved by any.   *Ven. and Ad.* 679.[1]

Sweetening the way with discourse on these and such-like matters, William Silence and his companion approached the village green of Shallow. The shades of evening were closing around the scene, but the humours of the holy-ale still continued in full career. Neither the diarist, nor the age in which he lived, was given to moralising; and yet I can trace in his pages certain foreshadowings of that public opinion by which assemblies of this kind were ultimately suppressed.[2] It is not necessary to believe

---

[1] These stanzas are quoted at length by Coleridge in his lectures on Shakespeare, as an example of 'affectionate love of nature and natural objects,' and the lecturer adds that the poems 'give us at once strong promise of the strength, and yet obvious proofs of the immaturity of his genius.' Coleridge's thoughts on Shakespeare, like those of Goethe and Ben Jonson, possess the rare interest attaching to the reflections of one man of genius upon the work of another. But when he descends to criticism, and proposes to amend the following passage,

Fal. Now, the report goes she has all the rule of her husband's purse; he hath a legion of angels.

Pist. As many devils entertain; and 'To her, boy,' say I.

> *Merry Wives*, i. 3. 58.

by reading 'As many devils enter (or enter'd) swine,' the lowest depth of conjectural emendation is reached, and Theobald has his ample revenge for the exclamation, 'What a noble pair of ears this worthy Theobald must have had.' His rejection of the lines in Mark Antony's speech,

> O world, thou wast the forest to this hart;
> And this, indeed, O world, the heart of thee.
>
> *Jul. Cæs.* iii. 1. 207.

on the ground that 'the conceit is a mere alien' is scarcely better. Many of Shakespeare's allusions to sport are alien to the context or the action of the play, although closely akin to the writer's thoughts, and an alien conceit on such a topic is, in itself, strong evidence of Shakespeare's workmanship.

[2] Mr. Hamilton, in his *Quarter Sessions from Queen Elizabeth to Queen Anne*, mentions an order of justices made in July 1595, declaring that 'Church or parish ales, revels, May games, plays and such other unlawful assemblies of the people of sundry parishes into one parish on the Sabbath Day and other times, is a special cause that many disorders, contempts of law, and other enor-

all that is said by Master Philip Stubbes in his *Anatomie of Abuses* (1583) in regard to the coarse and full-blown iniquities of his time. But it is impossible to study the plays, ballads, sermons, jest-books, and satires of the age without understanding that there was a dark as well as a bright side to merry England. It is hard to realise in these pagans of Shallow—with their coarse pleasures, their large jests, their rollicking country pastimes, their keen animal enjoyment of life, and their frank immorality—the sires and grand-sires of the puritans of the next century, whose mission it was to impart to the modern life of English-speaking men, even when blessed by an admixture of Celtic blood, a sad seriousness deeper rooted than the beliefs from which it sprang.

To trace even in outline the natural history of the evolution of Puritan from Pagan would far transcend the design of these pages. But I would note in passing certain things. In the first place, the picturesque pagans of the plays and jest-books were not the whole of England ; any more than the Sir Oliver Martexts and Sir Nathaniels, or the curates of the *Hundred Merrie Tales*, constituted the whole of the English Church. As there were Protestants before the Reformation, so, I am convinced, there were in England puritans before puritanism. One of the most entertaining of Erasmus' *Colloquies* describes a visit to the shrine of St. Thomas at Canterbury before its spoliation, in the company of an Englishman, Gratianus Pullus by name, who is described as no Wickliffite, although he had read

mities are there perpetrated and committed, to the great profanation of the Lord's Sabbath, the dishonour of Almighty God, increase of bastardy and of dissolute life, and of many other mischiefs and inconveniences, to the great hurt of the commonwealth.' They were accordingly prohibited on the Sabbath Day. 'In January 1599 the Justices took a long step further, and having discovered that many inconveniences " which with modestie cannot be expressed " had happened in consequence of these gatherings, they ordered that parish ales, church ales and revels should thenceforth be utterly suppressed. . . . An order of Easter 1607 declares that church ales, parish ales, young men's ales, clerks' ales, sextons' ales, and all revels are to be utterly suppressed. Yet we find so late as 1622 that the war against them was being still carried on.'

Wickliffe's books.[1] This Pullus has been identified with
Colet, Dean of St. Paul's, on the rather slender evidence of a
statement by Erasmus in another work,[2] that Colet was his
companion when he visited Canterbury. But whether the
Pullus of the dialogue is intended for Colet, or designed
by Erasmus to represent the typical Englishman in his
attitude towards relics and shrines, that keen observer must
have detected in the English character many germs of the
puritanism of a later day.

Again, amidst all the swinish excesses of the church-ale
and the foolishness of Sir Topaz, a visitor to Shallow Church
might have discovered a grain of seed destined to spring up
into a mighty tree, overshadowing the whole land. For in
the chancel of Shallow church there stood a roughly hewn
oaken desk, and to it was chained, in obedience to the
law (together with Foxe's *Book of Martyrs* and Jewel's
Apology) a certain Book, lately done into the vulgar
tongue, destined to furnish a great people, just quickening
to intellectual life, with all the thoughts, associations, and
aspirations which go to the formation of national character,
and to constitute for many years practically the whole of their
prose literature. And so it happened, in the words of Mr.
Green,[3] that England became the country of a book, and that
book was the Bible; and the prophecy of Miles Coverdale
was fulfilled, when he said that he would give to the people
of England something that would do away with the singing of
' *hey nony nony, hey troly loly*,' and such-like phantasies.

But we are still with the diarist in the age of ' *hey nony
nony*,' and if we would catch somewhat of its spirit, we
should do well to note the group by which he was encountered on his approach to Shallow Green; for, rude
though they be, they are of the number of those who show
' the very age and body of the time his form and pressure.'

---

[1] *Mendemus*. Vinclevita quispiam, opinor.

Ogygius. Non arbitror; etiamsi libros illius legerat, incertum unde nactus.
These words of Ogygius are certainly not suggestive of Colet, whose opinions
and literary resources were well known to Erasmus.

[2] *Modus orandi Deum*.   [3] *History of the English People*.

"Who and what are these?" asked Silence of Simple, whom he recognised as one of the three men-servants provisionally kept by his kinsman Abraham Slender. He was thus answered:

"'Master, there is three carters, three shepherds, three neat-herds, three swine-herds, that have made themselves all men of hair; they call themselves Saltiers, and they have a dance which the wenches say is a gallimaufry of gambols, because they are not in't; but they themselves are o' the mind, if it be not too rough for some that know little but bowling, it will please plentifully.'"[1]

This was Shallow's modest contribution to the dramatic spirit of the age. It was a time when play-acting was in the air, and men of all sorts and conditions caught the contagion, with varying symptoms.

We know how it showed itself in the parish of which Sir Nathaniel was curate. There the performers were more ambitious than the shepherds, neat-herds and swine-herds of Shallow; and with the assistance of the village pedant, Holofernes, the Nine Worthies were presented, Sir Nathaniel being cast for the part of Alexander the Great. We know also how mercilessly the performers were 'baited' by the great lords and ladies whom they would entertain, and how easily Alexander the Conqueror was overthrown by their raillery. 'There an't shall please you,' said Costard, elated with the receipt of his impersonation of Pompion the Big, 'a foolish mild man; an honest man, look you, and soon dashed. He is a marvellous good neighbour, faith, and a very good bowler; but for Alisander—alas, you see how 'tis, a little o'erparted.'[2]

Greater things than these were attempted in towns like Stratford-on-Avon. There you would find an entire company, with a scroll of every man's name, able to discharge you all the parts in such plays as *The most lamentable comedy, and most cruel death of Pyramus and Thisby.* We know how Nick Bottom, the weaver, Françis Flute,

---

[1] *Wint. Tale*, iv. 4. 331.   [2] *Love's L. L.* v. 2. 584.

the bellows-mender, Robin Starveling, the tailor, Tom Snout, the tinker, and Snug, the joiner—hard-handed men, that worked in Stratford—answered to the call of Peter Quince, the carpenter. Sweet Bully Bottom, who had simply the best wit of them all, and would discharge you any part, in any beard, albeit his chief humour was for ' Ercles' vein, a tyrant's vein,' was beyond all doubt a local celebrity, as well known in Stratford as Clement Perkes on the Hill, or William Visor in the village of Woncot.

In the eyes of Theseus and Hippolyta all this was mere tedious folly, necessary to be endured by persons of quality, and mitigated in some degree by the jests and merriment in which they were at liberty to indulge at the expense of the actors. ' The best in this kind,' said Theseus, ' are but shadows ; and the worst are no worse, if imagination amend them.' [1]

It needed, in truth, a poet's imagination to realise the debt owed by humanity to the base mechanicals of Stratford, and to the rude peasants of Shallow. Had not the drama been deeply rooted in the native soil, it could not have borne such excellent fruit. This is a law of nature in regard to all the arts. It was to the village festival and the goat-song in honour of Dionysus that we owe the sublimity of Æschylus, the grace of Sophocles, the humanity of Euripides, and the inexhaustible mirth of Aristophanes. And two thousand years later, in another period of marvellous intellectual growth ; from mysteries and miracles enacted on village scaffold or rood-loft in parish church—with their strange admixture of religion and broad farce, Termagant and Herod side by side ;—through the intermediate links of moralities, rude comedies like *Ralph Roister Doister* and *Gammer Gurton's Needle*, and bloody tragedies such as *Gorboduc* and *Titus Andronicus*, there was developed in less than the space of a lifetime the supreme art that culminated in *Hamlet* and *As You Like It*.

It is ever thus. Impenetrable is the mystery enshrouding

[1] *Mids. N. Dr.* v. 1. 212

the birth of individual genius. But we know that it cannot be grown to order, as an exotic in a hothouse. It thrives not on the patronage of the great, the largess of the rich, or the criticism of the learned. If it were otherwise the Victorian age would have far surpassed those of Elizabeth and Pericles in wealth of dramatic genius. How many itinerant ballad-singers went to make up one Homer? To how many rude masons and builders, each doing art-work perfect of its kind, do we owe the majesty of York Minster, the beauty of Lincoln, the strength of Ely, the grace of Salisbury, and the refinement of Westminster? How many village altar-pieces were painted in the days of Raphael? How many music-loving German peasants went to produce one Handel? The world may see another Shakespeare, but before then we should look for some assurance that the drama has again taken possession of the heart of the people, such as was afforded by the rude gallimaufry of gambols, enacted by disguised rustics on the village green of Shallow.

Born and bred amidst such surroundings, the poet's mind received a tincture stronger and more enduring than that by which in later life, through public means and public manners, his nature became subdued ' to what it works in, like the dyer's hand.' [1] For it is the vase of freshly-moulded clay that longest holds the rose-scent. And year by year, as autumn came round, he renewed his giant strength, like another Antæus, by contact with the earth from which he sprang.[2] Thus it came to pass that his images of country life and of field sports are as fresh and vivid in middle life as they were in the early days of *Venus and Adonis* and *Love's Labour's Lost*, or as we find them in the later years, when, again living amidst the scenes and pursuits of the ' age between sixteen and three-and-twenty,' [3] he wrote *The Tempest* and *Cymbeline*.

[1] Sonnet cxi.

[2] The tradition that Shakespeare spent each autumn with his family at Stratford is confirmed by the fact that he continued throughout his life to be described in legal documents as of Stratford, which he evidently regarded as his permanent abode. [3] *Wint. Tale*, iii. 3. 59.

And so by constant and lifelong devotion to nature—for sport is but one form of nature-worship—he kept alive in middle life the sensations of boyhood, and the child was the father of the man, his days being

> Bound each to each by natural piety.

It is in the simple and abiding facts of nature that the greatest and sanest intellects have sought and found refuge from the vain questionings and imaginings of the human mind, and from the lies that have been invented to quiet them. I do not know that this feeling has been better expressed in prose than by Charles Kingsley, when he wrote : ' Gladly would I give up history to think of nothing but dicky-birds—but it must not be yet. Some day, ere I grow too old to think, I trust to be able to throw away all pursuits save natural history, and die with my mind full of God's facts, instead of man's lies ; ' or in poetry than by Words- worth, when, complaining that the world is too much with us, he exclaims :

> Great God! I'd rather be
> A Pagan suckled in a creed outworn—
> So might I, standing on this pleasant lea,
> Have glimpses that would make me less forlorn.

Such glimpses can be had by all who seek for them where they may be found. It was thus when the world was young. The Preacher set his heart to search out by wisdom concerning all things done under heaven—the sore travail given by God to the sons of men. And with fullest know- ledge of the wisdom, madness, and folly of men, he pronounces all to be vanity and vexation of spirit. Then he turned to nature. ' And he spake of trees, from the cedar tree that is in Lebanon, even unto the hyssop that springeth out of the wall ; he spake also of beasts and of fowl, and of creeping things and of fishes.' His words have been lost to mankind. But of some things I am certain. What he spake of beasts and of fowl had nothing in common with the passages quoted in these pages ; for the literature of the children of Jacob shows

no trace of devotion to any of the sports of the field, loved by
Esau, not wisely but too well. Again, I feel sure that he
wrote of them in the spirit of the Canticles rather than in
that of Ecclesiastes; and lastly, I doubt not that what he
spake of nature, with what he wrote of men, led up to
one and the same 'conclusion of the whole matter: fear
God, and keep His commandments, for this is the whole duty
of man.'

The wisest and greatest of moderns gives the same
answer to the obstinate questionings by which the great king
of Israel was sorely perplexed some twenty-eight centuries
ago. In vain look you will to Shakespeare for any light
upon the great religious, social, and philosophical questions
of his day.

What was his creed? He has been variously described,
and with equal confidence, as a Roman Catholic and as a
Protestant; as a deist and as an atheist. An English lawyer
suspects, and a Frenchman of letters proves to his complete
satisfaction, that he was a Roman Catholic.[1] A Scottish
Bishop claims him as a faithful son of the English Church
of the Reformation.[2] Many lessons in true religion may
be learned from Shakespeare; but with regard to the con-
tending factions of the day he had nothing to teach us,
unless it be the easy-going toleration thus characteristi-
cally expressed by a certain clown: 'For young Charbon
the puritan and old Poysam the papist, howsome'er their
hearts are severed in religion, their heads are both one; they
may joul horns together, like any deer i' the herd.'[3]

What were his politics? He has been claimed as the
harbinger of the modern spirit. He has been described as
'incarnated uncompromising feudalism in literature;'[4] while

---

[1] *Historical Memoirs of English Catholics*, by Charles Butler (1819). *Shakespeare*, par A. L. Rio. (Paris) 1864.

[2] *Shakespeare's Knowledge and Use of the Bible*, by Charles Wordsworth,
Bishop of St. Andrews (1864); see also an article in the *Edinburgh Review* (Jan.
1866) entitled, *Was Shakespeare a Roman Catholic?*

[3] *All's Well*, i. 3. 55.

[4] Walt Whitman, quoted by Prof. Dowden (*Shakspere, His Mind and Art*).

according to Gervinus, ' no man fought more strongly against rank and class prejudice than Shakespeare,' who dared in the reign of James I. ' to speak of political freedom.' But of his proper opinions I can find no trace ;—unless, indeed, he has put them into the mouth of Sir Andrew Aguecheek, when he said :

> I had as lief be a Brownist as a politician.
> *Twelfth Night*, iii. 2. 33.

What was his philosophy? I doubt that he could have formulated his ideas after the fashion of any school. But that he never applied his mind to obtain some solution of the problems of life is not to be believed. What is life? What is matter, in itself, apart from our sensations? How came they into being? What is their appointed end? Is this vast universe nothing more than an aggregate of ever-shifting phenomena, capable of discovery by empirical science? Does materialistic philosophy leave nothing unaccounted for; and are the boastful words addressed by Lucretius to his master, and re-echoed by feebler imitators to-day, borne out by fact :

> Natura tua vi
> Tam manifesta patens, ex omni parte retecta est ?

What of

> Those obstinate questionings
> Of sense and outward things,
> Fallings from us, vanishings,
> Blank misgivings of a creature
> Moving about in worlds not realised,
> High instincts, before which our mortal nature
> Did tremble like a guilty thing surprised ?

What of the visions of prophets and seers, and revelations, in every age, of things unseen by the eye of sense? What of the store of ideas having no counterpart in the world of matter, the presence of which to the mind is a fact more certain than the objective existence of a material universe, inasmuch as they form part of our very consciousness?

Those whose minds are racked by questions like these will
look in vain to Shakespeare for definite answers. But they
may learn from him something better than cut-and-dry dog-
matism. They are taught the mental attitude which befits
them in regard to a whole universe of objects of thought,
not capable of being touched, tested, handled, or weighed
in balances of scientific construction. In inquiries into the
nature and origin of life, as in the subdivision of matter, an
ultimate point is at some time reached, beyond which research remains as fruitless after three centuries of Bacon as it
was after two thousand years of Aristotle. Such a point may
also be reached in the confines of the seen and unseen worlds,
beyond which if we would pass it must be under some
guidance other than that of philosophy. This is a great
truth, the realisation of which is *summa sapientia* ; and it
has never been better expressed than by words put into the
mouth of Hamlet, in the presence of a mysterious something,
for which the philosophy of Wittenberg could not account :

> There are more things in heaven and earth, Horatio,
> Than are dreamt of in our [1] philosophy.
>
> *Hamlet,* i. v. 167.

There is a middle course possible between, on the one
hand, denying the existence of these undreamed-of things,
and, on the other, wasting a lifetime in fruitless efforts to
give them form and definition. The practical mind of
Shakespeare was in little danger of falling into the latter
extreme, or of ignoring the attractions of the world of sense.
Perhaps, after all, if the diarist had faithfully recorded all
that was said in the course of his ride on Cotswold, we should
have had no richer inheritance than some stray thoughts of
outward things, not very different from those with which the

---

[1] Thus the Folio. The alteration of ' our ' into ' your,' adopted from the
Quartos by the Cambridge editors, is not only a departure from the true original
text, but, like many errors of the surreptitious copyists, mars a distinct point.
Hamlet and Horatio had been fellow students of philosophy at Wittenberg.

passages collected in these pages are conversant. If we seek for converse high

> Of providence, foreknowledge, will and fate :
> Fixed fate, free will, foreknowledge absolute. . . .
> Of happiness and final misery,
> Passion and apathy, and glory and shame ;

and would know where, and from whom, such discourse may be had, we may inquire of the great puritan poet, who of all the qualities of Shakespeare selects for admiration his 'native wood-notes wild.'

CHAPTER XII

A DAY'S HAWKING

Believe me, lords, for flying at the brook,
I saw not better sport these seven years' day.
                    Second Part of King Henry VI.

WHEN William Silence and his sister Ellen left old Silence's
house in order to take part in Master Petre's hawking, they
had little fear lest Abraham Slender should join the company,
and thus mar their plots.   Ellen Silence was in her brother's
confidence, and had made sure of this on the day before.
She was, as we know, the Justice's favourite god-daughter,
and she and her father were wont to dine at Shallow Hall
on Sundays.   Coming over to the Hall after Sir Topaz's
famous discourse had been brought to an inglorious end,
she found there to her surprise Master Will Squele and the
fair Anne.   Their presence was part of the Justice's deep-
laid scheme.   He was resolved that Abraham Slender should
lack no opportunity of pressing his suit, especially in view
of the dangerous proximity of William Silence.   Heartily did
Silence laugh as Ellen told what she had seen and heard;
how Abraham would not come in to dinner until Anne had
been sent to the garden to bid him; and with what grave
formality the message had been delivered.   Let us hear her
story in the very words of the speakers :

Anne. Will't please your worship to come in, sir ?
Slen. No, I thank you, forsooth, heartily ; I am very well.
Anne. The dinner attends you, sir.

Slen. I am not a-hungry, I thank you, forsooth. Go, sirrah, for all you are my man, go wait upon my cousin Shallow. (*Exit* Simple.) A justice of peace sometime may be beholding to his friend for a man. I keep but three men and a boy yet, till my mother be dead : but what though ? yet I live like a poor gentleman born.

Anne. I may not go in without your worship : they will not sit till you come.

Slen. I' faith, I'll eat nothing ; I thank you as much as though I did.

Anne. I pray you, sir, walk in.

Slen. I had rather walk here, I thank you. I bruised my shin th' other day with playing at sword and dagger with a master of fence ; three veneys for a dish of stewed prunes ; and, by my troth, I cannot abide the smell of hot meat since. Why do your dogs bark so ? Be there bears i' the town ?

Anne. I think there are, sir ; I heard them talked of.

Slen. I love the sport well ; but I shall as soon quarrel at it as any man in England. You are afraid, if you see the bear loose, are you not ?

Anne. Ay, indeed, sir.

Slen. That's meat and drink to me, now. I have seen Sackerson loose twenty times, and have taken him by the chain ; but, I warrant you, the women have so cried and shrieked at it, that it passed : but women, indeed, cannot abide 'em ; they are very ill-favoured rough things.   *Merry Wives*, i. 1. 275.

"Now, by all that's holy," said Silence, " I'll wager on the bear against the lady. If there be bears in the town, you will not see Abraham Slender to-day."

As he was so saying, they overtook Clement Perkes and his friend, wending their way from the Hill to take part in the day's sport in accordance with Petre's hospitable invitation of the day before. They went on foot, provided for the purpose of clearing obstacles with hawking poles, like to that the breaking of which well-nigh cost the eighth Henry his life in a Hertfordshire ditch.

" What say you, goodman Perkes," said Silence, "you know Master Slender and his ways. There are bears in the town. Think you that he will find it in his heart to leave them ? "

" I' faith that a' wont," said the honest yeoman, " a'd sooner leave to live than a'd quit the bear-garden."

' And so we fell to talking of bears and bear-baytings and bull-baytings, and what manner of men they be that haunte them.' These are the diarist's words.

When I read so far, I again hoped that I might be able to give to the world some words from the lips of the nameless stranger. Again I was doomed to disappointment. But though the diary is silent as to his words, we have a better and more enduring record of the thoughts of one of the party.

Who are the lovers and haunters of bear-baitings and such-like sports ?

(a) The knave, Autolycus :

Out upon him ! Prig, for my life, prig ; he haunts wakes, fairs, and bear-baitings . . . not a more cowardly rogue in all Bohemia.
Winter's Tale, iv. 3. 108.

(b) The fool, Abraham Slender, and his congener, Sir Andrew Aguecheek :

I would I had bestowed that time in the tongues that I have in fencing, dancing, and bear-baiting. *Twelfth Night*, i. 3. 97.

(c) The sot, Sir Toby Belch :

You know [said Fabian to the knight, of Malvolio] he brought me out o' favour with my lady about a bear-baiting here.
Sir To. To anger him we'll have the bear again ; and we will fool him black and blue, shall we not, Sir Andrew?
Sir And. An we do not, it is pity of our lives.
Twelfth Night, ii. 5. 8.

If it be true that the puritan Malvolio objected to the bear-baiting, not for the pain it gave the bear, but for the pleasure it afforded the sportsman, Sir Toby was even with him, and would have the bear back again, not so much for the sport's sake as to anger the puritan.

(d) The villain, Richard III. If he were not a frequenter of the bear-garden, he could not have said :

Rich. Oft have I seen a hot o'erweening cur
Run back and bite, because he was withheld;
Who, being suffer'd with the bear's fell paw,
Hath clapped his tail between his legs and cried;
And such a piece of service will you do,
If you oppose yourselves to match Lord Warwick.
Clif. Hence, heap of wrath, foul indigested lump,
As crooked in thy manners as thy shape!

2 *Hen. VI.* v. 1. 151.

Images from the bear-garden are for ever recurring to the mind of Richard. Thus he compares his father York, engaged in battle, to

a bear, encompass'd round with dogs,
Who having pinch'd a few and made them cry
The rest stand all aloof, and bark at him.[1]

3 *Hen. VI.* ii. 1. 15.

(e) The wretch, Thersites, to whose lips the cries of Paris-garden rise familiar, when Menelaus and Paris fight before his eyes:

Now, bull! now, dog! 'loo, Paris, 'loo! Now my double-henned sparrow! 'loo, Paris, 'loo! The bull has the game; ware horns, ho! *Troil. and Cres.* v. 7. 10.

(f) The monster, Aaron; 'I was their tutor to instruct them,' he boasts of Tamora's sons, whom Lucius had called barbarous beastly villains, like himself:

That bloody mind I think they learn'd of me,
As true a dog as ever fought at head.

Tit. Andr. v. 1. 101.

---

[1] This passage and the preceding are not to be found in the *Whole Contention of the Houses of York and Lancaster*, the older plays which were taken by Shakespeare as the foundation of his work. They are touches carefully added by the master hand of the artist, in limning the features of Richard's character. Richard's thoughts recur to bear-baiting; Hamlet's to recollections of woodcraft and falconry. These small matters, we may be sure, are not without significance. The incidents of bear-baiting were, of course, familiar to all, and references to bears, bear-herds, and the stake are not infrequent (*Twelfth N.* iii. 1. 129; 2 *Hen. VI.* v. 1. 144; *Jul. Cæs.* iv. 1. 48; *K. Lear*, iii. 7. 54; 2 *Hen. V.* i. 2. 192; etc.). Allusions of this kind are very different from the passages quoted above, which were intended to represent the speakers as habitual frequenters of the bear-garden.

(*g*) The common rabble, thus addressed :

You'll leave your noise anon, ye rascals : do you take the Court for Paris-garden? ye rude slaves, leave your gaping.

Hen. VIII. v. 4. 1.

Could Shakespeare have said in plainer language that bear-baiting was in his eyes a sport fit only for knaves, fools, sots, villains, wretches, monsters, or the common rabble?

And yet no pastime had, in his day, a stronger hold of the people of England than bear-baiting, and its kindred amusements of bull-baiting and cock-fighting. They had not in Shakespeare's eyes the charm of the honest sports of the field, though he could admire the pluck of the British mastiff. ' Foolish curs' (the Duke of Orleans calls them) ' that run winking into the mouth of a Russian bear and have their heads crushed like rotten apples!' [1]   Englishmen, indeed, have little more sense.   They never know when they are beaten ; or, as the Constable of France put it, some centuries before Napoleon, 'If the English had any apprehension they would run away.' [2]

Professional feeling may possibly have, to some extent, blinded the eyes of the play-house manager to the attractions of the bear-garden ; for there was traditional war between the play-house and the bear-garden at the Bankside, and neither would lose an opportunity of girding at the other.

However this may be, it is certain that Abraham Slender was not one of the company assembled in the courtyard of Petre Manor on the morn of the hawking party.   But William Silence's triumph was short-lived.   He had to learn by yet another instance that the course of true love never did run smooth.   Old Will Squele was there also. His cold reception of William Silence's greetings, and his manifest intention of keeping his daughter by his side, forbad all hope of a private interview on that day.   But his loss is our gain.   For if he had not been baulked in his expectation, Silence certainly would not have bestowed upon the sports

[1] *Hen. V.* iii. 7. 153.   [2] *Ibid.* 145.

of the day the close attention which we find reflected in the pages of his diary.

A fair scene met the eyes of the company assembled in the court-yard of Petre ·Manor. It was a glorious day in September, such as might well bring upon the giant in the immortal allegory his worst of fits. Bright ,colours glancing in the sun, and the merry sounds of hawks, dogs, and men, dispelled the gloom which usually hung around the mouldering courts of the ancient manor-house. The Lady Katherine, like most women of spirit, loved dress. The hardest part of her training was when she had to forego the gown elaborately fashioned by Feeble, the woman's tailor. We may be sure that the gossip of Petre Manor lost nothing in the telling, as he related at the Hill to Clement Perkes and his visitor the strange doings of the Squire. 'I never saw' (said poor Kate) 'a better fashioned gown, more quaint, more pleasing, nor more commendable.' [1] She wears this gown now. If you are curious as to such matters and look at the illustration in Turbervile's *Booke of Faulconrie*,[2] representing a great lady riding out a-hawking, you will find in her gown all the peculiarities against which Petre directed the shafts of his ridicule, and in particular ' the sleeves curiously cut.'

> *Pet.* What's this? A sleeve? 'Tis like a demi-cannon;
> What, up and down, carved like an apple tart?
> Here's snip and nip and cut and slish and slash,
> Like to a censer in a barber's shop;
> Why, what, i' devil's name, tailor, call'st thou this?
>
> *Tam. of Shrew*, iv. 3. 88.

If you study the curious old print· carefully, you may imagine, rather than discern, the place of the tiny velvet cap, from which the veil depends. It affords neither shade nor warmth. But what of that? For, as the Lady

---

[1] *Tam. of Shrew*, iv. 3. 101.

[2] The illustrations in this book and in the *Noble Arte of Venerie* are said to have been taken from an older French work. But the fact that they were reproduced by Turbervile proves that they represent with fair accuracy the English costumes of 1575.

Katherine explains : 'This doth fit the time, And gentle-women wear such caps as these.'[1] Fashion had not then decreed that ladies should ride out hunting or hawking in the austere rigidity of the modern riding-habit and hat, and indeed both sexes displayed in the field much of the bravery of apparel characteristic of the time.

The day was a favourable one for the sport. It was clear, without being too hot, and above all was calm. 'During windy weather it is only at a great risk of loss that hawks can be flown at any quarry.'[2] The careful falconer would not let a valuable haggard falcon, manned and reclaimed, like old Joan, go out in a high wind.

> Yet, by your leave, the wind was very high ;
> And, ten to one, old Joan had not gone out.
>
> 2 *Hen. VI.* ii. 1. 3.

But if you would get rid of an irreclaimable haggard, you would 'whistle her off and let her down the wind, to prey at fortune.'[3]

The hawks had not been fed that day, for it is true of beasts and birds of prey, as of mankind, that 'hunger will enforce them to be more eager,'[4] or 'as an empty eagle, sharp by fast.'[5]

> Look, as the full-fed hound or gorged hawk,
> Unapt for tender smell or speedy flight,
> Make slow pursuit, or altogether balk
> The prey wherein by nature they delight ;
> So surfeit-taking Tarquin fares.   *Lucrece,* 694.

Those that were required for the day's sport were placed, hooded, upon a wooden frame or 'cadge' carried by an attendant, called from his occupation a 'cadger.' His was the humblest task connected with the sport, and his title, like that of knave, became in time a term of reproach.

And so the company, some on horseback and some on foot, sallied from the court-yard, and made their way across

---

[1] *Tam. of Shrew,* iv. 3. 69.
[2] Salvin and Brodrick's *Falconry in the British Isles.*
[3] *Othello,* iii. 3. 262.   [4] *1 Hen. VI.* i. 2. 38.   [5] *Ven. and Ad.* 55.

the meadows to the great common-field lying between Petre Manor and the brook.

"And first," said Petre to Master Shallow, "I will show you a flight at the partridge. Here, in this cornfield, where the stubble grows high beside the balks, I dare swear a covey lies. The birds are yet young, and we may see some sport, and at the same time furnish the larder for supper. ' Where's my spaniel, Troilus ? ' [1] Here, Troilus, to it, to it." Troilus, the spaniel, beat the stubble, ranging far and wide over the acres [2] divided by the balks. Full of grass and weeds and standing high, before the days of reaping machines and careful tillage, it afforded ample cover, especially where it mingled with the rough grass covering the balks, or boundaries separating the acres of the extensive common-field.

The falconer, taking a falcon from the cadge and holding her on his fist, followed the dog. It was not long before Troilus acknowledged the presence of the game, by setting after the manner of well-trained spaniels. The falconer at once unhooded and cast off the falcon, whistling her from his fist. Mounting higher and higher in wide circles, she seemed to the ordinary looker on as though she would be lost for ever in the clouds, unless something were done to recall her attention to the game before her. Not so to the practised falconer, who held Troilus by the collar to prevent him from rushing in and springing the birds before the falcon had mounted to her full pitch.

It was hard to believe that the ever lessening spot between the company and the sun was a comrade of man, under his control, and taking an intelligent if not altogether disinterested part in his pastime. Yet so it was, and if Troilus' point had proved a false one, the falcon would have followed man and dog as they beat the extensive common-field, hawk and dog working together with one common end in view.[3] But Troilus was of the right sort, else his

---

[1] *Tam. of Shrew*, iv. 1. 153.　　　[2] 1 *Hen. IV.* i. 1. 25.

[3] See a description of the combined action of hawk and greyhound in pursuit of the antelope in Persia, *Quarterly Review*, xxxvi. 358.

name would not have been handed down to us, and there
was no mistake about his point.

At length the falcon, swinging round and round in
lessening circles, reached her full pitch, and hung steadily
with her head to the wind, some hundred and fifty yards
above the earth. In the language of falconry, she waited
on, 'towering in her pride of place.' [1] She was 'a falcon
towering in the skies.' [2]

Petre could claim, with Warwick the king-maker, that
he had perhaps some shallow spirit of judgment 'Between two hawks, which flies the higher pitch?' and he
might have added, with truth,

> Between two dogs, which hath the deeper mouth ;
> Between two blades, which bears the better temper ;
> Between two horses, which doth bear him best ;
> Between two girls, which hath the merriest eye ?
>
> <div align="right">1 <i>Hen. VI.</i> ii. 4. 10.</div>

Of the falcon now waiting on he would say that she is
not one to 'fly an ordinary pitch.' [3] She was the best of
his falcons, except old Joan, and was generally reserved for
'flying at the brook.' But Petre was impatient to show
the company what his hawks could do, and so he now flew
her in the field. As for old Joan, not a falcon in Gloucestershire could mount her pitch. But she was a thoroughly
trained and made heroner, and was never flown at any less
noble quarry.

Meanwhile the covey lay like stones beneath the shadow
of the bird of prey and the terror of her bells. The hawk
was always furnished with bells, attached to her legs. 'As
the ox hath his bow, sir,' says Touchstone, 'the horse his

---

[1] *Macbeth*, ii. 4. 12.   [2] *Lucrece*, 506.

[3] The word ' pitch,' signifying in falconry the height to which a falcon soars
or towers (1 *Hen. VI.* ii. 4. 11 ; 2 *Hen. VI.* ii. 1. 6 ; *Jul. Cæs.* i. 1. 78), was
used figuratively (*Rich. II.* i. 1. 109 ; *Tit. Andr.* ii. 1. 14 ; *Rom. and
Jul.* i. 4. 21 ; *Jul. Cæs.* i. 1. 78 ; Sonnet lxxxvi. 6), and came to mean height
in general (*Twelfth Night*, i. 1. 12 ; 1 *Hen. VI.* ii. 3. 55 ; *Rich. III.* iii. 7. 188 ;
Sonnet vii. 9). The point to which the long-winged hawk towers was also
called ' her place ' (*Macbeth*, ii. 4. 12).

curb, and the falcon her bells, so man hath his desires.' [1]
They served a twofold purpose. By their sound a falconer
could trace an erring hawk, while they struck terror to the
heart of the listening fowl.

> Harmless Lucretia, marking what he tells
> With trembling fear, as fowl hear falcon's bells.
>
> *Lucrece*, 510.

In partridge-hawking, while the falcon or tercel-gentle
was mounting to its pitch, the sound of its bells secured the
close lying of the covey, cowed, as were England's barons
by the king-maker.

> Neither the king, nor he that loves him best,
> The proudest he that holds up Lancaster,
> Dares stir a wing, if Warwick shakes his bells.
>
> 3 *Hen. VI.* i. 1. 45.

They were in hawking language 'enmewed,' and dare
not show themselves openly any more than could follies and
vices in the city of Vienna, under the stern rule of Angelo
the Deputy, of whom Isabella says,

> This outward-sainted deputy,
> Whose settled visage and deliberate word
> Nips youth i' the head and follies doth enmew [2]
> As falcon doth the fowl, is yet a devil.
>
> *Measure for M.* iii. 1. 89.

When Petre was satisfied that the falcon was steadily
waiting on, Troilus was allowed to spring the birds. The
falcon instantly selected her quarry from the covey, and,

---

[1] *As You L.* iii. 3. 80.

[2] The correction 'enew' adopted by Dr. Schmidt (*Shakespeare Lexicon*) and
Professor Baynes (*Shakespeare Studies*) is unnecessary and inept. The
secondary use of the word 'enmew' in the sense of 'to cause to lie close and
keep concealed, as hawk in mew,' is illustrated by a passage in Beaumont and
Fletcher's *Knight of Malta*, where a warrior besetting a town is compared to a
falcon mounting her pitch, and is said to 'inmew the town below him.' 'Enew'
is a term used in connection with flying at the brook. It is used by Drayton,
Turbervile, and Nash (*Quaternio*), apparently in the sense of driving the fowl
into the water. Hence, probably, its derivation in the Norman French language
of hawking. It is not as appropriate to the passage quoted in the text as the
original reading. It is more natural to speak of Angelo causing follies to lie
close, than of driving them into water.

directing her course by a few strokes, swooped downward
with closed wings. This is the stoop, or swoop, of the
long-winged hawk, by which it stuns or kills its prey. Of
such a deadly stoop thought Macduff, when he exclaimed of
Macbeth,

> O hell-kite ! All?
> What, all my pretty chickens and their dam
> At one fell swoop ? *Macbeth*, iv. 3. 217.

But the fatal blow was not then dealt. The partridge
singled out by the falcon happened to be the old cock-bird.
Partly by strength of wing and partly by craft, he eluded
the first onslaught of the enemy, and fled for shelter to a
neighbouring thicket, while the rest of the covey settled down
in a more distant part of the great common-field.

When the falcon recovered herself, she again mounted
into the air. The falcon does not fly after game in a stern
chase, as the greyhound courses the hare, or the short-winged
hawk pursues its quarry. She must needs soar aloft, and
then swoop down. Circling around, she marked with keen
eye the spot where the bird had taken refuge, and making
her point accordingly, waited on, high above the thicket, but
not rising to her full pitch.

Again the bird was put up by Troilus, and again the
falcon stooped from her pride of place, swift and resistless
as a thunderbolt. This time her aim was unerring. In the
language of falconry she ' stoop'd as to foot' her quarry ; [1]
and when Master Petre and the falconer rode up, she had
' soused ' [2] the partridge, and holding it firmly in her foot, she
had begun to devour, or in hawking language to tire on the
bird, after the manner of birds of prey :

> Even as an empty eagle, sharp by fast,
> Tires with her beak on feathers, flesh and bone.
> Shaking her wings, devouring all in haste,
> Till either gorge be stuff'd or prey be gone. [3]
> *Ven. and Ad.* 55.

[1] *Cymb.* v. 4. 116.   [2] See *K. John*, v. 2. 150.
[3] Cf. 3 *Hen. VI.* i. 1. 268 ; *Tim. of Ath.* iii. 6. 5; *Lucrece*, 417.

Had she been left to herself, 'twere long ere she had been
' disedged ' (or had the edge taken off her keen appetite) by
that on which she tired.[1] But as she was needed for further
flights, the falconer took the bird from her, rewarding her,
however, with the head, so as to stimulate her to further
exertion, and then having hooded her, replaced her on the
cadge.

The party then betook themselves to the division of the
common-field whither the rest of the covey had flown, dis-
cussing as they rode the incidents of the flight—somewhat
after the following fashion of a certain royal hawking party :

> *K. Hen.* But what a point, my lord, your falcon made,
>   And what a pitch she flew above the rest !
>   To see how God in all His creatures works !
>   Yea, man and birds are fain of climbing high.
> *Suf.* No marvel, an it like your majesty,
>   My lord protector's hawks do tower so well ;
>   They know their master loves to be aloft
>   And bears his thoughts above his falcon's pitch.
> *Glo.* My lord, 'tis but a base ignoble mind
>   That mounts no higher than a bird can soar.[2]
> *Car.* I thought as much ; he would be above the clouds.[3]
>
>   2 *Hen. VI.* ii. 1. 5.

The next flight was not so successful as the former.

"The birds are yet young," said Petre, "and may well
be taken by a tassel-gentle. I will now essay a flight with
one which I had of Master Edmund Bert in exchange for an
Irish goshawk. Here, Master Falconer, let's try what Jack
can do."

The falconer took the bird from the cadge, and followed
Troilus to the place where they had marked down the scattered covey. The dog forthwith began to set, and the falconer
unhooded and cast off the hawk ; but, as ill luck would have

---

[1] *Cymb.* iii. 4. 96 ; cf. *Rich. II.* i. 3. 296 ; *Hamlet,* iii. 2. 260.

[2] Cf. *K. John,* i. 1. 206.

[3] In the *Whole Contention* the hawking incident occurs. But the dialogue
has been re-written and materially changed by Shakespeare, in order no doubt
to bring it into accord with true falconry.

it, he forbore to hold Troilus back, and the dog, springing
forward, flushed the game before the hawk had mounted to
its full pitch. Downward swooped the hawk, but with uncertain aim, pursuing his quarry rather than striking it down,
and, in the end, missing it altogether. Petre and Silence
rode as hard as they could, but as the direction taken by the
partridge was down-wind, the danger of losing the tercel-
gentle was imminent.

" ' Had not your man put up the fowl so suddenly,' " said
Silence, " ' we had had more sport.' " [1]

" Hist, Jack, hist ! " cried Petre. " ' O ! for a falconer's
voice, to lure this tassel-gentle back again.' [2] . . . 'Hillo, ho,
ho, boy ! Come, bird, come.' " [3]

Thus shouted Petre, but the hawk heeded him not, and
they could hear the sound of his bells as he flew down-wind.
The falconer quickly came up, holloing " ' Jack, boy ! ho !
boy ! ' " [4] and soon succeeded in attracting the attention of the
erring tercel-gentle, partly by his voice, but mostly by use
of the lure. This was a sham bird, usually constructed of
pigeon's wings, to which was attached food for the hawk,
known as a train.[5] Attracted by the semblance of a bird,
and by the reality of a meal, the hawk soon descended to the
lure. So it was in due course removed, rehooded, and restored
to the cadge.

The flight of the falcon, whether at her quarry or to the
lure, is the very type of speed, confidence, and strength.
When Henry Bolingbroke would fight with Thomas Duke of
Norfolk, his onslaught, we are told, would be ' as confident
as is the falcon's flight Against a bird.' [6] And of Venus,

---

[1] 2 *Hen. VI.* ii. 1. 45.   [2] *Rom. and Jul.* ii. 2. 159.

[3] *Hamlet*, i. 5. 115.

[4] *Tam. of Shrew*, iv. 1. 42.

[5] ' Devilish Macbeth,' says Malcolm, ' By many of these trains hath sought
to win me into his power ' (*Macb.* iv. 3. 117). ' To train ' frequently occurs in
the sense of ' to allure ' (*Com. of Err.* iii. 2. 45 ; *K. John*, iii. 4. 175 ; 1 *Hen. IV.*
v. 2. 21 ; 1 *Hen. VI.* ii. 3. 35 ; *Tit. Andr.* v. 1. 104). The hunters of the wolf
are instructed in the *Noble Arte* how to ' lay down their traynes ' so as to allure
them to the place where they desire to find them.

[6] *Rich. II.* i. 3. 61.

when, hearing a merry horn, she believes her Adonis to be
still alive, we read,

> As falcon to the lure, away she flies;
> The grass stoops not, she treads on it so light.
>
> *Ven. and Ad.* 1027.

Several flights were then tried, with varying fortune,
until the bag contained two and a half brace of partridge.

Then said Petre, " By my faith, this hath been a deadly
day to the birds. Let us now stay our hands, and essay a
flight at some other quarry."

" Only two brace and a half of partridge," exclaims the
shooter of driven game, used to slaughter his birds by the
hundred ; brace, dozen and score were useful words in the
.reckoning of our forefathers, but they are out of date in the
tale of a modern battue ;—" Only two brace and a half of
partridges, what poor sport ! "

In a dialogue, after the fashion of old books of sport,
between *AUCEPS*, as the spokesman of falconry, and *CARNI-
FEX*, on behalf of modern shooters, each commending his
recreation, *AUCEPS* would, I think, have held his own. He
would have admitted at once that the art of fowling could
never, in his time, have attained to the slaughter of several
hundred birds by one man in a single day. A few, no doubt,
might be killed by bird-bolt,[1] shot from stone-bow,[2] or by
birding-piece,[3] if you could use it aright, and had skill to stalk
on until the fowl should sit,[4] and under presentation of the
stalking horse to shoot your bolt.[5] The creeping fowler
might approach the wild goose, or duck, or russet-pated
chough,[6] before it could spy him. But for one bird killed
by the discharge of his caliver, many ' a poor hurt fowl '
would ' creep into sedges,'[7] and if it had the good luck to
recover, it would be more wary in future, for what could
' fear the report of a caliver worse than a struck fowl or a hurt

---

[1] *Much Ado*, i. 1. 42 ; *Love's L. L.* iv. 3. 25 ; *Twelfth N.* i. 5. 100.
[2] *Twelfth N.* ii. 5. 51.　　　　　　[3] *Merry Wives*, iv. 2. 59.
[4] *Much Ado*, ii. 3. 95.　　　　　　[5] *As You L.* v. 4. 111.
[6] *Mids. N. Dr.* iii. 2. 20.　　　　　[7] *Much Ado*, ii. 1. 209.

wild duck,'[1] unless it were one of Falstaff's commodity of warm slaves ? As for those that were not hit, the fowler is not likely to meet with them again, after that they,

> Rising and cawing at the gun's report,
> Sever themselves and madly sweep the sky.
>
> *Mids. N. Dr.* iii. 2. 22.

Full many a fowler had good right to respond to the falconers' toast, as given by Petre : 'a health to all that shot and miss'd.'[2]

The fowler, it is true, had his 'springes to catch woodcocks,'[3] and his lime-twigs, familiar to the thoughts of the stranger from Stratford.[4] He would take birds at night by bat-fowling.[5] He had his nets, his pit-falls, and his gins.[6] But birds will become shy where bushes are constantly limed.

> The bird that hath been limed in a bush,
> With trembling wings misdoubteth every bush ;
>
> *3 Hen. VI.* v. 6. 13.

to say nothing of the disadvantage that the fowler, in order to use his bird-lime, net, or springe aright, must take pains to learn somewhat of the nature and habits of the bird he would take, "from which labour, Master CARNIFEX," AUCEPS would readily admit, "the shooter of driven game would seem, from what you say, to be wholly free ; although, indeed, the master and deviser of the drive doth stand in need of some such knowledge."

Hunger's prevention, he would add, is the end of fowling,[7] whereas falconry has ever been a gentle and noble art in the eyes of princes and honourable persons. Further, he would point out that ladies took delight in the gentle art of falconry, especially in the flight of the merlin, whereas it is not to be supposed that they would be present

[1] *1 Hen. IV.* iv. 2. 20.   [2] *Tam. of Shrew*, v. 2. 51.
[3] *Wint. Tale*, iv. 3. 36 ; *Hamlet*, i. 3. 115 ; *Ibid.* v. 2. 317.
[4] The liming of birds is alluded to by Shakespeare in thirteen passages.
[5] *Tempest*, ii. 1. 185.   [6] *Macbeth*, iv. 2. 34.
[7] Gervase Markham published in 1621 a book entitled *Hunger's Prevention ; or, the Whole Arte of Fowling by Water and Land*.

at the mere slaughter by the hundred of innocent birds, although he would readily admit that such slaughter was excusable, and even commendable, for the prevention of hunger.

Whereupon *CARNIFEX* would, with some indignation, explain that he did not shoot birds for the prevention of hunger; that each bird he shot cost him four or five times its value as an article of food; that his was the sport of princes, and right honourable, as well as honourable persons; that he wondered how it could be compared to taking of birds by bird-lime and springes, the sport (if it could be so called) of the rabble of towns; that as for ladies, they loved nothing better than walking with the guns; and, finally, that he would like to see *AUCEPS* try his hand at shooting the driven grouse, or the rocketing pheasant.

"I grant you," *AUCEPS* would reply, "that to shoot a bird flying is indeed more than I can attain unto. I have heard it said of one that he 'rides at full speed, and with his pistol kills a sparrow flying,'[1] but I believe it not. But what if he did? Is it to be said of the shooter with the bow who is 'clapped on the shoulder and called Adam,'[2] or of the skilful player at tennis, billiards, or bowls, that he excelleth in field sports because his aim is good? Then should Bankes be the greatest of horsemen, and the dancing-horse the noblest of steeds, because they have attained to do what Alexander and Bucephalus could not? Unless, indeed, it is to be taken that whatever endeth in the destruction of the greatest number of lives, even though it be to the profit of none, and without exercise of cunning or skill (save the mean handicraftman's skill of aim), is to be considered as the first of sports."

But whatever were the arguments used by the disputants, we may be certain that neither would have yielded one jot to the other. You may more easily induce a man to abandon the political principles and professions of a lifetime (if you go the right way about it) than change his opinions on

[1] *1 Hen. IV.* ii. 4. 379. [2] *Much Ado,* i. 1. 261.

matters of sport. Nay, it is easier to turn one from the faith of his forefathers. And so grouse and partridge will still be driven, and, in time, salmon and trout may be driven too, while the angler, stroke-all in hand and luncheon-basket by his side, sits beside some narrow channel through which the driven fish must needs pass. And the same reasons will be given. The fish have grown so wild and shy that they will not look at the most craftily constructed fly. Why, even now, an old and wary trout in an over-fished chalk-stream has been seen to rush away in terror from a natural fly alighting above his nose. Then it is so much more difficult to strike the salmon as he darts past you in the stream than when he closes his mouth for an instant on your hook. And some may be found old-fashioned enough to regret that yet another ancient sport had been degraded to the level of a mere game of skill.

"And now," said Petre, "for a flight at the brook. I know where we may take a mallard or a duck. But on our way thither we may perchance find a heron at siege. I would love well, Master Silence, that you should see old Joan stoop from her pride of place. Not another falcon in Gloucestershire flies a pitch like hers."

And hereupon the Lady Katherine conceived and promptly executed a scheme which the diarist afterwards noted as determining the whole course of his affairs. "For," he adds, "to the readye witte and spirit of that most admirable ladye do I owe all the happinesse of my lyfe."

Turning to Petre she said: "Thou knowest the country saying: 'The falcon as the tercel for all the ducks i' the river,'[1] by which I understand him that useth it to intend that he would wager as much on the lady as on her lord. Now, my lord, I challenge thee to this contest. Take thou thy falcons and tercel-gentles for flying at the brook, and leave to me the lady's hawks—this cast of merlins. I will keep by me Mistresses Ellen Silence and Anne Squele. Do thou take Master Squele and the rest of the worshipful

[1] *Troil and Cres.* iii. 2. 55.

company, and when we meet at dinner let's see which may
show the better sport."

"It's a wager," said Petre, adding in a whisper as he
placed one of the merlins on his wife's hand, "whichever
may show the better sport, I know who hath the keener wit."

Anne Squele took the other merlin, and, accompanied by
Ellen Silence, rode off in the direction of some fallows, the
favourite haunt of larks, while Petre, attended by falconer
and cadger, led William Squele and the rest of the company
through the woodlands towards the brook.

As the Lady Katherine had anticipated, Master Ferdinand
Petre found some excuse for following their party. Attaching himself to Ellen, he left Katherine and Anne free to
cloak their meaning by ' talking of hawking,'[1] like Cardinal
Beaufort and the good Duke Humphrey of Gloucester.

Not a suspicion crossed the mind of Will Squele. He
welcomed the move as relieving him from all trouble in the
matter of keeping watch on his daughter. Nor did Silence
realise at the moment that the Lady Katherine had brought
to the settlement of their affairs that superabundant energy
which, thwarted, misdirected, and misunderstood, had brought
her into trouble and disrepute in her maiden years. The
stream which had fretted and chafed against each opposing
pebble became a useful motive power, once its collected
waters were turned into a fitting channel—all the more
valuable by reason of the volume of force which had been
wasted before.

Her quick woman's wit had divined that a crisis was at
hand. She had noted the attitude of Squele towards William,
and the misery which Anne vainly tried to hide. And so
she rightly concluded that if she and her husband were to
be of service to their friend, immediate action must be taken.

"Let's have some sport by the way," said Petre, "as we
ride through this woodland. 'I have a fine hawk for the
bush.'[2] Here, give me that Irish goshawk, and let Master

---

[1] 2 *Hen. VI.* ii. 1. 50.   [2] *Merry Wives*, iii. 3. 247.

Squele have on his fist the sparrow-hawk I had of Master Bert."

The way to the brook lay through a thickly wooded valley, and the hawks were carried with their hoods lightly fastened, in anticipation of a flight at rabbit or bird.

What degree of success they attained I cannot say. The diarist has failed to note the flights at the bush with the particularity bestowed on the doings of the falcon and tercel-gentle. The flight of the short-winged hawk, though swift and deadly, is not so attractive or suggestive as the lofty tower and resistless stoop of the falcon. They are not (in the language of falconry) hawks of the tower, or of the lure, but of the fist. They fly after their quarry from the hand, whither they return when the flight is over. To them their master's hand takes the place of the branch from which, in their wild state, they watch for their prey.

Most parts of the country are frequented by the kestrel or windhover, and by the sparrow-hawk. The observer, comparing the actions of these common birds, can form some idea of the difference between the practice of the falconer and the astringer. The kestrel, though the most ignoble of long-winged hawks, still possesses the characteristics of its race. It hovers in the air, waiting on, until some unhappy field mouse emerges from its hiding-place, and then it stoops on its victim. The sparrow-hawk, on the other hand, lurches from tree to tree, and having selected its quarry, pursues it in a stern chase, like shot discharged from a fowling-piece, a similitude which was present to the godfathers of the 'musket' when they named it after the male sparrow-hawk, the smallest hawk employed in falconry.

And so we see that every long-winged hawk, though base and degraded as the puttock or kite,[1] is a *falco* still, and of the same order as the eagle, that 'o'er his aery towers, To souse annoyance that comes near his nest.'[2] It is a different

---

[1] Imogen thus compares the nobility of Posthumus, the 'poor but worthy gentleman' of her choice, with the baseness of Cloten, 'I chose an eagle, And did avoid a puttock' (*Cymb.* i. 1. 139).   [2] *K. John*, v. 2. 149.

creature from the *accipiter*, or short-winged hawk; and though one falcon may fly a higher pitch than another, as one man excels his fellows in thought or action, yet are they alike subject to the conditions of a common nature which makes the whole world kin. ' The king is but a man as I am,' said King Henry to the soldier John Bates. ' The violet smells to him as it doth to me; the element shows to him as it doth to me; all his senses have but human conditions; his ceremonies laid by, in his nakedness he appears but a man; and though his affections are higher mounted than ours, yet, when they stoop, they stoop with the like wing.' [1]

But though the eye of the diarist found little in it to admire or record, there were many who took delight in the flight of a well-trained hawk, pursuing its quarry with unerring aim through the thickest bush; and in the days of the diarist, as in those of Chaucer, the keenest sportsmen, as well as the noblest in the land, would often ride abroad ' with grey goshawk in hand.'

The woodland was soon passed, and the hawks were returned to the cadge, in anticipation of the great event of the day.

Crossing a wide stretch of open country, the company at length reached a long winding valley, where the brook had been dammed up and converted into a pond, somewhat after the fashion of the water where the hart was taken. It was stocked with large trout.

With the exception of certain human consciences, there is nothing in nature so marvellous as the elasticity of the organisation of the trout, and its power of adapting itself to altered surroundings. It has no fixed principles in the matter of size and weight. Leave it in a rocky mountain stream, and it will live and die among its fellows a two-ounce trout. Transfer it to a pond productive of insect life, and it thinks nothing of reaching the weight of five or six pounds. Having attained to such eminence, it devours its less weighty kith and kin, if they should cross its path. And

[1] *Hen. V.* iv. 1. 104.

so this pond supplied Petre Manor with fish, especially in
the season of Lent.   When, however, Petre last returned
home, he shrewdly suspected that it had

> been sluiced in's absence,
> And his pond fish'd by his next neighbour, by
> Sir Smile, his neighbour.   *Wint. Tale*, i. 2. 194.

Petre's disposition was not jealous or suspicious, like that of
poor Leontes, in matters great or small.   But he never believed in any of the Smile family.   They were, he would
say, too sweet to be wholesome.   And his suspicions were
probably well founded.

Now this pond held not only trout fit for the dish, but
hosts of smaller fry, and eels, affected by the heron.   About
two miles southward there was a well-stocked heronry,
separated from the brook by a stretch of open wold.   No
better country could be desired for the sport of flying at the
heron.   Towards the end of February, or early in March,
the herons begin to 'make their passage.'   It is then their
custom to sally forth in the morning to distant rivers and
ponds in search of food.   Towards evening they leave their
feeding grounds, and return to the heronry.   The falconer
stations himself in the open country, down-wind of the
heronry, and as the bird flies over him on its homeward way,
the falcons are cast off, and the flight begins.

This is the sport of taking herons on the passage.   It was
commonly practised in spring, but at other seasons of the
year excellent sport might be had if a heron could be found
at siege, and in the hope of such good fortune the company
made for the pond.

Petre, like Bertram, had a 'hawking eye.' [1]   He quickly
discerned a heron, busily engaged in fishing, and half concealed by willows growing thickly around the pond.   He
at once made ready for action.   Old Joan was a noted
heroner.   She was never flown at any other quarry, and
she had been brought out on the chance of finding a heron

[1] *All's Well*, i. 1. 105.

at siege. Taking with him Joan and another well-trained haggard falcon, and loosing their hoods so as to be ready for a flight, Petre (who loved to fly his hawks himself) left the company at a short distance, and dismounting approached the heron, being careful to keep under the wind, and concealing himself behind his horse.

At last the wary heron spied him, and, slowly rising, left the siege. As soon as he had flown a couple of hundred yards, the falcons were unhooded and cast off. Old Joan sighted him at once, the other falcon joined in, and the flight began.

The heron took in the position at a glance. The heronry lay up-wind, and was distant at least two miles. He could never succeed in making this point, flying in the teeth of the wind and pursued by two swift and eager falcons. The country on every side was bare, and afforded no prospect of shelter. Driven from earth in despair, he sought shelter in the clouds. Lightening himself by throwing overboard the result of the morning's fishing, he ascended to the heavens in spiral curves, making wide circuits as he mounted aloft. The higher the heron mounted, the higher soared the falcons. This is what the old falconers celebrate under the name of the 'mountey.' What circles they describe! There goes old Joan. Turning her back on the quarry, she rushes into the wind for full half a mile, and then, sweeping round in a vast circle, is carried high above the heron. The company can see them still, but it takes a sharp eye to 'know a hawk from a handsaw,' [1] even though the wind is southerly. If it were north-north-westerly, the birds, carried forward by the wind, would fly between the spectator and the sun, and to tell hawk from heron would be harder still. [2] They can just see

[1] *Hamlet*, ii. 2. 397.

[2] The heron was also called heronshaw (heronsewe in Chaucer's *Squier's Tale*, and herounsew in John Russell's *Boke of Nurture*, circ. 1430), easily corrupted into handsaw. Shakespeare does not hesitate to put into the mouths of his characters vulgar corruptions of ordinary language, current in the stable or in the field. Thus Lord Sands talks of springhalt (stringhalt), and Biondello of fashions (farcy) and fives (vives). In the edition of *Hamlet* by Mr. Clarke

old Joan close her wings, and precipitate herself with fell swoop
on the heron.   By a swift movement he narrowly escapes
the blow.   Meanwhile the second falcon has mounted over
both.   Stooping downward she dashes a few feathers from
the heron's wing, and drives him nearer to the earth.   Old
Joan, by ringing into the wind, has more than recovered her
advantage, and is preparing for a deadly stoop.   The three
birds are now nearer to the ground, and in full view of the
company, who have followed as best they could, on foot and
on horseback, the course of the flight, carried by the wind
about a mile from the spot where the heron was found.
They are in time to see the finish.   Joan's second swoop hit
the heron hard.   Her mate renews the attack.   In a moment
Joan is bound to the heron.   The second falcon comes in,
and the three birds descend steadily to the ground.

The falcons have learned by experience to let go the
heron as they approach the ground.   They thus avoid concus-
sion, and the danger of being spitted by the heron on
his sharp, sword-like bill—a formidable weapon of defence.
But the contest on the ground, which might have been
fraught with danger to the falcons, was soon put an end to by
the falconer, who seized the heron, and rewarding the falcons,
hooded them, and restored them to the cadge.

Then followed some flights at the brook.   This sport, in

and Mr. Aldis Wright, we find the suggestion that the north-westerly wind would
carry the hawk and the handsaw between the falconer and the sun, with the consequence that they would be indistinctly seen, while it would be easy to tell
the difference between them when the wind was southerly.   I believe this to be
the origin of the saying.   It was probably a common one in Shakespeare's time,
which naturally fell out of use with the practice of falconry.   In aid of this
suggestion, I may add that in an article on *Falconry in the British Isles* in the
Quarterly Review (1875), an account of a flight at the heron is quoted from an
old French writer, who describes the heronshaw as mounting directly towards
the sun, *pour se couvrier de la clarté*.   The soothsayer in *Cymbeline* (iv. 2. 350)
notes as a portent that Jove's bird, the Roman eagle, ' vanished in the sunbeams.'
This annoyance must have occurred constantly on a bright morning with a
strong north-north-westerly wind.   The angler who, under similar conditions, in
order to have the wind in his favour, fishes with the glare of the sun in his eyes,
can sympathise with Hamlet when he describes himself as ' mad north-north-
west.'   When the wind is southerly he can tell a rise from a ripple.

the opinion of some, ranked higher than heron hawking. For, as Turbervile says, ' although it [a flight at ye hearon] be the most noblest and stately flight that is, and pleasant to behold, yet is there no suche art or industrie therein as in the other flights. For the hawke fleeth the hearon moved by nature, as against hir proper foe ; but to the river she fleeth as taught by the industrie and diligēce of the falconer.'

Whatever be the cause, I can find in the diary no record of the sport, and I must console myself with the knowledge that flights at the brook did not differ essentially from those in the field at partridge, although the mallard, being larger and stronger on the wing, afforded better sport, and, indeed, could not be successfully flown except by well-trained haggard falcons.

CHAPTER XIII

A DEAD LANGUAGE

Talking of hawking. . . . *Second Part of King Henry VI.*

SHORTLY before eleven o'clock—the dinner hour at Petre Manor—the company reassembled in the old court-yard. Petre could, as we know, give an excellent account of the morning's sport. He was in high spirits, not only on this account, but by reason of some intelligence rapidly conveyed to him by his wife, who rode into the court-yard with her party shortly after the rest of the company had returned from flying at the brook. It is needless to say that they had nothing to show in the way of results, and Petre would doubtless have made merry at their expense, had he not feared to arouse suspicions in the mind of Will Squele. For the performances of Petre's merlins were well known to every Cotswold man, and the Lady Katherine and Anne Squele were too expert in the gentle art of falconry to come back empty-handed, had there not been some good reasons for the marring of their sport.

A few words sufficed to put William Silence in possession of Petre's scheme, and of the arrangements which Katherine had made with Anne for carrying it into effect. It only remained for William to make the necessary preparations on his part, and for all to meet at the solemn hunting of the deer with cross-bow and greyhound, proclaimed by the Justice for the following day.

The details of this scheme are so interwoven with the nature of the sport in which they were to engage, that I deem it best to allow the Justice's plot and Petre's counter-plot to unfold themselves side by side with the incidents of the solemn hunting. I do so the more readily inasmuch as, in not anticipating the events of the morrow, I am following the example of the diarist, from whose notes I can gather little beyond the facts that he excused himself from staying to dinner with his friends, and busied himself in preparation for what was to prove the most eventful day in his life.

Scanty as are the notes of the diarist, they may have served to impart to the reader some knowledge of the favourite sport of our forefathers—a pursuit interesting in itself, and deserving special attention, inasmuch at it has left its mark plainly traceable on the literature of the Elizabethan age. Even those who cared nothing for the sport do not fail to bear witness in their writings to the estimation in which falconry along with the other sports of the field—but in a pre-eminent degree—was then generally held.

Each popular sport or pastime tends to develop a language of its own, affected by its votaries, but generally distasteful to the outside public. The non-sporting guest at a country house in a hunting county, or the uninitiated visitor at a golfing hotel, conscious of missing the point of tales and allusions, commonly falls into the error of hurling at the offending sport the strong condemnation which ought to be directed against his own ignorance.

The language of falconry was picturesque, unique, and lent itself readily to poetical imagery. It was borrowed by men of letters, and affected by men of fashion, at one of the most interesting periods of our history. Incorporated with the literature of the day, it forms part of our inheritance from the Elizabethan age. As a sporting language it is long since dead ; although, like Latin, it may be spoken here and there by a few learned professors. But three hundred years ago 'small Latin' was not more fatal to the reputation of a scholar than was ignorance of the language of falconry to the character of a gentleman. To 'speak the hawking language' was, according to Ben Jonson, affected by those 'newer men,' who aped the manners of the older gentry.[1]

[1] *Speech according to Horace.*

It was to qualify himself for gallants' company by skill in this tongue that Master Stephen, having bought a hawk, hood and bells, desired a book to keep it by.[1] For those who were not to the manner born had to acquire this language by painful study. Hence the immense popularity and ready sale of books of sport in the Elizabethan age, a subject dealt with at greater length in a note.[2]

Even those who professed ignorance or dislike of the sport are found writing in the language of the day. Sir Philip Sidney is credited with the saying that of all sports, next to hunting, he hated hawking most.[3] And yet in Arcadia the falcon and goshawk are flown and the ' Sport of Heron ' is affected by princes. Nor does he ignore the detested sport of hunting. For the stag is pursued with hounds, 'their crie being composed of so well-sorted mouths that any man would perceive therein som kinde of proportion, but the skilful woodmen did finde a music.'

Spenser may have been of the same mind with his friend and patron Sidney. But his pages prove that he was well skilled in the hawking language, and many apt illustrations evidence familiarity with the sport.

The traces of this forgotten tongue discernible in the prose and poetry of the sixteenth and seventeenth centuries take the form, sometimes of set descriptions, and oftener of incidental allusion. Of the former, the best known are Drayton's description of the sport of flying at the brook, in the twentieth song of his *Polyolbion* (1612–22) ; Nash's oft-quoted passage in praise of hawking in *Quaternio ; or, a*

---

[1] *Every Man in his Humour.*   [2] See Note, *The Book of Sport.*

[3] The following passage in Spenser's *Elegy* upon the death of Sir Philip Sidney, under the name of Astrophel, may, in its curious language, refer to Sidney's professions, as it certainly does to his practice, with regard to field sports :

> Besides, in hunting such felicitie,
> Or rather infelicitie he found,
> That every field and forest far away
> He sought, where salvage beasts do most abound :
> No beast so salvage but he could it kill,
> No chase so hard, but he therein had skill.

Fourefold Way to a Happy Life (1633); Massinger's lifelike picture of the sport in which we have taken part with Master Petre of flying at the ' hearon put from her seige ' and at 'the partridge ' sprung in *The Guardian* (1633); Heywood's colloquy between two lovers of falconry in *A Woman Killed with Kindness,* with its profusion of technicality suggestive of careful study in the book of sport; and Fletcher's imitation of Shakespeare's falconry, in his sequel to the *Taming of the Shrew,* entitled *The Woman's Prize.*

Elaborate descriptions of this kind introduced for a set purpose afford little evidence of practical knowledge of the sport; of which indeed Drayton confessed ignorance in his *Illustrations* prefixed to the fifth song of *Polyolbion.*   More suggestive are the casual illustrations and the borrowed phraseology which we light on here and there, often where we should least expect them. ' Since I was of understanding to know we know nothing, my reason hath been more pliable to the will of faith : I am now content to understand a mystery without a rigid definition in an easy and Platonic description.' [1] Here we recognise Sir Thomas Browne the philosopher; but when he adds ' and thus I teach my haggard and unreclaimed reason to stoop into the lure of truth,' the sportsman stands confessed ; and the further thought is suggested that the falconer sets more store on one reclaimed haggard than on many eyesses that need no reclaiming.

In was no doubt a kindly remembrance of his early years at Montgomery Castle, where he learned the proverb ' the gentle hawk half mans herself,'[2] that suggested to the saintly George Herbert, writing a poem on Providence, the thought, ' Birds teach us hawking.'

It so happens that not one of the playwrights between whose authorship and that of Shakespeare controversy has arisen among critics, gives any proof of practical interest in falconry, or in any other sport of the field.   It had been well for them and for letters if it had been otherwise.   But the dissipation of town life had stronger attractions.   Marlowe

---

[1] *Religio Medici,* 1642.   [2] *Iacula Prudentum.*

—son of a Canterbury shoemaker—was killed in a tavern brawl in his thirtieth year; but not until he had, in his mighty line, created English blank verse, and given the world a richer harvest of finished work than Shakespeare at the same time of life, though not such rare buds of promise. Greene, before he took his degree at Cambridge, travelled in Italy and Spain, where he practised ' such villainy as is abominable to declare,' and after a chequered career as schoolmaster, student of physic, priest and dramatist, died miserably at about the same age as Marlowe, denouncing with his dying breath, as an upstart crow beautified with his feathers, one who bestowed upon poor Greene and his revilings the rather doubtful boon of immortality, in return for some indifferent plays adapted to his use. Fletcher was son of a Bishop of London, at one time a favourite of the Queen's, of whom we read that he was especially skilled in riding the great horse. The dramatist died of the plague at the age of forty-nine, and little is known of his private life. His plays show that he had skill in hawking language, as we should expect from his birth and breeding, but he gives little evidence of interest in this or in any other field sport. His occasional allusions to sport have not—except in the single instance already mentioned, where he deliberately and avowedly imitated Shakespeare's work—the unmistakable flavour which distinguishes the thoroughly Shakespearian allusion, and they are usually introduced with an evident view to dramatic effect. ' Sporting Kyd ' has not made good his title to the character pleasantly bestowed on him by Ben Jonson, so far as his language is concerned.

Now, inasmuch as Marlowe, Greene, Fletcher and Kyd happen to be the dramatists whose workmanship needs to be discriminated from Shakespeare, it follows that any points of contrast become of importance. I have in a note pursued the train of thought thus suggested, and pointed out a use which may be served by Shakespeare's allusions to field sports and kindred matters, by way of test, and in aid of criticism, when it has to be decided whether any particular play or passage is the work of Shakespeare or of some contemporary dramatist.

It was not until late in life that Ben Jonson—town bred by his stepfather, a master bricklayer—was introduced to a sport, the strange fascination of which he had often noted with wonder. He was not surprised when Master Stephen bought a hawk, hood and bells, and lacked nothing but a book, whereby he might keep his hawk and learn the hawking language; for Master Stephen was a fool. But when he found a wise man seriously follow hawking he could not understand it, until one day he visited in Warwickshire Sir Henry Goodyere, a gentleman of the King's Privy Chamber, the friend and patron of Drayton, described by Camden as ' a knight memorable for his virtues,' to whom he writes :

> Goodyere, I'm glad, and grateful to report
> Myself a witness of thy few days sport;
> Where I both learn'd why wise men hawking follow,
> And why that bird was sacred to Apollo :
> She doth instruct men by her gallant flight,
> That they to knowledge so should tower upright,
> And never stoop, but to strike ignorance ;
> Which if they miss yet they should re-advance
> To former height, and there in circle tarry
> Till they be sure to make the fool their quarry.[1]

Who were these wise men, whose love of hawking amazed Ben Jonson ? I know of one, who in all respects answers the description; that wise man, namely, of whom Jonson wrote in his *Discoveries*, 'I loved the man, and do honour his memory, on this side idolatry, as much as any.'

There was, indeed, in the Elizabethan age, another wise man of transcendent genius, also well known to Jonson, who happened to be a man of birth and breeding, but who differed from his fellows in his attitude towards the sports and pastimes of the day, and in whose mind the allusions collected in these pages would have excited no emotion, unless it were one of distaste. When Francis Bacon took all knowledge for his

---

[1] *Epigrams.*

province, his *omne scibile* comprehended none of the
mysteries in which the writer of these passages found
unceasing delight. This is not to be wondered at. The
'age between sixteen and three and twenty'[1] was passed by
him in pursuits far different from those which engaged the
lifelong affection of Shakespeare. Had he been so inclined,
the delicacy of his health in early life would have forbidden
him to indulge in violent exercises. We should not have
looked for any indication of such tastes, had he possessed
them, in his philosophical works; although I doubt that
Shakespeare could have written the *Natural History*, or
the *New Atlantis*, without his speech in some degree
bewraying him. It is in Bacon's *Essays*—the recreation (as
he calls them) of his other studies—that we expect to find
evidence of his lighter pursuits. And so it is. He writes
lovingly of gardens, trees, flowers, aviaries, and fountains.
He discourses on foreign travel, and condescends to such toys
as masques, triumphs, dancing, and acting to song; but he
never writes of horse, hawk, or hound. In the essay on
Building, indeed, at the end of a long list of possible wants
in a site for a great mansion, he mentions 'want of places at
some near distance for sports of hunting, hawking, and races.'
But beyond this general and almost inevitable reference to
field sports, and a very commonplace reference to the greyhound and the hare in the essay on *Discourse*, he has nothing
to tell us about any of them, not even when he speaks of the
exercises proper to be taken for the regimen of health and
in aid of studies, a topic which led the studious recluse,
Burton, to discourse with interest—though as an outsider—
on hawking, hunting and fishing as cures for melancholy, and
inspired him to expand Dame Juliana Barnes' commendation of angling into a passage not unworthy of Isaac
Walton.[2]

---

[1] *Wint. Tale*, iii. 3. 59.

[2] 'But he that shall consider the variety of baits, for all seasons, and pretty
devices which our anglers have invented, peculiar lines, false flyes, severall
sleights, &c., will say that it deserves like commendation, requires as much study
and perspicuity as the rest, and is to be preferred before many of them; because

Bacon's attitude towards field sports, so far as it can be gathered from his writings and from the known course of his life, was probably that of his kinsman Burleigh, of whom Fuller tells the following tale : ' When some noblemen had gotten William Cecil, lord Burleigh and Treasurer of England, to ride with them a hunting, and the sport began to be cold : "What call you this ? " said the Treasurer. "Oh, now,"said they, "the dogs are at fault." "Yea," quoth the Treasurer, "take me again in such a fault, and I'll give you leave to punish me ! " Thus as soon may the same meat please all palates as the same sport suit with all dispositions.'

Sudden and complete was the downfall of hawking and of the hawking language. Falconry naturally declined during the years of the civil war and the Commonwealth, with other sports and pastimes. But in the case of this sport—once the great national field sport of England—its revival after the Restoration was but an expiring flicker. No stronger evidence of its decay could be given than the fact that in the year 1718 a book entitled the *Compleat Sportsman* was published by one Giles Jacob, in which he states that he took no notice of the diversion of hawking, because it was so much disused in his time, ' especially since sportsmen are arrived at such perfection in shooting.' Hedgerows and enclosures have taken part with gun and dog in the extinction of falconry, and although there never has been a time when hawks were not flown by lovers of the sport in some part of the British Isles, it cannot be said to have ranked among our national field sports during the last two centuries.

But although the falcon, and the gentle art to which she

hawking and hunting are very laborious, much riding and many dangers accompany them ; but this is still and quiet ; and if so be the angler catch no fish, yet he hath a wholesome walk to the brook side, pleasant shade by the sweet silver stream ; he hath good ayr, and sweet smells of fine fresh meadow flowers ; he hears the melodious harmony of birds ; he sees the swans, herons, ducks, water-hens, coots, &c., and many other fowl with their brood, which he thinketh better than the noyse of hounds or blast of horns, and all the sport that they make ' (*Anatomy of Melancholy*, Part 2, ii. 4).

gave her name, are too picturesque in their accessories, and lend themselves too readily to poetic treatment, to lose their place in literature, they hold it with a difference. Dryden is the latest English classic who writes the hawking language with the accuracy of Chaucer, Spenser, and Shakespeare. Thenceforward the noble falcon is unsexed and degraded to the level of her tercel; surely because it was men who held the pen. Such an outrage could not have been perpetrated in an age of falconry. You will always find it tacitly assumed by the lords of creation, in the absence of practical experience, that the falcon must needs be of their sex; such is the innate nobility of the bird.

Homer loves to compare the earthward descent of his goddesses to the downward swoop of the long-winged (τανυπτέρυγι) hawk. He was far too keen an observer of the animal world, especially in its relation to sport, to overlook the superiority of the female of the race, if it had been made manifest to him in practical experience. When, therefore, we find that his falcons are males, we may fairly infer that the language, as well as the art, of the falconer was unknown in the Grecian communities among whom he lived.[1]

Scott had, in common with Homer and with Shakespeare, an intense love of nature and of country life; a sentiment which is, according to him, a common feature of genius.[2] He was a sportsman, too, although less catholic in his tastes than Shakespeare. When, therefore, we find his goshawks

---

[1] ἴρηξ (translated 'falcon' in Liddell and Scott's *Lexicon*) is masculine. George Chapman, translating the *Iliad* in 1602, when the hawking language was still a living one, could not think or write of a falcon otherwise than as a female, and instinctively restored her proper sex; thus rendering the Greek words descriptive of the quarry upon which ἴρηξ ὠκύπτερος is described as swooping (ὄρνεον ἄλλο), ' a fowl not being of *her* kind ' (*Il.* xiii. 62). The hawk called κίρκος, also a long-winged hawk, is ἐλαφρότατος πετεηνῶν (Il. xxii. 139) and δεξιὸς ὄρνις (*Odyss.* xv. 525). In Latin *falco* and *accipiter* are both masculine. I have not been able to fix the period in the development of the English tongue and of the art of falconry, when the nobler bird appropriated to herself the name of falcon. In Chaucer's *Assembly of Fowles*, the falcon is female, and her mate a tercelet, the form in which the word still appears in French.

[2] *Life of Swift.*

soaring high, and hovering, after the fashion of a long-winged falcon towering in her pride of place, and when we note that his 'falcons' are often males,[1] even if flown at the heron (a flight only to be essayed with a cast of haggard falcons), we need no further evidence that falconry was unknown in his time ; and from this and other tokens we may infer that he was less attracted by the sports and pastimes of antiquity than by other features of those bygone times which he has reproduced with such lifelike reality—a unique example in letters of an antiquary inspired by the creative genius of a poet.

The language of hawking must now, like the dead tongues of antiquity, be painfully acquired by laborious research. And here the student encounters peculiar difficulties. If in his study of Homer he would learn the precise meaning of some unfamiliar word, he turns to his *Liddell and Scott* in full assurance of finding the necessary explanation and illustrations. Reading his *Faerie Queen*, he meets the word tassel-gent, and is informed by Mr. Todd in a foot-note, accurately, but irrelevantly, that 'tassell is the male of goshawk.' If he has brought to his literary studies some knowledge of natural history, it strikes him as strange that Juliet should choose as the type of her lover the male of an inferior race of hawks. To remove all doubt as to the accuracy of his information he consults Nares's *Glossary*, a work specially designed for the illustration of Shakespeare. There he reads ' Tassel, or Tassel-gentle. The male of the goss-hawk, properly tiercel, supposed to be called gentle from

---

[1] In *The Abbot, Ivanhoe,* and *Rob Roy.* It is really as incorrect to call a falcon 'he' as to speak of a bull as 'she,' and yet illustrious examples in letters might be cited as authorities for the solecism. For example, Tennyson published a poem entitled *The Falcon,* of which the noble bird is the central figure, and consistently a male. In a poem by Mr. William Morris bearing the same name, the same unsexing occurs ; and even the great lexicographer thus misquotes a line from Macbeth, 'A falcon towering in his pride of place.' In time these examples may justify the use of the word 'falcon' as a neutral term, but hitherto neither dictionaries nor writers on natural history give any sanction to an abuse of language which breaks the continuity of literary usage, and falsifies the traditions of an ancient and picturesque national pastime.

its docile and tractable disposition,' and Juliet's meaning
utterly eludes his grasp.

Fully assured by the passages quoted at page 150 that
the word ' bate ' conveyed to the minds of the speakers some
definite meaning upon which they thought it worth while to
dwell, and even to play, he turns for enlightenment to the
works of a recognised authority, Mr. Strutt.   He reads in
Sports and Pastimes of the English People that a hawk
was said to bate 'when she fluttered her wings to fly after
her game.'   His perplexity is not lessened when the same
authority informs him, in the glossary to *Queen Hoo Hall*,
that ' when a hawk is said to bate, he leaves the game.'

Mr. Strutt's authority as an antiquary stands high, and
he has certainly collected, in his various works, a great deal
of interesting information.   But in regard to falconry and all
other mediæval field sports, he is a most untrustworthy
guide.   His romance, *Queen Hoo Hall*, is interesting from
the fact that it was completed and edited by Scott, whose
well-known hunting song, 'Waken lords and ladies gay,'
shines as a gem of purest ray serene in a rather indifferent
setting.   If this earliest essay (1808) turned Scott's mind in
the direction of romance-writing, the world owes to Strutt a
debt which may well outweigh many heresies in falconry and
woodcraft,[1] such as we should not have expected to find in a
tale written by a professed antiquary.

When professed antiquaries confuse a hawk's jesses with

---

[1] Different kinds of hounds and of deer are mixed up in inextricable confusion.   For example, ' ban dogs ' are confounded with hounds.   ' A hart
(sic) of the second year,' described as a ' velvet-headed knobbler,' breaks cover
instead of the harboured stag.   This latter was ' a buck (sic) of the first head ; '
it is coursed by greyhounds for a couple of miles, and afterwards by ' a
sufficient number of slowhounds.'   It would be easy to fill pages with equally
absurd explanations of old-world sporting terms, extracted from various notes
and glossaries.   They are of little significance, save when they mar the point
of a simile or allusion.   If, for instance, ' jesses ' meant ' the leathers that fasten
on the hawks' bells ' (as explained by Mr. Church in a note to the *Faerie Queen*)
a beautiful and familiar passage would have absolutely no significance.   It
is satisfactory to note that the glossary to the edition of Shakespeare in
most general use (*The Globe* edition) is generally the most accurate in matters
of falconry and woodcraft.

her bells; when so keen a sportsman as the author of *The Moor and the Loch* tells us that of Scottish hawks 'the largest is the goshawk, the young males of which are called falcon-gentles, and were once thought a distinct species;'[1] and when even Charles Kingsley's peregrine, forgetful of tower and stoop, shot 'out of the reeds like an arrow' after the manner of a short-winged hawk, and having 'singled one luckless mallard for the block, caught him up, struck him stone dead with one blow of his terrible heel, and swept his prey with him into the reeds again,'[2] we need not marvel at the mistakes of lesser men. But it is worth noting that the hawking language, once spoken by the card with absolute accuracy, is the only dead language of antiquity which it is considered allowable to write without any regard to the meaning of its words; an indulgence which authors are tempted to allow themselves, partly from consciousness of the ignorance of their readers, and partly by reason of the vague, pleasurable ideas of mediæval sport and gallantry associated with its terminology, however recklessly misapplied.[3]

It is a pleasanter task to point out where a knowledge of this dead tongue may be acquired. Mr. Harting's *Ornithology of Shakespeare* is the work of a practical falconer, who has in his *Bibliotheca Accipitraria* applied himself to the historical and antiquarian aspect of the sport. The study of Mr. Lascelles' contribution to the Badminton Library, of Messrs. Salvin and Brodrick's *Falconry in the British Isles*, Messrs. Freeman and Salvin's *Falconry*, and Mr. Freeman's *How I became a Falconer* among the modern, and among the older writers, of the works of Turbervile, Latham, and Bert, will supply all that is necessary for literary purposes.

---

[1] *The Moor and the Loch, containing minute instructions in all Highland Sports*, by John Colquhoun.

[2] *Hereward the Wake*, chap. xx.

[3] Dr. Drake, in his valuable work on *Shakespeare and his Times*, describes the haggard as 'a species of hawk wild and difficult to be reclaimed.'

Those who have pursued such a course of study, and thus
miliarised themselves with the tongue, have detected various
ces of the hawking language scattered through the works
Shakespeare.   Many terms of art employed by him with
ultless accuracy have been explained and illustrated in the
regoing pages.   Others of less obvious significance are
llected in a note entitled *The Language of Falconry.*

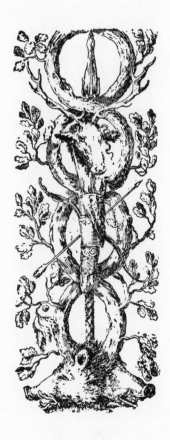

CHAPTER XIV

THE TAKING OF THE DEER

Ros. Well, then, I am the shooter.
Boyet. And who is your deer? *Love's Labour's Lost.*

'IT is a thievish forme of hunting to shoote with gunnes
and bowes, and greyhounde hunting is not so martial a
game' as 'the hunting with running houndes,' which is
'the most honourable and noblest sort thereof.'

This saying is part of the 'kingly gift' bestowed on his
ill-fated son by the British Solomon, who added to his skill
in kingcraft a knowledge of woodcraft which might, had
we power to test it, prove equally profound.

The sentiment may be just, but it would not have been
approved in Gloucestershire. In that county, indeed, if we
may believe its historian, a kind of hunting more thievish
still was winked at, and if there be any truth in the story that
Shakespeare took refuge with kinsfolk in Gloucestershire
after a misadventure in the matter of deer, he could not
have fled to a better sanctuary.[1]

---

[1] 'The last anecdote I have to record of this chase [Michaelwood] shows
that some of the principal persons in this county (whose name I suppress
where the family is still in existence) were not ashamed of the practice of
deer-stealing. Henry Parmiter of Stone, an Attorney-at-Lawe; Giles . . .
then of Stone, Attorney-at-law; Giles . . . then of . . . George Smallwod,
then of Dursley, and seven others, all men of metall and good woodmen (I mean
old notorious deer-stealers) came in the night time to Michaelwood with deer-
nets and dogs to steele deer' (Fosbrooke's *History of Gloucestershire*, quoting

But, indeed, the taking of a deer was in those days nowhere regarded as a serious offence, except possibly by him to whom the deer belonged. It ranked distinctly higher than cony-catching, and yet Simple evidently regarded it as a feather in his master's cap that he had 'fought with a warrener.'[1] No offence was intended to Aaron the Moor, but rather the contrary, when it was asked of him,

> What, hast thou not full often struck a doe,
> And borne her cleanly by the keeper's nose?
>
> *Tit. Andr.* ii. 1. 93.

The reformed deer-stealer would, in after life, speak of his escapades, much as Mr. Robert Sawyer or Mr. Benjamin Allen might relate the capture of an occasional knocker in the hot days of youth. 'There is another kinde of coursing,' the author of the *Noble Arte of Venerie* is not ashamed to write, 'which I have more used than any of these; and that is at a deare in the night; wherein there is more arte to be used thā in any course els. But because I have promised my betters to be a friend to al Parkes Forrests and Chaces, therefore I will not here expresse the experience which hath bene deerer unto me, particularly, that it is meete to be published generally.' 'To steal deer' was classed with robbing orchards, carousing in taverns, and dancing about maypoles, as belonging to a class of exploits—venial in unruly youths, but unfit for grave scholars.[2] 'Our old race of deer-stealers,' wrote Gilbert White, 'are hardly extinct yet; it was but a little while ago that over their ale they used to recount the exploits of their youth.' About the beginning of the century, 'unless he was a hunter, as they affected to call themselves, no young person was allowed to be possessed of manhood or gallantry.'[3]

It is, however, in the lawful taking of deer with cross-

Smith MS.). Mr. Malone, in his *Life of Shakespeare*, has collected several passages illustrative of the opinion of the age as regards deer-stealing and kindred adventures.

[1] *Merry Wives*, i. 4. 28.

[2] *Overthrow of Stage Playes*, 1599.   [3] *Nat. Hist. of Selborne.*

bow and greyhound that we are about to engage, a pastime
upon which in the days of our diarist no cloud of royal
disfavour rested, for it is recorded of Elizabeth that on
one day in the year 1591, at Cowdray in Sussex, her grace
saw from a turret ' sixteen bucks, all having fayre lawe,
pulled downe with greyhounds in a laund or lawn.' [1] It was
also highly appreciated by her subjects for practical reasons.
For as Sir Thomas Elyot had remarked some years before,
' kylling of dere with bowes or grehunds serveth well for
the potte (as in the commune saynge), and therefore it muste
of necessitie be some tyme used. But,' he adds, ' it contayneth
therin no commendable solace or exercise, in comparison
to the other fourme of hunting, if it be diligently perceiued.'

The solemn hunting, big with the fate of William
Silence, as well as of many a fat and seasonable buck, had
been proclaimed in honour of Petre and his bride. It was
customary with the lords of the manor of Shallow periodi-
cally to announce an observance of this kind, not only for
love of sport and venison, but in order to assert their lawful
rights. For by the custom of the manor each tenant was
bound to find one man three times a year to drive the deer
to a stand, to be taken whenever the lord should please.[2]
This particular hunting, however, was designed by the
Justice to serve a further purpose. It was intended to afford
an opportunity to Abraham Slender of pressing his suit,
and finally securing Anne beyond possibility of escape. The
conditions under which the sport was practised rendered it
suitable for such a purpose, and also for the counter-plot
designed by Master Petre, who looked forward with eagerness
to the enjoyment of seeing the engineer hoist with his own
petard, especially when that engineer was Master Shallow.

Meanwhile, it is needful to know something about the
sport, in order to understand how readily it lent itself to the

---

[1] Nichols's *Progresses.*

[2] The burgesses of Bishop's Castle held of the See of Hereford by a similar
tenure : ' Omnes Burgenses de Bishop's Castle in com. Salop. debent invenire
unum hominem ter per annum, ad Stabliamentum pro venatione capienda,
quando Episcopus voluerit ' (Blount's *Antient Tenures*).

designs of the opposing parties. This knowledge is not easy of attainment, for the killing of deer in a pale with crossbows and greyhounds is a thing of the past, and the books of sport treat generally of hunting the deer with running hounds, and do not concern themselves with the details of a pastime, which, indeed, needed no explanation to contemporary Englishmen.

You may, however, obtain all necessary information from Shakespeare, for throughout his life he loved to dwell upon the sport and its humours.

In his earliest comedy, *Love's Labour's Lost*, you may find a lively picture of the pastime ; in the eyes of Sir Nathaniel, ' Very reverend sport, truly ; and done in the testimony of a good conscience.' [1] It was on the death of the deer killed by the Princess of France—' a buck of the first head,' according to Sir Nathaniel, but only ' a pricket' in the eyes of the matter-of-fact Dull—that Holofernes composed an 'extemporal epitaph,' in which he tells us : ' To humour the ignorant, call I the deer the princess killed a pricket.' [2]

The preyful princess pierced and prick'd a pretty pleasing pricket,
  Some say a sore ; but not a sore, till now made sore with shooting.
The dogs did yell ; put L to sore, then sorel jumps from thicket
  Or pricket sore, or else sorel, the people fall a-hooting.
If sore be sore, then L to sore makes fifty sores one sorel.
Of one sore I an hundred make by adding but one more L.
                                        Love's L. L. iv. 2. 58.

And in the earliest tragedy the composition of which is in any degree Shakespeare's, a ' general hunting ' [3] is recog-

---

[1] *Love's L. L.* iv. 2. 1.   [2] *Ibid.* 49.

[3] This would seem to mean a hunting, not only with cross-bow and greyhound, but with running hounds also. Aaron points to the former when he speaks of singling out and striking home a dainty doe ; Titus Andronicus to the latter, in the words,

  The hunt is up, the morn is bright and grey,
  The fields are fragrant and the woods are green :
  Uncouple here, and let us make a bay.   ii. 2. 1.

Holinshed writes of ' a genrall huntyng with a toyle raysed, of foure or five

nised by Aaron the Moor as affording rare opportunity for strategy and wile.

> My lords, a solemn hunting is in hand ;
> There will the lovely Roman ladies troop :
> The forest walks are wide and spacious ;
> And many unfrequented plots there are
> Fitted by kind for rape and villainy ;
> Single you thither then this dainty doe,
> And strike her home by force, if not by words ;
> This way, or not at all, stand you in hope.
>
> *Tit. Andr.* ii. 1. 112.

Nor did advancing years or London life quench his passion for the sport. It would seem to have gained new strength after he had finally taken up his abode at Stratford, for again in *Cymbeline*, one of his latest plays, as in his earliest, we find a hunting proclaimed with all the rites of woodcraft. ' Up to the mountains,' cries Belarius to Cymbeline's disguised sons ;

> he that strikes
> The venison first shall be the lord o' the feast ;
> To him the other two shall minister ;
> And we will fear no poison, which attends
> In place of greater state.   *Cymb.* iii. 3. 73.

And when the sport is over,

> You, Polydore, have proved best woodman, and
> Are master of the feast.   Cadwal and I
> Will play the cook and servant, 'tis our match.
>
> *Ibid.* iii. 6. 28.

It is fortunate that we can draw upon this storehouse of information, for the diarist was too much occupied with the main issue of the day to note the incidents of sport, and these pages would be well-nigh blank, had not its events been recorded by another chronicler.

The scene of the hunting was the park into which the great hart should have been driven on the memorable day of the chase across Cotswold, had not Abraham Slender other-myles in lengthe, so that many a deere that day was brought to the quarrie.' As to this meaning of the word quarry, see *post*, p. 245.

wise determined. Within the pale great numbers of fallow
deer were enclosed. In those days herds of deer of both kinds
—red as well as fallow—roamed at large, especially throughout woodland districts like Arden, where the 'poor dappled
fools' ranked as 'native burghers of this desert city.'[1] But
here and there a 'park ribbed and paled in' confined the
deer with barrier impassable, save by some errant buck, of
whom the keeper might say, as Adriana of her husband,

> too unruly deer, he breaks the pale
> And feeds from home.
>
> *Com. of Err.* ii. 1. 100.

We may learn from the instance of the Cotswold hart to
compare the fate of the deer confined within a pale, with the
chances of escape open to his fellow when hunted at force
across an unenclosed country ;—a thought which occurred to
the mind of Talbot, surrounded by the outnumbering hosts
of France :

> How are we park'd and bounded in a pale,
> A little herd of England's timorous deer,
> Mazed with a yelping kennel of French curs !
>
> 1 *Hen. VI.* iv. 2. 45.

There is, however, a difference, for

> Our Britain's harts die flying, not our men.
>
> *Cymb.* v. 3. 24.

In the 'chiefest thicket of the park' the Justice would
often take his stand, making his way thither, as did King
Edward and his huntsmen, 'under the colour of his usual
game.'[2]

For the sport, however, of hunting with cross-bow and
greyhound, a park like the Justice's was specially fitted.
The 'thick grown brake'[3] and close coppice afforded
abundant covert for the deer. Here and there were 'wide
forest walks,' and many a fair 'laund,' across which the
deer when driven presented a fair mark to the arrow of the
shooter. 'Then, forester, my friend,' asks the Princess,

---

[1] *As You L.* ii. 1. 22. [2] *3 Hen. VI.* iv. 5. 3, 11.

[3] *Ibid.* iii. 1. 1.

> where is the bush
> That we must stand and play the murderer in ?
>
> *Love's L. L.* iv. 1. 7.

We may learn the answer to this question from two keepers, as, in accordance with a stage direction, they enter a chase, with cross-bows in their hands, and thus converse :

First Keep. Under this thick-grown brake we'll shroud ourselves ;
For through this laund anon the deer will come,
And in this covert will we make our stand,
Culling the principal of all the deer.
Sec. Keep. I'll stay above the hill, so both may shoot.
First Keep. That cannot be ; the noise of thy cross-bow
Will scare the herd, and so my shoot is lost.
Here stand we both, and aim we at the best.

> 3 *Hen. VI.* iii. 1. 1.

'I am glad,' said Falstaff, when he saw that Ford's scheme for his discomfiture was not an unmixed success, as regards its author, 'though you have ta'en a special stand to strike at me, that your arrow hath glanced.' [1]

A special stand,[2] we now know, was a hiding place constructed in the thickest brake, commanding the laund across which the deer were expected to pass, and affording concealment, 'in the ambush' of which the shooter might 'strike home.' [3]

> Why hast thou gone so far,
> To be unbent when thou hast ta'en thy stand,
> The elected deer before thee ?   *Cymb.* iii. 4. 110.

Thus asked Imogen of Pisanio, when he failed to execute his deadly purpose. It was a question to be asked, for when the deer are driven by the stand, then comes the moment for action.

First you must choose aright, in woodcraft as in love ;

> When as thine eye hath chose the dame,
> And stall'd the deer that thou shouldst strike,
> Let reason rule things worthy blame.
>
> *The Passionate Pilgrim,* xix.

---

[1] *Merry Wives,* v. 5. 247.
[2] Cf. *Measure for M.* iv. 6. 10, which savours of woodcraft.
[3] *Measure for M.* i. 3. 41.

Unless this is done well, all will go ill. 'End thy ill aim before thy shoot be ended,' pleads Lucrece with Tarquin, appealing, but in vain, to the better instincts of woodcraft;

> He is no woodman that doth bend his bow
> To strike a poor unseasonable doe.
>
> *Lucrece*, 580.

At the time of the Justice's hunting, in the month of September, the skilled woodman, 'culling the principal of all the deer,' would pick out a 'buck, and of the season too.'[1] Later on in the year, when bucks were no longer seasonable venison, he would 'single out a dainty doe, And strike her home.'[2] He would stall as 'fat a deer' as might be, and one 'in blood';[3] no rascal, or worthless deer, a term of venery which has passed into common use as a word of reproach. In making this choice he must depend on his practised eye. You cannot judge by the antlers alone. As a rule the better the head, the fatter the deer. But there are exceptions, and you cannot always judge of the deer by his antlers. As Touchstone says,

> Horns? Even so. Poor men alone? No, no; the noblest deer hath them as huge as the rascal.[4]   *As You L.* iii. 3. 56.

But in shooting or coursing, 'at a deare in the night,' no such careful discrimination is possible, and, as Falstaff has it,

> When night-dogs run all sorts of deer are chased.
>
> *Merry Wives*, v. 5. 252.

Roger Ascham[5] compares 'a father that doth let loose his son to all experiences,' to 'a fond hunter that letteth slippe a whelpe to the hole herde. Twentie to one he shall fall vpon

---

[1] *Merry Wives*, iii. 3. 169.   [2] *Tit. Andr.* ii. 1. 117.
[3] 1 *Hen. IV.* v. 4. 107.
[4] Touchstone's intimate knowledge of woodcraft is illustrated by an incident of the deer-stalking season of 1893. A stag bearing twenty points on his antlers was shot in Glenquoich Forest by Lord Burton, who sent to the *Field* a drawing of the head, writing that the deer was ' in the worst condition I have ever seen, and covered with warbles.' He was, in short, a rascal, though bearing huger horns than the noblest deer that had fallen to the rifle within living memory.
[5] *Scholemaster*, 1570.

a rascall, and let go the faire game.   They that hunt so, be
either ignorant persones, preuie stealers, or night walkers.'

And the foremost deer, that leads the herd, may be a rascal
after all, and ' worst in blood to run ' if it came to the pinch.
For it is not the best of men, or of deer, that push themselves
in front of their fellows.   Thus said Menenius Agrippa to
the self-asserting citizen, whom he called the great toe of the
mutinous assembly :

> *Men.* For that, being one o' the lowest, basest, poorest,
>   Of this most wise rebellion, thou go'st foremost;
>   Thou rascal, that art worst in blood to run,
>   Lead'st first to win some vantage.   *Coriol.* i. 1. 161.

Hence we learn that it needs a wary and practised eye
to detect the rascality of the big-horned, self-asserting brute,
who to win some vantage thrusts himself in front of the
herd ; and herein consists the woodman's art.

Having stalled his deer, the hunter, if he be indeed a
woodman, will ' strike home,' and kill outright, for, as the
Princess of France tells the forester,[1]

>   mercy goes to kill,
>   And shooting well is then accounted ill.
>   Thus will I save my credit in the shoot ;
>   Not wounding, pity would not let me do't.
>   *Love's L. L.* iv. 1. 24.

In shooting with the cross-bow, it was no easy matter to
kill outright, and the wounded deer was a common incident
of the chase, and topic of discourse.

>   Why, let the stricken deer go weep,
>   The hart ungalled play ;
>   For some must watch, while some must sleep :
>   So runs the world away.   *Hamlet,* iii. 2. 282.

' I found her,' says Marcus Andronicus of poor Lavinia,
—ghastliest object in that ghastly tragedy—to his brother
Titus, who cannot refrain from a familiar pun,

---

[1] The same idea underlies the concluding lines of Sonnet cxxxix.

>   Since I am near slain,
>   Kill me outright with looks and rid my pain.

straying in the park,
Seeking to hide herself, as doth the deer
That hath received some unrecuring wound.
Tit. It was my deer; and he that wounded her
Hath hurt me more than had he kill'd me dead.
Tit. Andr. iii. 1. 88.

To course the wounded deer, greyhounds were held in
leash, close by the stands, 'swift as breathed stags, ay,
fleeter than the roe.'[1] And in an enclosed park, most of
the stricken deer were in this way picked up and saved from
a lingering death.

The venison thus obtained was accounted ill killed, a
matter of some moment when it was intended as a present
to bespeak good will, or 'bribe buck,' as it was commonly
called. 'Divide me like a bribe buck, each a haunch,' said
Falstaff to the merry wives; 'I will keep my sides to myself,
my shoulders for the fellow of this walk, and my horns I
bequeath your husbands. Am I a woodman, ha? Speak
I like Herne the hunter?'[2]

When last the Justice sought a wife for Abraham Slender,
and desired Master Page's consent to his marriage with
sweet Anne Page, he sought to obtain his good will by
sending him a bribe buck.

Page. I am glad to see your worships well. I thank you for
my venison, Master Shallow.
Shal. Master Page, I am glad to see you; much good do it
your good heart! I wished your venison better; it was ill killed.
Merry Wives, i. 1. 80.

But in the deep recesses of the unenclosed forest the
stricken deer, mortally wounded but not killed outright,
'their round haunches gored . . . with forked heads' were
doomed to a lingering death, such as that which moved
the melancholy Jaques to moralise on the spectacle of the
stricken hart in Arden, 'left and abandoned of his velvet[3]
friends.'

[1] *Tam. of Shr.* Ind. 2. 49.   [2] *Merry Wives*, v. 5. 27.
[3] The covering of the newly-grown antlers is called 'velvet.'

> ' Ay,' quoth Jaques,
> ' Sweep on, you fat and greasy citizens ;
> 'Tis just the fashion : wherefore do you look
> Upon that poor and broken bankrupt there ? '

It was a piteous sight, the death of the stricken deer :

> Under an oak whose antique root peeps out
> Upon the brook that brawls along this wood ;
> To the which place a poor sequester'd stag,
> That from the hunter's aim had ta'en a hurt,
> Did come to languish, and indeed, my lord,
> The wretched animal heaved forth such groans
> That their discharge did stretch his leathern coat
> Almost to bursting, and the big round tears
> Coursed one another down his innocent nose
> In piteous chase ; and thus the hairy fool,
> Much marked of the melancholy Jaques,
> Stood on the extremest verge of the swift brook,
> Augmenting it with tears.   *As You L*. ii. 1. 31.

It will have occurred even to those less evilly disposed than was Aaron the Moor, that the sport which we have described was one affording many opportunities for ' policy and stratagem.'

The Justice's stratagem was to place Anne in Abraham Slender's stand. There he was to press his suit. If she demurred, Slender was to get over her scruples by carrying her off bodily with the aid of William Visor, who owed the Justice a good turn and had in readiness a stout horse to carry them to his house at Woncot, where Sir Topaz waited to make them man and wife.

William Silence was to be disposed of by placing him in a distant stand with Petre and the Lady Katherine. It seemed clear to the wisdom of the Justice that the honour of the position assigned to him, and the duty of entertaining the principal guests, would keep him out of harm's way for the day. For himself, he would best provide for the amusement of the company by seeing to the driving of the deer, leaving the shooting of them to younger hands.

Petre's stratagem was equally simple. " Do you and

Mistress Anne take your stand in the same bush. Have a good horse in readiness. 'I have been with Sir Oliver Martext, the vicar of the next village,'[1] for I dared not to open the matter to Sir Topaz. He loveth not Sir Topaz, and is consumed with envy by reason of the portent and the church-ale. He will attend you at goodman Perkes's. There you may be made fast enough or ere you be missed to the hunting. Good lord, 'twill be rare sport when you present yourselves to the company assembled at the quarry of the slaughtered deer. I warrant you this day's work, if it be an evil one for the bucks, will make two hearts right merry. Nay, Master Silence, I mean not you and Mistress Anne. That remains for proof hereafter. But Master Squele will joy inwardly, and Master Slender will scarce refrain from rejoicing outwardly. This business of the Justice's was never to their minds."

"But in what manner will you dispose of Abraham Slender?" asked Silence. "It is true that his heart is not in the matter. But he is bound to do the Justice's will in this, as in other matters."

"Let him be put in the stand with my wife," said Petre, "a hundred marks my Kate will keep him still enough till all be over. She will discourse him so learnedly of bears, tell him such marvellous tales of Sackerson, and praise his woodcraft so discreetly, that he will forget all about Mistress Anne in his desire to display his skill in shooting before a lady of such excellent discernment."

To carry out this scheme, the aid of the forester was needed. It was by his directions that the company were to be conducted to the special stands assigned to them. This aid, however, might be bought. In those days (I write of three hundred years ago) there could be found foresters and keepers willing to accept gold at the hands of their masters' guests. 'Take this for telling true.' So saying, the Princess in *Love's Labour's Lost* rewards the forester, who leads her to what he describes as 'a stand where you may make the fairest

[1] *As You L.* iii. 3. 43.

shoot.'[1]   When Cloten would gain admittance to Imogen, he
bethinks him thus :

> I know her women are about her ; what
> If I do line one of their hands ?   'Tis gold
> Which buys admittance ; oft it doth ; yea, and makes
> Diana's rangers false themselves, yield up
> Their deer to the stand o' the stealer.
>
> *Cymb.* ii. 3. 71.

I know not whether this thought was suggested by the
venality of Master Shallow's forester.   But it is certain that
he was somehow induced to lend his aid.   It was arranged
that he should himself attend to the driving of the deer
leaving to assistants the placing of the company in their
stands.   Thus it would be easy to persuade the Justice afterwards that these varlets mistook his directions, and he would
escape scot free.

And now that we know something of the sport, and of
the plots and counter-plots to which it gave birth, let us
return to the never-to-be-forgotten spot where each of us
first made the acquaintance of the Gloucestershire Justices—
the court 'before Justice Shallow's house.'[2]   And when
you once again stand in the old court-yard, be not
surprised to find unchanged the stage direction, 'Enter
Shallow and Silence meeting.'   They have so met at any
time these fifty-five years, and have spoken the same words.
They would do so still, were they yet alive.

Shal. Come on, come on, come on, sir ; give me your hand, sir ;
give me your hand, sir ; an early stirrer, by the rood !   And how
doth my good cousin Silence ?
Sil. Good morrow, good cousin Shallow.

> 2 *Hen. IV.* iii. 2. 1.

There is no need for the Justice to inquire after his god-
daughter Ellen, or William, formerly of Oxford but now o
Gray's Inn, for they are here to answer for themselves, and
by some strange coincidence Master Ferdinand Petre arrives

---

[1] *Love's L. L.* iv. 1. 18.   [2] 2 *Hen. IV.* iii. 2.

in their company. The next arrivals who receive the effusive greetings of the Justice are Will Squele and his daughter Anne. Shortly afterwards the guests of the day, Master Petre and the Lady Katherine, ride into the court-yard, followed by attendants holding in leash a brace of greyhounds which had accompanied the Justice's invitation. This attention was customary where special honour was intended, and for some reason or other Petre was courted by the Justice with singular observance.

Third Serv. Please you, my lord, that honourable gentleman, Lord Lucullus, entreats your company to-morrow to hunt with him, and has sent your honour two brace of greyhounds.
Tim. I'll hunt with him; and let them be received,
Not without fair reward. *Timon. of Ath.* i. 2. 192.

Petre's enjoyment of the scene was due, no doubt, to the expectation of outwitting the Justice and his nephew—for he loved not your Shallows or your Slenders—and (in justice it ought to be added) to the prospect of serving a friend, and rescuing Anne Squele from the fate to which her father was ready to consign her.

" Good morning, Master Slender," said Petre, when he had escaped from the greetings of the Justice.

" Give you good morrow, sir," said Slender.

" By my word, Master Slender, you are indeed furnished as a hunter. Mistress Anne, have a care that he slay not a hart."

" Ha, ha, ha, most excellent, i' faith," said the Justice, " the word hart hath a double meaning. It signifieth the heart of man, or woman, too, for the matter of that, as well as a warrantable male of the red deer. Very singular good ; well said, Master Petre, well said."

" Master Slender," said Anne, " is too good a woodman to bestow a thought on ought but the deer when a solemn hunting is proclaimed."

" But," said Petre, " Mistress Anne, what if you be his deer? You know 'tis the burden of many an old song.

> For, O, love's bow
> Shoots buck and doe." [1]
>
> *Troil. and Cres.* iii. 1. 126.

"In faith, Mistress Anne says but the truth, for when a solemn hunting is proclaimed——"

I know not what awkward avowal on Slender's part was interrupted by the Justice.

"Ha, ha, ha, Master Petre, you can do it, you can do it. I commend you well, very good, i' faith!"

Marvel not at the success of Petre's poor and threadbare wit. He was a great man in those parts. Moreover, the jests had stood the test of time. They were familiar to the ear, requiring no effort of the intellect to comprehend them, and so they were highly esteemed in Gloucestershire and elsewhere, and I have no doubt from their frequent recurrence that they were an unfailing source of merriment in the playhouse.

It was not without design that Petre entertained the company with these and suchlike jokes, for an opportunity was thus afforded to the Lady Katherine of drawing Anne aside, and instructing her as to the part which she was to play in the drama of the day.

"'Go, one of you, find out the forester,'" [2] said the Justice at length to the tenants and retainers who crowded the court-yard, some holding greyhounds in leash, some supplied with cross-bows [3] for the use of the shooters, while others were

---

[1] The male of the fallow deer is commonly called a buck, the female a doe, and the young a fawn. In the strict language of venery, the male is called in ' the first year a fawn, the second year a pricket, the third year a sorel, the fourth year a sore, the fifth year a buck of the first head, the sixth year a great buck.'—*Gentleman's Recreation.*

[2] *Mids. N. Dr.* iv. 1. 108.

[3] At the time of our diarist, the cross-bow had superseded the long-bow as an instrument of woodcraft, to the great sorrow of sportsmen of the old school, as well as of those who were concerned for the ancient defences of the realm. ' Verily, I suppose,' writes Sir Thomas Elyot (*The Gouernor*, 1531), ' that before crosse bowes and hand gunnes were brought into this realme by the sleighte of our enemies, to thentent to destroye the noble defence of archery, continued use of shotynge in the longe bowe made the feate so perfecte and

ready to act as drivers of the deer, in accordance with the custom of the manor. The forester having been found made his report to the Justice as to the whereabouts of the various herds of deer, and suggested that while the company were being conducted by his assistants to their special stands, he should with the Justice superintend the work of the drivers.

Think not that I have imported into the sport of our ancestors a modern term of art. The drivers are an institution as old as the famous hunting with 'bomen' and 'greahondes' proclaimed on the hills of Cheviot, and celebrated in the ballad of which Sir Philip Sidney wrote, 'I never heard the old song of Percie and Douglas that I found not my heart moved more than with a trumpet.'

> The dryvars thorowe the woodes went,
>   For to reas the dear;
> Bomen bickarte uppone the bent
>   With thar browd aras cleare;
> Then the wyld thorowe the woodes went,
>   On every syde shear,
> Greahondes thorowe the greves glent,
>   For to kyll thear dear.

And so the drive began, and before it ended many a fat and seasonable buck bit the dust. Some were killed outright as they fled past the marksmen; others, wounded only by the arrow, were coursed and pulled down by greyhounds.

At length the mort was sounded, and the day's hunting was at an end. The company then left their stands, and assembled at the quarry, where the slaughtered deer were exposed to view.

This word has, in its time, borne several meanings.

exacte amonge englisshe men, that they then as surely and soone killed suche game whiche they listed to have as they now can do with the crosse bowe or gunne, and more expeditely and with the lasse labour they dyd it.' The preamble of an act passed ' for avoidyng shoting in crosbowes' states that the 'king's subjects daily delite them selfes in shoting of crosbowes, whereby shoting in long bowes is the lesse used ' (6 *Hen. VIII.* c. 13; 33 *Hen. VIII.* c. 6).

Derived, like most terms of venery, from Norman French, it originally signified the square (*carré*) whither the slaughtered deer were brought when the chase was over, for the purpose of being viewed and broken up. When the hunting on the Cheviot hills was over, and a hundred fat deer lay dead,

> The blewe a mort uppone the bent,
> The semblyd on sydes shear,
> To the quarry then the Persè went
> To se the bryttlynge off the deare.

Or, as the ballad modernised by a contemporary of the diarist has it,

> Lord Percy to the quarry went
> To view the slaughtered deere.

The word was next applied to a heap of slaughtered game, such as was collected in the quarry. 'This quarry cries on havoc,' said Fortinbras, viewing the dead bodies of Hamlet, Laertes, and the King.[1] 'I'ld make a quarry,' said Coriolanus,

> With thousands of these quarter'd slaves, as high
> As I could pick my lance.   *Coriol.* i. 1. 202.

And finally, about the time of the diarist, it came to bear the meaning in which it is commonly used by modern dealers in antique phraseology—that is to say, living game as an object of chase.[2]

It was, however, in its original sense that the Justice used the word when he invited the company to assemble at the quarry, and to partake in the ceremonies which marked the close of a solemn hunting.

It fell to Master Petre, as the guest of highest degree, to decide who was first woodman. He had no difficulty in awarding the palm to Abraham Slender. Tried by all the tests of woodcraft, he was clearly first. He had culled the

---

[1] *Hamlet*, v. 2. 375.

[2] The word 'quarry,' signifying the reward of the hounds at the death of a beast of venery (see *ante*, p. 100), is a different term of woodcraft. It is derived from the French *curée*, a word still applied to the part of the deer given to the hounds.

principal of all the deer driven past his stand, and had
killed his quarry outright, not one needing to be pulled
down by greyhounds. He is, in short, one who 'handles
his bow like ' a woodman, not like ' a crowkeeper.' [1]

The company were so merry that the absence of William
Silence and Anne Squele was not observed, and to this
merriment Petre contributed of set purpose. The part that
he then played was afterwards assigned to another humourist
of a different type.

Pet. [*Jaques*] Let's present him to the [Justice] like a Roman
conqueror ; and it would do well to set the deer's horns upon his
head, for a branch of victory. Have you no song, forester, for this
purpose ?

For. Yes, sir.

Pet. [*Jaques*] Sing it ; 'tis no matter how it be in tune, so it
make noise enough.

SONG.

For.   What shall he have that kill'd the deer ?
     His leather skin and horns to wear.
          Then sing him home ;
             [The rest shall bear this burden.
     Take thou no scorn to wear the horn ;
     It was a crest ere thou wast born :
          Thy father's father wore it,
          And thy father bore it :
     The horn, the horn, the lusty horn
     Is not a thing to laugh to scorn.

                    As You L. iv. 2. 3.

" ' Bid my cousin Ferdinand come hither,' " [2] cried Petre,
as the merriment subsided ; " it appertaineth to my office to
declare who has proved worst woodman, as well as best.
Come, Master Ferdinand, you have liberty to speak for
yourself, only I pray you, let it be in the vulgar tongue, so
that you be understanded of the company. What deer hath
fallen to your arrow this day ? "

" This dearest dear," said Master Ferdinand, taking
Ellen Silence by the hand, and leading her to where her

---

[1] *K. Lear*, iv. 6. 87.   [2] *Tam. of Shrew*, iv. 1. 154.

father stood between Justice Shallow and Petre. "Were there ten thousand royal harts in yonder quarry, they would be as nothing in comparison with the queenly heart that hath fallen to me this day."

"Well said, indeed," said Shallow, "well said indeed. Robert Shallow commends you. 'Tis well, i' faith, that the words hart and deer have a double meaning, else many an ancient and merry jest had been lost. But, Master Ferdinand, you have chosen well. I' faith you have chosen well, and, cousin Silence, by yea and nay, you may no more call 'your fairest daughter and mine . . . a black ousel,' as you have used this many a day past, as often as we might meet."

"Silence gives consent," said Petre, waving his hand in the direction of the worthy Justice, Ellen's father, who seemed deprived of all power of speech by the suddenness of the event—things were not expected to occur suddenly in Gloucestershire—"well, cousin Ferdinand, if thou hast failed to win the horns as best woodman, be of good cheer, thy forehead may be furnished yet." [1]

While these scenes were being enacted, two figures, having dismounted from horseback, emerged from the shadow of the wood, and, crossing the laund where the quarry had been formed, approached the group of merrymakers. These were William Silence and Mistress Anne Silence, formerly Squele, his wedded wife.

And here, at the supreme moment of his life, the pen of the diarist, ready enough in chronicling trifles, seems to falter and to fail him. But we are not without a better and more enduring record of what was said and done. For, many years afterwards, the scene beside the quarry, and the story of sweet Anne's discomfiture of Justice Shallow,

[1] I know no surer proof of the genuineness of the diary and the correctness of the theory propounded in these pages in regard to its origin, than the wearisome iteration therein of poor jests about harts, deer, and horns. For you may find in Shakespeare a play on the words 'deer' and 'hart' repeated some dozen times, while jests and allusions on the subject of horns, such as those in which Petre indulged, occur nearly thrice as often. 'I question whether there exists a parallel instance of a phrase, that like this of "horns" is universal in all languages, and yet for which no one has discovered even a plausible origin' (Coleridge, *Lectures on Shakespeare*).

of Abraham Slender, and of her selfish father, recurred to the
memory of one who never troubled himself to construct a
plot when he could find one ready to his hand. He had
been commanded by his Queen to write a play wherein
Falstaff should be presented as a lover, for the delectation
of the Court. The surroundings must needs be English.
It were idle then to turn to Italian novel, and the incident
was scarcely worthy of the dignity of a history. In these
straits he bethought him of the fortunes of an old Gloucestershire acquaintance. So pleased was he with the notion,
that he brought the whole company from Gloucestershire to
Windsor for the occasion, and gave the world one comedy,
and only one, the scene of which is laid in England.

Thus it comes to pass that the story of the taking of the
deer concludes in words worthier of the occasion than some
meagre notes hastily written on the last page of the Diary
of William Silence.

Squele [*Page*]. My heart misgives me, here comes William
Silence [Fenton]. How now, Master ?
Anne. Pardon, good father ! . . .
Squele. Now, mistress, how chance you went not with Master
Slender ? . . .
William [*Fenton*]. You do amaze her ; hear the truth of it.
You would have married her most shamefully,
Where there was no proportion held in love.
The truth is, she and I, long since contracted,
Are now so sure that nothing can dissolve us.
The offence is holy that she hath committed ;
And this deceit loses the name of craft,
Of disobedience, or unduteous title,
Since therein she doth evitate and shun
A thousand irreligious cursed hours,
Which forced marriage would have brought upon her.
Petre [*Ford*]. Stand not amazed ; here is no remedy ;
In love the heavens themselves do guide the state ;
Money buys lands, and wives are sold by fate. . . .
Squele. Well, what remedy ? [William], heaven give thee joy !
What cannot be eschew'd must be embraced. . . .
Heaven give you many, many merry days !
Merry Wives, v. 5. 225.

CHAPTER XV

THE HORSE IN SHAKESPEARE

Nay, the man hath no wit that cannot, from the rising of the lark to the lodging of the lamb, vary deserved praise on my palfrey. It is a theme as fluent as the sea; turns the sands into eloquent tongues, and my horse is argument for them all.

King Henry V.

' 'TIS now fifty and four yeares since these words were writ, and ten yeares since my deare wife receiued at the hands of Captaine Anthony Petre (then of the householde of the Lord Deputy) by way of remembrance from his mother the Ladye Katherine—now well stricken in yeares, but of great repute for zele in good workes and aulmsdedes—that Boke in which are written many things whereof we may say with Tully *senectutem oblectant, pernoctant nobiscum, peregrinantur, rusticantur.* And as I think over those neuer-forgotten tymes, I call to minde the commandement of olde; *hospitalitatem nolite oblivisci, per hanc enim latuerunt quidam angelis hospitio receptis.* 'Tis passing strange how little I can remember of our discourse in those dayes, and that little appertayneth rather to horse, hawke and hound than to weightier matters. And indede as a solace for my declining years, now (as I may saye) in the sear and yellow leaf, I have bethought me to collect what he hath written, and what I can call to minde that he did saye, in regard to those sports and pastimes wherein we delighted, and in the which he excelled all others of his yeares with whom I have ever chaunced to mete. Of this my design I haue hitherto accomplished naught beyond noting in the margents certaine passages relating to the Horse, and the conceipt of a fourfold diuision, somewhat after the fashion of Maister Thomas Blundeuill, his boke on horsemanshippe,[1] which I have followed, but after the manner of a disciple rather than of a slaue.

' In the first part I would declare concerning the choosing of Horses, and the order of their breeding ; in the second of how to diet and to breake the Great Horse, and therein of his nature and disposition, and how to make him a horse of seruice. Thirdlie, I would discourse of the whole arte of riding the Great Horse, and fourthlie (and lastly) to what diseases Horses be subject, together with the names of such diseases, and the kindlie and proper termes meet to be used in discoursing concerning the Horse and his furniture. Suche is my designe, in the accomplishment of whiche I meane to perseuere

> Dum res et ætas et sororum
> Fila trium patiuntur atra.'

* * * * * * *

Whether it was due to advancing years, to the troubles which burst on the land of his adoption in the following year (1641), or to the arrest of the fell sergeant death, I know not ; but these are the last words written by the hand of the diarist of which I have any knowledge.

When I read this postscript my first thought was to rescue from the rubbish of Sir William's tower that priceless volume, noted by the diarist's hand, the existence of which was, to my mind, conclusively proved. I admit that his words are ambiguous. I confess that a friend of great

---

[1] *The foure chiefest Offices belonging to Horsemanship*, that is to saie, the office of the Breeder, of the Rider, of the Keeper, and of the Ferrer. In the first part whereof is declared the order of breeding of Horses. In the second how to breake them and to make them Horses of seruice. Conteining the whole Art of Riding, latelie set forth and now newlie corrected, and amended of manie faults escaped in the first printing as well touching the Bits as otherwise. Thirdlie, how to diet them, as well when they rest as when they trauell by the way. Fourthlie, to what diseases they be subject, together with the causes of such diseases, the signes how to knowe them, and finallie how to cure the same. London, 1580.

literary attainments, to whom I showed the diary and the postscript, regarded the writer as simply one of a numerous class of adventurers invited to settle in Ireland in 1586 after the forfeitures in Munster, many of whom came from the south-western counties of England. As to the postscript, he conjectures that it may refer to a collection of the works of Gervase Markham (who served in Ireland under Essex, with his brothers Francis and Godfrey, and may thus have been known to the diarist), bound together, as was not uncommon, and comprising not only his *Discourse of Horse-manshippe* (1593), *Cavalarice* (1607), and *Maister-Peece of Farriery* (1615), but his *Country Contentments* (1611) and the *English Hous-wif, compairing the inward and outward vertues which ought to be in a compleat woman* (1615), by the last of which the volume was specially recommended to the wife of the diarist. He regards an allusion to *King Lear*, more than thirty years after the publication of the play, as in no way significant ; adding that by quoting its author as he quotes a classic, the diarist rather negatives the notion that he was an acquaintance. I mention this opinion, not that it is entitled to serious consideration, but as an illustration of the truth that high literary attainments do not necessarily confer that power of dealing with circumstantial evidence by which alone such questions can be solved as the authorship of the letters of Junius, the personality of the man in the iron mask, the relations of Swift to Stella, the origin of the round towers of Ireland, and, I would humbly add, the identification with William Shakespeare of the nameless stranger who three hundred years ago was a partaker of the sports and pastimes of Gloucestershire gentlemen.

I give in his own words the answer of the owner of Sir William's tower to my earnest letter of inquiry :—

There used to be a lot of rubbishy old books in Sir William's tower. The covers made capital gun-wads. Don't you remember cutting them up yourself ages ago, with the machine we used to work in the old muzzle-loading times ? The leaves must have been used by the housemaids for lighting fires, for I cannot now find even the Continuation of Rapin. I am certain that an old Shake-speare was burned, because I remember our getting into a scrape about it. My mother said it was a shame, when she saw the leaves in the grate. We told her it was no harm, for it was all marked and scribbled over, besides being badly printed and rottenly spelt, and my father said it was no great matter, as there was a newer one much better bound in the library. If this is any use to you, you can have it. But there is a smaller one that would easily go by book post, by a Mr. Bowdler; you could return it when you have done with the old rubbish I left you.

I spare the reader all expression of my sorrow and remorse, and in lieu of vain words, I present to him the result of an endeavour to repair the ravages of my thought-less youth, and to re-construct the work which perished with Sir William's folio of 1623. And I bid him to remem-ber that the diarist's notes would have recorded actual facts, and to reflect how much fine writing and ecstatic transcen-dentalism must have been lost to the world if learned com-mentators had been subject to the like restriction.

And so I proceed, adopting the fourfold division of the diarist.

I

FIRSTLIE, CONCERNING THE CHOOSING OF HORSES, AND THE ORDER OF THEIR BREEDING

As soon as the adventurer from Stratford could afford it with prudence, (but no sooner, I am certain) he thus resolved; in the words of Pericles, Prince of Tyre,

> I will mount myself
> Upon a courser, whose delightful steps
> Shall make the gazer joy to see him tread.
>
> *Pericles*, ii. 1. 163.

But that which was a joy to the gazer was mortification to the less fortunate fellows of the owner of the courser,[1] and

[1] According to Dr. Murray's new *Dictionary of the English Language*, it was not until the seventeenth century that the word ' courser ' conveyed any suggestion connected with the race-course. Originally applied to the great horse, it had in Shakespeare's time become a term of general application, seldom, however, used, except in poetry.

when he followed it up by the acquisition of landed property and armorial bearings, one of them could restrain himself no longer, and so he put into the mouth of a cavilling scholar these words :

> England affords those glorious vagabonds
> That carried earst their fardels on their backes
> Coursers to ride on through the gazing streetes,
> Looping it in their glaring satten sutes,
> And Pages to attend their maisterships,
> With mouthing words that better wits have framed
> They purchase lands, and now Esquiers are made.[1]

The last couplet is supposed to point the reference unmistakably to Shakespeare, to whose father a grant of arms was made (probably at the instance of the poet) in 1596, and who bought a house and land at Stratford in the following year. To my mind, the courser is no less suggestive. I believe that its advent preceded by many years the acquisition of either land or armorial bearings, and a sly hit at the envy of his fellows may have been intended when in touching up Greene's *True Contention* he made Jack Cade thus address the Lord Say :

> Thou dost ride in a foot-cloth, dost thou not ?
> *Say.* What of that ?
> *Cade.* Marry, thou oughtest not to let thy horse wear a cloak, when honester men than thou go in their hose and doublets.
>
> 2 *Hen. VI.* iv. 7. 51.

However this may be, to buy this courser he must needs go to Smithfield. This great London mart had not the best of characters. ' Where's Bardolph ? ' asked Falstaff.

> *Page.* He's gone into Smithfield to buy your worship a horse.
> *Fal.* I bought him in Paul's, and he'll buy me a horse in Smithfield ; an I could get me but a wife in the stews, I were manned, horsed, and wived.[2]   2 *Hen. IV.* i. 2. 55.

---

[1] *The Returne from Pernassus*, acted in 1602.

[2] Smithfield was a mart for horses from the reign of Henry II. Later on, Froissart tells us that Wat Tyler, Jack Straw, and John Ball ' assembled their company to commune together in a place called Smithfield, where every Friday there is a market of horses ' (*Chronicles*, Lord Berners' translation). Here

These words record a personal experience in horse-dealing, the key to which—as to most of Shakespeare's allusions to horses and sport—may be found where least you would expect it; in this instance in a Roman play.

When Octavius Cæsar was taking leave of his sister Octavia, wedded to Mark Antony, the aspect of his countenance was noted by two lookers on : by his friend Agrippa, and by Domitius Enobarbus who followed the fortunes of his rival Antony. They spoke as follows :

Eno. (*aside to Agr.*) Will Cæsar weep ?
Agr. (*aside to Eno.*) He has a cloud in's face.
Eno. (*aside to Agr.*) He were the worse for that, were he a horse ;
So is he, being a man. *Ant. and Cleop.* iii. 2. 51.

Enobarbus' grim jest would have prospered better in the ear of a Smithfield horse-courser than it has fared with some of the critics. Mr. Grant White explains it as ' an allusion to the dislike which horse fanciers have to white marks or other discolorations in the face of that animal.' The horse-courser could have told him that the words meant the exact opposite. The horse with a cloud in his face was one with no white star. Fitzherbert, in his *Boke of Husbandrie,* commends the white star. ' It is an excellent good marke also for a horse to have a white star in his forehead. The horse that hath no white at all upon him is furious, dogged, full of mischiefe and misfortune.' [1] Thus Gervase Markham ; but

was held the celebrated fair, the humours of which are drawn to the life by Ben Jonson in his *Bartholomew Fair,* the comedy which won for him the title of ' rare Ben Jonson.' ' You are in Smithfield,' says Waspe to his master, ' you may fit yourself with a fine easy-going street nag for your saddle again Michaelmas term, do.' Dan Jordan Knockem, one of the characters in this play, is a horse courser, or jobber, a class which ranked lower in public estimation than the horse-master, who either bred the horses he sold, or bought them as young, unbroken colts (Fitzherbert, *Boke of Husbandrie*). Fitzherbert, one of the Justices of the Court of Common Pleas *tempore* Hen. VIII. proclaims himself a horse-master. Burton (*Anatomy of Melancholy*) bears testimony to the evil repute of Smithfield, and it was a common saying that ' a man must not make choyce of three things in three places : of a wife in Westminstre ; of a servant in Paules ; of a horse in Smithfield ; lest he chuse a queane, a knave, or a jade ' (*The Choice of Change,* 1598). [1] *Cavalarice,* G. Markham.

in the common language of the stable, such a horse was said to have a cloud in his face. *Equus nebula (ut vulgo dicitur) in facie, cujus vultus tristis est et melancholicus, jure vituperatur*, says the learned Sadleirus in his work, *De procreandis etc. equis* (1587).[1]

But Smithfield taught the lesson *fronti nulla fides.* The horse carefully chosen for his fair white brow developed in time the fateful cloud. For the Smithfield horse-courser had skill to make a false star in the forehead, and the old masters of farriery did not scruple to tell him how the trick might be done, so as to deceive the unwary—for they taught also how to distinguish the artificial from the natural white. And so the purchaser, notwithstanding all his care, might find himself the owner of such a steed as Emily bestowed on Arcite :

> a black one, owing
> Not a hair-worth of white,[2] which some will say
> Weakens his price, and many will not buy
> His goodness with this note ; which superstition
> Finds here allowance.[3]

It may have been for good cause that the superstition of the clouded face found allowance with the author of these lines and of *Antony and Cleopatra*, for the story of the showy black courser with the ill-omened cloud was perhaps a personal reminiscence of what happened to the writer in very deed,

[1] From Sadler's words *ut vulgo dicitur*, the expression ' cloud in the face ' seems to have been in general use. Those who had not Shakespeare's intimate knowledge of the language of the stable probably used it without any clear idea of its meaning, as Burton may have done when he wrote 'every louer admires his mistress, though she be very deformed of herselfe—thin leane chitty face, haue clouds in her face ' (*Anatomy of Melancholy*).

[2] ' A coal black without any white ' is, according to Markham (*Maister-peece*), ' a cholerick horse ' partaking ' more of the fire than of the other elements.' Homer had sound views in regard to the forehead, for at the funeral games in honour of Patroclus, the horse noted by Idomeneus was one

ὃς τὸ μὲν ἄλλο τόσον φοῖνιξ ἦν, ἐν δὲ μετώπῳ
λευκὸν σῆμ' ἐτέτυκτο περίτροχον, ἠΰτε μήνη.

Il. xxiii. 454.

[3] *Two Noble Kinsmen*, v. 4. 50. As to Shakespeare's share in the authorship of this play, see Note, *Critical Significance of Shakespeare's Allusions to Field Sports*.

but fortunately with a less tragical result as regards the
rider. As Arcite, mounted on this horse, was

> Trotting the stones of Athens, which the calkins
> Did rather tell than trample ; for the horse
> Would make his length a mile, if't pleas'd his rider
> To put pride in him ; as he thus went counting
> The flinty pavement, dancing as 'twere to the music
> His own hoofs made,

a sudden spark flew. forth, with this result :

> The hot horse, hot as fire,
> Took toy at this, and fell to what disorder
> His power could give his will, bounds, comes on end,
> Forgets school-doing, being therein train'd
> And of kind manage ; pig-like he whines
> At the sharp rowel which he frets at rather
> Than any jot obeys ; seeks all foul means
> Of boisterous and rough jadery, to disseat
> His lord that kept it bravely : when naught serv'd,
> When neither curb would crack, girth break, nor differing
>   plunges
> Disroot his rider whence he grew, but that
> He kept him 'tween his legs, on his hind hoofs
> On end he stands,
> That Arcite's legs, being higher than his head,
> Seem'd with strange art to hang ; his victor's wreath
> Even then fell off his head ; and presently
> Backward the jade comes o'er, and his full poise
> Becomes the rider's load.

'Furious, dogged, full of mischiefe and misfortune,' in
the words of Gervase Markham, was this ill-starred steed ;
and though 'proper palfreys black as jet'[1] might please
the eye in the sallet days when the showy black courser
was bought, and when *Titus Andronicus* was thought worth
adapting, we can trace, along with the development of the
mighty genius of Shakespeare, the growth of a sounder
judgment in the matter of horseflesh. Later on, roan Barbary, and the Dauphin's prince of palfreys, are more to his
mind ; proving him to be of the same opinion with Master

[1] *Tit. Andr.* v. 2. 50.

Blundevill, who tells us that 'a fair rone' is among all kinds 'most commendable, most temperat; strongest and of gentlest nature.' Of this roan we shall hear more anon, for it also is a personal reminiscence.

But there is more to be looked to, if you would choose your horse aright, than his white marks, his colour, or even than that 'ostrich feather,' of which Blundevill says that the horse that hath it 'either on his forhead, or on both sides of his maine, or on the one side, or else behind on his buttockes, or in anie place where he himself cannot see it, can never be an euill horse.' For, he wisely adds, 'though the horse be neuer so well coloured and marked, yet is he little worth unlesse his shape be accordinglie.' And I am certain that the author of *Venus and Adonis*, though he may have had reason to rail at Smithfield in the matter of the clouded face, made no mistake in regard to shape, provided he carried in his eye the points which he had noted in Adonis's trampling courser :

> So did this horse excel a common one
> In shape, in courage, colour, pace, and bone.

> Round-hoof'd, short-jointed, fetlocks shag and long,
> Broad breast, full eye, small head and nostril wide,
> High crest, short ears, straight legs and passing strong,
> Thin mane, thick tail, broad buttock, tender hide :
> Look, what a horse should have he did not lack.
>
> Ven. and Ad. 293.

This is a picture of the perfect English horse, drawn with pen and ink, as

> when a painter would surpass the life,
> In limning out a well-proportioned steed.[1]
>
> Ibid. 289.

[1] Professor Dowden asks in regard to this passage, 'Is it poetry, or a paragraph from an advertisement of a horse sale ? ' (*Shakspere, his Mind and Art*). And in truth it is scarcely more poetical than Blundevill's catalogue of points in his chapter entitled, *What shape a good horse ought to have*, from which I give the following extract, in his own words, but in the order of the description in *Venus and Adonis* : 'Round hoofe ; pasterns short ; his joints great with long feawter locks behind which is a signe of force ; his breast large and round ;

In the horse of to-day these qualities, inherited from his native-born ancestors, would be deemed underbred.

For in the year of Shakespeare's death (1616) there occurred an event of signal importance in the history of the horse ; a history, by the way, in antiquity beggaring the puny records of human life on this planet, and stretching back to palæozoic ages, when Hipparion roamed the plains with, as yet, no thought of consolidating the several divisions of his foot into a hoof, to the manifest advantage of horse, groom, and farrier. In that year there was imported into England the first of those Arabian horses from whom the modern thoroughbred traces his descent. In earlier times a cross between an eastern horse —usually a Barb—and an English mare was not uncommon. It was an idea familiar to the mind of Iago.[1] The stock thus produced was of high repute.[2] But it was not until the middle of the seventeenth century that a systematic attempt was made to produce a sub-species of a distinct and permanent character by judicious crossing of the best native with the best Arabian strains. This was the origin of the thoroughbred, happily combining the highest qualities of the two unmixed races from which it sprang, and

his eyes great; his iawes slender and leane ; his nostrils so open and puffed up as you may see the read within, apt to receiue aire ; his necke bending in the midst ; his eares small or rather sharp ; his legs straight and broad ; his maine should be thin and long ; his taile full of haires ; and his rumpe round.' Was the line of *Venus and Adonis* ending ' full eye, small head, and nostril wide ' ringing in the ears of Michael Barrett, when among the qualities of the perfect English mare he included ' a small head, full eye, wide nostril? ' (*The Vineyard of Horsemanship*, 1618). Ben Jonson obviously parodies this passage in *Bartholomew Fair*, when he makes Knockem the horse-courser speak thus of Mrs. Littlewit, ' Dost thou hear, Whit ? Is't not pity my delicate dark chestnut here, with the fine lean head, large forehead, round eyes, even mouth, sharp ears, long neck, thin crest, close withers, plain back, deep sides, short fillets, and full flanks ; with a round belly, a plump buttock, large thighs, knit knees, strait legs, short pasterns, smooth hoofs and short heels, should lead a dull honest woman's life, that might live the life of a lady? ' But rare Ben was just then in a mocking mood, and he had his fling at *The Tempest*, *The Winter's Tale*, and *Titus Andronicus* in the Induction to this play. These ebullitions, however, did not interrupt a friendship which on the part of Ben Jonson approached (so he tells us) to idolatry.

[1] *Othello*, i. 1. 112.   [2] Blundevill.

in its best form unrivalled throughout the world for speed, courage, and beauty.

In Tudor times neither the race-horse, the carriage-horse, the cart-horse, the hack nor the hunter, as we now understand the terms, were in existence. There were in use horses of various kinds, home-bred or imported, more or less suited to the several purposes for which they were employed. There were 'the Turke, the Barbarian, the Sardinian, the Napolitan, the Jennet of Spaine, the Hungarian, the high Almaine, the Friezeland horse, the Flanders horse, and the Irish hobbie.' The last-mentioned had not attained the quality and reputation of his descendants ; but still he was ' a prettie fine horse, having a good head and a bodie indifferentlie well proportioned, saving that manie of them be slender and pin-buttocked, they be tender mouthed, nimble, light, pleasant, and apt to be taught, and for the most part they be amblers, and therefore verie meete for the saddle and to travell by the way.' They were, however, ' somewhat skittish and fearfull, partlie perhaps by nature, and partlie for lacke of good breaking at the first.' [1]

Of these breeds the diarist would, I think, have selected two only for special notice, the English horse and the Barb. The Stratford youth who limned out the shapes of the handsome home-bred courser came, in later years, to know and to celebrate the rare qualities of the eastern horse. If in the former task his verse is somewhat prosaic, this would seem to be the result of sympathy with its subject-matter ; for his prose becomes instinct with the poetry of motion when inspired, like the Dauphin of France, by the exquisite paces of the ' wonder of nature.'

Dau. I will not change my horse with any that treads but on four pasterns. Ça ha ! He bounds from the earth as if his entrails were hairs ; le cheval volant, the Pegasus, chez les narines de feu ! When I bestride him, I soar, I am a hawk : he trots the air : the earth sings when he touches it : the basest horn of his hoof is more musical than the pipe of Hermes.

---

[1] Blundevill, *Foure Chiefest Offices.*

Orl. He's of the colour of the nutmeg.

Dau. And of the heat of the ginger. It is a beast for Perseus : he is pure air and fire ; and the dull elements of earth and water [1] never appear in him, but only in patient stillness while his rider mounts him : he is indeed a horse ; and all other jades you may call beasts.

Con. Indeed, my lord, it is a most absolute and excellent horse.

Dau. It is the prince of palfreys ; his neigh is like the bidding of a monarch and his countenance enforces homage. . . . I once writ a sonnet in his praise and began thus : ' Wonder of Nature.'

Hen. V. iii. 7. 11.

I believe that this roan Barb—prince of palfreys—came into Shakespeare's possession somewhere about the year 1592. Thenceforth a change comes over the poet's conception of the perfect horse. The fiery courage and elastic tread of the eastern horse—transmitted to the thoroughbred of to-day— must have been a revelation to one accustomed to the some- what wooden paces of the thickset, straight-pasterned courser of Stratford. ' This roan shall be my throne,' he would say,

---

[1] This reference to the elements has more significance than appears on the surface. The old writers on horses or farriery classify horses according to the element which is supposed to predominate in their composition. I quote from Blundevill ; but they are all of the same mind with Shakespeare, and give the preference to ' pure air and fire.' ' He is complexioned according as he doth participate more or lesse of any of the iiii Elements. For if he hath more of the earth than of the rest, he is melancholie, heauie, and faint hearted, and of colour a blacke, a russet, a bright or darke dunne. But if he hath more of the water then is he flegmatike, slowe, dull, and apt to lose flesh, and of colour most commonlie milke white. If of the aire, then he is sanguine, and therefore pleasant, nimble, and of colour is comonlie a bay. And if of the fire, then is he cholerike, and therefore light, hot, and fierie, a stirer, and seldom of anie great strength, and is wont to be of colour a bright sorrell. But when he doth participate of all the foure elements, equallie, and in due proportion, then is he perfect, and most commonlie shall he be one of the colours following,' among which we find ' a faire rone.' The due proportion in which the four elements should participate is thus defined by the Dauphin : ' he is pure air and fire, and the dull elements of earth and water never appear in him, but only in patient stillness while his rider mounts him ' (*Hen. V.* iii. 7. 22), and he is a fair roan. ' I am fire and air,' says Cleopatra ; ' my other elements I give to baser life ' (*Ant. and Cleo.* v. 2. 292). Gervase Markham (*Maister-peece*) deals with this subject at greater length, detailing the diseases to which horses of each com- plexion are most subject.

in the words of Hotspur, who could abide the 'forced gait
of a shuffling nag' as little as 'mincing poetry.'[1]   We meet
this roan Barb again in the person of the roan Barbary on
which Henry Bolingbroke made his triumphal entry into
London—

> Mounted upon a hot and fiery steed,
> Which his aspiring rider seem'd to know.
>
> *Rich. II.* v. 2. 8.

Proudly he bore his proud rider, and with the sympathetic
instinct of the eastern race shared his master's pride, and
seemed to know his feelings, as the tired horse imitates his
rider.   There is little difficulty in identifying the same
favourite with the red roan[2] courser, plainly of eastern race,
'of the colour of the nutmeg,[2] and of the heat of ginger,'
whose praises we have heard the Dauphin sing.   Indeed, if
I were disposed to adopt the language of criticism, I should
class the historical plays as the roan Barbary group.   In the
tragedies we meet with Barbary horses now and then, but
'the bonny beast he loved so well,'[3] the prince of palfreys, is
no more.   Can we wonder that the period when they were
written was, in Professor Dowden's language, a period of
depression and gloom?

But although the eastern horse had his peculiar charm,
I conclude from the testimony of the best judges that, of
the various unmixed races then in use, the English was the
best and most serviceable.. 'The true English horse, him I
mean that is bred under a good clime, on firme ground, in a
pure temperature, is of tall stature, and large proportions.'[4]
Thus Gervase Markham expresses the opinion of those who

---

[1] 1 *Hen. IV.* iii. 1. 133.

[2] A nutmeg when grated is suggestive of the colour known as red roan.

[3] 2 *Hen. VI.* v. 2. 12.

[4] 'Yorkshire doth breed the best race of English horses' (Fuller, *Worthies*).
So say all the old writers, including Shakespeare, for in a letter written to the
Lord Chamberlain the horses for which he sent are described as 'well chosen,
ridden, and furnished.   They were young and handsome, and of the best breed
in the north' (*Hen. VIII.* ii. 2. 2).

were best competent to judge—an opinion which he supports by several instances of rare merit in English horses.

But native-bred horses did not always, or indeed commonly, attain this standard of excellence. The herds that roamed over heaths, forests, and moors seem to have degenerated into mere ponies. 'The great decay of the generation and breeding of good and swift and strong horses' is deplored in the preambles of 27 Hen. VIII. c. 6, and 32 Hen. VIII. c. 13. The altitude and height prescribed by these statutes, thirteen handfuls for mares and fifteen for horses, tell their own tale, and even this standard for horses was afterwards lowered to thirteen hands in regard to certain 'marishes or seggy grounds' in Cambridgeshire and elsewhere.

These statutes (which in Elizabeth's reign had been suffered to fall into desuetude) were not successful in raising the standard of the native breed. 'Horses are abundant, yet, although low and small, they are very fleet,' wrote Herr Rathgeb in 1602 ; and to the same effect is the testimony of Hentzner, who visited England in 1592, 'the horses are small, but swift.'

Horses of this class did very well for hunting and hawking 'nagges, and for ambling roadsters.' But the great horse, or horse of service, fit for warfare and the use of princes, was in danger of becoming extinct.

'The necessarie breeding of horses for service whereof this realm of all others at this instant hath greatest neede' was urged on Elizabeth's ministers, and not without success. Blundevill tells us that when he determined with himself 'to have translated into our vulgar tongue the foure bookes of Grison treating in the Italian tongue of the Art of riding and breaking great horses . . . my L. Burleigh high Treasurer of England . . . of his Lordship's goodnesse vouchsafed to peruse my first draught, and misliked not the same : ' and that it was at the instance of the Lord Robert Dudley, Earl of Leicester, 'Maister of the Queenes Maiesties horses,' that the writer substituted for this translation his complete and original treatise in the vulgar tongue on *The Foure Chiefest Offices of Horsemanship.*

In dedicating this work to 'his singular good Lord, the Lord Robert Dudley, Earle of Leicester,' the author appeals to the patriotism as well as self-interest of 'Noblemen and gentlemen of this realme having Parkes or ground impaled meete for such use' that these enclosures 'might not wholie be emploied to the keeping of Deere (which is altogether a pleasure without profite), but partlie to the necessarie breeding of Horses for service.'

The timely adoption, under similar circumstances, of the system of breeding in enclosures, has rescued from degeneracy the Exmoor pony, a beautiful and interesting survival of the indigenous English horse, in the miniature form common in moorland and mountainous districts. The process of natural selection cannot be looked to for the production, or survival, of what is fittest for the artificial needs of mankind, and when the breeding of horses was left pretty much to chance, we cannot be surprised to find complaints of the degeneracy of the race.

Master Blundevill's appeal to the noblemen and gentlemen of England to turn their enclosures to practical use in improving the breeding of horses, and the statutes which I have quoted, lead to the conclusion that horse-breeding in England was in his time generally conducted after the haphazard fashion still in use in open and unenclosed countries.

Under such conditions 'compaynys of beestys' of various kinds roamed the hillsides and wastes. Each 'company' had its kindly and proper term, which no gentleman, if he had the smallest regard for his character, would dream of misusing. According to the *Boke of St. Albans*, you should apply the word 'herd' to deer, and 'drove' to cattle, but you must be careful to speak of a 'stode of maris,' a term of art which, in the phrase 'stud farm,' retains to the present day its special application to the mare. You should likewise speak of a 'Ragg (rage) of coltis, or a Rake' (race). The word 'herd' had become in Shakespeare's time of more general applica-

tion, although it was still the appropriate term to designate
a company of deer.[1] And those who were particular in the
use of language, when applying this general term to a company of beasts for whom usage had provided a more specific
designation, were careful to explain themselves ; after the
manner of Shakespeare, describing an experiment which he
tried, or saw tried, upon a race of colts, full of rage upon the
Cotswold hills.

> *Jes.* I am never merry when I hear sweet music.
> *Lor.* The reason is, your spirits are attentive :
> For do but note a wild and wanton herd,
> Or race of youthful and unhandled colts,
> Fetching mad bounds, bellowing and neighing loud,
> Which is the hot condition of their blood ;
> If they but hear perchance a trumpet sound,
> Or any air of music touch their ears,
> You shall perceive them make a mutual stand,
> Their savage eyes turn'd to a modest gaze
> By the sweet power of music ; therefore the poet
> Did feign that Orpheus drew trees, stones and floods ;
> Since nought so stockish, hard and full of rage,
> But music for the time doth change his nature.[2]
>
> *Merch. of Ven.* v. 1. 69.

[1] *As You L.* ii. 1. 52; *All's Well*, i. 3. 59 ; 1 *Hen. VI.* iv. 2. 46; 3 *Hen. VI.*
iii. 1. 7. In the *Jewell for Gentry* (1614), largely taken from the *Boke of St.
Albans*, ' ragg ' appears as ' ragge.' The word ' race ' appears in the form
' rake.' We learn that if the colt's head be restrained, he will hardly be
' brought to rake coolely.' I have not met with the word ' ragg ' in the form ' rage.'
Strutt (*Sports and Pastimes of the English People*) renders it ' rag.' But Strutt
is an untrustworthy guide in such matters. See the next succeeding footnote as
to the use of the word ' rage ' in reference to colts.

[2] In Shakespeare's time the wod ' race,' althrough retaining (as we have
seen) its primary application to a company of colts, was used to designate a
breed or kind of horses, distinguished with reference either to the country
whence they originally came, or to the person by whom they were bred. The
former use of the word is illustrated by the passage from Blundevill quoted
above, and in the eighth chapter of his book on the breeding of horses he
mentions a custom ' used even at this present daie at Tutberie, whereas the
Queene's Maiestie hath a race.' Elsewhere he calls to witness in support of
some statement, ' not onlie the Queenes Maiesties race, but also other men's
races and speciallie Sir Nicholas Arnolds race.' · We can thus understand why
Duncan's horses, beauteous and swift, were called the ' minions of their race '
(*Macbeth*, ii. 4. 15). There was no need for Theobald to read ' minions of the

' The mares of this kind or race,' writes Blundevill of the Libian race,' as the authors write, be so delighted with musicke, as the heardman or keeper, with the sound of a pipe, maie lead them whither he will himselfe ; ' a device borrowed by Ariel when he would mislead Caliban and the drunken varlets of the King of Naples :

race ; ' very probably and poetically, according to Johnson, and with the full approval of Steevens, who writes, ' I prefer " minions of *the* race," *i.e.*, the *favourite* horses on the race-ground ; ' an emendation and explanation, however, which I regard as doubly objectionable, inasmuch as they not only needlessly alter the text, but attribute to Shakespeare an allusion to a pastime which he absolutely ignores. Nor need Malone have tampered with the printing of Sonnet li., by introducing needless brackets, and thereby spoiling the sense. The sympathy of horse with his rider is the subject of the preceding Sonnet. The beast that bears the poet from his friend plods dully on, tired with his rider's woe. But when he returns, there is no horse so swift as to keep pace with the poet's desire :

> Therefore desire, of perfect'st love being made,
> Shall neigh, no dull flesh in his fiery race.

As we have seen (p. 261 n.), horses were classed according to the element which was supposed to dominate in their composition. The Dauphin's palfrey was ' pure air and fire,' as distinguished from the ' dull elements of earth and water ' (*Hen. V.* iii. 7. 22). And so desire is likened to a steed, of a race or breed so compact of fire as to admit of no dull flesh in its composition. Malone, followed by the Cambridge editor, isolated the words ' no dull flesh,' thus printed in the *Globe* :

> Shall neigh—no dull flesh—in his fiery race.

Traces of the terms ' rage ' and ' ragerie ' as applied to colts may be found in early literature. Thus Chaucer, of old January, ' He was al coltish, ful of ragerie ' (*Marchantes Tale*). Thence it came to be used generally of rough horse-play. The word is now obsolete (see Todd's *Johnson's Dictionary*) in this sense, but in Shakespeare's time it was still in use, with no doubt a suggestion of its original application. In the lines quoted above the words ' full of rage ' describe the mad bounds and neighing of the unhandled colts. Prince Hal's coltish humours suggest to his father the ragery of an uncurbed and unhandled colt :

> His headstrong riot hath no curb,
> When rage and hot blood are his counsellors.
>
> *2 Hen. IV.* iv. 4. 62.

And there is a reminiscence of this use of the word, coupled with a characteristic quibble, in the Duke of York's advice with regard to Richard,

> The king is come ; deal mildly with his youth ;
> For young hot colts being raged do rage the more.
>
> *Rich. II.* ii. 1. 69.

The word ' raged ' is obelised in the *Globe*, although correctly explained in the Glossary appended to the edition of 1891, as ' chafed, enraged.'

I beat my tabor ;
At which like unback'd colts, they prick'd their ears,
Advanced their eyelids, lifted up their noses
As they smelt music : so I charmed their ears
That, calf-like, they my lowing follow'd through
Tooth'd briers, sharp furzes, pricking goss and thorns,
Which entered their frail shins ; at last I left them
I' the filthy-mantled pool beyond your cell.

Tempest, iv. 1. 175.

But even under this haphazard system of breeding, good
results were obtained when conditions were favourable.
'Witnesse Gray Dallavill, being the horse upon which
the Earle of Northumberland roade in the last rebellion of
the North ; witnesse Gray Valentine wch dyed a Horse never
conquered ; the Hobbie of Maister Thomas Carleton's, and
at this houre most famous Puppey, against whom men may
talke, but they cannot conquer.'[1]   Witness Sir Andrew
Aguecheek's good horse ' grey Capilet,'[2] and more famous
still, Richard's ' white Surrey,'[3] whose name bespeaks him
of the same race and colour.

Shakespeare has noted with a distinguishing mark each
of the several classes of horse in general use in his time.

First in importance was the great horse, or horse of
service, meet for the wars or for the tourney.   To ride the
great horse, according to the order of the manage, was
esteemed among the necessary accomplishments of a gentleman.   He is ' Mars fiery steed,' whereof to ' sustain the
bound and high curvet' was a part of manly honour.[4]   He
is a ' fiery Pegasus,'[5] and to turn and wind him was, as we
shall see anon, the greatest achievement of noble horsemanship.

A horse of no ordinary power was needed to sustain the
weight of a knight in full armour, in addition to the cum-
brous furniture and heavy plates which the charger bore for
his own protection.   The Clydesdale of to-day approaches

---

[1] Markham, *Cavalarice*.   [2] *Twelfth N.* iii. 4. 315.   [3] *Rich. III.* v. 3. 64.
[4] *All's Well*, ii. 3. 299.   [5] *1 Hen. IV.* iv. 1. 109.

most nearly to the great war-horse of our ancestors, from which this noble animal has been developed by careful breeding through many generations.   The High Almain or German horse was 'stronglie made and therefore more meete for the shocke [1] than to pass a cariere, or to make a swift manege, because they be verie grosse and heauie.' Of the same class, we are further told by Blundevill, was the Flanders horse, 'sauing that for the most part he is of a greater stature and more puissant. The mares also of Flanders be of a great stature, strong, long, large, faire, and fruitfull, and besides that will endure great labour.'   The momentum imparted to these huge animals in the career must have enhanced considerably 'the grating shock of wrathful iron arms.' [2]   We shall hear more of the career and swift manage when we come to the third division of the diarist.

Here may be noted the excellence of the Neapolitan horses.[3]   Although not so meet for the shock as the heavier horses of Flanders and Germany, for the lighter exercises of the manage they were unequalled.   'In mine opinion,' writes Blundevill, 'their gentle nature and docilitie, their comelie shape, their strength, their courage, their sure footmanship, their well reining, their loftie pace, their

[1] This word is used by Shakespeare. Compare 1 *Hen. IV.* i. 1. 12; *Hen. V.* iv. 8. 114; *Rich. III.* v. 3. 93; and (metaphorically) *Rich. II.* iii. 3. 56.

[2] *Rich. II.* i. 3. 136.

[3] The Neapolitans were famous not only for horses, but for horsemanship. 'At this day,' writes Peacham in his *Compleat Gentleman* (1627), 'it is the onely exercise of the Italian Nobility, especially in Naples, as also of the French, and great pitty of no more practised among our English Gentry.' It is not therefore without design that Portia is made thus to describe her Neapolitan suitor:

Por. I pray thee, over-name them; and as thou namest them, I will describe them; and according to my description, level at my affection.

Ner. First, there is the Neapolitan prince.

Por. Ay, that's a colt indeed, for he doth nothing but talk of his horse; and he makes it a great appropriation to his own good parts, that he can shoe him himself. I am much afeard my lady his mother played false with a smith.

Merch. of Ven. i. 2. 39

Theobald, unaware that the word Neapolitan would, to Shakespeare, naturally suggest 'colt,' reads 'dolt.' 'Hapless Shakespeare!'

cleane trotting, their strong gallopping, and their swift running well considered (all which things they haue in maner by nature) they excel numbers of other races, euen so farre as the faire Greihounds the fowle Mastiffe Curres.'

With the disuse of defensive armour and with changes in the mode of warfare, the great horse became quite out of fashion. But he was not, like a rusty mail, condemned to hang in monumental mockery. For the blood of the Tudor war horse runs in the veins of the heavy draught horses of to-day, and in the best specimens of this class we may trace many characteristics of their famous progenitors.

Next in importance, and in far more general request, was the roadster. He was an ambling, not a trotting horse. In Tudor times all travellers, and most goods, were conveyed on horseback. Coaches had been but lately introduced, and were unknown outside the great cities. Carts labouring heavily through the mire were in use, but only for short distances. Many of the roads were little better than tracks impassable save for the packhorse or the hackney roadster, and even the best of them in the pre-macadamite ages were rough and uneven. To the wayfarer who had to travel his weary miles under such circumstances, a horse trained to the easy pace known as the amble was almost a necessity. 'Take away the ambling horse,' writes Blundevill, ' and take away the olde man, the rich man, the weake man, nay generally all men's travels ; for coaches are but for streets, and carts can hardly passe in winter.'

The word amble did not then, as now, denote a slow and easy trot. It was an artificial pace, in which the horse moved simultaneously the fore and hind legs on each side, a mode of progression which may be now studied in animals differing as widely in other respects as the African camel and the American pacer. In teaching the horse to amble, the legs on each side were attached by means of trammels.[1] Some

<hr />

[1] Macbeth's words,

> If the assassination
> Could trammel up the consequence, *Macbeth*, i. 7. 2,

are thus paraphrased by Johnson : ' If the murder could terminate in itself, and

horses took more naturally to this pace than others, notably
your Irish hobby, which was therefore in much request for
an ' ambling gelding.' [1] The movement in the trot of the
thick-set, straight-pasterned horse of unmixed native breed
was a very different motion from the smooth trotting of the
well-bred saddle-horse of to-day ; and the hardness (as it was
called) of this pace, compared with the amble, made the
journey appear long and tedious. ' Sir,' said Benedick to
Claudio, ' your wit ambles well ; it goes easily.' [2] Rosalind
expressed the general sense of the riders of her day when
she noted as wearisome the hard pace of a trotting horse.

Time travels in divers paces with diverse persons.   I'll tell you
who Time ambles withal, who Time trots withal, who Time gallops
withal, and who he stands still withal.

Orl. I prithee, who doth he trot withal?

Ros. Marry, he trots hard with a young maid between the con-
tract of her marriage and the day it is solemnized : if the interim
be but a se'n night, time's pace is so hard that it seems the length
of seven year.

Orl. Who ambles Time withal ?

Ros. With a priest that lacks Latin and a rich man that hath
not the gout, for the one sleeps easily because he cannot study
and the other lives merrily because he feels no pain, the one
lacking the burden of lean and wasteful learning, the other knowing
no burden of heavy tedious penury ; these Time ambles withal.

Orl. Who doth he gallop withal ?

Ros. With a thief to the gallows, for though he go as softly as
foot can fall, he thinks himself too soon there.

Orl. Who stays it still withal ?

Ros. With lawyers in the vacation ; for they sleep between
term and term and then they perceive not how time moves.[3]

As You L. iii. 2. 326.

restrain the regular course of consequences.'   The manner in which the regular
course of a horse was restrained by strapping together the legs on each side—
' which is called among horse-men trammelling '—will be found fully described
in Gervase Markham's *Cheap and Good Husbandry.*

[1] *Merry Wives*, ii. 2. 319.   [2] *Much Ado*, v. 1. 159.

[3] Mr. Hunter substitutes ' amble ' for ' trot,' and *vice versâ*, supposing that
the ' se'ennight ' appeared seven years from the slowness of the pace, and not
from its hardness ; a double error, for there is no reason to suppose that the
ambler was slower than the trotting horse.   In fact, some of the fastest movers

But if the ambling gelding was preferred for swift and easy travelling on the road, the foot-cloth horse served for show. He was a trotting horse, like the great horse, which, no doubt, served this purpose in the piping days of peace. In ' the chequir roul of nombre of all the horsys '[1] appertaining to the Earl of Northumberland in 1512, among his ' clothsell hors,' we find mention of ' a great double trotting-hors called a curtal for his lordship to ride when he comes into townes.' Of such a clothsell curtal thought Lafeu, an old lord, when he said,

> I'ld give bay Curtal and his furniture,
> My mouth was no more broken than these boys',
> And writ as little beard.   *All's Well*, ii. 3. 65.

A great personage entering a town in state would exchange his ambling nag for a trotting horse, called a clothsell horse or foot-cloth horse from the sell or saddle adorned with foot-cloth, well known to us from pictures of the day ; as

> the duke, great Bolingbroke,
> Mounted upon a hot and fiery steed
> Which his aspiring rider seem'd to know,
> With slow but stately pace kept on his course,
> Whilst all tongues cried ' God save thee, Bolingbroke ! '
> *Rich. II.* v. 2. 7.

On such a trotting horse Lord Hastings rode through London when warned of his doom.

> Three times to-day my foot-cloth horse did stumble,
> And started,[2] when he look'd upon the Tower,
> As loath to bear me to the slaughter-house.
> *Rich. III.* iii. 4. 86.

With this knowledge we may more perfectly understand

of the present day are pacers, and would have been by our ancestors called amblers. I have been told that in some parts of Asia where a good deal of travelling is done on horseback, the horses are frequently amblers, in the strict sense of the term.

[1] Quoted, Sidney's *Book of the Horse.*

[2] Thus the Folio, using an apt term in speaking of the horse. The *Globe* and Cambridge editors read ' startled.'

the bitterness of Jack Cade when he accused Lord Say of
riding on a foot-cloth horse, and why it was that a trotting
horse was associated with the idea of pride.

> *Edg.* Who gives anything to poor Tom ? whom the foul fiend
> hath led through fire and through flame, and through ford and
> whirlipool, o'er bog and quagmire ; that hath laid knives under his
> pillow, and halters in his pew ; set ratsbane by his porridge ; made
> him proud of heart, to ride on a bay trotting-horse over four-inched
> bridges, to course his own shadow for a traitor.
>
> *K. Lear*, iii. 3. 51.

The great horse was always a trotter,[1] and I have no
doubt served, in times of peace, as a foot-cloth horse. But
after the introduction of the eastern horse, his ' delightful
steps ' brought him into request on state occasions. Bolingbroke, as we have seen, rode a Barb, and of the same race,
I doubt not, was the ' hot horse, hot as fire,' on which Arcite
was mounted when, ' trotting the stones of Athens,' he
verified the superstition of the clouded face.[2]

The horses used in hunting and hawking were mostly of
native breeding, and of very various degrees of merit. But
a cross between an English mare and a Barbary horse was
highly esteemed for speed and endurance. It was commended by Blundevill to him that delighteth in those sports,
' to the intent he maie have such Coltes of him as will be
able to continue in such extreame exercises as to gallop the
Bucke, or follow a long winged Hawke. Either of which exercises killeth yœrelie in this realme manie a good Gelding.'

From this and other references to the hunting horse of
the day, I conclude that it had shared in the general decay
of the native-bred horse, before its regeneration by an admixture of eastern blood. In the dialogue already quoted,
entitled *the Cyuile and Vncyuile Life* (1579), Vallentine the
courtier complains to Vincent the country-gentleman that
' many Gentlemen there are that spend yearly so much hay

---

[1] According to the old writers it was not considered meet that horses of
service should amble.

[2] *Two Noble Kinsmen*, v. 4, *ante*, p. 257.

and corne upon huntinge and hawkinge Iades as would maintayne halfe a dozen able horses to serue their Prince. . . Also (if you marke it well) it is (besides the necessity) a better and more commendable sight to see a Gentleman ride with three fayre horses, then fifteene of those vncumly Curtalles ' ; an estimate of the common hunting and hawking jade that Vincent does not see his way to dispute.

Much of the hunting and hawking of the day was done on foot, and a very ordinary nag sufficed for the requirements of the rider, unless indeed for such rare and ' extreame exercises ' as the hunting at force of the Cotswold hart, or keeping in sight a cast of falcons, as hawk and handsaw are borne into the sunbeams by a keen north-north-westerly wind.[1]

Humbler but useful tasks were performed by the post-horse,[2] the cart-horse, or fill-horse,[3] whose life would seem to have been a hard one. ' Whip me ? ' says Pompey to good old Escalus,

> No, no ; let carman whip his jade :
> The valiant heart's not whipt out of his trade.
> *Measure for M*. ii. 1. 269.

The pack-horse,[4] with his pack-saddle [5] laden with merchandise, was a familiar object, not only on the highway, but on numerous tracks known as pack-horse roads, which are still pointed out in various parts of the country. His pace was neither trot nor amble, but a fast walk, known as a foot pace. ' If you will chuse a Horse for portage,.that is, for the Pack, or Hampers, chuse him that is exceeding strong of Body and Limbs, but not tall, with a broad back, out ribbs, full shoulders and thick withers, for if he be thin in that part, you shall hardly keep his back from galling.' [6] In this task the carriers whom we have met in the Rochester inn yard do not seem to have succeeded. ' I prithee, Tom,' said the First Carrier to his fellow, ' beat Cut's saddle, put

---

[1] See *ante*, p. 214.
[2] 2 *Hen. IV*. Ind. 4 ; *Rich. III*. i. 1. 146 ; *Rom. and Jul*. v. 1. 26.
[3] *Merch. of Ven*. ii. 2. 100.   [4] *Rich. III*. i. 3. 122.
[5] *Coriol*. ii. 1. 99.   [6] Markham, *Cheap and Good Husbandry*.

a few flocks in the point ; poor jade is wrung in the withers out of all cess.' [1]

Nothing has, heretofore, been said of the running-horse, or as we should now call him, the race-horse. And this for a sufficient reason. He is the only horse in whom, and in whose doings, Shakespeare took no interest, and the horse-race is the only popular pastime to which no allusion can be found in his writings. It is true that the Turf and the thoroughbred are institutions of later date, for which we are indebted to the Stuarts, not to the Tudors. It is true that these institutions had not, as yet, filled the country with ruined gamblers, and flooded the horse-market with worthless weeds, in order that here and there a horse might be bred of the rarest power to gallop for a couple of miles, carrying on his back a boy or attenuated man. Nevertheless, the popularity of horse-race and running-horse is attested by the literature of the Elizabethan age. Full knowledge of the sport is brought home to Shakespeare with certainty, for horses as well as greyhounds were ' outrun on Cotsall.' In the Cotswold games, celebrated in later years under the auspices of Mr. Robert Dover, the horse-race held a foremost place. Its several incidents, differing little from those of to-day, are commemorated by the contributory poets in their verses, and by the artist who designed the curious frontispiece illustrative of the games.[2]

The impulse to match horse against horse is probably coeval with the subjugation of the animal by man. It is certainly older than the passion for Olympic dust, or for the later day triumphs of the Turf. Traces of this primeval instinct—faint and far between—may be discovered in

---

[1] 1 Hen. IV. ii. 1. 6.

[2] The date of the publication of Annalia Dubrensia was 1636. But according to Anthony Wood, Dover carried on for forty years those games (Athenæ Oxon.) of which he appears to have been the restorer, not the founder. The horse-race is taken as a matter of course, not as a new or exceptional item in the programme. The Annalia Dubrensia fixes its place among English sports with the same certainty as Homer's description of the games in honour of Patroclus proves the chariot race to have been a usual pastime in the heroic age.

Shakespeare. In a wit-combat between Romeo and Mercutio, Romeo exclaims, ' Switch and spurs, switch and spurs ; or I'll cry a match,' whereupon Mercutio, ' Nay, if thy wits run the wild-goose chase, I have done.' [1] There was no need for a critic to substitute ' goats ' for ' goose,' for Mercutio had clearly in his mind a ' way our Ancestors had of making their Matches,' thus described by Nicholas Cox : ' The Wild goose chase received its name from the manner of the *flight* which is made by *Wild geese*, which is generally *one after another* ; so the two Horses after the running of Twelvescore *Yards* had liberty which horse soever could get the *leading* to *ride* what *ground* he pleas'd : the *hindmost* Horse being bound to follow him within a certain *distance* agreed on by Articles, or else to be *whipt* up by the *Triers* or *Judges* which rode by, and whichever Horse could distance the other won the Match.' [2]

There is also a distant recognition of the match or wager, as something heard of rather than seen, in *Cymbeline*, one of Shakespeare's latest plays. Imogen, about to fly to Milford, inquires of Pisanio how many score of miles may be ridden in a day. Pisanio suggests that one score would be enough for her.

> *Imo.* Why, one that rode to's execution, man,
>   Could never go so slow : I have heard of riding wagers,
>   Where horses have been nimbler than the sands
>   That run i' the clock's behalf. But this is foolery :
>   Go, bid my woman feign a sickness ; say

[1] *Rom. and Jul.* ii. 4. 73.

[2] *Gentleman's Recreation*, 1674. The writer tells us that this chase fell into disuse, being ' found by experience so *inhumane* and so destructive to *Horses*, especially when two *good* horses were matched.' It was popular in the time of Burton, for he writes (*Anatomy of Melancholy*, 1632), of ' riding of great horses, running at ring, tilts and turnements, horse-races, wild goose chases, which are the disports of greater men, and good in themselves, though many gentlemen by that meanes gallop quite out of their fortunes.' The running of train-scents with hounds succeeded the wild goose chase as a mode of deciding matches, and it, in turn (according to Cox), ' afterwards was chang'd to *three heats*, and a *straight course*.'

> She'll home to her father : and provide me presently
> A riding suit, no costlier than would fit
> A franklin's housewife.   *Cymb.* iii. 2. 72.

The match or wager between two horses is plainly different from the horse-race, in which several competitors strive for the mastery, as at the Cotswold games. And in the horse-race Shakespeare shows no interest whatever. It occupies the unique position of a sport recognised by Bacon [1] and ignored by Shakespeare ; so let it pass.

II

SECONDLIE HOW TO DYET THE GREAT HORSE, AND THEREIN OF HIS NATURE AND DISPOSITION, AND HOW TO MAKE HIM A HORSE OF SERVICE

'My horse,' said Mark Antony, 'is

> a creature that I teach to fight,
> To wind, to stop, to run directly on,
> His corporal motion govern'd by my spirit.

For that, he says, ' I do appoint him store of provender.' [2]

Bottom, the weaver, may have overrated his gifts as an actor, but in the character of a four-footed beast of burden he proves that an ass can discourse most wisely on provender ; thereby suggesting that we should do well to take a hint even from an ass in a matter which he thoroughly understands, as Zeuxis took hints from a cobbler on the painting of a shoe. ' Say, sweet love,' asks Titania, ' what thou desirest to eat.'

Bot. Truly, a peck of provender : I could munch your good dry oats. Methinks I have a great desire to a bottle of hay : [3] good hay, sweet hay, hath no fellow.

---

[1] *Essay of Building* (1625).   [2] *Jul. Cæs.* iv. 1. 29.

[3] ' A bottell of haie,' according to Blundevill, is the allowance prescribed by Camerarius for a horse at each feed. Bottle, in this sense, meant a bundle, and survives in the saying, ' Look for a needle in a bottle of straw.' This use of the word ' bottle,' like many other words, phrases, and modes of pronunciation, has survived from the Tudor age to the present time in parts of Ireland. Witnesses examined before me in the counties of Tyrone and Cork have spoken of ' bottling ' straw and hay, and have explained that they meant to express the idea of forming it into bundles.

Tita. I have a venturous fairy, that shall seek
The squirrel's hoard, and fetch thee new nuts.
Bot. I had rather have a handful or two of dried peas.

Mids. N. Dr. iv. 1. 33.

Bottom's views on the subject of dry provender are
sound. But unsound reasons may be given for sound conclusions ; witness the carriers loading their pack-horses in
the Rochester inn-yard, to bear London-wards Kentish
turkeys, and ' a gammon of bacon and two razes of ginger to
be delivered as far as Charing Cross,' while they converse
after the manner of their kind :

Sec. Car. Peas and beans are as dank here as a dog, and
that is the next way to give poor jades the bots. This house is
turned upside down since Robin Ostler died.
First Car. Poor fellow, never joyed since the price of oats
rose ; it was the death of him.

1 *Hen. IV.* ii. 19.

If carriers on the Kentish road were ignorant of the
natural history of the bot (which we know to be the offspring of eggs, attached to certain leaves and swallowed by
the horse), they erred in good company. We read in
Blundevill that bots are engendered most commonly by
' fowle feeding,' and Markham,[1] referring to the opinion of
his ' masters, the old antient farriers,' attributes their
presence in the body of the horse to ' foul and naughty
feeding.'

' My brother Jaques he keeps at school,' complains
Orlando of his unjust and cruel brother,

and report speaks goldenly of his profit : for my part, he keeps
me rustically at home, or, to speak more properly, stays me here
at home unkept ; for call you that keeping for a gentleman of my
birth, that differs not from the stalling of an ox ? His horses are
bred better ; for, besides that they are fair with their feeding, they
are taught their manage, and to that end riders dearly hired.

As You L. i. 1. 5.

' Fair with their feeding,' in this lies the whole art of

[1] *Maister-peece of Farriery.*

horse-keeping. Fair provender should be fairly apportioned to the work done, noting the different conditions of the 'soiled horse,'[1] 'the fat and bean-fed horse,'[2] the 'hot and fiery steed,'[3] the 'hollow pamper'd jade,'[4] and the horse that is truly tired, to which you must offer neither oats nor beans, but 'barley broth . . . a drench for sur-rein'd jades.'[5]

If you neglect this maxim, the result will be disaster. Your fat and bean-fed horse, overfed and underworked, may point a moral. 'The times are wild,' said Northumberland,

> contention, like a horse
> Full of high feeding, madly hath broke loose
> And bears down all before him.   *2 Hen. IV.* i. 1. 9.

Thus it came about that Duncan's horses,

> Beauteous and swift, the minions of their race,
> Turn'd wild in nature, broke their stalls, flung out,
> Contending 'gainst obedience, as they would make
> War with mankind.
> *Old M.* 'Tis said they eat each other.
> *Ross.*   They did so, to the amazement of mine eyes
> That look'd upon't.   *Macbeth,* ii. 4. 14.

For if the story is (as we are told) ' a thing most strange and certain,' the explanation of the portent may be found in overfeeding and underwork, the ruin of many as beauteous and swift as they, ignoring the ' hot condition of their blood.'[6]

But the horse of service, if hard work is looked for, must be highly fed. ' The confident and over-lusty French ' before Agincourt noted how their own 'steeds for present service neigh,' and comparing their 'hot blood' with the starved condition of the English, and of their horses reduced to chewing grass, made sure of easy victory, and mockingly suggested finding the English, and giving ' their fasting horses provender,' so as to make the fight a fair one.

> Their poor jades
> Lob down their heads, dropping the hides and hips,
> The gum down-roping from their pale-dead eyes,

---

[1] *K. Lear,* iv. 6. 124.   [2] *Mids. N. Dr.* ii. 1. 45.
[3] *Rich. II.* v. 2. 8.   [4] *2 Hen. IV.* ii. 4. 178.
[5] *Hen. V.* iii. 5. 19.   [6] *Merch. of Ven.* v. 1. 74.

And in their pale dull mouths the gimmal bit
Lies foul with chew'd grass, still and motionless;
And their executors, the knavish crows,
Fly o'er them, all impatient for their hour.
Description cannot suit itself in words
To demonstrate the life of such a battle
In life so lifeless as it shows itself.   *Hen. V.* iv. 2. 46.

The Frenchmen soon learned that a gallant horse, though
half starved, is a different animal from

pack-horses,
And hollow pamper'd jades of Asia,
Which cannot go but thirty miles a-day.
2 *Hen. IV.* ii. 4. 177.

For even in regard to the beast that perisheth, there is
somewhat more to be thought of than abundance of meat
and drink.   There is the quality of its spirit.   King Harry
said of his force ' our hearts are in the trim,' [1] and when
this is so, it is a long way to the end of man, horse, or
hound.

Avoiding the extremes of overfeeding, and starvation,
and taking care that your horses are fair with their feeding,
you will have them ' taught their manage.'

In training any animal—not excepting man—it is before
all things needful to understand the nature and disposition
with which you have to deal.   For, notwithstanding wide
differences between individuals, there has been given to each
species of created beings a separate and individual nature.
And so it is that we understand each other (in Bishop
Butler's words) when we speak of such a thing as human
nature.   Brute creatures, according to this great thinker,
need not to be trained up in the way they should go, ' nature
forming them by instincts to the particular manner of life
appointed them, from which they never deviate.'   But if
you would have a brute creature deviate from his particular
appointed manner of life to another, for which nature has
supplied the capacity but not the needful instincts, you

[1] *Hen. V.* iv. 3. 115.

must train him as you would a child. For example, the whole nature of the horse, physical, intellectual, and moral,[1] proves him 'created to be awed by man,' and 'born to bear.'[2] But in this he is perfected, not by instinct, but by training, and here comes in the similitude between man and beast, on which Shakespeare loved to dwell.

The horse has been chosen by two lovers of the race for illustration of human character and conduct; by Swift[3] in a single work, in the way of contrast, and for purposes of bitterest satire; by Shakespeare, constantly, with a kindly and tolerant feeling towards both creatures, and in the pursuit of that truly eclectic philosophy which turns even adversity to sweet uses, and

> Finds tongues in trees, books in the running brooks,
> Sermons in stones, and good in everything.
>   *As You L.* ii. 1. 16.

Many are the sermons for which the horse and his training supply him with the text; short, practical, and to the point.

Thus Gardiner, Bishop of Winchester, when he advised

---

[1] If you take exception to the application of the word 'moral' to what is called the brute creation, I refer you to a suggestive passage in Bishop Butler's *Analogy*, where he describes as both invidious and weak an objection taken to certain of his arguments for the immortality of the soul, by reason of their applicability to brutes as well as to mankind.

[2] *Rich. II.* v. 5. 91.

[3] 'He was also a tolerable horseman,' writes Sir Walter Scott, 'fond of riding, and a judge of the noble animal, which he chose to celebrate, as the emblem of moral merit, under the name of Houynhnhnm' (*Life of Swift*). His earliest misadventure was at Kilkenny College, where he expended all his little store of money in buying a mangy horse on its way to the knacker's yard (Sheridan's *Life of Swift*), but soon repented of his bargain when the poor brute dropped down dead. Stella's horse, Johnson, is remembered amidst all the varying interests of his London life. It was not from Shakespeare that Swift learned to love the horse. 'He never once alludes to the writings of Shakespeare, nor, wonderful to be told, does he appear to have possessed a copy of his works.' (*Life*, by Sir Walter Scott.) In this respect he differed widely from his biographer and editor. Apart from conscious imitation or discipleship in the same branch of literature, it would be hard to name any man of creative genius so thoroughly interpenetrated with the thoughts and the very language of another as Scott is with those of Shakespeare.

vigorous measures against heretics, reminded the Council that the first care of the trainer is to get the mastery of his horse; until this has been achieved, gentleness is out of place.

> For those that tame wild horses
> Pace 'em not in their hands to make 'em gentle,
> But stop their mouths with stubborn bits, and spur 'em,
> Till they obey the manage. If we suffer,
> Out of our easiness and childish pity
> To one man's honour, this contagious sickness,
> Farewell all physic : and what follows then ?
> Commotions, uproars, with a general taint
> Of the whole state.   *Hen. VIII.* v. 3. 21.

But though it is necessary to prove who is master, care must be taken to avoid unnecessary violence, as children should not be provoked to wrath, but brought up in due nurture and admonition.

'The king is come,' says the Duke of York of poor Richard,

> deal mildly with his youth ;
> For young hot colts being raged [1] do rage the more.
>   *Rich. II.* ii. 1. 69.

Above all things, allow plenty of time for growth, and do not begin your training too soon.

> Who wears a garment shapeless and unfinish'd,
>   Who plucks a bud before one leaf put forth ?
> If springing things be any jot diminish'd,
>   They wither in their prime, prove nothing worth :
> The colt that's back'd and burden'd being young
> Loseth his pride and never waxeth strong.
>   *Ven. and Ad.* 415.

[1] In a footnote at p. 265, it is shown that the word 'rage' was a kindly and proper term to be used in speaking of colts; and in Shakespeare's time the play upon this word in the text conveyed to the ears of a Tudor horseman some meaning now lost. That the words stand in need of explanation is evident from the following list of conjectural emendations taken from the notes to the *Cambridge Shakespeare*, which retains the original text, without obelising the word 'raged' as in the *Globe* Edition; 'inrag'd' (Pope) ; 'being 'rag'd' (Hanmer) ; 'being rein'd' (Singer) ; 'being urg'd' (Collier) ; 'being chaf'd' (Jervis) ; 'being curb'd' (Keightley) ; 'be-wringed' (Bulloch) ; 'being rous'd' (Herr).

This is a text upon which, if time and place did serve, much might be said. How many springing things of rarest promise wither in their rⁿime, or prove nothing worth in after years, from overwork in youth? The evil was not so rife three hundred years ago as in these days of competitive examinations, open scholarships, and forced culture. Shakespeare's wisdom is not of an age, but for all time, and of all his object-lessons from the animal world there is none more deserving of being laid to heart than the poor spiritless jade, unequal to sustained effort, once a promising colt, but hopelessly ruined for life, inasmuch as he was backed and burdened, being young, by an impatient master, too eagerly desirous of immediate results.

But the discipline of punishment is not the whole of training. There is the discipline of reward. The manage had not only its needful corrections, but its helps and cherishing, by hand, leg, and voice. Shakespeare calls them 'aids'[1] and 'terms of manage.'[2] He has given us examples.[3] It is when the Dauphin cries 'Ça ha!' to his prince of palfreys that he 'bounds from the earth as if his entrails were hairs.'[4] Adonis addressed to the duller courser of Stratford not only his stern 'Stand, I say,' but his 'flattering Holla.'[5] Richard II. bemoaned roan Barbary's forgetfulness of the hand that 'made him proud with clapping him,' the royal hand from which the ungrateful jade had often eaten bread.[6]

Hermione pleaded on behalf of mankind in general, and her own sex in particular, that they too might have their aids and rewards, and she insists on the ill effects of correcting when you ought to cherish.

---

[1] *A Lover's Complaint*, 117.   [2] 1 *Hen. IV*. ii. 3. 52.

[3] The old writers are at one with Shakespeare in this matter of 'helps and corrections of the voyce.' Michael Baret (*Vineyard*, 1618), in addition to 'Backe, I say, Stand, and such like,' is of opinion that 'Will, you Roague; Ah, thou Traytor; So, thou Villaine; or such like, will helpe to bring him into the more subiection, so that he doe not perceive the man to be timerous.' According to the *Art of Riding* (1584), 'a cowardly horse must be corrected courteously.'

[4] *Hen. V*. iii. 7. 13.   [5] *Ven. and Ad*. 284.   [6] *Rich. II*. v. 5. 85.

> Cram's with praise, and make's
> As fat as tame things : one good deed dying tongueless
> Slaughters a thousand waiting upon that.
> Our praises are our wages : you may ride's
> With one soft kiss a thousand furlongs ere
> With spur we heat an acre.   *Wint. Tale,* i. 2. 91.

In the commonwealth of Utopia 'they do not only fear their people from doing evil by punishments, but also allure them to virtue with rewards of honour.'[1] Socrates suggested as his desert, a sentence of maintenance at the public expense in the Prytaneum, and public rewards as well as punishments are hinted at in the Republic of his disciple Plato—surely the most dismal of ideal communities, where the domestic virtues are impossible, and poetry and fiction are unknown. In the kingdom of Lilliput, whoever can prove that he has strictly observed the laws of his country for a certain time, may add to his name the title of *snilpall* or legal, and draw a certain sum of money out of a fund appropriated for that use ; the image of Justice, in Lilliputian Courts of Judicature, is formed with a bag of gold open in her right hand, and a sword sheathed in her left, to show that she is more disposed to reward than to punish. Those people thought it a prodigious defect of policy among us when told that our laws were enforced only by penalties without any mention of reward. And yet, despite philosophers ancient and modern, Swift's observation still holds true : 'Although we usually call reward and punishment the two hinges upon which all government turns, yet I could never observe this maxim to be put in practice by any nation except that of Lilliput.' It remains for some social reformer in the future, by means of a system of public rewards out of money voted by Parliament, at once to provide infinite possibilities in Committee of Supply, agreeably to diversify the labours of a going Judge of Assize, and to give practical effect to the philosophy of Socrates, Plato, More, Swift, and

---

[1] More's *Utopia*, ch. ix. Robinson's translation, 1551.

the wisdom which Hermione derived from long experience and intimate knowledge of the nature of the horse.

The comparison of the body politic to a horse, and of a ruler to its rider, is a favourite one with Shakespeare. 'The estate is green and yet ungoverned,' said Buckingham,

> Where every horse bears his commanding rein,
> And may direct his course as please himself.
>> *Rich. III.* ii. 2. 128.

'The times are wild,' said Northumberland in the days of Hotspur's rebellion,

>> contention like a horse
> Full of high feeding, madly hath broke loose
> And bears down all before him. 2 *Hen. IV.* i. 1. 9.

Similes of this kind, however, are among the commonplaces of literature. Shakespeare's application of his experience of the horse is commonly of a more direct and personal character.

In studying mankind, we must regard not only individual men, and human nature in the abstract, but also certain types, or varieties, in accordance with which the dissimilar atoms constituting the sum total of humanity seem to arrange themselves.

The study of these types, or Characters, was much affected by our early satirists.[1] Shakespeare is a dramatist, not a satirist, and he presents us not with characters, but with living men and women. But these men and women sometimes classified their fellow-creatures, as we might. And in so doing, moved by some common impulse even when alike in nothing else, when they would illustrate their

---

[1] The *Characters* of Bishop Hall, better known as a divine than as a satirist, may be read with interest at the present day. He was followed by the ill-fated Sir Thomas Overbury, a Gloucestershire man, who published in 1614 his *Characters ; or, Witty Descriptions of the Properties of Sundry Persons*, and in imitation of his work John Earle, afterwards Bishop of Salisbury, wrote *Micro-cosmographie; or, a Peece of the World discovered in Essays and Characters* (1628), displaying, in Hallam's opinion, ' acute observation, and a happy humour of expression.'

meaning, they sought in field or stable a counterpart to each human character.

Take, for instance, the Hollow Man. Who does not know him? Loud-voiced, confident, self-asserting, in the eyes of the ignorant the type of the ideal Strong Man. But call on him in the needful time of trial, and he will fail to respond.

> There are no tricks in plain and simple faith;
> But hollow men, like horses hot at hand,
> Make gallant show and promise of their mettle;
> But when they should endure the bloody spur,
> They fall their crests, and, like deceitful jades,
> Sink in the trial. *Jul. Cæs.* iv. 2. 22.

This hollow deceitful jade is far removed from the ideal horse, typical of a very different man. *Troilus and Cressida* was written shortly after the appearance of Chapman's translation of the Iliad. This work of genius—uncouth and rugged, but instinct with the heroic spirit—must have been a revelation to one possessed of 'small Latin and less Greek,' and striving to attain a full understanding of the great masters of the old civilisation. It may well be that the Father of Poets was thus made known to the greatest of his sons, as he was long afterwards revealed to another of the chosen race:

> Oft of one wide expanse had I been told
> That deep-brow'd Homer rul'd as his demesne:
> Yet did I never breathe its pure serene
> Till I heard Chapman speak out loud and bold;
>
> —Then felt I like some watcher of the skies
> When a new planet swims into his ken.

Shakespeare's Latin and Greek may have needed the aid of English translations, but, however this may be, he succeeded in clothing his conceptions of classical antiquity in flesh and blood, and presenting them with a living reality unattained by his learned contemporary and critic, Ben Jonson. Among his presentations of the men and women who live in the Iliad, none is so natural or so Homeric (the words mean the same thing) as Ajax the Strong Man; truest, if not greatest, among the heroes of the Iliad.

Achilles had withdrawn in wrath to his ships, reckless of the slaughter of his fellows and of the ruin of the Achæan cause. Then was the occasion, and the man was found in Ajax. Plain, sparing of words, but when needful speaking straight to the point, he was in all respects the opposite of the Hollow Man. So far was he from making gallant show and promise of great qualities, that he seemed to conceal them even from himself. In search of a parallel for his absence of self-consciousness, Shakespeare, like Homer, turns instinctively to the 'great and sane and simple race of brutes.' [1]

In the scene in which Ulysses unfolds to Achilles the consequences of his withdrawal, he insists that a man can hardly be called lord of the qualities with which he is endowed, nor can he be said really to know them, until by communicating his parts to others, he beholds them 'form'd in the applause where they're extended.' Wrapt in this thought, he apprehends one, unknown even to himself, whom chance is about to make famous, so as even to dim the recollection of great Achilles' deeds.

> The unknown Ajax.
> Heavens, what a man is there! a very horse,
> That has he knows not what. Nature, what things there are
> Most abject in regard and dear in use!
> What things again most dear in the esteem
> And poor in worth! Now shall we see to-morrow—
> An act that very chance doth throw upon him—
> Ajax renown'd. *Troil. and Cres.* iii. 3. 125.

Ajax goes about his work with as little self-conscious affectation as an honest horse, who simply does his kind. 'Thou sodden-witted lord!' says Thersites, 'thou hast no more brain than I have in mine elbows; an assinego may tutor thee: thou scurvy-valiant ass! thou art here but to thrash Trojans.' [2]

---

[1] *Pelleas and Ettarre;* see *Iliad*, xi. 556, xiii. 702. 'This man, lady,' says one to Cressida, of Ajax, 'hath robbed many beasts of their particular additions' (*Troil. and Cres.* i. 2. 19). [2] *Troil. and Cres.* ii. 1. 47.

The lies currently told and believed of a great man are no small aid towards forming an estimate of his real character ; a branch of study in which singular advantages may be enjoyed by the future historian of the present age, provided always he has skill to discern lies from truths. The Greeks before Troy, in default of modern institutions, had to be content with their Thersites. According to him, Ulysses was a dog-fox, and Ajax a stupid beast of burden, whom it were gross flattery to compare in intellect with a horse. 'Thy horse will sooner con an oration than thou learn a prayer without book. Thou canst strike, canst thou? A red murrain o' thy jade's tricks.'[1] Sent by Achilles to Ajax with a letter, he exclaims : 'Let me bear another to his horse; for that's the more capable creature.'[2] But neither he nor Ulysses can think of the Strong Man[3] without the idea of the horse presenting itself to their minds ; nor can Nestor, who thus complains :

> Ajax is grown self-will'd, and bears his head
> In such a rein, in full as proud a place
> As broad Achilles.   *Ibid.* i. 3. 188.

Not that Ajax was devoid of the fiery spirit to which the word 'rage,'[4] in a meaning now lost, was formerly applied, with special reference to the horse. Among the Trojan heroes depicted in the house of Collatinus,

> In Ajax' eyes blunt rage and rigour roll'd ;
> But the mild glance that sly Ulysses lent
> Show'd deep regard and smiling government.
>   *Lucrece*, 1398.

---

[1] *Troil. and Cres.* ii. 1. 18.   [2] *Ibid.* iii. 3. 309.

[3] Gervinus in his note on *Troil. and Cres.* remarks, ' that in single instances we stumble, as it were, upon a psychological commentary. The hand is masterly with which, in the delineation of Ajax, physical strength is exhibited strengthened at the expense of mental power; the abundance of similes and images with which the rare but simple nature is described is inexhaustible; the discernment is wonderful with which all animal qualities are gathered together to form this man, at once both more and less than human.' All these qualities, and Shakespeare's concentrated experience of man and horse are gathered together in the words ' a very horse That has he knows not what.'

[4] As to this application of the words ' rage ' and ' ragerie,' see the note to p. 265.

His rage was real, not figured like the Hollow Man's. It was also in keeping and harmony with the other parts of his nature.   He was not like

> some fierce thing replete with too much rage,
> Whose strength's abundance weakens his own heart.
>
> *Sonnet* xxiii.

He was there to thrash Trojans.   He knew it, and did his work in simple good faith, thoroughly, as an honest horse fulfils his daily task.

In describing the Stedfast Man as one 'breathed, as it were, To an untirable and continuate goodness'[1] there is a suggestion of the stable.   For in the stable language of the day a horse with what is now known as staying power was called a continuer.

> *Bene.* I would my horse had the speed of your tongue, and so good a continuer.   *Much Ado*, i. 1. 142.

And there is something more than mere suggestion in the line

> As true as truest horse, that yet would never tire.
>
> *Mids. N. Dr.* iii. 1. 98.

Nearly akin to the Hollow Man is he whom we have met in the course of our pilgrimage, travelling under the name of Mr. Talkative, ready to discourse of all matters, sacred or profane.   'What shall we do to be rid of him?' asked Faithful.   Let us hear the answer of his fellow pilgrim, translated into the language of the stable.

'Enter Tranio, brave,' full of brave words, and classical allusions :

> *Gre.* What! this gentleman will out-talk us all.
> *Luc.* Sir, give him head ; I know he'll prove a jade.
>
> *Tam. of Shrew*, i. 2. 248.

But the selfsame trial which reveals the jade in Mr. Talkative reveals also the True Man, or woman.   Paulina denounced Leontes in unmeasured terms for his cruel ill-treatment of

---

[1] *Timon of Ath.* i. 1. 10.

the gentle Hermione and of her innocent child. To the jealous king she was ' a callat of boundless tongue,' and her husband Antigonus was ' worthy to be hanged that wilt not stay her tongue.' But Antigonus knew better :

> La you now, you hear :
> When she will take the rein I let her run ;
> But she'll not stumble.   *Wint. Tale*, ii. 3. 50.

Then there is the Wrathful Man. He is best treated as Mr. Talkative, and given his head, for

> anger is like
> A full hot horse, who being allow'd his way,
> Self-mettle tires him.   *Hen. VIII*. i. 1. 132.

More dangerous still is the Brute, who gives way to the baser passions of his nature. It were well to restrain him if you can, but be not too sanguine of success, for

> What rein can hold licentious wickedness
> When down the hill he holds his fierce career ?
>   *Hen. V*. iii. 3. 22.

If curb and rein fail, there is nothing for it but to leave him also to himself, for

> O, deeper sin than bottomless conceit
> Can comprehend in still imagination !
> Drunken Desire must vomit his receipt,
> Ere he can see his own abomination.
> While Lust is in his pride, no exclamation
>   Can curb his heat or rein his rash desire,
>   Till like a jade Self-will himself doth tire.
>   *Lucrece*, 701.

But neither man nor horse can be finally disposed of by classing them simply as good or bad. There are infinite varieties of either species. There is, for example, the Bore— no need to enlarge on him. He too has his counterpart in the horse ;

> O he is as tedious
> As a tired horse, a railing wife,
> Worse than a smoky house.
>   1 *Hen. IV*. iii. 1. 160.

And there are the Headstrong, the Forward, and the Wayward, for each of whom a different treatment is prescribed. The Headstrong is not, like the Brute, absolutely unmanageable. And for him must be provided 'the needful bits and curbs' to which the Duke of Vienna likened the 'strict statutes and most biting laws,'[1] put in force by his deputy Angelo, a similitude somewhat like that which presented itself to the mind of Claudio, when he compared the body public to

> A horse whereon the governor doth ride,
> Who, newly in the seat, that it may know
> He can command, lets it straight feel the spur.
>
> *Measure for M.* i. 2. 164.

But the free and forward horse needs neither the stimulus nor the discipline of the spur.

> How fondly dost thou spur a forward horse!
>
> *Rich. II.* iv. 1. 72.

And even should forwardness degenerate into waywardness there is no need to have recourse to strict or biting methods. A word of manage spoken in season, how good is it! 'Backe, I say. Stand and such like' are among the terms of manage recommended by old writers. 'Will, you Roague. Ah! thou Traytor. So thou, Villaine, or such like it, will help to bring him into the more subjection, so that he do not perceiue the man to be timerous.'[2] Celia knew this when she said to Rosalind, 'Cry "holla" to thy tongue, I prithee; it curvets unseasonably.'[3]

Then there are the Indifferent. They find their counterpart in the whole equine race. It is best so. The horse is designed by nature to bear whatever burden may be placed upon his back, kindly, but with the smallest amount of individual preference. To this end his affectionate but shallow nature is no less adapted than his physical structure. The horse has his likings and dislikings, a lasting memory of injuries, and a kindly feeling towards master and groom.

---

[1] *Measure for M.* i. 3. 20. [2] Michael Baret, 1618.
[3] *As You L.* iii. 2. 257.

But he is generally indifferent to the personal element in his surroundings.   Lovers of the horse, disposed to rail at the fickleness of a favourite, can sympathise with poor dethroned Richard II. in his indignation at the forgetfulness of roan Barbary :

Groom.   I was a poor groom of thy stable, king,
          When thou wast king ; who, travelling towards York
          With much ado at length have gotten leave
          To look upon my sometimes royal master's face.
          O, how it yearn'd my heart when I beheld
          In London streets, that coronation day,
          When Bolingbroke rode on roan Barbary,
          That horse that thou so often hast bestrid,
          That horse that I so carefully have dress'd !
K. Rich. Rode he on Barbary ?   Tell me, gentle friend,
          How went he under him ?
Groom.   So proudly as if he disdain'd the ground.
K. Rich. So proud that Bolingbroke was on his back !
          That jade hath eat bread from my royal hand ;
          This hand hath made him proud with clapping him.
          Would he not stumble ?   Would he not fall down,
          Since pride must have a fall, and break the neck
          Of that proud man that did usurp his back ?
          Forgiveness, horse !   Why do I rail on thee,
          Since thou, created to be awed by man,
          Wast born to bear?   *Rich. II.* v. 5. 72.

Richard was a thoughtful, if not a practical, student of the horse, and in these words he has suggested the secret of man's dominion.   Captain Lemuel Gulliver's master wondered ' how we dared to venture upon a Houynhnhnm's back ; for he was sure that the weakest servant in his house would be able to shake off the strongest Yahoo, or, by lying down, and rolling on his back, squeeze the brute to death.'   The answer is a simple one.   The dominion of man over the horse, like that of a governing race of men over an inferior, rests entirely on prestige.   One is born to command.   The horse, by reason of his nervous and impressionable nature, is ' created to be awed.'   Take away the awe, and the advantage is on the side of the horse. Reverse the order of nature,

take from man the higher faculties which we call reason and
transfer them to the horse ; this done, a Houynhnhnm is a
possibility, and a Yahoo a certainty.

III

*THIRDLIE OF THE WHOLE ARTE OF RIDING THE
GREAT HORSE*

It could not be otherwise than that Shakespeare's favourite
character, in whom some have seen reflected the image of
his creator,[1] should be devoted to the horse; not with the
foolish affection of Richard II.—who marvelled that roan
Barbary, fed with bread from his royal hand, could bring
himself to carry Henry Bolingbroke proudly—but after a
fashion thoroughly practical, in accordance with his genius.

'I saw young Harry with his beaver on,' Sir Richard
Vernon reports to Hotspur,

> Rise from the ground like feather'd Mercury,
> And vaulted with such ease into his seat,
> As if an angel dropp'd down from the clouds,
> To turn and wind a fiery Pegasus
> And witch the world with noble horsemanship.
>
> <div align="right">1 <i>Hen. IV.</i> iv. 1. 104.</div>

This world-witching horsemanship differs as widely from
the impetuosity of Hotspur as from the sentimentality of
poor Richard, who, notwithstanding his attention to roan
Barbary, was conscious of ' wanting the manage of unruly
jades.'[2] The contrast between the characters of Henry of
Monmouth and of Harry Hotspur foreshadows the destiny

---

[1] Gervinus discusses the conjecture 'that Shakespeare conferred upon
Prince Henry many essential qualities of his own nature,' and concludes that
' in the most essential respects the character of our poet was reflected in Prince
Henry ' (*Shakespeare Commentaries*).   There is a singular interest attached to
self-portraits by great artists, such as Holbein, Rembrandt, Reynolds and
Murillo, and imagination busies itself in labelling certain pen-and-ink sketches
with names great in literature.   Thus *David Copperfield* becomes DICKENS ;
Maggie Tulliver, GEORGE ELIOT ; *Childe Harold*, BYRON ; and *Henry of Monmouth*, SHAKESPEARE.   It is at all events certain that if Shakespeare's counterfeit presentment were limned by himself, it must needs take the form of an
equestrian portrait.   [2] *Rich. II.* iii. 3. 179.

appointed to each ; fame and empire to the one ; to the other failure, and a rebel's grave. Each was brave, and each was a horseman. But they were unlike in horsemanship as in gallantry. Hotspur, true to his name, might have appropriated to himself John of Gaunt's dying saying, ' He tires betimes that spurs too fast betimes.' [1] He too, like Richard, had a favourite roan.

Hot. Hath Butler brought those horses from the sheriff ?
Serv. One horse, my lord, he brought even now.
Hot. What horse ? A roan, a crop-ear, is it not ?
Serv. It is, my lord.
Hot.   That roan shall be my throne.
Well, I will back him straight ; O esperance !
Bid Butler lead him forth into the park.

1 Hen. IV. ii. 3. 70.

But Hotspur's roan had other work to do than eat bread from his master's hand. ' Give my roan horse a drench,' he would cry. This was after killing ' some six or seven dozen of Scots at a breakfast ; ' [2] and sorely the poor beast needed his ' barley-broth,' which many even now agree with Shakespeare in approving as ' a drench for sur-rein'd jades.' [3] In dreams he would urge his bounding steed to the field with ' terms of manage.' Waking he would rail on ' the forced gait of a shuffling nag,' [4] as no better than ' mincing poetry,' and deride Owen Glendower, calling him ' as tedious as a tired horse.' [5]

But this bluster and impetuosity gave as little promise of the noble horsemanship wherewith Henry of Monmouth could witch the world and woo a wife, as of the mental and moral qualities which won him his place in history. ' If I could win a lady,' he tells Katherine of France in his blunt way, ' by vaulting into my saddle with my armour on my back, under the correction of bragging be it spoken, I should quickly leap into a wife. Or if I might buffet for my love, or bound my horse for her favours, I could lay on like a butcher and sit like a jack-an-apes, never off.' [6]

¹ *Rich. II.* ii. 1. 36.   ² 1 *Hen. IV.* ii. 4. 115.   ³ *Hen. V.* iii. 5. 19.
⁴ *Ibid.* ii. 3. 52 ; iii. 1. 134.   ⁵ 1 *Hen IV.* iii. 1. 159.   ⁶ *Hen. V.* v. 2. 142.

As 'for these fellows of infinite tongue that can rhyme themselves into ladies' favours, they do always reason themselves out again;' and Henry's estimate of the lasting impression made on the female heart by the qualities in which he was conscious of excelling, is borne out by the experience of the sad, pale, deserted maid, who recalls among the perfections of her faithless betrayer,

Well could he ride, and often men would say
' That horse his mettle from his rider takes :
Proud of subjection, noble by the sway,
What rounds, what bounds, what course, what stop he makes ! '
And controversy hence a question takes,
Whether the horse by him became his deed,
Or he his manage by the well-doing steed.

But quickly on this side the verdict went :
His real habitude gave life and grace
To appertainings and to ornament,
Accomplish'd in himself, not in his case :
All aids, themselves made fairer by their place,
Came for additions : yet their purpose trim
Pieced not his grace, but were all graced by him.

A Lover's Complaint, 106.

In Tudor times to excel in horsemanship ranked highest among courtly graces. The King of Denmark was a murderer and a usurper, but he had not forgotten the princely accomplishments of his youth. And when he would stimulate Laertes by a report of the praise bestowed on his skill in fence by a gentleman of Normandy, he knew how to enhance the value of his commendation.

Two months since,
Here was a gentleman of Normandy :—
I've seen myself, and served against, the French,
And they can well on horseback ; but this gallant
Had witchcraft in't ; he grew into [1] his seat ;

[1] Thus the Folio. The first Quarto has 'unto,' precisely the error which we should expect from a surreptitious copyist, incapable of appreciating the vigour and truth of the original. The Cambridge Edition follows the Quarto.

And to such wondrous doing brought his horse,
As had he been incorpsed and demi-natured
With the brave beast ; so far he topp'd my thought,
That I in forgery of shapes and tricks,
Come short of what he did.
Laer.   A Norman was't ?
King. A Norman.
Laer. Upon my life, Lamond.
King.   The very same.
Laer. I know him well ; he is the brooch indeed,
And gem of all the nation. [1]   *Hamlet*, iv. 7. 82.

Had the diarist completed his self-appointed task, we might have learned much of the horsemanship of his day. More elaborate than the exercises of the military riding school, and less fantastic than the tricks of the circus, the manage of our ancestors afforded excellent training for nerve and temper, as well as for hand and eye.

Blundevill, in his second book, devoted to an exposition of the art of riding the great horse, describes seven stages in the course of his education, each of which has been noted by Shakespeare.

First you must pace him ; this is the elementary teaching upon which the higher education of the manage must be

---

[1] It is not without design that this picture of ideal horsemanship is drawn by the hand, not of Hamlet, but of his uncle. Shakespeare's men of action, Henry V., Hotspur, Mark Antony, the Dauphin of France, and the King of Denmark (among whose sins irresolution found no place) are his horsemen. It is so in history, from Alexander the Great to Oliver Cromwell. Hamlet was visited by recollections of the chase. He had a practical knowledge of falconry, a sport which, in its ordinary pursuit, required but little physical exertion. But his thoughts do not dwell on horsemanship, an exercise to which I would venture to apply the following words written by Goethe, and Englished by Thomas Carlyle : ' The fencing tires him,' Wilhelm Meister says, ' the sweat is running from his brow ; and the Queen remarks, *He's fat and scant of breath.* Can you conceive him to be otherwise than plump and fair-haired ? Brown-complexioned people in their youth are seldom plump. And does not his wavering melancholy, his soft lamenting, his irresolute activity, accord with such a figure ? ' The horse, in Shakespeare's words, takes his mettle from his rider, and I fear that Hamlet, had he essayed to turn and wind a fiery Pegasus, would have proved ' wanting the manage of unruly jades,' like one who resembled the high-souled Prince of Denmark only in so far as he was infected by the fatal evil of irresolution.

founded. It does not come by nature, and the Lord Lysi-machus of Mytilene understood what was meant when it was said to him of Marina, ' My lord, she's not paced yet ! you must take some pains to work her to your manage.'[1]

Although the horse in a state of nature will walk, trot, and gallop, yet he must needs be ' paced' if he is to acquit him-self well under artificial conditions, while the amble and the ' false gallop' are purely artificial movements. Master Michel Baret published in 1618 a book entitled *An Hippo-nomie, or Vineyard of Horsemanship*, in which he sets forth ' how to bring any horse of what age and disposition soeuer to a faire and commendable pace, onely by the hand : ' a matter in which he is compelled respectfully to ' digresse ' from his master, Gervase Markham, who insists on the use of the trammel in teaching horses to amble, and in which he differs also from Shakespeare, who in a passage already quoted (*ante*, p. 281) suggests that wild horses need bit and spurs for discipline, as well as pacing in the hand.

The false gallop, or artificial canter, was denoted by the Latin term *succussatura*, and the idea of jolting would be naturally associated with that pace in the case of the straight-pasterned, thickset horse of his day. With this knowledge we understand why Touchstone calls doggerel rhymes ' the very false gallop of verses.'[2]

' Secondlie,' says Blundevill, ' you must teach him to be light at stop.' If the great horse knows not the stop, his performances are as crude and unpleasing as poetry read without regard to rhythm or punctuation. ' This fellow does

---

[1] *Pericles*, iv. 6. 68.

[2] *As You L.* iii. 2. 119. Sadler, in his work *De procreandis etc. equis* (1587), gives the following account of the false gallop : ' Noverit plene equus a succussatura ad celeriorem paulo progressum, a celeriore ad citatiorem cursum ascendere, et commutatis vicissitudinibus, a citatiore ad sedatiorem progressum iterum descendere, quoties et quandocumque equiti videbitur, antequam se ver-tere illum doceatis. At, ut clare anglice dicam, my meaning is that your horse knows thorowly from his trot to rise to his false gallope, from his false gallope get to a swifter, and then from this swifter to descend again to his false gallope, and trot againe by turnes when and as oft as the rider shall thinke good, before you teach him to turne.'

not stand upon points,' said Theseus, when Peter Quince had thus delivered himself of his prologue; whereupon Lysimachus of Athens caps his pun with a better. ' He hath rid his prologue like a rough colt; he knows not the stop.'[1] But the stop artistically performed was a joy for ever. 'What stop he makes,' men would say, as they gazed with admiration on the beauteous but false-hearted gallant, bemoaned in *A Lover's Complaint.*

' Thirdlie, to advance before, and yerke behinde.' And inasmuch as this yerking is an artificial development of a motion to which the horse is by nature occasionally too prone, Gervase Markham counsels to make your horse ' yerk out behind, yet so as it may be perceived it is your will, and not the horse's malice,' as it was on the field of Agincourt when the wounded steeds of the French

> Fret fetlock deep in gore and with wild rage
> Yerk out their armed heels at their dead masters,
> Killing them twice.   *Hen. V.* iv. 7. 82.

The fourth of Blundevill's stages in the courser's progress, ' to turne, readilie, on both hands with single turne and double turne,' leads up to the fifth, which is ' to make a sure and readie manege.' The twenty-nine pages devoted by Blundevill to the mysteries of single turns, whole turns, double turns; manage with half rest, with whole rest, or without rest; and the needful helps and corrections for these complicated evolutions, are fairly summed up in two lines already quoted:

> To turn and wind a fiery Pegasus,
> And witch the world with noble horsemanship.
>   1 *Hen. IV.* iv. 1. 109.

We now arrive at the last stage, and the most important, either in the lists or in warfare; 'sixthlie, to passe a swift cariere.' There is no term of manage which occurs so often in Shakespeare as the ' career,' and there is none the original meaning of which has been more obscured by its popular use in the language of the present day. In truth, when we

[1] *Mids. N. Dr.* v. 1. 118.

speak of a career, we mean something not only different from
what Shakespeare intends by the word, but its exact opposite.
We mean something that continues for an indefinite time.
He meant something that soon comes to an abrupt ending.
‘ When your horse is perfect in the manages beforesaid,
you may then pass a *career* at your pleasure, which is to
run a horse forthright at his full speed, and then making him
stop quickly, suddenly firm, and close on his buttock.’[1]   The
length of the career was four or five score yards at the most.

The essential characteristic of the career, wherein it
differed from the ordinary gallop, was its abrupt ending,
technically known as ‘ the stop,’ by which the horse was
suddenly and firmly thrown upon his haunches.   Wherever
Shakespeare uses the word, this stop is present to his mind.
Leontes, skilled, I doubt not, in the stop and in the career,
spoke terms of manage when he marked ‘ stopping the
career Of laughter with a sigh,’ as ‘ a note infallible Of
breaking honesty.’[2]

A swift gallop with a sudden stop is not unlike the
humour which led Henry of Monmouth to be a madcap
for once.   ‘ The king hath run bad humours on the knight ;
that’s the even of it,’ said Nym, when told of Falstaff’s
sickness unto death.

Pist. Nym, thou hast spoke the right ;
  His heart is fracted and corroborate.

Nym. The king is a good king ; but it must be as it may ; he
  passes some humours and careers.[3]   *Hen. V.* ii. 1. 127.

---

[1] Blundevill.   Dr. Schmidt explains the word ‘ career ’ as meaning a race.
According to the *Glossary* to the *Globe* edition (1880), ‘ careire ’ means ‘ the
curveting of a horse.’   The word had no special significance when so spelled.
According to the *Glossary* to the edition of 1891 ‘ career ’ means a ‘ course run
at full speed.’   Dr. Johnson gives, ‘ a course, a race.’   The technical meaning
of the word, as a term of manage, seems to have long since dropped out of
remembrance.

[2] *Wint. Tale,* i. 2. 287.   Nearly akin to a stop recorded long ago, as a note
infallible of Dido’s breaking honesty,
Incipit effari, mediaque in voce resistit.

[3] A sudden flash of humour is compared by Benedick. to the career of the
manage (*Much Ado,* ii. 3. 250).   This term of manage is used by Bardolph in
speaking of Slender, who having drunk himself out of his five sentences, ‘ and

The king was, as we have seen, a consummate horseman. He knew that before you venture to pass a swift career, you should know when and how to stop, and so, in words already quoted, he warned the Governor of Harfleur of the consequences of letting loose upon the town an unbridled soldiery.

> What rein can hold licentious wickedness
> When down the hill he holds his fierce career?
>
> *Ibid.* iii. 3. 22.

When the great horse has passed through the intermediate stages of training, and can pass a swift career, he is, according to Blundevill, perfect as a horse of service ; that is to say, fit for war, or for its gentle and joyous image in times of peace, the tournament. It was in the lists that the career came into practical use. ' Sir, I shall meet your wit in the career, an you charge it against me,' said Benedick, when he would pick a quarrel with Claudio ;—' in most profound earnest, and I'll warrant you for the love of Beatrice.' [1]

When Henry Bolingbroke, Duke of Hereford, was about to fight Mowbray, Duke of Norfolk, in the lists at Coventry, the Duchess of Gloucester accepted him as a champion of her cause :

> O, sit my husband's wrongs on Hereford's spear,
> That it may enter butcher Mowbray's breast !
> Or, if misfortune miss the first career,
> Be Mowbray's sins so heavy in his bosom,
> That they may break his foaming courser's back,
> And throw the rider headlong in the lists,
> A caitiff recreant to my cousin Hereford !
>
> *Rich. II.* i. 2. 47.

---

being fap, sir, was, as they say, cashiered ; and so conclusions passed the careers ' (*Merry Wives*, i. 1. 183). Various commentators have tried to make sense of these words, but that they are intended for nonsense is suggested from Slender's next words, ' Ay, you spoke in Latin then too ; but 'tis no matter.' The technical meaning of the stop, as the end of a swift career, was often present to Shakespeare's mind. Read in this light, the word ' stop,' common enough, acquires a new significance ; as when Prince Henry says of a king's career, ' Even so must I run on, and even so stop' (*K. John*, v. 7. 67) ; see also *Wint. Tale*, ii. 1. 187 ; *Cymb.* i. 6. 99.   [1] *Much Ado*, v. 1. 134, 198.

There is perhaps a play on the word manage, as well as an allusion to the lists, in Boyet's answer to Biron, when, accused of having brought about by contrivance the encounter of wit in which the King of Navarre and his lords were signally defeated by the Princess and her ladies, he pretends no longer, but straightforwardly admits the impeachment:

Boyet.   Full merrily
     Hath this brave manage, this career, been run.
Biron. Lo, he is tilting straight! Peace! I have done.
                                   Love's L. L. v. 2. 481.

'Although the rules before taught,' continues Blundevill, 'do suffice to make a horse of service; yet if your horse be light, a stirrer, and nimble of nature, you maie besides these, for pleasure's sake, teach him manie other proper feates.' Henry of Monmouth plainly agreed with Gervase Markham in thinking these 'salts and leaps right pleasant to behold,' when he spoke of bounding his horse for his lady's favours; and, as we have learned from *A Lover's Complaint*, men would say of the perfect horseman, 'what rounds, what bounds, what course, what stop he makes.'

Among these salts and leaps the corvette, or curvet, was highly esteemed. It was 'a certaine continuall pransing and dansing up and downe still in one place, like a beare at a stake, and sometimes sideling to and fro, wherein the horse maketh as though he would faine run, and cannot be suffered.' 'France is a dog hole,' says the braggart Parolles to Bertram, when he would incite him to the wars, and to 'sustain the bound and high curvet Of Mars's fiery steed,'[1] an accomplishment, by the way, which Markham describes as 'not generally used in the wars, yet not utterly useless for the same.'

Although different ends were aimed at by horsemen in Tudor times and at the present day, the means which they employ, their 'aids,' corrections, and cherishings are as un-

[1] *All's Well*, ii. 3. 299.

changeable as the natures of man and of horse. The 'riding rod,' as the whip is called by Blundevill, and by Philip the Bastard; [1] 'the needful bits and curbs;' [2] the 'terms of manage' [3] by which the horseman chides or encourages his horse; and the 'filed steel,' [4] 'the spur to prick the sides,' [5] have all the same uses now as they had three hundred years ago; whence it follows that Shakespeare's hints with regard to their management are as fresh and useful now as when they were written.

Take, for instance, the spur. You will find in Shakespeare almost all that is well said by Whyte Melville in a chapter of his *Riding Recollections,* entitled *The Abuse of the Spur,* to which he has prefixed the words of Hermione, already quoted.[6] We have already, in the pursuit of the Cotswold hart, witnessed a verification of the old saw; 'How fondly dost thou spur a forward horse!' [7] and of the death-bed prophecy of old John of Gaunt; 'He tires betimes that spurs too fast betimes.' [8]

But the spur, though often abused, has its necessary use, and there is a golden mean between Richard II., with his sentimental irresolution, and the 'jauncing' rider, whose spur-galled jade bears on his flanks the marks of needless severity.[9]

> I was not made a horse;
> And yet I bear a burden like an ass,
> Spur-gall'd and tired by jauncing Bolingbroke.
>
> *Rich. II.* v. 5. 92.

[1] *King John,* i. 1. 140.
[2] *Measure for M.* i. 3. 20.
[3] 1 *Hen. IV.* ii. 3. 52.
[4] *Twelfth N.* iii. 3. 5.
[5] *Macbeth,* i. 7. 25.
[6] *Ante,* p. 283.
[7] *Rich. II.* iv. 1. 72.
[8] *Ibid.* ii. 1. 36.
[9] Thus the Folio. 'Spur-galled' was a word in common use in farriery. Markham gives a prescription for the sore spot on the flank of the 'spur-galled' horse. The *Cambridge* Edition reads 'spurr'd, gall'd' with one of the Quarto editions, denounced by the editors of the Folio as stolen, and corrupt; and in so doing sacrifices yet another term of art unappreciated by surreptitious copyist, but dear to Shakespeare's heart. The attitude of the editors towards the Folio is well illustrated by their note: 'Though spur-galled is an extremely probable correction, we adhere to our rule of following the higher authority whenever it seems to yield a reasonable sense.'

'Most men,' says Whyte Melville, 'stoop forward, and let their horses' heads go, when engaged in this method of compulsion, and even if their heels *do* reach the mark, by no means a certainty, gain but little with the rowels compared to all they lose with the reins.'   Precisely after this fashion

> came spurring hard
> A gentleman, almost forspent with speed,

who, stopping 'to breathe his bloodied horse' and ask the way to Chester, brought the news of Hotspur's overthrow and death.

> He told me that rebellion had bad luck
> And that young Harry Percy's spur was cold,
> With that, he gave his able horse the head,
> And bending forward struck his armed heels
> Against the panting sides of his poor jade
> Up to the rowel-head, and starting so
> He seemed in running to devour the way,
> Staying no longer question.   *2 Hen. IV.* i. 1. 36.

These words are intended to suggest the reckless riding of a runaway, spurring his jade after the common fashion of most riders, and not the noble horsemanship that turns and winds a fiery Pegasus by the combined action of heel, rein, hand, and voice.   This was the effect produced by the description on the mind of Lord Bardolph, who dubs the rider as

> some hilding fellow that had stolen
> The horse he rode on, and, upon my life,
> Spoke at a venture.   *Ibid.* 57.

'Not one man in ten,' says the writer from whom I have quoted, 'knows *how* to spur a horse.'   Shakespeare had observed precisely the same thing in the tilting field, and noted it as the cause of the failure of a bad rider to get his lance home, in a direct line, against his adversary's breast, with the result that, in the language of the tourney, it 'breaks across.'   'O, that's a brave man!' says Celia of Orlando, in a mocking vein.

> He writes brave verses, speaks brave words, swears brave oaths and breaks them bravely, quite traverse, athwart the heart

of his lover ; as a puisny tilter, that spurs his horse on one side,
breaks his staff like a noble goose.   *As You L.* iii. 4. 43.

Shakespeare had considered well a question suggested in
the same chapter ; ' Granted then, that the spur may be
applied advantageously in the school, let us see how far it is
useful on the road, or in the hunting field.'   Arcite's horse,
taught in ' school doing, being therein trained, and of kind
manage,' takes fright on the stones of Athens.   His rider
gives him the spur, whereat,

> pig-like he whines
> At the sharp rowel, which he frets at rather
> Than any jot obeys.   *Two Noble Kinsmen*, v. 4.

To that ill-advised spurring, and to the ' boisterous and rough
jadery ' which followed, Arcite owed his death, and, so far,
Shakespeare teaching by example, and Whyte Melville by
precept, are at one as to the dangers which ensue from
careless or unskilful use of the spur.

But Shakespeare shows truer wisdom and deeper insight
when he teaches how the spur may be used as well as abused
on the road, as in the school.   His chapter is a short one,
but little can be added to it.   Angelo, entrusted by the Duke
with the government of Vienna during his absence, no
sooner takes his seat as deputy, than he puts into force
' strict statutes and most biting laws,' which had for years
lain in desuetude ' for terror, not to use.'   Claudio, the first
victim of his severity, discusses whether

> the body public be
> A horse whereon the governor doth ride,
> Who, newly in the seat, that it may know
> He can command, lets it straight feel the spur.
>   *Measure for M.* i. 2. 163.

There are horses—and good horses too—who need no
constant application of the spur, but whose whole nature
seems to change according as they bear one like to him
whom Arviragus described as

> A rider like myself, who ne'er wore rowel,
> Nor iron on his heel !   *Cymb.* iv. 4. 39.

or a master who, having let them know that he can command, spares further to use the spur.

'Some people tell you they ride by "balance," others by "grip." I think a man might as well say he played the fiddle by "finger" or by "ear." Surely in either case a combination of both is required to sustain the performance with harmony and success.'[1] Shakespeare has expressed the same idea in two words. Lamond, the gentleman of Normandy, 'to such wondrous doing brought his horse, As had he been incorpsed and demi-natured With the brave beast;'[2] incorpsed, by virtue of the firm grip whereby he 'grew into his seat;' demi-natured, by perfect balance, adjusting itself to every motion of the horse, with that complete sympathy of man and beast, of mind and muscle, on which Shakespeare loves to dwell; whether it be roan Barbary rejoicing in his rider's pride, or 'the beast that bears me, tired with my woe.'[3] And the conclusion of the whole matter, the end towards which the horseman ever strives, is expressed in one short sentence, put into the mouth of Mark Antony, 'his corporal motion govern'd by my spirit.'[4]

IV

FOURTHLIE (AND LASTLY), TO WHAT DISEASES HORSES BE SUBJECT, TOGETHER WITH THE NAMES OF SUCH DISEASES, AND THE KINDLIE AND PROPER TERMES, MEET TO BE USED IN DISCOURSING CONCERNING THE HORSE AND HIS FURNITURE

'He's mad,' says Lear's fool, 'that trusts in the tameness of a wolf, a horse's health, a boy's love, or a whore's oath.'[5] 'O stumbling jade,' cries the ruffian in *A Yorkshire Tragedy* to his falling horse, 'The spavins overtake thee! The fifty diseases stop thee.'[6]

---

[1] Whyte Melville, *Riding Recollections.*   [2] *Hamlet*, iv. 7. 87.
[3] *Sonnet* L.   [4] *Jul. Cæs.* iv. 1. 33.   [5] *K. Lear*, iii. 6. 20.
[6] As to Shakespeare's authorship of *The Yorkshire Tragedy*, see note on the *Critical Significance of Shakespeare's Allusions to Field Sports.* 'There is an

Petruchio, according to Gremio, would marry for money
' an old trot with ne'er a tooth in her head, though she have
as many diseases as two and fifty horses.' [1]

How many diseases two and fifty horses may be supposed
to share between them can be gathered from the allowance
bestowed upon a single animal. And if the enumeration in
Venus and Adonis of ' what a horse should have ' smacks of
the auctioneer, the following tale of what he should not
have, but often has, is no less suggestive of the veterinary
surgeon.

It was one of Petruchio's strange humours to come to
his wedding, not only ' a very monster in apparel,' [2] but
mounted on a ' horse hipped with an old mothy saddle and
stirrups of no kindred ; besides, possessed with the glanders
and like to mose in the chine ; troubled with the lampass,
infected with the fashions, full of windgalls, sped with
spavins, rayed with the yellows, past cure of the fives,
stark spoiled with the stagger, begawn with the bots,
swayed in the back and shoulder-shotten ; ne'er legged
before.' [3]

This extraordinary catalogue of unsoundnesses is not, like
Ben Jonson's sporting terms, copied from a book. It is

old book entitled *The Fifty Diseases of a Horse*, by Gervase Markham.' So
wrote Hazlitt in his edition of the *Doubtful Plays of Shakespeare*. I have not
been able to verify this reference. There is no mention of this work in Mr.
Huth's *Works on Horses and Equitation* (1887), nor does it appear in the
six pages of the catalogue of books in the British Museum which are devoted
to Markham.

[1] *Tam. of Shrew*, i. 2. 80.   [2] *Ibid*. iii. 2. 61.

[3] *Tam. of Shrew*, iii. 2. 49. Never, when contracted to ne'er, is constantly
printed in the Folio ' nere,' both in compound words and singly ; *Two Gent*. iv.
1. 30 ; *Tam. of Shrew*, i. 1. 77 ; *Ant. and Cleo*. iii. 1. 33, &c. As the spelling
of the Folio must be corrected, I prefer to reject a superfluous final ' e ' with
Malone than to introduce a foreign ' a ' with the Cambridge editors, especially as
near-legged conveys no distinct meaning, while ne'er-legged plainly signifies
what would be called in stable language ' gone before.' It has been suggested
that by the term near-legged the dangerous action is intended that causes a
horse, not to stumble, but to hit himself and fall. I doubt that the word would
have been understood as suggesting a defect of this kind by one possessed of
Shakespeare's practical knowledge, whereas the ' ne'er legged ' horse is bound
to stumble, even without the additional infirmities enumerated in the text.

unmistakably racy of the stable. If Shakespeare had learned his farriery from Blundevill, as Jonson copied his hunting language from the *Noble Arte*,[1] he would have written of mourning, not 'mosing,' of the chine ; a disease akin to glanders, the name of which is 'borrowed of the French tongue, wherein it is called Mortdeschyen, that is to say, the death of the backe.'[2]

As to the word 'fashions,' he must have picked it up from some blacksmith at Stratford. For the proper name of this troublesome ulcer was 'farcin,'[3] commonly known as 'the farcy, of our ignorant smiths called the fashions.'[4] No one but an ignorant smith, or one bred in a stable, would speak of 'the fives.' If he had even a smattering of the book-learning of farriery, he would have known that the 'vives' are 'certaine kernels growing under the horse's eare. . . . The Italians call them vivole.'[5] The phrases 'shoulder-shotten' and 'ne'er legged before' are more suggestive of the stable than technically correct.

It must likewise have been from some 'ignorant smith' that he learned to miscall the affection known as stringhalt, when he made Lord Sands—a homely Englishman, surveying the capering and grimacing of gallants returned from France, juggled by her spells into strange mysteries and new customs, and marvelling at the action of their legs—exclaim :

> One would take it,
> That never saw 'em pace before, the spavin
> Or springhalt reign'd among 'em.
>
> *Hen. VIII.* i. 3. 11.

The tradition that Shakespeare, in extremity of need, turned to horses as a means of earning his bread, and in some employment connected with their care made a name

---

[1] Mr. Gifford comments on this fact in his notes to the hunting scenes in *The Sad Shepherd*. A comparison of these carefully elaborated passages with Shakespeare's casual allusions to similar topics is not without interest.

[2] Blundevill. Fitzherbert (*Boke of Husbandrie*) quotes a French saying,

> Morte de longe, et d'eschine
> Sont maladies saunce medicine.

[3] Blundevill.   [4] Markham's *Maister-peece*.   [5] Blundevill.

which others thought worth pirating, gains some confirmation from the constant and needless occurrence in his plays of the language of the groom, the farrier, and the horse-master, and still more from his use of familiar corruptions and cant phrases current in the stable and in the blacksmith's shop. The tradition is not one of the kind which invention loves to weave around names great in letters, and the most philosophical way of accounting for its existence may possibly be to accept it as true. But whether the story be true or false, the fact remains that Shakespeare's works are a perfect mine of what our diarist calls 'the kindlie and proper termes meet to be used in discoursing concerning the horse and his furniture.'

Spurs, bits and reins are topics common to all writers who deal in metaphor, and I have not noted the many passages in which they are so employed by Shakespeare. But from what other poet or dramatist may we learn how to use aright these aids to horsemanship?

There is a certain particularity and distinctness in Shake-speare's casual mention of the most ordinary 'furniture' of the horse. Thus, for example, it is said of the famished horses of the English army before Agincourt,

> in their pale dull mouths the gimmal bit
> Lies foul with chew'd grass, still and motionless.
>
> *Hen. V.* iv. 2. 49.

What is a gimmal[1] bit? And why is it put into the mouths of the English horses? The former question has been satisfactorily answered by Archdeacon Nares.[2] 'A bit in which two parts or links were united as in the gimmal ring,' quoting Coles, *Gimmal, annulus gemellus*. Blundevill's *Four Chiefest Offices* contains plates representing fifty different bits, some of extraordinary severity. Some are in one piece, with ports like the modern bit; others are

---

[1] 'Iymold' in the Folio. Johnson reads 'gimmal,' and that this emendation is merely a correction in spelling appears from the passages quoted in Nares' *Glossary*.

[2] *Glossary* in verb.

jointed in the middle, although used with a curb-chain, somewhat after the fashion of the modern pelham. These softer gimmal bits would naturally be used in active service, the severer instruments of torture being reserved wherewith to turn and wind a fiery Pegasus in the exercises of the manage. Shakespeare knew well that Henry V. would have none but gimmal bits for service in the field.

Petruchio's screw, infected with a fair proportion of the fifty diseases, had ' a half-checked [1] bit and a head-stall of sheep's leather which, being restrained to keep him from stumbling,[2] hath been often burst, and now repaired with knots ; one girth six times pieced and a woman's crupper of velure, which hath two letters for her name fairly set down in studs, and here and there pieced with packthread.' [3]

The crupper [4] was necessary in order to keep in its place the ungainly saddle of the day, and considerable pains were expended on its ornamentation. The engraving in Turbervile's *Booke of Falconry*, of a great lady taking part with her attendants in flying the heron, represents an elaborate

---

[1] The Folio has ' half-check'd,' corrected in the third folio to 'halfe chekt,' and in the fourth to ' half chekt.' The reading half-cheeked adopted by the Cambridge editors was first suggested by Singer. There were in use long cheeks and short cheeks ' suitable to the proportion of the horse's neck ; knowing that the long cheek raises up the head, and the short pulls it down ' (*The Perfect Horseman*, by Lancelot Thetford, 1655). Markham (*Cavalarice*) writes of ' the straight cheek broke into two parts.' But the term half-cheek does not appear to have been in use. The fact that the editors of the third and fourth folios troubled themselves to alter the spelling, leaving the word unchanged, suggests that the word half-checked applied to a bit was then intelligible. It may have been the vulgar stable equivalent of one of the many terms of art enumerated by Blundevill ; possibly the half-scatch bit. Of certain bits, not so complete as others, ' Grison,' he tells us, ' calleth them but halfe bits, as the halfe canon, the halfe scatch, the halfe cat's foot, etc.' At all events, of two unintelligible words, I prefer the Folio's to Singer's. The *Globe* (1891) reads ' half-checked,' but that this is a misprint appears from the *Glossary* ; ' half-cheeked *adj.* ; a half-cheeked bit was perhaps a bit of which only one part remained ;' *obscurum per obscurius*.

[2] The horse was ' ne'er legged before,' and therefore in special danger of stumbling.

[3] *Tam. of Shrew*, iii. 2. 57.

[4] *Com. of Err.* i. 2. 56 ; *Tam. of Shrew*, iv. 1. 84.

and ornate crupper, which may well have been of velure (velvet) with the owner's name ' fairly set down in studs.'

The saddlery of the day was more ornate than that now in use, and was commonly ornamented with devices in studs. It is the ' studded bridle ' of Adonis' horse that Venus fastens to a bough, when her favourite would not ' rein his proud head to the saddle bow ' ;[1] and Christopher Sly is offered, should he be disposed to ride, horses trapped with ' harness studded all with gold and pearl.'[2]

A complete catalogue of Shakespeare's stable phrases would be tedious, but not without significance, for surely, in the whole history of literature, never did tragedies, comedies, histories and poems furnish such a vocabulary. He delighted, moreover, in saws and proverbs, racy of the stable, of which some are in common use, but others are peculiar to himself. If Lear's fool had not noted a horse's abhorrence of any greasy matter, it would never have occurred to him to say of one devoid of sense; ' 'Twas her brother that, in pure kindness to his horse, buttered his hay.'[3] It is he who noted the madness of trusting in ' a horse's health,'[4] and it is to the selfsame fool that we owe, among many other excellent precepts :

> Ride more than thou goest . . .
> And thou shalt have more
> Than two tens to a score.
>
> *K. Lear*, i. 4. 134.

In Tudor times the beggar on horseback, though not so frequent a spectacle as at the present day, must have been quite as entertaining to the well-constituted mind. The proverb in general use, particular enough as to the ultimate destination of the equestrian mendicant, takes no note of his horse. Shakespeare's mind was moved to pity by the fate of the nobler animal, for the Duke of York thus addresses the ' she-wolf of France ' :

---

[1] *Ven. and Ad.* 14, 37.   [2] *Tam. of Shrew*, Ind. 2. 44.
[3] *K. Lear*, ii. 4. 127.   [4] *Ibid.* iii. 6. 19.

> It boots thee not, proud queen,
> Unless the adage must be verified
> That beggars mounted run their horse to death
>   *3 Hen. VI.* i. 4. 126.

Stray thoughts of horse and stable are for ever recurring
to all sorts of people. To Nym, ' Though patience be a
tired mare, yet she will plod ' ;[1] to Dogberry, ' An two men
ride of a horse, one must ride behind ; '[2] to Menenius, when he
exclaims that compared to good news of Marcius, ' the most
sovereign prescription in Galen is but empiricutic, and, to
this preservative, of no better report than a horse-drench ';[3]
and again, when he says of Marcius, ' He no more remembers
his mother now than an eight-year-old horse ';[4] to Enobarbus,
when, hearing that Cleopatra would accompany Antony to
the field, he reflects

> If we should serve with horse and mares together,
> The horse were merely lost; the mares would bear
> A soldier and his horse.   *Ant. and Cleo.* iii. 7. 8.

To the old groom whom we know as Petruchio's ' ancient,
trusty, pleasant servant Grumio,' and who, when his horses
were called for, was wont to reply with a stable pleasantry,
' Ay, sir, they be ready ; the oats have eaten the horses ; '[5] to
the Lord Chamberlain, when he tells Lord Sands, ' Your
colt's tooth is not cast yet ' ;[6] to Touchstone—' As the ox
hath his bow, sir, the horse his curb and the falcon her bells,
so man hath his desires ';[7] to Maria, ' My purpose is,
indeed, a horse of that colour ';[8] to Hamlet, when he exclaims, 'let the gall'd jade wince, our withers are unwrung';[9]
to Master Ford, ' I will rather trust . . . a thief to walk my
ambling gelding than my wife with herself ';[10] to Moth,
when the tag of the morris-dance song,—' The hobby-horse
is forgot '—suggests, ' The hobby-horse is but a colt, and your

---

[1] *Hen. V.* ii. 1. 25.
[2] *Much Ado,* iii. 5. 40.
[3] *Coriol.* ii. 1. 127.
[4] *Ibid.* v. 4. 16.
[5] *Tam. of Shrew,* iii. 2. 207.
[6] *Hen. VIII.* 1. 3. 48.
[7] *As You L.* iii. 3. 80.
[8] *Twelfth N.* ii. 3. 181.
[9] *Hamlet,* iii. 2. 253.
[10] *Merry Wives,* ii. 2. 316.

love perhaps a hackney ';[1] to Beatrice, when her gentle-
woman would run on :

Beat. What pace is this that thy tongue keeps?
Marg. Not a false gallop.[2]   *Much Ado*, iii. 4. 93.

To the Duke of York, when he reminded Northumberland
that the time was when King Richard would have checked
his insolence—he would, he says, 'shorten you for taking
so the head, your whole head's length ';[3] to Falstaff, when
he thus addresses Prince Harry—'what a plague mean
ye to colt me thus?' and to the Prince, when he replies,
'Thou liest; thou art not colted, thou art uncolted ';[4] to
Brutus, who says of Coriolanus, as of a high spirited
horse, 'being once chafed, he cannot be rein'd again to tem-
perance ';[5] to Hortensio when he said of Katherine, 'There
be good fellows in the world,' 'an a man could light on them,
would take her with all faults, and money enough ';[6] and
(I suspect) to Capulet, when he bids Juliet :

> Fettle your fine joints 'gainst Thursday next,
> To go with Paris to Saint Peter's Church.
>   *Rom. and Jul.* iii. 5. 154.

Posthumus must have had experience of the sudden
seizure to which horseflesh is occasionally subject when he

---

[1] *Love's L. L.* iii. 1. 30. The word 'hackney' in the diarist's time conveyed no suggestion of the kind of action now associated with the name. It is
the same word as the French *haquénée*, originally signifying (according to
Littré) *cheval ou jument docile et marchant ordinairement à l'amble.* The
derivation appears to be uncertain (but see Skeat's *Etymological Dictionary*).
It was used in the English language, at all events since the time of Chaucer
(*Romaunt of the Rose*), to denote a small useful nag, of the kind usually employed
on the road. This being the class of horse commonly let out on hire, the
secondary meaning of a hired animal, in common use, became attached to the
word. This is, of course, the suggestion intended to be conveyed by Moth.
The transfer from horse to vehicle was easy, and the phrase 'hackney coach'
is a familiar one. In time the word 'hackney' and its abbreviated form 'hack'
came to be employed without reference to the horse, as when we speak of a
hackneyed metaphor, or a hack scribe. The modern use of the word as
descriptive of a class of horse is somewhat akin to its original meaning, with
certain ideas superadded in regard to shape and action.

[2] For the meaning of this term of art, see *ante*, p. 296.

[3] *Rich. II.* iii. 3. 12.   [4] *1 Hen. IV.* ii. 2. 39.

[5] *Coriol.* iii. 3. 27.   [6] *Tam. of Shrew*, i. 1. 133.

exclaimed in his amazement, ' How come these staggers on
me ? ' [1]

' Bots on't ' was strong language current at the time,
not, however, in the mouth of fishermen, except at Penta-
polis ; [2] and the phrase rises so naturally to the lips of
Proteus of Verona as to suggest a pun on the word boots—
surest evidence of familiarity.[3]

It is only in the stable that ' a huge hill of flesh,' like
Falstaff, would be known as a ' horse-back-breaker.' [4] Indeed, by the great ungainly saddles of the day (even without
the additional twenty stone contributed by a Falstaff), many
a ' poor jade ' like the carrier's horse at Rochester was
' wrung in the withers [5] out of all cess,' and the stable boys
(whether Shakespeare's or another's) often heard the injunction, ' I prithee, Tom, beat Cut's saddle, put a few flocks in
the point.' [6]

It is not quite clear what Scarus meant, when he called
Cleopatra ' You ribaudred nag of Egypt,' [7] nor have commentators thrown much light on the ' arm-gaunt steed '
soberly mounted by Mark Antony, ' who neighed so high,'
according to Alexas,

<blockquote>
that what I would have spoke
Was beastly dumb [8] by him.   Ibid. i. 5. 48.
</blockquote>

It is still a matter of uncertainty how the ' garboils ' which
baffled Antony, skilled in the manage of unruly jades, come
to be described as ' uncurbable ' ;

<blockquote>
As for my wife,
I would you had her spirit in such another ;
The third of the world is yours ; which with a snaffle
You may pace easy, but not such a wife.
</blockquote>

---

[1] *Cymb.* v. 5. 233.   [2] *Pericles*, ii. 1. 24.
[3] *Two Gent.* i. 1. 25.   [4] 1 *Hen. IV.* ii. 4. 268.
[5] See *Tit. Andr.* iv. 3. 47, and *Hamlet*, iii. 2. 253.
[6] 1 *Hen. IV.* ii. 1. 6.   [7] *Ant. and Cleo.* iii. 10. 10.
[8] Thus the Folio, intelligible, if somewhat obscure. What Alexas would
have spoken was dumb by reason of the neighing of the beast. The Cambridge
edition reads ' dumb'd,' adopting what seems to be a needless emendation of
Theobald's.

Eno. Would we had all such wives, that the men might go
to wars with the women !

Ant. So much uncurbable, her garboils, Cæsar,
Made out of her impatience, which not wanted
Shrewdness of policy too, I grieving grant
Did you too much disquiet; for that you must
But say, I could not help it.   *Ant. and Cleo.* ii. 2. 61.

But whatever be the meaning of these passages, it is clear
that they all had their origin in the stable.

Shakespeare's allusions to horse, hound, hawk and deer
contrast in mere point of frequency with those of any other
writer, in ancient or modern times. Some of these references
are in themselves of an ordinary kind, and only acquire
significance from their frequent occurrence, and from the
circumstance that they are seldom suggested by any necessary action of the drama, but seem to spring forth out of
the abundance of the poet's heart. Others are of a
different character, and especially characteristic of Shakespeare.

The foregoing pages have been written in vain if the
reader has not been helped towards an understanding of
the nature and significance of Shakespeare's allusions to
field sports. But it may be useful, before parting company
with the diarist and his labours, to note the essential elements of the distinctively Shakespearian allusion.

I should not account as such any which does not present
one or more of the following characteristics :

I. A secret of woodcraft or horsemanship :

II. An illustration therefrom of human nature and conduct :

III. A lively image :

IV. A conceit ; or

V. An irrelevance ; by which I mean an idea somewhat
out of place with its surroundings.

To illustrate my meaning I select, out of many, six
examples of each of these classes.

I. A secret of woodcraft or horsemanship :

(1) The only sovereign plaster for ' venomed sores ' is the hound's ' licking of his wound.' [1]

(2) Beware of a horse with no white in his face. [2]

(3) You cannot judge of the quality of the deer by his horns alone. He may have huge antlers, and yet be a worthless ' rascal.' [3]

(4) How to avoid scaring a herd of deer by the noise of the cross-bow. [4]

(5) Choose a falcon or tercel for flying at the brook, and a hawk for the bush. [5]

(6) If you are tired or out of sorts, so will your horse be also. [6]

Under this head range also the many precepts on the breeding, choosing, riding and breaking of horses, and on the manning and training of hawks, collected in these pages, including an enumeration of the points of a horse and of a hound, and of a fair number of the fifty diseases known to the veterinary surgeon.

II. An illustration of human nature and character :

(1) ' Hollow men, like horses hot at hand, make gallant show and promise of their mettle,' but, when the time of trial comes, they, ' like deceitful jades, sink in the trial.' [7]

(2) Beware of self-asserting impostors, who, like rascal deer worst in blood to run, push themselves to the front of the herd, and so deceive the unwary. [8]

(3) There are men too who, ' like coward dogs, most spend their mouths when what they seem to threaten runs far before them,' and there are those who need, like Roderigo, to be trashed for too quick hunting. [9]

(4) A man may be quick of apprehension, and yet be an

---

[1] *Ven. and Ad.* 915 (p. 78).

[2] *Ant. and Cleo.* iii. 2. 51 ; *Two Noble Kinsmen*, v. 4 (p. 255).

[3] *As You L.* iii. 3. 56 (p. 237).

[4] 3 *Hen. VI.* iii. 1. 5 (p. 236).

[5] *Troil. and Cres.* iii. 2. 55 (p. 209).

[6] *Sonnet* 1. ; *Love's L. L.* iv. 2. 131 (p. 82).

[7] *Jul. Cæs.* iv. 2. 23 (p. 285).   [8] *Coriol.* i. 1. 161 (p. 238).

[9] *Hen. V.* ii. 4. 68 ; *Oth.* ii. 1. 312 (pp. 37, 39).

untrustworthy guide; like a 'hound that runs counter, and yet draws dry-foot well.'[1]

(5) There are men and women, as there are horses, who need bit and spur, while there are others who may truly say 'you may ride's with one soft kiss a thousand furlongs, ere with spur we heat an acre.'[2]

(6) In training youth, as in training horses, avoid the extremes of severity and of laxity.[3] And, above all, do not begin too young, for 'the colt that's back'd and burden'd, being young, loseth his pride and never waxeth strong.'[4]

III. A lively image; such as:

(1) Queen Margaret's description of Edward and Richard as 'a brace of greyhounds, having the fearful flying hare in sight, with fiery eyes, sparkling for very wrath.'[5]

(2) Talbot's comparison of his few troops surrounded by the French multitude to 'moody mad and desperate stags,' who 'turn on the bloody hounds with heads of steel, and make the cowards stand aloof at bay.'[6]

(3) 'The poor frighted deer that stands at gaze, wildly determining which way to fly,' apt image of Lucrece, in mutiny with herself, 'to live or die, which of the twain were better.'[7]

(4) Uncontrollable and licentious wickedness is compared to a runaway horse, which no rein can hold 'when down the hill he holds his fierce career.'[8]

(5) War differs as widely from dull, sleepy, lethargic peace as a hound who has hit off the scent, and becomes 'sprightly walking, audible, and full of vent,' from his fellow, standing listlessly, at a fault, or hopelessly trying to pick out a cold scent.[9]

(6) The barons overawed by Warwick cower like par-

---

[1] *Com. of Err.* iv. 2. 39 (p. 65).

[2] *Measure for M.* i. 3. 20; *Wint. Tale,* i. 2. 95 (p. 282).

[3] *Rich. II.* ii. 1. 69 (p. 281).

[4] *Ven. and Ad.* 419 (p. 281).   [5] *3 Hen. VI.* ii. 5. 129 (p. 174).

[6] *1 Hen. VI.* iv. 2. 50 (p. 59).   [7] *Lucrece,* 1149 (p. 34).

[8] *Hen. V.* iii. 3. 22 (p. 45).   [9] *Coriol.* iv. 5. 237 (p. 53).

tridges enmewed and terrified by a hawk, and none 'dares stir a wing if Warwick shake his bells.' [1]

IV. A conceit, for example :

(1) The Dauphin's valour, according to the Constable of France, was 'a hooded valour, and when it appears, it will bate (abate).' [2]

(2) The elaborate conceits on the words 'pricket' and 'sorel' in Holofernes' 'extemporal epitaph.' [3]

(3) 'You are over˙ boots in love,' says Proteus to Valentine. '*Pro.* Over the boots, nay, give me not the bots (boots). *Val.* No, I'll not, for it boots thee not.' [4]

(4) The puns on 'an old hare hoar' in which Mercutio indulged. [5]

(5) 'He was furnished as a hunter,' said Celia of Orlando. 'Oh, ominous!' exclaimed Rosalind, 'he comes to kill my heart.' [6]

(6) Lavinia seeking to hide herself was likened by Marcus Andronicus to a wounded deer, whereupon Titus puns ' It was my deer (dear).' [7]

Indeed, puns on words connected with the chase, especially on the words 'hart' and 'deer,' and conceits in regard to horns, are almost beyond counting.

V. An irrelevance, often in the form of an anachronism ; as when :

(1) Lucrece appeals to Tarquin, as to an English sportsman, to mend his ill aim before his shoot is ended, and spare a poor unseasonable doe.[8]

(2) Mark Antony compares Cæsar's assassins to hunters, standing round where the hart was bayed and slain, signed in his spoil, and crimsoned in his lethe ; that is, blooded after the fashion of English sportsmen.[9]

(3) Flavius, when by plucking growing feathers from Cæsar's wing he would 'make him fly an ordinary pitch.' [10]

[1] *3 Hen. VI.* i. 1. 45 (p. 202).   [2] *Hen. V.* iii. 7. 121 (p. 151).
[3] *Love's L. L.* iv. 2. 58 (p. 233).   [4] *Two Gent. of Ver.* i. 1. 25 (p. 312).
[5] *Rom. and Jul.* ii. 4. 136 (p. 173).   [6] *As You L.* iii. 2. 258 (p. 30).
[7] *Tit. Andr.* iii. 1. 89 (p. 238).   [8] *Lucrece,* 580 (p. 237).
[9] *Jul. Cæs.* iii. 1. 204 (p. 64).   [10] *Ibid.* i. 1. 77 (p. 161).

(4) And so too Pandarus of Troy, when he says to Cressida, 'You must be watched ere you be made tame, must you?'[1]

(5) The Lord Lucullus pays court to Timon of Athens after the fashion of Shallow of Gloucestershire, by sending him two brace of greyhounds, and entreating his company to hunt with him.[2]

(6) Demetrius suggests to the mind of Aaron the Moor recollections of the same county, with its parks and keepers and deer stealers, when he asks whether he has not 'full often struck a doe, and borne her cleanly by the keeper's nose?'[3]

The Shakespearian allusion, even when it does not involve an anachronism, is seldom introduced of set purpose, to suit the context or situation, and is as often out of season as in season, in point of dramatic propriety.

---

[1] *Troil. and Cres.* iii. 2. 45 (p. 149).   [2] *Tim. of Ath.* i. 2. 193 (p. 243).
[3] *Tit. Andr.* ii. 1. 93 (p. 231).

NOTE I

THE CRITICAL SIGNIFICANCE OF SHAKESPEARE'S ALLUSIONS TO FIELD SPORTS

WHEN I began to collect and to arrange the allusions to field sports and to horses scattered throughout the writings of Shakespeare, nothing was further from my mind than to enter the field of criticism. But as my work progressed, I discerned more and more clearly the true nature of these allusions, how they for the most part well up spontaneously as from the poet's inmost soul, and are seldom suggested by the plot or character in hand at the moment, with which, indeed, they are often out of keeping. And according as I became better acquainted with the works of his contemporaries, it was more and more evident that this peculiar mode of thought does not happen to be shared by other dramatic writers of his age. Thus the thought was suggested that the presence or absence of this distinctive note might be of some aid in distinguishing the workmanship of Shakespeare from that of certain other dramatists with whom Shakespearian criticism is mainly concerned. From the admitted writings of Shakespeare it is never wholly absent. In the admitted works of Fletcher, Greene, Kyd, or Marlowe, or in certain of the anonymous plays attributed to Shakespeare, it is never found.

Again, in the course of my work, I found myself in the presence of certain matters of fact by which an inquiry was suggested. These facts are that in no single instance has the authority of the Folio been displaced by the result of my inquiries, and that the knowledge thus obtained has often unexpectedly tended to support the testimony of its editors. I was thus led to investigate the sufficiency of the reasons which have led critics, almost without exception, to reject the Folio in favour either of some earlier Quarto edition, or of a certain compound known as the Received Text, the result of the labours of many generations of more or less intelligent emendators. How far the Text differs from the Folio can be realised only

by those who have been at the pains to compare even so conservative a text as that of the Cambridge Editors with what was given
to the world by Shakespeare's fellows as having been printed
from the 'true original copies.'

Hence this note. Upon certain matters of criticism, meet only
for the decision of experts, I disclaim any right to express an
opinion; but I would remind the reader that in criticism, as in the
administration of the law, the determination of questions of nicety,
fit only for experts, often depends upon some cardinal matter of
fact, to be determined by weighing testimony and balancing
probabilities. When such an issue is evolved, legal experts stand
aside for a while, until the question of fact has been answered, yea
or nay, by laymen empanelled to decide upon the evidence submitted to them. Jurors differ widely in intelligence and indepen-
dence, and Courts are accustomed to regard the finding of a jury
upon even a doubtful question of fact with a superstitious reverence
never accorded to any other merely human pronouncement. But
speaking generally, I suppose that few thinkers, and fewer men of
practical experience, believe that the administration of the law
would be bettered by the universal substitution of trained lawyers
for those who are now called in from the counting-house or from
the farm to answer questions of fact upon which may depend the
devolution of an estate, or the graver issues of life or death. It
would, I think, be well for criticism if it were possible to submit
broad issues of fact—with proper instructions—to men of fair intelligence and general culture (for the jury should be a special one)
bound to decide in accordance with evidence; not in the technical
sense in which the term is understood in Courts of Justice, but as
comprehending (in the words of Bentham), ' any matter of fact, the
effect, tendency, or design of which, when presented to the mind,
is to produce a persuasion concerning the existence of some other
matter of fact,'—a philosophical definition of evidence towards
which its legal significance is slowly but surely gravitating.

But for two remarkable circumstances, Shakespearian criticism
would never have exercised so many minds and filled so many
volumes. One is the fact noted by the editors of the Folio, that
Shakespeare had not 'the fate common with some to be exequtor
to his owne writing.' That the author of *Othello* and *As You Like
It* should not have deemed those works worthy of the editorial care
bestowed on *Venus and Adonis* and *Lucrece*; that he used them
simply as a means of making money, and when that purpose had
been served, took no further heed of them; that notwithstanding

the publication and rapid sale of pirated and inaccurate copies, he was never moved, during the years of retirement at Stratford, to take even the initial step of collecting and revising for publication the manuscripts of his plays ; and that, so far as their author was concerned, they might be stolen, travestied, or perish altogether ; are surely among the strangest facts in the history of literature. There is the further circumstance that Shakespeare was not only an original dramatist, but a theatrical manager, who commenced authorship as Johannes-fac-totum, and who never hesitated to turn the work of others to profitable use, re-writing it to a greater or less extent, according as it suited the purposes of the theatre with which he was connected.   Thus it is that we have not the authority of Shakespeare for the fact of his authorship of any one of the plays attributed to him, or for the authenticity of any particular edition. Thus it also is that Shakespearian criticism is not restricted to recension of a text, however corrupt, admittedly printed from an authentic manuscript.   It must, before approaching this task, determine questions of no small difficulty.   It must, in the first place, settle the canon of Shakespeare's works.   It must define, as best it can, his share in each drama admitted to this canon ; and it must also decide between rival claimants to the title of 'true original copy.'

THE FOLIO OF 1623

Seven years after Shakespeare's death a volume was published which, if the professions of its editors may be believed, supplied to a certain extent the want of an authorised edition.   In the First Folio, John Heminge and Henry Condell, fellow-actors with Shakespeare, custodians of his manuscripts, and legatees under his will, gave to the public, under the auspices of Ben Jonson, what purported to be a complete collection of his works printed from the true original copies received by them at the hands of the poet. If this profession be true, it narrows considerably the field of controversy.   Shakespeare's authorship, in whole or in part, of the thirty-four plays included in the Folio would be conclusively established, leaving to criticism the task of estimating as best it could his share in the composition of each individual play.   No doubt would remain as to the edition which represented most clearly the finished work of the author.   This edition would necessarily form the basis of the text, and criticism would have occupied itself in correcting manifest errors, and in the emendation of such passages as were unintelligible or obviously corrupt, by reference to the less authentic issues, or by conjectural emendation. On the other hand, if the testimony of the editors of the Folio is discredited, and if the Quartos are admitted as of equal or greater authority, questions of authorship and of textual criticism are, so to speak, altogether at large, to be determined without regard to authority. It is therefore evident that the question of the authority of the Folio underlies the whole of Shakespearian criticism.

Who, then, were the editors of the First Folio, and how far are they entitled to credit? These men, Heminge and Condell, were precise in their statements and in their claims. The plays are stated on the title page to be 'published according to the True Originall Copies.' 'We have collected them,' the editors say in the dedication to the Earl of Pembroke and the Earl of Montgomery, 'and done an office to the dead to procure his Orphanes Guardians; without ambition either of selfe-profit or fame: onely to keepe the memory of so worthy a Friend and Fellow alive, as was our Shakespeare, by humble offer of his playes to your most noble patronage.' The claim thus put forward to a close relationship with the author is supported by the evidence of Shakespeare himself. By his will he left to his 'fellows John Hemynge, Richard Burbage and Henry Cundell twenty-six shillings and eight pence apiece to buy them rings.' Richard Burbage, the celebrated actor, the impersonator of Shakespeare's greatest characters, died in 1619, and the volume was published in 1623 by the surviving objects of the author's affectionate remembrance, under the auspices of Ben Jonson. It was he who wrote the lines introducing to the reader the Droeshout portrait, engraved on the title page. It was to his genius we owe the noble commendatory verses prefixed to the Folio, of which it is enough to say that they are not unworthy of their theme.

These editors were not only the trusted friends of Shakespeare, but, as joint proprietors of the Globe Theatre, they were the lawful holders of his manuscripts. They knew with regard to each play which copy embodied the author's final workmanship, and had the best title to be called the true original.

It is not indeed the custom of those who discredit the Folio to question the knowledge of its editors. It is their common honesty and their veracity which are in dispute. 'There is no doubt,' writes Mr. Spalding (*Letter on Authorship of Two Noble Kinsmen*), 'but they could at least have enumerated Shakespeare's works correctly: but their knowledge and their design of profit did not suit each other.' They must, he points out, be presumed to have known perfectly what works were, and what were not, Shakespeare's. But these men were ' unscrupulous and unfair ' in their selection, their whole conduct ' inspires distrust ' and justifies a critic in throwing the First Folio entirely out of view as a ' dishonest ' (and, I would add, a hypocritical) ' attempt to put down editions of about fifteen separate plays of Shakespeare, previously printed in quarto, which, though in most respects more accurate than their successors, had evidently been taken for stolen copies.'

Somewhat similar is the language held by the editor of the latest and best edition of Shakespeare's works, Mr. W. Aldis Wright. Led by the result of critical research to adopt the quartos of several plays as the true original copies, he has to dispose of the assertions of the editors of the Folio.　He does not hesitate to convict them of *suggestio falsi*, in conveying to the public the idea that the Folio was printed from original manuscripts received by them at the author's hands.　This sounds better than the vernacular ;—lie. But there is no use in mincing matters, and if the suggestion of the editors of the Folio was false in fact, it must have been false to their knowledge, and their fraudulent puffing of their own wares coupled with their ' denunciation of editions which they knew to be superior to their own ' would, if proved, fully justify the plainer language used by Mr. Spalding.

Great allowance must be made for speculators in the regions of criticism, philosophy, antiquity, or theology, who find themselves face to face with a fact too stubborn to accommodate itself to some conclusion, the result of life-long study.　The critic who, after infinite labour and research, has satisfied himself that the quarto is the true original of Shakespeare's *Hamlet*, has to deal with the fact that two intimate friends of the author, possessed of special means of knowledge, assert the contrary, and that their assertion is endorsed by some whom it would be scarcely possible to deceive, and who have no motive to aid or abet in deceiving others.　There are but two courses open to one who finds himself in such a position : either to reconsider in the light of testimony the conclusion to which he has been led by a process of reasoning, or to denounce and discredit the inconvenient witnesses.　The former course was (after the use of some strong language) followed by Mr. Jonathan Oldbuck of Monkbarns when his learned identification of the Prætorium in his Roman camp at the Kaim of Kinprunes, the result of long and careful study of castrametation, was interrupted by Edie Ochiltree : ' Prætorian here, Prætorian

there, I mind the bigging o't.' The latter is the ordinary course
of Shakespearian criticism.

That the editors of the Folio failed in their duty is well known ;
if, indeed, the term editing can be applied to the process of handing over to the printer what were probably hastily-finished and
ill-written manuscripts, and leaving them to take their chance.
But a careless editor is not necessarily a fraudulent knave, and it
is needful to discriminate. It is not, however, surprising that the
manifold and glaring defects of the Folio should have blinded the
eyes of many generations of critics to the true position of that
edition, and to its claims upon their attention.

These shortcomings are fairly enumerated by a writer in the
Quarterly Review (July 1892), in a successful vindication of
Theobald's claim to rank as ' The Porson of Shakspearian criticism.' ' Words, the restoration of which is obvious, left unsup-
plied ; unfamiliar words transliterated into gibberish ; punctuation
as it pleases chance ; sentences with the subordinate clauses
higgledy-piggledy or upside down ; lines transposed ; verse printed
as prose, and prose as verse ; speeches belonging to one character
given to another ; stage directions incorporated in the text ; actors'
names suddenly substituted for those of the *dramatis personæ* ;
scenes and acts left unindicated or indicated wrongly—all this
and more makes the text of the First Folio one of the most por-
tentous specimens of typography and editing in existence.' All
this is true, but it is beside the question of the honesty of the two
play-actors who had not the wit to call in literary aid in the discharge of a task for which they were incompetent. It does,
however, explain the disfavour with which the Folio was regarded
by critics, in whose eyes those literary enormities assumed gigantic
proportions.

LATER EDITIONS

In the succeeding Folio editions of 1632, 1664, and 1685 little
was done to amend the text. A few errors were corrected, and
others were perpetrated. But in the century following the publication of Rowe's octavo edition in 1709 some of the keenest
intellects of the age devoted their energies to the text of Shakespeare, and the result of their labours is collected in the well-known
Variorum edition (21 vols.), published in 1821 by James Boswell ;
a monumental work, in which is embodied the result of the
labours of Rowe, Pope, Theobald, Warburton, Hanmer, Johnson,

Capell, Steevens, Malone, Monck Mason, and many others of lesser note.

Of these, by general consent, Pope is the least successful, and Theobald, the victim of his remorseless satire, the happiest, in the matter of conjectural emendation. The others may be ranked as critics in the inverse order of their literary reputation. Differing widely in other respects, they agreed in operating upon a certain thing which they treated as the text of Shakespeare. This they amended with a greater or less degree of success, sometimes by brilliant and certain conjectures, sometimes by wild and reckless guesses, and sometimes by collation with the Folios and Quartos, classed together as apparently of equal authority and called the old editions, as compared with the received text. But I cannot find that the Folio ranked higher with any of them than as a source from which emendations, more or less probable, might be drawn.

As might have been expected, the methods of investigation and criticism current in the present century brought into prominence the question of the Folio's claim to authority. It would be impossible within the limits of a note to consider the attitude with regard to the Folio of the chief modern editors—Collier, Halliwell, Dyce, Knight, Staunton, Grant White, and the Cambridge editors. Suffice it to note that no one would now venture to edit Shakespeare without regard to the old copies. Some, indeed, have gone further. Mr. Knight's edition is founded on the text of the Folio, to which he adheres with superstitious tenacity, rejecting emendations which are certain and necessary. Mr. Grant White, in his historical sketch of the text of Shakespeare prefixed to the edition of his works edited by him (Boston, 1865), writes of the Folio : ' Indeed, such is the authority given to this volume by the auspices under which it appeared, that had it been thoroughly prepared for the press and printed with care, there would have been no appeal from its text; and editorial labour upon Shakespeare's plays, except that of an historical or exegetical nature, would have been not only without justification but without opportunity.'

I pass at once to the preface of the Cambridge editors, taking it as a fair statement of the creed of modern conservative Shakespearian criticism. In their preface to the first edition the editors plainly state that they accept the Folio only in the absence of an earlier edition. ' This' [the Folio] ' we have mainly adopted, unless there exists an earlier edition in quarto, as is the case in more than one-half of the thirty-six plays.' In a preface to a reprint of certain quartos they add : ' In the great majority of cases where a previous Quarto exists, the Quarto and not the Folio is our best authority.' Of the Folio edition of *Love's Labour's Lost* they write that it is ' a reprint of this Quarto [that of 1598], differing only in its being divided into Acts, and, as usual, inferior in accuracy.' Except in the case of *King Lear*, where they admit a substantial rivalry between the Folio and an earlier edition, the Quarto is accepted as the higher authority, the Folio being sometimes dismissed with the remark that it is, as usual, inferior in accuracy, or in other instances accounted for, as being a reprint of some spurious edition. And ' the most unkindest cut of all ' is, appropriately enough, dealt in the preface to *Julius Cæsar* : ' *Julius Cæsar* was published for the first time in the Folio of 1623. It is more correctly printed than any other play, and may perhaps have been (as the preface falsely implies that all were) printed from the original manuscript of the author.'

In short, the authority of the Folio is uniformly rejected, the assertions of its editors discredited, and it is adopted as the foundation of the text only in the absence of another edition.

The editors, it is true, open a door of escape for the ' setters forth ' of the Folio : ' It is probable that this deception arose not from deliberate design on the part of Heminge and Condell—whom, as having been Shakespeare's friends and fellows, we like to think of as honourable men—but partly at least from want of practice in composition, and from the wish rather to write a smart preface in praise of the book than to state the facts simply and clearly. Or the preface may have been written by some literary man in the employment of the publishers, and merely signed by the two players.'

I have little doubt as to how my imaginary special jurors would dispose of the suggestion by which it is attempted to establish the honesty of the editors at the expense of their intelligence, if any literary advocate had the hardihood seriously to press it on their attention. That the setters forth of so high an enterprise, in which they had so great an interest—honourable or corrupt—should have signed dedication or preface without reading either, could scarcely be believed, even if attested by respectable witnesses. As a gratuitous hypothesis it is plainly inadmissible. Besides, the theory must be so far extended as to free the editors from responsibility for the title page, for it is there that they are hopelessly committed to the most damaging assertion, namely : that the plays are 'published according to the True Originall Copies.' The theory is specially inapplicable to this particular dedication and preface, inasmuch as they are obviously not mere literary flourishes, but plain statements with regard to matters of a personal nature. The most important of these statements can be traced to the editors, and is certainly not the invention of their supposed literary man. 'His mind and hand,' they write, 'went together : And what he thought he vttered with that easinesse that we haue scarse receiued from him a blot in his papers.' This saying, which was probably current in the profession, was no doubt specially brought home to Ben Jonson when he co-operated with Heminge and Condell in the publication of the Folio. 'I remember,' he wrote many years after, 'the players have often mentioned it as an honour to Shakespeare, that in his writing (whatsoever he penned) he never blotted out a line' (*Discoveries*).

The theory which convicts the editors as knaves is deserving of more attention than that which lets them escape as fools, who published without looking at title page or preface. And for this reason—there have been editors capable of the imposition practised upon the public according to the former theory ; there never were men capable of the folly suggested by the latter.

But, after all, why should these men be disbelieved? what corrupt or dishonest motive can be attributed to them with reasonable probability? They profess to have published the plays of their friend and fellow without ambition of self-profit or fame. Mr. Halliwell-Phillips (*Outlines of the Life of Shakespeare*) points out with some force that in giving unreservedly to the public valuable literary property of which they were sole proprietors, they made a sacrifice for which the profits on the sale of the Folio would not compensate them. They were believed by those who had the best means of forming an opinion as to their credit, and succeeded in imposing on the simple guileless Ben Jonson, who was induced to lend the authority of his great name to their undertaking.

BEN JONSON AND THE FIRST FOLIO

In truth, I have never been able to discover the part assigned to Ben Jonson in the literary frauds associated with the name of Shakespeare. He was too clever and knew too much to be a dupe. I presume he is included in the indictment as a co-conspirator. In order to estimate the value of Ben Jonson's imprimatur we do well to inquire what manner of man he was in himself, and what were his relations to his contemporaries.

He was a man of great and varied genius, a scholar, a dramatist, and a poet. On occasions only too rare, he showed himself capable of writing English prose in grandeur approaching that of Milton. He was, in Mr. Swinburne's happy phrase, a giant, but not of the number of the gods. He was a man of the world, and on familiar terms with many of his contemporaries. He journeyed into Scotland to visit Drummond of Hawthornden, who committed to writing some of his pointed and caustic sayings. He had the rare good fortune to be on terms of intimacy with the two greatest men of his own, or of any age.

If Scotland had furnished this earlier Jonson with another Boswell, the world would have had a richer entertainment than the scanty crumbs picked up by Drummond of Hawthornden. But such as they are, in default of better they are worth preserving. ' At his hither coming Sir Francis Bacon said to him, He loved not to sie Poesy goe on other feet than poeticall Dactylus and Spondaeus.' With keen eye he had noted his little mannerisms. ' My Lord Chancelor of England wringeth his speeches from the strings of his band.' He had also gauged the immensity of his genius. It is to Jonson that we owe our only account of Bacon's manner of speaking, a passage which often does duty as a commonplace, descriptive of true eloquence. In Bacon's prosperity Jonson had addressed him, in well-chosen language of poetical compliment, as one

> Whose even thread the fates spin round and full
> Out of their choicest and their whitest wool.

But Jonson was not of the race of flatterers (with whom are busy mockers) who,

> like butterflies,
> Show not their mealy wings but to the summer.
> *Troil. and Cres.* iii. 3. 78.

It was after Bacon's fall that the spirit of Jonson was touched to a finer issue, and he wrote these noble words : ' My conceit of his person was never increased towards him by his place or honours : but I have and do reverence him for the greatness that was only proper to himself, in that he seemed to me ever, by his work, one of the greatest men, and most worthy of admiration that had been in many ages. In his adversity I prayed that God would give him strength ; for greatness he could not want.'

Of Shakespeare, Jonson was in a still greater degree the companion, the critic, and finally the panegyrist. In their ' wit-combates' at the Mermaid Tavern he held his own. While Shakespeare was yet alive, a prosperous gentleman, he did not escape the lash of Ben Jonson's tongue. Jonson was by common consent a keen and even a censorious critic. He was, according to Dryden, a most severe judge of himself as of others. If he had a giant's strength, he was wont to use it ' as a giant.' This is probably a truer estimate of his character than Drummond's : ' a great lover and praiser of himself ; a contemner and scorner of others.'

I never could understand why Jonson's criticism of Shakespeare should have exposed him to stupid attacks, and to the still stupider defence of an editor and biographer who would have us believe that Jonson never thought of Shakespeare when he laughed at servant-monsters, tales, tempests, and suchlike drolleries. Why should not Jonson be allowed to do his kind ? It was surely more to the discredit of some other contemporaries of Shakespeare that they do not appear to have been conscious of his existence. It would indeed have been unpardonable if Jonson had nothing more to say of Shakespeare. But in his declaration ' I loved the man and do honour his memory on this side idolatry as much as any ; ' and in his immortal words,

He was not of an age, but for all time,

we have the true measure of Jonson's estimate, and his carping criticism is only of importance as indicative of his nature and habits. He was scarcely the man who from easy-going good-fellowship would endorse without inquiry any statement which the editors were fraudulent enough to put into their preface, or indolent enough to allow their literary man to write for them. As to this imaginary literary man, I cannot help thinking that, if he had any real existence, he would probably have suggested to the editors the possibility of printers' errors, and the desirability of preparing for publication copies which were designed for another and a different purpose.

LEONARD DIGGES

But another name, not wholly unknown, is involved in this discreditable business :

Shake-speare, at length thy pious fellows give
The world thy Workes ; thy Workes, by which outliue

Thy Tombe, thy name must ; when that stone is rent
And Time dissolues thy Stratford Moniment
Here we aliue shall view thee still.

Thus wrote Leonard Digges.   Although his only claim to immortality is his association with the editors of the Folio to which his
verses are prefixed, he was well known at the time, and finds a
place in Wood's *Athenæ*.   He was the typical man about town
and play-goer of the day.   In some further verses in praise of
Shakespeare subsequently printed, he shows keen interest in the
stage, and knowledge of dramatic matters.   A man like Digges, of
literary habits and independent means, with a special interest in
the stage and a passionate admirer of Shakespeare, must have been
acquainted with the Quarto editions of his plays.   It is strange
that he should have associated himself with the dishonest or careless publication of inferior copies, commending it to the world as a
collection of the poet's works which it owed ' at length ' to the
pious offices of his fellows.

It seemed needful to collect and summarise the principal facts
connected with the publication of the Folio, before proceeding to
develop and illustrate the statement that the result of the studies
and inquiries undertaken in order to explain the allusions collected
in these pages, has in every instance tended to support its
authority.   .

It must be admitted that the credit of its editors would be completely shattered if they were proved to have included in the Folio
any play which was not, in part at least, the work of Shakespeare ;
for this is a matter about which they could not be mistaken ; and
those who believe them guilty of palming upon the public as
works of Shakespeare, printed from his original manuscript, the
compositions of other dramatists, are quite consistent in repudiating
the Folio and denouncing its editors.

Accusations of this kind have been brought againt these men,
and with a light heart.   In the case indeed of one play, *Titus
Andronicus*, a verdict of guilty has been brought in with a nearer
approach to unanimity than I have observed in any branch of
literary criticism.

TITUS ANDRONICUS

Johnson could write in 1765, ' All the editors and critics agree
with Mr. Theobald in supposing this play spurious.   I see no
reason for differing from them.'   And Hallam in 1837, ' *Titus
Andronicus* is now by common consent denied to be in any sense

a production of Shakespeare' (*Literature of Europe*). It is not
too much to say that in regard to this play there is opposed to the
entire voice of criticism *quod semper, quod ubique, quod ab omnibus*,
simply the assertion of the editors of the Folio; for although
Professor Dowden and Gervinus doubt, and Collier and Knight
with some German critics believe, it is plain that neither their
faith nor their scepticism would have been exercised upon this play
had it not been included in the Folio. The case is therefore an
interesting one for the application of the suggested test.

Titus Andronicus was first published under Shakespeare's name
in the Folio of 1623. The Quarto edition appeared anonymously.
We can fix approximately the date of its original production.
Bartholomew Fair was first acted in 1615. In the Induction Ben
Jonson has his laugh at the 'servant monster' in *The Tempest*, the
humours of the watch in *Much Ado About Nothing*, and generally
at ' those that beget tales, tempests, and such like drolleries ; ' and
in the humorous *Articles of the Fair* it is agreed that ' he that will
swear that *Jeronimo* or *Andronicus* are the best plays yet, shall
pass unexcepted at here as a man whose judgment shows it is
constant, and has stood still these five-and-twenty or thirty years.'
These words proved that *Andronicus* was in 1615 classed with
Jeronimo as a familiar example of the old-fashioned bloody tragedy,
in vogue some quarter of a century earlier. Jonson is not to be
understood as fixing the date with accuracy, but taking the lowest
figure, twenty-five years, *Titus Andronicus* must have been before
the public since 1589 at latest. If written by Shakespeare, it was
written at the stage of intellectual development which produced
Venus and Adonis and *Love's Labour's Lost*.

In 1598 Francis Meres published a work entitled *Palladis
Tamia*, or *Wit's Treasury*, in which he pronounces that ' Shakespeare among ye English is the most excellent in both kinds for
the stage; for comedy, witnes his *Gentlemen of Verona*, his *Errors*,
his *Loue Labors Lost*, his *Loue Labours Wonne* (*All's Well*), his
Midsummer's Night Dreame, and his *Merchant of Venice;* for
tragedy, his *Richard the 2*, *Richard the 3*, *Henry the 4*, *King John*,
Titus Andronicus, and his *Romeo and Juliet*.' The evidence
afforded by this enumeration of *Titus Andronicus* with eleven other
plays, all undoubtedly genuine, is thus summarily disposed of by
Mr. Hallam : ' In criticism of all kinds we must acquire a dogged
habit of resisting testimony, when *res ipsa per se vociferatur* to the
contrary.'

In applying this principle of criticism, somewhat dangerous in its practical application, it behoves us to listen with the utmost care to the voice in which *res ipsa* speaks.

Its accents, no doubt, sound differently in different ears, but certain notes are unmistakable. It may safely be stated (1) that scarcely a trace of Shakespeare is apparent in the first act, (2) that frequent evidences of a different hand become discernible in the subsequent treatment of the principal characters. Was this the hand of Shakespeare, the Shakespeare (be it remembered) not of *Hamlet* and *Lear*, but of *Venus and Adonis* ; the hand of Johannes-Factotum in his earliest attempts at dramatic adaptation?

At the commencement of the second act the attention of the Shakespearian student is at once arrested by the opening lines of the speech of Aaron the Moor. His love, Tamora, Queen of the Goths, has become Empress of Rome.

> Advanc'd above pale envy's threatening reach,
> As when the golden sun salutes the morn,
> And, having gilt the ocean with his beams,
> Gallops the Zodiac in his glistering coach,
> And overlooks the highest-peering hills.

From this image, borrowed from the dawn, Aaron digresses to the falconer's art :

> Then, Aaron, arm thy heart, and fit thy thoughts,
> To mount aloft with thy imperial mistress,
> And mount her pitch, whom thou in triumph long
> Hast prisoner held.

While Aaron thus soliloquises, the sons of Tamora come upon the scene, competitors for the love of Lavinia, the ill-starred daughter of Titus Andronicus. One of them, in justification of his design upon her, thus appeals to Aaron's personal experience in woodcraft :

> What, hast not thou full often struck a doe,
> And borne her cleanly by the keeper's nose ?

Aaron, with imagination full of the incidents of a solemn hunting of the deer, suggests :

> My Lords, a solemn hunting is in hand ;
> There will the lovely Roman ladies troop :
> The forest walks are wide and spacious ;
> And many unfrequented plots there are
> Fitted by kind for rape and villany :
> Single you thither then this dainty doe,
> And strike her home by force, if not by words.—ii. 1. 112.

The hunting in hand was, as afterwards explained, a 'general hunting in this forest' (ii. 3. 59), with running hounds as well as crossbow and greyhounds. Accordingly, the stage direction, 'A cry of hounds and horns winded in a peal,' follow these words of Andronicus:

> *Tit.* The hunt is up, the morn is bright and grey,
> The fields are fragrant and the woods are green:
> Uncouple here and let us make a bay,
> And wake the emperor and his lovely bride
> And rouse the prince, and ring a hunter's peal,
> That all the court may echo with the noise.—ii. 2. 1.

The Empress Tamora is then invited to see the sport:

> *Sat.*   Madam, now shall ye see
> Our Roman hunting.
> *Marc.*   I have dogs, my lord,
> Will rouse the proudest panther in the chase,
> And climb the highest promontory top.
> *Tit.*   And I have horse will follow where the game
> Makes way, and run like swallows o'er the plain.

But the Empress Tamora was intent on other thoughts:

> *Tam.* My lovely Aaron, wherefore look'st thou sad,
> When everything doth make a gleeful boast?
> The birds chant melody on every bush,
> The snake lies rolled in the cheerful sun,
> The green leaves quiver with the cooling wind
> And make a chequer'd shadow on the ground:
> Under their sweet shade, Aaron, let us sit,
> And, whilst the babbling echo mocks the hounds,
> Replying shrilly to the well-tuned horns,
> As if a double hunt were heard at once,
> Let us sit down, and mark their yelping noise;
> And, after conflict, such as was supposed
> The wandering prince and Dido once enjoy'd,
> When with a happy storm they were surprised
> And curtained with a counsel-keeping cave,
> We may each wreathed in the other's arms,
> Our pastimes done, possess a golden slumber;
> Whiles hounds, and horns, and sweet melodious birds
> Be unto us as is a nurse's song
> Of lullaby to bring her babe asleep.—ii. 3. 10.

But Aaron, bent on the destruction of the Emperor's brother, Bassianus, is deaf to her advances; as was Adonis to Venus, when her imagination suggested the music of the cry:

Then do they spend their mouths : Echo replies,
As if another chase were in the skies.

Ven. and Ad. 695, see *ante*, p. 181.

Bassianus appearing on the scene, Aaron departs to mature
his revenge. His parting admonition to Tamora—' be cross with
him '—is thus carried out :

Bas. Who have we here ? Rome's royal empress
Unfurnish'd of her well-beseeming troop ?
Or is it Dian, habited like her,
Who hath abandonèd her holy groves
To see the general hunting in this forest ?
Tam. Saucy controller of our private steps !
Had I the power that some say Dian had,
Thy temples should be planted presently
With horns, as was Actæon's ; and the hounds
Should drive upon thy new-transformed limbs,
Unmannerly intruder as thou art !

The word ' drive,' puzzling to critics (one of whom suggests
' thrive '), is to this day a technical term of the hunting language,
expressive of the eagerness and spirit of the hound.

'Twere long to tell the dull tale of death and mutilation that
follows, unrelieved, save here¯ and there ; as when one tells
Andronicus that his unhappy daughter was found cruelly mutilated :

straying in the park,
Seeking to hide herself, as doth the deer
That hath received some unrecuring wound.

and he replies with a play on words, familiar to the ear :

Tit. It was my deer ; and he that wounded her
Hath hurt me more than had he kill'd me dead.—iii. 1. 88.

Or when he gives a lesson in shooting :

Tit. Sir boy, now let me see your archery ;
Look ye draw home enough, and 'tis there straight.—iv. 3. 2.

As the dismal tale progresses these bright spots become fewer
and fewer, and the fifth act relapses into the dulness of the first,
save for an instant when Aaron, with the villain's liking for the
bear-garden, compares himself to

As true a dog as ever fought at head.—v. 1. 102.

The reader of the foregoing pages must have recognised in
these passages many touches of nature, already selected in these

pages, as characteristic of his handiwork, from the undoubted works of Shakespeare. The general hunting; the music of the bay; the effect of echo mocking the hounds and doubling the chase (described in almost the same words as in *Venus and Adonis*); the ill-timed, but irresistible, pun on the word deer; the images borrowed from country life; and finally the reminiscence of the stricken doe often borne cleanly by the keeper's nose: must it not be said of these in the words borrowed by Hallam from Lucretius: *res ipsa per se vociferatur ?*

It may be asked, what induced Shakespeare to expend his time upon a ghastly tale of horrors, unredeemed before his touch by any passages of poetical beauty? Ben Jonson supplies the answer. It suited the taste of the age. There were old-fashioned playgoers, even a quarter of a century after its production, who would swear that it and *Jeronimo* were the best plays yet. In the cant of the present day, there was money in it; and whether we like it or not, we must admit that this consideration had always weight in determining Shakespeare's choice.

But there is another question to be asked. If Shakespeare had no part in its composition, what induced the editors to print it as his? The poorer the play, the less the temptation to foist it upon the public as Shakespeare's. The deception would be less likely to succeed, and the danger of discrediting their collection would be considerable, especially in the case of an old and once popular piece, the authorship of which was as well known to Ben Jonson, to Leonard Digges, and to all persons interested in the drama, as to the editors themselves.

The admission of *Titus Andronicus*, or of any disputed play, into the Shakespearian canon decides no more than that Shakespeare had sufficient share in its composition to justify an editor in printing it in a collection of his works. For it must never be forgotten that Shakespeare was not only an author, but an appropriator and adapter of plays, and that he was an adapter before he was an original author. In regard to this very play an ancient tradition has been recorded according to which it was the work of an unknown author, adapted by Shakespeare, and tradition does not always lie.

SHAKESPEARE'S METHOD OF ADAPTATION

We are fortunately not without means of becoming acquainted with the method by which he adapted such like plays to his use; knowledge which can be turned, as we shall see, to practical use.

In *The Taming of the Shrew* we possess an adaptation and development, undoubtedly by Shakespeare, of an older play which is, no less certainly, the work of another hand. This latter is *The Taming of a Shrew* published in 1594, and reprinted by the Shakespeare Society in 1844 ; an excellent and spirited comedy by an unknown author, which furnished ready to Shakespeare's hand the humours of the drunken Sly, and the leading idea and many of the details of his Katherine and Petruchio scenes.

Shakespeare's *Taming of the Shrew* teems with allusions to sports, to horses and to their fifty diseases. These allusions are of two kinds : Some form part of the necessary action of the play. Of these the rudimentary germs may be found in the older play, but without the distinctively Shakespearian characteristics discernible in the ultimate development. Others are casual, self-suggested, and independent of the plot. These latter are without exception confined to the work that is undoubtedly Shakespeare's.

Thus, Petruchio's old groom—the ' ancient trusty pleasant servant ' whom we know as Grumio—tells us that his master is ready to marry for money an old trot, ' though she have as many diseases as two and fifty horses.' And when asked if the horses are ready he answers in stable language : ' Ay, Sir, they be ready, the oats have eaten the horses.' And stable language is not found only in the mouths of grooms, for we have already noted Lucentio's : ' Sir, give him head, I know he'll prove a jade,' and Biondello's marvellous catalogue of glanders, windgalls, spavins, staggers, and half a dozen other ills that horse-flesh is heir to. Petruchio's spaniel Troilus, his exclamation : ' O slow-wing'd turtle ! shall a buzzard take thee?' and the falconer's cry of ' Jack, boy ! ho, boy ! ' suggests that Petruchio knew what he was about when he took in hand to man a haggard. There is also the sporting talk in Lucentio's house of fowling, coursing, and of the deer at bay, with Tranio's ' good swift simile, but somewhat currish ' when he said :

> Lucentio slipp'd me like his greyhound
> Which runs himself, and catches for his master.—v. 2. 46–58.

Not a trace of any of these allusions is to be found in the *Taming of a Shrew*.

In the old play, as in Shakespeare's revised version, a lord returning from hunting discovers Sly lying drunk by the roadside.

> Here breake we off our hunting for to-night ;
> Cupple uppe the hounds and let vs hie vs home
> And bid the huntsman see them meated well,
> For they have all deserved it well to-day.

Shakespeare's version will be found *ante*, p. 78. Clowder is to be coupled, but Merryman, the embossed hound, is to be otherwise treated. In the old play all are to be alike coupled and all deserve their meat equally well. Shakespeare had ridden—or perhaps run —home too often with the hounds to be content with such colourless stuff. He knew well that the master and his huntsmen would dispute and finally quarrel over the performance of each particular hound. To him, as to them, a pack did not mean so many couples of hounds and nothing more. It was an aggregate of individuals, whose several performances were deserving of as serious and detailed criticism as the successive speakers in a full-dress debate in the House of Commons. Silver, the lord observed, had ' made it good at the hedge corner, in the coldest fault.' Belman, according to the huntsman, had cried upon it at the merest loss, and twice pick'd out the dullest scent. He was in truth the better dog. ' Thou art a fool,' rejoins the lord, who had his particular fancies ; ' if Echo were as fleet I would esteem him worth a dozen such.' A better example could not be found of the difference between Shakespeare's notions of woodcraft and the compositions of contemporary dramatists, on the rare occasions when they handled such matters.

In the old play Sly is offered lusty steeds, more swift of pace than winged Pegasus :

> And if your Honour please to hunt the deere,
> Your hounds stand readie cuppled at the doore,
> Who in running will o'ertake the Row
> And make the long breathde Tygre broken winded.

This would never do : who ever heard of coupling hounds to be used in coursing, for this is meant by overtaking in running? The greyhound in Tudor times had his collar, not his couple. And what about hawking? And so Shakespeare, with the echo of the bay sounding in his ears, re-wrote, after his fashion, the passage thus :

> Dost thou love hawking ? thou hast hawks will soar
> Above the morning lark : or wilt thou hunt ?
> Thy hounds shall make the welkin answer them,
> And fetch shrill echoes from the hollow earth.
> *First Serv.* Say wilt thou course ? Thy greyhounds are as swift
> As breathed stags, ay, fleeter than the roe.

The author of the old play, though evidently no sportsman, knew, as every one of his day knew, that hawks were kept in mews, and that they were tamed by hunger. It was an obvious thought to compare the taming of a shrew by starvation to the discipline of the hawk. And this is the result:

> I'le mew her up as men do mew their hawkes,
> And make her gentlie come vnto the lure.
> Were she as stuborne and as full of strength
> As were the Thracian horse Alcides tamde,
> That King Egeus fed with flesh of men,
> Yet would I pull her downe and make her come
> As hungry hawkes do flie vnto there lure.

Now hawks are mewed up for moulting and not to teach them to come to the lure. It is in the manning of the haggard falcon, by watching and by hunger, and not in her mewing or in her training to the lure, that Shakespeare saw a true analogue to the taming of the shrew; so borrowing from the old writer an excellent idea, badly worked out, he wrote:

> My falcon now is sharp and passing empty;
> And till she stoop she must not be full-gorged
> For then she never looks upon her lure.
> Another way I have to man my haggard,
> To make her come and know her keeper's call;
> That is, to watch her, as we watch those kites
> That bate, and beat, and will not be obedient.

It has been already noted (*ante*, p. 155) that this passage contains no less than ten technical terms of art, and its falconry is approved as faultless by the latest writer upon the sport.

KING HENRY VI

With the knowledge thus acquired of Shakespeare's method as an adapter, I approach the question of the authorship of the three parts of *King Henry VI*. Passing by the first part, for the present, I find the second and third parts to be adaptations and developments of two older plays, which we fortunately possess. These are (1) *The first part of the Contention betwixt the two famous houses of Yorke and Lancaster* (published in 1594 and reprinted by the Shakespeare Society in 1844) upon which the second part of *King Henry VI.* is founded; and (2) *The True Tragedie of Richard the Third* (published and reprinted at the same dates) which was developed into the third part of *Henry VI.*

As regards these plays, the problem is more complicated than in the case of *The Taming of the Shrew*, for although the work

which appears for the first time in the edition of 1623 is undoubtedly Shakespeare's, opinion is divided as to the authorship
of the earlier plays : Johnson, Steevens, Knight, Schlegel, Tieck,
Ulrici, Delius, Oechelhaüser, and H. von Friesen being in favour
of Shakespeare's authorship; and Malone, Collier, Dyce, Courte-
nay, Gervinus, Kreyssig, and the French critics in favour of
Greene's or Marlowe's authorship (Dowden, *Shakspere, his Mind
and Art*).

A comparison of these old dramas with the plays as printed
in the Folio, discloses precisely the same process as that by which
the comedy of 1594 was transmuted into *The Taming of the Shrew*.
Certain passages are re-written and become instinct with life and
racy of the soil.   Vague or inaccurate allusions become truthful
and striking, `and some distinctively Shakespearian touches are
added.

In the *First part of the Contention* Suffolk compared Duke
Humphrey to a fox who must be killed to save the lamb :

> Let him die, in that he is a Foxe,
> Lest that in liuing he offend vs more.

Here is no hint of the laws of woodcraft which distinguish
vermin like the fox from beasts of venery to whom fair law is
allowed ; and so it was re-written :

> And do not stand on quillets how to slay him :
> Be it by gins, by snares, by subtlety,
> Sleeping or waking; 'tis no matter how
> So he be dead.   *2 Hen. VI.* iii. 1. 257.

It was part of the plot of the original drama that Duke
Humphrey and Cardinal Beaufort should quarrel as they returned
with the King and Queen from hawking.   In the *First part of the
Contention* the Queen has a hawk on her fist :

> *Queene.* My lord, how did your grace like this last flight ?
> But as I cast her off the wind did rise,
> And twas ten to one, old Ione had not gone out.
> *King.* How wonderful the Lord's workes are on earth,
> Euen in these silly creatures of His hands !
> Vncle Gloster, how hie your hawk did sore,
> And on a sodaine soust the Partridge downe !
> *Suffolk.* No maruele, if it please your Maiestie,
> My Lord Protector's Hawke done towre so well ;
> He knowes his maister loues to be aloft.

This was not to Shakespeare's mind.   Partridge hawking

might be good sport, but highflying emulation is best illustrated by the 'mountey,' when a cast of haggard falcons are flown at the heron or mallard, and not by the downward swoop of the falcon on the partridge. And so he re-wrote the passage thus:

Queen. Believe me, lords, for flying at the brook,
I saw not better sport these seven years' day:
Yet, by your leave, the wind was very high;
And, ten to one, old Joan had not gone out.
King. But what a point, my lord, your falcon made,
And what a pitch she flew above the rest!
To see how God in all His creatures works!
Yea, man and birds are fain of climbing high.
Suffolk. No marvel, an it like your majesty,
My lord protector's hawks do tower so well;
They know their master loves to be aloft
And bears his thoughts above his falcon's pitch.

Ibid. ii. 1. 1.

In *The True Tragedy*, a scene being laid in a forest, two keepers enter with bows and arrows, one of whom says to his fellow:

Keeper. Come, let's take our stands vpon this hi'l,
And by and by the deere will come this waie.

These dull and lifeless lines sufficed to suggest to the adapter recollections and images, which were not present to the imagination of the author. He saw, in his mind's eye, the thickgrown brake, the covert for the stand; the laund across which the deer will come; the woodman's art in ' culling the principal of all the deer ;' and he wrote the lines printed at p. 236, concluding with a secret of woodcraft thus imparted:

Sec. Keep. I'll stay above the hill, so both may shoot.
First Keep. That cannot be ; the noise of thy cross-bow
Will scare the herd, and so my shoot is lost.
Here stand we both, and aim we at the best.

3 Hen. VI. iii. 1. 1.

The additions which we find in the Folio are no less characteristic than the alterations. Among these may be noted Queen Margaret's comparison of Edward and Richard to

a brace of greyhounds
Having the fearful flying hare in sight,
With fiery eyes sparkling for very wrath.

Ibid. ii. 5. 129.

In another passage, Richard makes use of what we have learned to be a term of venery (*ante*, p. 32), when he tells Clifford that he has ' singled ' him alone, and when he says to Warwick coming on the scene :

> Nay, Warwick, single out some other chase ;
> For I myself will hunt this wolf to death.　　*Ibid.* ii. 4. 12.

In the old play Eleanor Duchess of Gloucester simply makes her exit.　In the revised version Buckingham remarks :

> She's tickled now ; her fume needs no spurs,
> She'll gallop far enough to her destruction.　　*2 Hen. VI.* i. 3. 154.

Here we discern the horseman, as we detect the falconer in King Henry's desire that his wife might be revenged on

> that hateful duke,
> Whose haughty spirit, winged with desire,
> Will cost my crown, and like an empty eagle,
> Tire on the flesh of me, and of my son !　　*3 Hen. VI.* i. 1. 268.

These alterations and additions closely resemble those which were introduced into *The Taming of the Shrew*.　But when we compare the Histories in their older form with the play of 1594 upon which that comedy was founded, a difference is at once perceived.　We find in these Histories allusions of the spontaneous and self-suggested kind, which we have noticed as constantly occurring in the works of Shakespeare.　You will find in *The Taming of a Shrew* no such reminiscences as the following :

> Neither the king, nor he that loues him best,
> The proudest burd that holds vp Lancaster,
> Dares stirre a wing, if Warwike shake his bels.
> 　　　　　　　*True Tragedie* (3 *Hen. VI.* i. 1. 45).
> *Cliff.* I, I. So strives the Woodcocke with the gin.
> *North.* So doth the Cunnie (Coney) struggle withe the net.
> 　　　　　　　*True Tragedie* (3 *Hen. VI.* i. 4. 61).
> Who finds the partridge in the puttock's neast,
> But will imagine how the bird came there,
> Although the kyte soare with vnbloodie beake.
> 　　　　　*First part of the Contention* (2 *Hen. VI.* iii. 2. 192).
> So doues doe pecke the Rauen's piersing tallents.
> 　　　　　　　*True Tragedie* (3 *Hen. VI.* i. 4. 41).

These passages, though few in number, are distinctly Shakespearian, and unlike the undoubted workmanship of either Greene or Marlowe.　They support the conclusion that Shakespeare had some part, probably not a large one, in the older dramas,

which he finally revised and altered, thus converting them
into the second and third parts of *Henry VI.*, as printed in
the Folio. This conclusion accords with Greene's oft-quoted
denunciations of Shakespeare, as ' an vpstart crow beautified
with our feathers, that, with his *Tygre's heart wrapped in a
player's hyde*, supposes hee is able to bombast out a blanke verse
as the best of you ; and beeing an absolute Johannes-fac-totum,
is in his owne conceit the onely Shake-scene in a Countrie.'
The line here parodied :

O tiger's heart, wrapt in a woman's hide !

occurs not only in 3 *Hen. VI.* i. 4. 138, but in *The True Tragedy*.
Greene's denunciation of Shakespeare would have no point unless
he meant to convey that Johannes-fac-totum foisted a ridiculous
line of his own composition into a play which he had stolen. ' His
angry allusion to Shakespeare's plagiarism is best explained,' says
Hallam—I would suggest only explained—' by supposing that he
was himself concerned in the two old plays which had been
converted into the second and third parts of *Henry VI.*' The
superior workmanship of certain parts of the older Histories, compared with the acknowledged writings of Greene, has led some
critics to assign these plays to Marlowe. But, great though
Marlowe was as poet and master of the English language, he
has left nothing behind him suggestive of capacity to write the
Jack Cade scenes—more Shakespearian than Shakespeare's
undoubted additions to the plays of which they form part.

These historical dramas exhibit precisely the kind of patch-
work which we should expect to find in the earlier handiwork
of Johannes-fac-totum. ' A vast number of early English dramas
once acted with success, but never printed, have entirely perished,
nor is it improbable that there may have been among them some
rifacimenti by Shakespeare of plays in which Greene and his
friends were largely concerned ' (Dyce, *Account of R. Greene and
his Writings*).

The first part of *Henry VI.* may be shortly dealt with. lt was
published as Shakespeare's in the Folio of 1623. No former
edition is known, nor is there in existence any earlier drama from
which it was adapted. Two opinions with regard to its authorship deserve consideration. By some it is regarded as in no part
the work of Shakespeare. Others believe that he had some share
in its composition, assigning to him by general consent the scene
in the Temple Garden, and certain portions in which Talbot plays

a part. If these parts are excepted, the play is absolutely barren of allusions of the kind with which we are dealing. In the Temple Gardens, however, we seem to meet with an old friend in the person of Warwick :

> Between two hawks, which flies the higher pitch ;
> Between two dogs, which hath the deeper mouth . . .
> I have, perhaps, some shallow spirit of judgment.—ii. 4. 11.

If Shakespeare had for the purposes of his trilogy of *Henry VI.* appropriated an old play, and did in truth alter it in certain important particulars, the editors of the Folio were certainly justified in printing it in their collections. Nay, they would be bound to do so, inasmuch as the History of King Henry VI. would not otherwise have been presented to their readers in the form in which Shakespeare would desire them to have it.

KING HENRY VIII

That Shakespeare had sufficient share in the authorship of *Henry VIII.* to justify its inclusion in the Folio is generally admitted. The portions of the play attributed to him are : Act I. Scenes 1 & 2 ; Act II. Scenes 3 & 4 ; Act III. Scene 2 (in part) ; Act V. Scene 1. 'Mr. Spedding and Mr. Hickson (1850) independently arrived at identical results as to the division of parts between Fletcher and Shakespeare. Mr. Fleay (1874) has confirmed the conclusions of Mr. Spedding (double endings forming in this instance his chief test) ; Professor Ingram has further confirmed them by his weak-ending test, and Mr. Furnivall by the stopt-line test' (Dowden, *Shakspere, his Mind and Art*).

In the first of these scenes we soon find ourselves in the company of a sportsman in the person of Norfolk, who, when he would chide the impetuosity of Buckingham, appeals to his experience of horsemanship and woodcraft (*ante*, pp. 38, 44). The language is so characteristic of Shakespeare, and of him alone, that it points to the same conclusion as that to which Dr. Ingram is led by the weak-ending, Mr. Spedding by the double-ending, and Mr. Furnivall by the stopt-line test. In Act III. Scene 2, Surrey's allusion to the sport of daring larks is suggestive. Lord Sands's comparison of the French courtiers to horses among whom 'the spavin or springhalt reign'd,' suggests that Shakespeare may have added some touches to the third scene of the first act. Otherwise the play is singularly barren in reminiscences of sport or of horsemanship. Thus the allusion test, while it fully justifies the inclusion of the play in the Folio, supports the conclusion that it is, in the main, the work of some dramatist whose mind was full of other thoughts than those which rose unbidden to the mind of Shakespeare.

There is not one of the thirty-four plays included in the Folio which fails to yield specimens of the true Shakespearian allusion. The veins with which they are intersected are of varying degrees of richness. But the metal is the same throughout.

For instance, *The Two Gentlemen of Verona* has been quoted but seldom, and yet even this play affords evidence that its author was concerned in the hunting of hares and the keeping of horses. To none but a sportsman would the simple words ' Run boy, run ; run and seek him out' (iii. 1. 189) suggest ' Soho, soho ! ' followed by the inevitable play on the word hare ; and who but a horsemaster or farrier troubles himself about the bots, or would think of it as suggested by the phrase ' over boots in love ' ? (i. 1. 24.)

It would of course be absurd to exclude any well-authenticated drama from the Shakespearian canon on the ground that it afforded no evidence of Shakespeare's sporting tastes. But the fact that no such drama is to be found in the Folio is of some importance in estimating the value of the test under consideration in these pages.

PLAYS NOT INCLUDED IN THE FIRST FOLIO

While the authority of the Folio would be seriously shaken if it were shown that its editors, possessed of full knowledge, had included in it any spurious play, the same results would not follow from the establishment of the authenticity of a drama not included in their edition. If Mr. Spalding had rightly rejected 1 *Henry VI.* and *Titus Andronicus*, he would have been justified in his conclusion :—' the editors then were unscrupulous and unfair as to the works which they inserted.' But the fair-minded reader will not, I think, adopt such a conclusion from the omission of *Pericles* from the first folio and from the addition thereto of *Troilus and Cressida* after the table of contents was printed. In his opinion, the ' whole conduct of these editors inspires distrust, but their unacknowledged omission of those two plays deprives them of all claim to our confidence ' (*Letter on Authorship of Two Noble Kinsmen*).

There are many conceivable reasons for the omission from the Folio of a genuine play. One indeed is suggested by Mr. Spalding himself. The editors may have been unable to procure the manuscript. Their particularity in adding *Troilus and Cressida* at the last moment, and at a sacrifice of the symmetry of their edition, so far from proving them 'unscrupulous and unfair,' seems rather to indicate an earnest desire to make their collection as complete as circumstances would permit. Exclusion from the folio is certainly *prima facie* evidence of non-authenticity. But, in our ignorance of the circumstances connected with any particular play, it cannot be pushed so far as to amount to a pronouncement of the editors upon the authenticity of a piece which may have escaped their recollection, or, more probably, may have been, at the moment, impossible of procurement. Any play, therefore, attributed to Shakespeare, though not included in the Folio, is a fair subject for the application of any test by which his workmanship may be discerned.

Twelve dramas in all, not included in the Folio, have been either printed under Shakespeare's name, or otherwise attributed to him. The copies of the third Folio, dated 1664, contain seven plays never before printed in Folio, viz.: *Pericles; The London Prodigal; Thomas Lord Cromwell; Sir John Oldcastle; The Puritan Widow; A Yorkshire Tragedy;* and *Locrine.* In 1634 a play entitled *The Two Noble Kinsmen* was published, and described as 'written by the memorable Worthies of their Time, Mr. John Fletcher and Mr. William Shakespeare Gent.' In addition to these, two plays published anonymously, *Arden of Feversham* (1592) and *Edward III.* (1596) have been attributed to Shakespeare in whole or in part, and it has been suggested that he is responsible for a play called *Fair Em* published anonymously in 1631, and for *The Birth of Merlin*, printed with the names of Shakespeare and Rowley in 1662.

PERICLES

Pericles has been long since admitted to the canon by general consent, and is always printed among Shakespeare's works. 'Whoever reads *Pericles* with attention' (Gervinus writes), 'readily finds that all these scenes in which there is any naturalness in the matter, or in which great passions are developed—especially the scenes in which Pericles and Marina act—stand forth with striking power from the poorness of the whole. Shakespeare's hand is here unmistakable.' Here it is also that we find the indications of his presence with which we are now concerned. It is Pericles who announces—quite gratuitously so far as the action is concerned—his intention to mount him

Upon a courser, whose delightful steps
Shall make the gazer joy to see him tread.—ii. 1. 164.

Of Marina it is said to the Lord Lysimachus, by one whose calling does not suggest familiarity with the language of the manage :

My lord, she's not paced yet ; you must take some pains to work her to your manage. iv. 6. 67.

And the parts of the play from which Pericles and Marina are absent are barren of reminiscences of this kind.

A YORKSHIRE TRAGEDY

A Yorkshire Tragedy was one of four plays acted at the Globe on the same day under the name of *All's One.* It was founded upon a domestic murder recorded in Stowe's Chronicle (1604). The three other plays produced with it were not, apparently, thought worthy of publication. But *A Yorkshire Tragedy* was entered at Stationers' Hall and printed in 1608, with Shakespeare's name. 'This,' says Mr. Hallam, 'which would be thought good evidence in most cases, must not be held conclusive ' (*Literature of Europe*). This most careful critic expresses no opinion beyond the general statement that he cannot perceive the hand of Shakespeare in any of the anonymous tragedies. Mr. Collier, on the other hand, writes : ' The internal evidence, however, of Shakespeare's authorship is much stronger than the external, and there are some speeches which could scarcely have proceeded from any other pen ' (*History of Dramatic Poetry* ; see also Mr. Fleay's *Chronicle of the English Drama*). Most critics pronounce against the authenticity of the play ; Malone professing himself unable to form a decided opinion.

Here, then, is an instance in which the test which I have suggested may be usefully applied, and by the result of the application its practical value may be, in some degree, estimated.

The play consists of a single act. In the first scene a servant arrives on horseback.

Sam. . . Boy, look you walk my horse with discretion. I have rid him simply ; I warrant his skin sticks to his back with very heat. If he should catch cold and get the cough of the lungs, I were well served, were I not ?

The husband, the chief actor in the ghastly drama, has ruined himself by gambling. ' That mortgage,' he tells his wife, ' sits like a snaffle upon mine inheritance, and makes me chew upon iron.' In his despair he kills his beggared children and stabs his wife. As he escapes his horse falls.

Hus. O stumbling jade, the spavin overtake thee !
  The fifty deseases stop thee !
  Oh, I am sorely bruised ! Plague founder thee !
  Thou runn'st at ease and pleasure. Heart of chance !
  To throw me now, within a flight o' the town,
  In such plain even ground too ! 'S foot a man
  May dice upon it, and throw away the meadows,
  Filthy beast !

Who but Shakespeare would have compared the ruined owner of a mortgaged estate to a proud horse, fretfully champing and grinding his teeth upon an iron snaffle? In the spavin, and the fifty diseases of horseflesh, do we not again recognise his Roman hand? 'As many diseases as two and fifty horses ; ' such was the form this saying took in the mouth of Grumio. Can we wonder that the author of the stable directions for treatment of the hide-bound jade first achieved fame in the matter of the care of horses? The horse's skin cleaveth fast to his back, says Blundevill, ' when the horse after some great heat hath beene suffered to stand long in the raine or wet weather.' The passages collected by Mr. Collier are suggestive. So are certain verbal quibbles and obscurities in this play. But ' the fifty diseases stop thee,' affords stronger evidence to my mind, and I confess to a considerable degree of satisfaction when I found that Shakespeare's authorship of this play is not only evidenced by passages of the kind which I have quoted, but supported by strong external evidence, and accepted, on other grounds, by high authority. It is easy to understand why an unimportant one-act piece was either overlooked by the editors of the Folio, or deliberately excluded from a collection of Comedies, Histories, and Tragedies.

TWO NOBLE KINSMEN

That Shakespeare had some part in the composition of *The Two Noble Kinsmen* has, since the publication in 1833 of Mr. Spalding's letter upon the authorship of that play, been generally admitted by critics, but with gradually increasing reluctance. Mr. Spalding, who was confident in his opinion when he published his letter in 1833, was less decided in 1840; and in 1847 he wrote, 'The question of Shakespeare's share in this play is really insoluble ' (*Edinburgh Review*, July, 1847). In Professor Dowden's words, ' The parts ascribed to him seem to grow less like his work in thought, feeling, and expression, as we, so to speak, live with them. The resemblance which at first impressed us so strongly seems to fade, or if it remains, to be at most something superficial' (*Introduction to Shakspeare*). Mr. Hallam also seems to have yielded a reluctant assent to Mr. Spalding's arguments. But still the assent has not been withdrawn, and a position held with varying degrees of confidence by Coleridge, Ingram, Spalding, Dyce, and Furnival can scarcely be regarded as in dispute. But an interesting question remains as to the nature and extent of Shakespeare's part in the work. Were the subject chosen, the plot devised, and portions of the play written by Shakespeare in collaboration with Fletcher? Or did Shakespeare operate upon the work of Fletcher, as we have seen him do with the originals of *The Taming of the Shrew*, *Titus Andronicus*, and *Henry VI.*, adding bits here and there, sometimes whole scenes, sometimes stray words or phrases?

The Two Noble Kinsmen is founded upon *The Knight's Tale* of Chaucer. It is a dramatic representation of the well-known story of Palamon and Arcite, to which is added a poor underplot conversant with the love and madness of the jailer's daughter. If it be in any part Shakespeare's work, it is the only play in which he was concerned containing nothing in poetic merit equal to several passages in the original work upon which it is founded. *Troilus and Cressida* is an indifferent play, founded upon the greatest of all poems. And yet we feel that there is something in Ulysses' speeches to Achilles (Act iii. 3) beyond the powers even of Homer. *The Knight's Tale* contains some noble passages. What can be finer, in its terrible truthfulness, than the line : ' We moste endure, this is the short and plain ' ? And Arcite's dying speech unites pathos, nobility of sentiment, and beauty of expression, in no common degree. There is no passage in *The Two Noble Kinsmen* comparable to these, and notwithstanding all the praise that has been bestowed on this play, notably by De Quincey, who calls it ' perhaps the most superb work in the language,' I confess to sharing the feeling thus expressed by Dr. Ingram : ' In reading the (so-called) Shakespearian part of the play, I do not often find myself in contact with a mind of the first order ' (*Shakespeare Society's Transactions*, Part II.).

But good or bad or indifferent, is any part of the play the workmanship of Shakespeare? Let us see how *res ipsa loquitur*. The story is a simple one. The two noble kinsmen, Palamon and Arcite, are nephews of Creon, Tyrant of Thebes. They become the prisoners of the hero Theseus, who, interrupting his marriage festivities with Hippolyta, marches to Thebes in order to avenge the barbarous treatment by Creon of the bodies of three vanquished kings, whose widowed queens have moved his pity. Cast into prison, the kinsmen bewail their fate.

> *Pal.* . . . . . O, never .
> Shall we two exercise, like twins of honour
> Our arms again, and feel our fiery horses
> Like proud seas under us ! . . . . .
> . . . . . To our Theban hounds
> That shook the aged forest with their echoes
> No more now must we hallow.
>
> *Two Noble Kinsmen*, ii. 2. 17.

Emilia, sister to Hippolyta, walking in the garden, is seen from the prison window by Palamon, who forthwith falls in love with her. His example is straightway followed by Arcite, each asserting his right to win her, if he may. Arcite is set at liberty, at the suit of Pirithous, but banished the kingdom. He returns in humble disguise, and attracts the attention of Theseus at some country games by his skill in wrestling and running. Asked by Theseus of his conditions and habits, he claims

> A little of all noble qualities ;
> I could have kept a hawk, and well have holla'd
> To a deep cry of dogs. I dare not praise
> My feat in horsemanship, yet they that know me
> Would say it was my best piece ; last and greatest,
> I would be thought a soldier. *Ibid.* ii. 5. 10.

He has the good fortune to be assigned by Pirithous as servant to Emilia.

> *Pir.* I'll see you furnish'd, and because you say
> You are a horseman, I must needs entreat you
> This afternoon to ride ; but 'tis a rough one.
> *Arc.* I like him better, prince, I shall not then
> Freeze in my saddle. *Ibid.* ii. 5. 44.

Emilia takes strong note of him, and, in his words,

> presents me with
> A brace of horses ; two such steeds might well
> Be by a pair of kings back'd, in a field
> That their crown's title tried. *Ibid.* iii. 1. 19.

Meanwhile, Palamon has .broken .prison by the aid of the jailer's daughter, who loves him to distraction. The two noble kinsmen meet in a forest near Athens, and after some contention agree that their claims to Emilia must be settled in a mortal combat. Horns are winded :

Arc.   You hear the horns
                Enter your musit, lest this match between 's
                Be crossed or met.   .   .   .   .   .

       .   .   .   . .   ` Plainly spoken !
                Yet·pardon me hard language; when I spur
                My horse, I chide him not; content and anger
                In me have but one face.—iii. 1. 96.

(The word ' musit, or muset,' used in *Venus and Adonis* [*ante*, p. 181], is thus explained in Nares' *Glossary* : ' The opening in a fence or thicket, through which a hare, or other beast of sport, is accustomed to pass. *Muset*, French.')

There is some rather tedious by-play—in the course of which the jailer's daughter goes mad for love of Palamon—only necessary to be noted, inasmuch as it brings Theseus and his company into the forest, hunting :

Thes. This way the stag took.

The schoolmaster Gerrold composes a hunting song, as did Holophernes :

                May the stag thou hunt'st stand long,
                And thy dogs be swift and strong,
                May they kill him without lets,
                And the ladies eat his dowsets.—iii. 5. 154.

Thereupon ' wind horns ' and exeunt the company.

(The word ' let ' has been explained, *ante*, p. 42. The dowcets (*testes*) of the deer were esteemed a delicacy. Directions for serving them are contained in John Russel's *Boke of Nurture, circ.* 1460.)

Palamon and Arcite meet, and exchange courtesies. Arcite recalls Palamon's prowess in the field on the day when the three kings fell.

                I never saw such valour ; when you charg'd
                Upon the left wing of the enemy,
                I spurr'd hard to come up, and under me
                I had a right good horse.
Pal.   You had indeed
                A bright bay, I remember.—iii. 6. 74.

As they fight, Theseus and his hunting party come up. Disdaining to fly, they stand confessed—Palamon and Arcite—and avow their love for Emilia, who, aided by the entreaties of Hippolyta and the generous Pirithous, dissuades Theseus, by whom they had been condemned to death. Finally it is decreed that they are to go to their own country, and return to Athens in a month, attended each by three fair knights, and do battle for the hand of Emilia, who is to be the victor's prize; the vanquished to lose his head and all his friends. In the combat Arcite conquers, and Emilia, who professes herself unable to choose between two so noble suitors, abides the result. Palamon has laid his head on the block when Pirithous enters, and tells the story of Arcite's death in the speech quoted at p. 257. Arcite lives long enough to transfer to Palamon the hand and affections of the accommodating Emilia.

If throughout this play we fail to recognise the Shakespeare of Heaven (to borrow Hallam's phrase), there are many and certain traces of the Shakespeare of earth; of Shakespeare the hunter, the falconer, and, above all, the horseman. Gerrold's hunting song, 'The Theban hounds that shook the aged forest with their echo;' Arcite's 'holla to a deep cry of dogs;' his words to Palamon, 'Enter your musit;' Palamon's comparison of a fiery horse to a proud sea, swelling beneath the rider; Arcite's preference of a rough horse—'I shall not then freeze in my saddle;' his explanation why he uses no hard language—'when I spur my horse I chide him not;' Palamon's recollection of 'the right good horse' ridden by his noble kinsman—'A bright bay, I remember'—are all suggestive, inasmuch as they are thoroughly Shakespearian, and utterly unlike the workmanship of Fletcher. But as evidence of Shakespeare's handiwork their accumulated force is not greater than that of a single speech put into the mouth of Pirithous, and quoted at page 257. Critics have found in the defects as well as the merits of this passage unmistakable evidence of Shakespeare's handiwork. But they have failed to note its most distinctive characteristics, although the description of the horse reminded Mr. Spalding, in a general way, of passages in *Venus and Adonis*. He thinks the speech bad, but undeniably the work of Shakespeare. 'The whole manner of it is that of some of his long and over-laboured descriptions. It is full of illustration, infelicitous but not weak; in involvement of sentence and hardness of phrase—no passage in this play comes so close to him.' This is all true. Other writers have manifested these qualities in a greater or less degree, but this speech is different in kind from any to be found in the works of any dramatist but Shakespeare. It is the narrative of a tragic event, the catastrophe of the play, from the point of view not of the dramatist, of the poet, or of the moralist, but of the practical horseman. The horse ridden by Arcite was hot—hot as fire. He had a cloud in his face : Enobarbus, as we have seen, thought a horse the worse for that. Pirithous recalls that ' many will not buy his goodness with this note,' and, taught by the event, allows their superstition. The horse was utterly above himself. I cannot attempt to spoil by paraphrasing the description of the slow progression of a prancing bean-fed horse :

> Trotting the stones of Athens, which the calkins
> Did rather tell than trample ; for the horse
> Would make his length a mile, if 't pleased his rider
> To put pride in him ; as he thus went counting
> The flinty pavement, dancing as 'twere to th' music
> His own hoofs made.

He is not really frightened at the spark, mark you, but after the fashion of an over-fresh horse makes some trifling occurrence the occasion of his misdoing :

> Took toy at this, and fell into what disorder
> His power could give his will.

Then follows the catastrophe. His rider, knowing him to be ' trained and of kind manage,' essays the discipline of the spur. But the horse has gone too far. He forgets school-doings. Pig-like he whines at the sharp rowel, which he frets at rather than any jot obeys.

Had Arcite been ' disseated ' by the ' boisterous and rough jadery ' that followed, or had he slipped off his horse (an operation not easy with the saddle of the day) no serious harm would have ensued. But Arcite, like Lamond of Normandy, ' grew into his seat,' and his horse, plunge he never so wildly, could not

> Disroot his rider whence he grew, but that
> He kept him 'tween his legs.

Finally, the brute rears, falls back on Arcite, who expires, having delivered a dying speech.

The lines of Chaucer which suggested this passage—for subtle insight into the nature of the horse and secrets of horsemanship, not to be equalled in the whole of literature—are simply these :

> Out of the ground a fury [al-fire] infernal sterte
> From Pluto sent, at requeste of Saturne,
> For which his hors for fere gan to turne,

And lepte aside and`foundred as he lepe ;
And ere that Arcite may take any kepe,
He pight him on the pomel of his hed,
That in the place he lay as he were ded,
His brest to-brosten with his sadel bow.

Whatever we may think of the merits of *The Two Noble Kinsmen,* of the description of Arcite's fall it must be said, *aut Shakespeare, aut diabolus.*

This and the other passages which I have quoted are found for the most part in the portions of the play which critics have, on other grounds, attributed to the hand of Shakespeare. But here and there isolated passages occur, as they may be found in the Shakespearian additions to the older editions of *The Taming of the Shrew* and *Henry VI.* They suggest that *The Two Noble Kinsmen,* as we now have it, is not the result of collaboration between Fletcher and Shakespeare, but of a process similar to that which we have observed in the case of the plays referred to ; appropriation, with or without the consent of the original author, and subsequent alterations and additions.

' No intelligent reader of *Locrine, Mucedorus, The London Prodigal, The Puritan, The Life and Death of Thomas Cromwell, The History of Sir John Oldcastle, Fair Em, The Birth of Merlin,* can suppose that a single line was contributed to any one of these plays by Shakespeare. It is conceivable that touches from his hand may exist in *A Yorkshire Tragedy,* and even in *Arden of Feversham.* But the chance that this is actually the case is exceedingly small. We may therefore set down *King Edward III.* and *The Two Noble Kinsmen* as doubtful plays ; the rest for which an idle claim has been made should be named pseudo-Shakespearian.'

Thus writes Professor Dowden, in his *Introduction to Shakespeare.* This passage may well stand as a summary of the result, not only of the higher criticism, but of the matter-of-fact test suggested in these pages ; with certain unimportant modifications. In the case of *The Two Noble Kinsmen* and *A Yorkshire Tragedy* the only doubt of which this test admits is as to the extent of the part taken by Shakespeare in the composition of these plays. The admission of *Arden of Feversham* into the list of doubtful plays receives no encouragement whatever. The claims of *Edward III.* are distinctly strengthened by the discovery of such passages as the following :

Edw. What, are the stealing foxes fled and gone,
Before we could uncouple at their heels ?
War. They are, my liege, but, with a cheerful cry,
Hot hounds, and hardy, chase them at the heels.

Fly it a pitch above the soar of praise.

What think'st thou that I did bid thee praise a horse ?

Jemmy, my man, saddle my bonny black.

As when the empty eagle flies,
To satisfy his hungry griping maw.

Thou, like a skittish and untamed colt,
Dost start aside, and strike us with thy heels ?

And reins you with a mild and gentle bit.

Dare a falcon when she's in her flight,
And ever after she'll be haggard-like.

A nimble-jointed jennet
As swift as ever got thou didst bestride.

To die is all as common as to live :
The one in choice, the other holds in chase.

If I could hold dim death but at a bay.

Of the plays rigidly excluded by Professor Dowden, I have examined *Locrine, The Puritan, The Life and Death of Thomas Cromwell, The History of Sir John Oldcastle,* and *The Birth of Merlin.* I found them, one and all, barren of results, until I reached *The Birth of Merlin.* I had not read very far until I became conscious of traces, faint and far between, but still noticeable, of the master's hand in the structure and style of certain passages. Those passages I refrain from quoting. I deal only with facts. Even were I disposed to discuss matters of opinion in regard to style, I should be warned off by the knowledge that certain German critics have discovered in *Locrine* evidences of Shakespeare's handiwork, even at his best. It is, however, a fact, that Cador thus addressed certain astonished priests: ' Why do you stand at gaze ? ' (see *ante,* p. 34) ; that the words ' So ho, boy, so ' (ii. 1), plainly suggest the same idea to a certain clown as they did to Mercutio (*ante*, p. 173); that Merlin's name suggests the inevitable pun: ' I do feel a fault of one side; either it was that sparrowhawk, or a cast of Merlin's, for I find a covey of cardecus sprung out of my pocket ' (iv. 1), and again, in the same scene:

> *Merl.* Why ask, ye gentlemen? My name is Merlin.
>
> *Clown.* Yes, and a goshawk was his father, for ought we know; for I am sure his mother was a windsucker.

(The kestrel, or windhover; used as a form of reproach, Nares' *Glossary*.)

Moreover, Prince Uter Pendragon thus describes his attack on a castle:

> I have sent
> A cry of hounds as violent as hunger
> To break his stony walls; or, if they fail
> We'll send in wildfire to dislodge him thence,
> Or burn them all with flaming violence. iv. 5.

The devil being addressed as ' hell-hound ' asks:

> What hound so'er I be
> Fawning and sporting as I would with thee,
> Why should I not be strok'd and play'd withal? v. 1.

And the Prince thus describes his amazement at sight of Artesia:

> For having overtook her;
> As I have seen a forward blood-hound strip
> The swifter of the cry, ready to seize
> His wished hopes, upon the sudden view,
> Struck with astonishment at his arrived prey,
> Instead of seizure stands at fearful bay. ii. 1.

These passages are not in the manner of the ordinary Elizabethan playwright, and they suggest the possibility that this play is one of those in the revision and production of which Shakespeare may have taken some part. Even if this were so we have no cause of complaint with the editors of the Folio on the ground of its exclusion from their collection, for his share in the authorship was probably a small one.

The evidence suggested by these pages may not commend itself to all minds as of the same degree of weight. But, so far as it goes, it tends in the direction of acquitting Masters Hemming and Condell of the rank offence of palming upon the public as the work of Shakespeare productions which they knew to be spurious. If the general result is to credit the editors of the Folio with an honest endeavour to make their collection as complete as might be, the question of their truthfulness in professing to have made use of the true original copies may be approached without suspicion. This profession may be challenged, but it is entitled to the respectful hearing commonly accorded to the testimony of a witness, who, having been assailed as perjured, and subjected to searching cross-examination, has passed through the ordeal unscathed. If the editors of the Folio are truth-telling in the matter of the Canon, there is no reason to suspect them of lying with regard to the Text.

Now there is one feature which the true original copy of a play of Shakespeare's could scarcely fail to possess. It may have been ill-written, and not easily decipherable by printer or copyist. Its grammar may have been uncertain, its chronology inexact, its geography faulty, and its metaphors occasionally mixed. But in the matter of woodcraft, venery, and horsemanship, its language was beyond all doubt absolutely correct. A term of art misused in the Folio, and rightly applied in a Quarto, would supply a piece of evidence worthy of being submitted to a literary jury, and an accumulation of such instances might be the foundation of a high degree of probability.

It is impossible to cite any such instance. Furthermore, several passages have been noted in the foregoing pages where the copyist for a Quarto, through ignorance or inattention, appears to have missed the point of some characteristic allusion preserved in the Folio. And they contain a greater number of instances, scarcely less significant, where some word or phrase of the Folio, condemned by critics as hopelessly corrupt, has been rescued from the hands of the common emendator ; or where some comparatively meaningless expression is suddenly clothed with beauty and significance in the light thrown upon it by some long-forgotten sport. Take, for example, in *Coriolanus*, the serving-man's description of war as ' spritely walking, audible, and full of vent ' (p. 53). So long as these words were unintelligible, the copy in which they appeared might fairly be suspected as unauthentic. But the discovery that ' vent ' was a term of art in use among sportsmen at once converts apparent nonsense into a lively and characteristic image. Again, when it is said of Malvolio ' Sowter will cry upon't for all this, though it be as rank as a fox,' an apparently insensible speech gains significance when it is brought home to us that Sowter is not a Leicestershire fox-hound, but an Elizabethan running-hound, in pursuit of the favourite quarry of the day—the hare—foiled by the rank scent of the vermin fox (p. 50). Many words and phrases, recklessly amended, or abandoned as hopelessly corrupt, have, I venture to think, been similarly illustrated. (See pages 50, 51, 53, 54, 82, 145–147, 156, 177, 182, 202, 265, 266, 268, 270, 271, 291, 294, 298, 301, 305, 308).

For instance, we have seen how completely the gentle crafts of the falconer and the astringer, with their needful terms of art, have fallen into oblivion, together with all knowledge of the sex of the noble falcon, and of the differing nature and habits of the long-winged falcon and short-winged hawk. A revival of this learning not only illustrates, but justifies certain obscure passages and readings. The bating of the estridge or goshawk is an image which none but a practical astringer would be likely to employ, but it makes sense out of a passage in the Folio which, as applied by critics to the ostrich, is unmeaning as it stands, and absurd as commonly amended (p. 156) ; and the recognition of this long forgotten astringer, who bore to the estridge the same relation as the falconer to the falcon, rescues from excision or emendation the stage direction, ' Enter a gentle astringer,' clothing it with a special significance in its application to the Court of France (p. 145).

In the instances in which it has been possible to compare the readings of the Folio and of a Quarto, where a term of art of woodcraft, falconry, or horsemanship was concerned, I have generally found the text of the Folio to be more in accordance with the language of ancient writers upon the mysteries of sport than either the readings of the Quarto or the conjectural alterations of critics. From the nature of the case these instances could not be expected to be numerous. The evidence, however, which they afford gains significance from the circumstance that no single instance to the contrary has presented itself in the course of my research.

It was by the accumulation of instances in support of the authenticity of the Folio which was presented by passages collected with a very different purpose, that I was led to examine the evidence forthcoming on the one side and on the other. I found the investigation to present a repetition of a very old story, with which Judges are better acquainted than are literary critics, although it is deserving of equal attention on the part of both. It is the conflict between, on the one hand, evidence of matters of fact, which I will call Testimony, and Opinion on the other hand, known in Courts of Justice as Expert Evidence. I have already collected some of the positive testimony in support of the assertions of the editors of the Folio. Their case depends upon matters of fact ; such as the action or non-action of the editors and of their contemporaries, viewed in the light of surrounding circumstances, and of the several degrees of knowledge which the various witnesses possessed. It is encountered mainly by criticism, that is to say, by Opinion, or expert evidence.

Now it would be unwise to particularise at one's leisure, in its application to expert witnesses, the general condemnation passed by King David in his haste upon mankind generally ; and all temptation in that direction must be steadily resisted. Expert evidence is generally worthless, not because the witness forswears himself, but because the particular matter which he proves—his individual opinion—is commonly of little value. It is valueless, because it affords an unsafe foundation for action ; and its insecurity arises from the fact that an equally positive opinion on the other side is generally obtainable in regard to any really doubtful matter ; that is to say, precisely where trustworthy guidance is needed.

It seems to me that the worthlessness of Opinion as compared with Testimony is being slowly but surely discovered by critics. This tendency is sometimes described as a growing preference for the historical method. The most casual student of the Homeric question cannot but have observed the rehabilitation of the Testimony of tradition and reputation, and the rejection of the Opinion of clever experts, whose powers of estimating the value of evidence may be gauged by the fact that they deem it more in accordance with probability that Greece should have produced, at about the same period, some twenty ballad-mongers in genius surpassing the rest of mankind, than that there should have been one Homer. The same tendency is discernible in the contest that rages around the question of the authenticity of the books of the New Testament. Dr. Salmon, in his *Historical Introduction to the New Testament*, notes the successive abandonment by destructive criticism of positions which were once held to be impregnable, but which, being based upon expert evidence, proved untenable when assailed by the force of Testimony and by evidence of positive fact.

Suppose, then, a verdict to be found in support of the testimony of Masters Hemming and Condell, what ought to be the result, beyond the vindication of their character for honesty and truthfulness ? Not certainly blind and obstinate adherence to the readings of the Folio, and summary or indiscriminate rejection of the Quartos.

It must never be forgotten that not one of the copies in the possession of Hemming and Condell, true original though it may have been, had been either written or revised by its author with a view to publication. These copies were provided and kept for the use of the theatre. They were, in all probability, revised and altered from time to time, from considerations, not of literary perfection, but of theatrical expediency. So long as Shakespeare was connected with the theatre, changes in his plays were probably made by him. But in the interval between his retirement about the year 1600 and the publication of the Folio in 1623, we have no security that the true originals were unprofaned by other hands. These considerations explain many things that would otherwise be unintelligible. Certain of the Quartos contain passages, undoubtedly Shakespeare's, which are not to be found in the Folio. Where this is the case, we may reasonably conclude that the stolen manuscript was surreptitiously copied before the revision of the true original. Some, at all events, of these passages, even though excised by Shakespeare himself for acting purposes, would probably have been restored, had he as the 'executor of his own writings' revised them for the press. For all such passages the Quartos are our only authority.

Furthermore, the Quartos, though denounced by Hemming and Condell as stolen, surreptitious, maimed and deformed, are not denied to be copies. The Quarto of one play only (*King Henry V.*) appears to have been made up from notes taken during the performance at the theatre. The practice of begging, borrowing, or stealing acting copies of popular dramas appears to have been a common one. In an old pamphlet by Nash, called *Lenten Stuff with the Prayse of the Red Herring* (1599) the author assures us that in a play of his called *The Isle of Dogs*, 'foure acts without his consent or the leaste guesse of his drift or scope were supplied by the players.' Mr. Farmer, in a note to his *Essay on the Learning of Shakspeare*, writes: 'When a poet was connected with a particular playhouse, he constantly sold his writings to the company, and it was their interest to keep them from a number of rivals. A favourite piece, as Heywood informs us, only got into print when it was copied by the ear, "for a double sale would bring on a suspicion of honestie."'

It must be remembered, in favour of the Quartos, that the setters-forth of these editions, however dishonestly the copies may have been come by, would be led by self-interested motives to make their edition as perfect as might be ; and that the editors of the Folio might, in perfect good faith, exaggerate the maiming and deforming of copies, which they knew to be stolen and surreptitious, and which they probably did not go to the trouble of collating with the true originals.

But there were insuperable difficulties in the way of the printers of the Quartos, strove they never so earnestly after truthfulness. The experience of every lawyer tells him how little reliance can be placed on an uncompared copy of a draft, be it the original ever so legibly written. Add the elements of haste and concealment, consequent on the patching together of acting parts obtained from different players, and the defects of the Quartos are fully accounted for.

I am not without hope that some Shakespearian scholar, fully equipped for the task, may yet, by judicious use of Folio, of Quarto, and of the labours of countless emendators, give to the world what will be at once the ideal and the real Shakespeare : the nearest possible approach to the true original.

The order of its development may be thus tentatively suggested. Take Mr. Lionel Booth's accurate reprint of the Folio. Trust no text, received or otherwise, notwithstanding professions of adherence to the Folio. The trail of the Quarto is over them all. Why even in Mr. Grant White's *Hamlet*, Lamond, the perfect horseman, grows *unto*, not *into*, his seat (see *ante*, p. 294). Modernise the spelling, and correct obvious misprints. Supply, where needful, *dramatis personæ*, division into acts and scenes, adopting (for convenience) those in the *Globe* edition, but restoring certain characteristic stage directions. Add from the Quartos the passages omitted from the Folio. But include the additions in brackets, thus restoring what was, in all probability, Shakespeare's handiwork, and, at the same time, informing the reader of the subsequent excision of the passage.

When so much of the task has been performed, the result will be a text containing many words wholly unintelligible, and many passages obviously corrupt. The critic must therefore gird himself for the needful task of emendation. And here all that he requires is the possession of two things : a judgment, critical in the etymological sense of the term, that is to say, capable of discerning; and a copy of *The Cambridge Shakespeare*, in the notes to which he will find an exhaustive collection of various readings and conjectural emendations.

In the use of these materials he will lay down for his guidance certain general principles. He will not condemn a passage because it violates rules of grammar, as they are now observed ;

for Shakespeare's grammar is not our grammar, as the student of
Mr. Abbott's work, so entitled, may learn. Nor will he amend it
because the exuberance of Shakespeare's fancy leads him into a
confusion of metaphors, which in the case of one of my fellow-
countrymen would be called a bull; as where Hamlet speaks of
taking up arms against a sea of troubles. If the words are
intelligible he will let them stand. The fact that they were printed
in the Folio affords a better assurance that they are the very words
written by Shakespeare than any amount of ingenuity on the
part of the emendator. If they make nonsense, and if a Quarto
edition exists, he will turn to it; for the copier, though never
so dishonest or surreptitious, may have avoided an error into
which the printer of the Folio has fallen. For example, the King
of Denmark says of the French that they ' ran well on horseback.'
For this unmeaning ' ran ' Theobald read ' can,' and an ingenious
conjecture is converted into certainty when we find ' can ' in the
Quarto. Again, in the passage quoted (p. 302) descriptive of the
reckless riding of a runaway, the Folio reads thus :

> With that, he gave his able horse the head,
> And, bending forward, struck his able heels
> Against the panting sides of his poor jade.
>
> 2 *Hen. IV.* i. 1. 43.

The repetition of the word ' able ' is an obvious error of a kind
not uncommon in writing or copying, into which most of us have
occasionally fallen. But what is the right word ? The answer is
at once supplied by the Quarto, and ' armed' is with absolute
certainty introduced into the text.

But in the greater number of cases the Quarto—if there be
one—gives no assistance, and the editor is left to the guidance of
his critical verifying faculty. He must distinguish as best he can
between the reasonably certain and the merely probable emendation. The former he will unhesitatingly introduce into the text.
The latter, be it never so attractive, must be ruthlessly relegated to
a footnote—the corrupt portion of the text being either obelised
or printed in italics. In deciding between the certain and the
probable, the trained critical faculty of the expert will have regard
to the general consent of editors ; *quod semper, quod ubique, quod
ab omnibus.*

From wanton emendations—by which I mean those introduced
for the purpose of improving sense, not of correcting nonsense—
he will rigidly abstain, be their authors ever so eminent. Of

this class are Pope's correction of 'south' for 'sound' in the lines :

> It came o'er my ear like the sweet sound
> That breathes upon a bank of violets,
> Stealing and giving odour ;

and Scott's suggested substitution of 'cud' for 'food' in the passage :

> Chewing the food of sweet and bitter fancy.

Emendations, however, of this class need cause him no care, for they have been by the Cambridge editors one and all excluded from the text, and relegated to foot-notes.

He will have more trouble with conjectural readings of another kind, where the Folio is corrupt and the emendation more or less plausible.   How, for example, ought he to deal with the following case ?   It may be a shock to the non-critical lover of Shakespeare to learn that the oft-quoted phrase in Mistress Pistol's account of the death of Falstaff, 'a' babbled of green fields,' was never fathered on Shakespeare until the last century, when Theobald, by a famous emendation, made sense of the Folio's nonsense : ' his Nose was as sharpe as a Pen, and a Table of greene fields.' The conjecture was brilliant, and the words are so poetical that they have passed into literature, and are repeated as an isolated expression, to be treasured for its own sake, apart from any consideration of dramatic propriety.   The literary quality of this phrase, so far from recommending it, seems to tell against its acceptance as a certain emendation ; for the words which we are accustomed to hear from the lips of Mistress Pistol, formerly Quickly, are of a more homely, if not of a coarser kind.   The conjecture 'and a' talked of green fields ' (possibly written 'and a' talke ') involves less change, and has the advantage (regarded as an emendation) of being more in the speaker's ordinary style. This is a case in which the Quarto may be fairly appealed to.

The Quarto of *King Henry V.* was (as has been observed) printed from notes taken during the performance.   This is how Mrs. Quickly's speech was taken down :

> His nose was as sharpe as a pen :
> For when I saw him fumble with the sheetes,
> And talk of floures, and smile vpo his fingers ends
> I knew there was no way but one.

The word 'talk' somehow caught the copyist's ear, and he mixed it up with the Folio's 'play with flowers.'   It is hard to suppose that such a striking expression as Theobald's—the most noteworthy in the whole passage—would have altogether eluded his grasp. Now in this, and in similar cases, the editor, I venture to suggest, best discharges his duties by obelising or italicising the corrupt word or passage, and giving the reader in a foot-note his choice of conjectural emendations. The passages so marked would be but few. The text would not be marred, while the reader would be fairly dealt with. If I quote Tibbald admiringly, I prefer to do so wittingly, having been afforded reasonable means of discerning between him and Shakespeare.

In this part of the labour there is little in the work of the Cambridge editors of which even the most conservative of critics can complain. Had only their labours been expended upon the true originals, the result would not have fallen far short of the Ideal Shakespeare. There is, unhappily, much virtue in that ' if.' In the play of *Hamlet* alone, the *Globe* edition, founded on the labours of the Cambridge editors, departs from the Folio in favour of the Quarto in some eighty passages, exclusive of corrections of spelling and punctuation. The variance in many instances is unimportant. But to my mind the exact words in which Shakespeare embodied his greatest thoughts are of even stronger interest than the precise manner in which his grandfather spelled his name, or, indeed, than any of the miscellaneous information collected—in default of better—by the pious labours of many generations.

Each of the great English Universities has given its name to an edition of Shakespeare. The Cambridge Shakespeare is familiar to the readers of these pages. The Oxford Shakespeare was edited by Mr. Craig, a graduate of the University of Dublin. Excellent editions both, but one thing they lack—they are neither of them based upon the Folio. It remains for the University of Malone and Monck Mason in the last century, and of Ingram and Dowden in the present, by restoring to the world the True Originals purged of their original imperfections, to realise in the Dublin edition the Ideal Shakespeare.

NOTE II
THE BOOK OF SPORT

The upstart gentleman of the Tudor age, with his innate vulgarity and his affectation of field sports, afforded a constant topic to the dramatist and satirist. Then, for the first time, admission to the ranks of Esquire and Gentleman became easy, or, as Harrison

calls it in his description of England (1577), 'good cheape.' He
tells us how the number of 'gentlemen whose ancestors are not
knowen to come in with William Duke of Normandie' was constantly swelled by accessions, not only from the professions, but
from the growing class of *novi homines*. Their ambition to 'be
called master, which is the title that men giue to Esquiers and
gentlemen, and reputed for a gentleman,' was no less keen than
the competition of their representatives of to-day for knighthoods
and baronetcies. To these men the Book of Sport was an absolute necessity. The *novus homo* (called by the plain-spoken
Master Stubbes in his *Anatomie of Abuses*, 'a dunghill gentleman,
or gentleman of the first head'), although he might (in Harrison's
words) 'for monie haue a cote and armes bestowed vpon him by
heralds,' could never pass muster until he had acquired the shib-
boleth of the class. There is always some recognised outward
and visible sign. At one time it is prowess in arms ; at another
in gallantry ; then it happened to be correct use of the language
of sport. This form of speech, largely founded on Norman
French, was traditional among those of gentle birth. But the
'gentleman of the first head,' who was not to the manner born, and
who had not, like Shakespeare, served an apprenticeship to sport,
and thus gained admission to the mystery, must needs acquire it
by study, like a foreign language. To him the Book of Sport
served as grammar, dictionary, and exercise-book in one. The
task was no trifling one. There was a separate word for every
conceivable act, done by, or to, each beast of venery or of the chase,
and for every incident of sport ; with an endless array of appropriate verbs, nouns, and adjectives, the misapplication of any one of
which stamped the offender as no gentleman. You might speak
of 'flaying' a deer without losing caste, although the correct phrase
was 'take off that deer's skin ; ' but if the Second Lord in *All's Well*
had used this word instead of saying 'We'll make you some sport
with the fox ere we *case* him,' he would have quickly discovered
that it is not for virtues only that men are whipped out of court.

Many of these terms have survived to the present day, and
lingering traces may yet be discerned of the old-world ideas associated with them. We still speak of a herd of deer, a bevy of ladies,
a congregation of people, a host of men, a flight of pigeons, a brace
and leash of greyhounds, a couple of hounds, a litter of whelps,
a covey of partridges, a swarm of bees, a cast of hawks, a flight of
swallows, a stud of mares, a drove of cattle, and a flock of sheep.
Few of us are conscious that in so speaking we are correctly using

the gentle terms appropriated by the *Boke of St. Albans* to the various ' compaynys of beestys and fowlys.' And even now—so inveterate are ideas wrought into our blood—while the misuse of scientific terms suggests nothing more than ignorance, we can hardly avoid associating the idea of vulgarity with a man who would speak of a flight of partridges, a flock of grouse, or a pair of hounds.

Such survivals, however, are but faint echoes of the ideas of our forefathers ; and if (as I believe) the Warwickshire gentry of the day agreed with Jonson and Spenser in applying to their neighbour the term ' gentle,' I am certain that their verdict was won rather by his accurate use of the hunting and hawking language than by a regard to any mental or moral qualities. For Shakespeare's sporting vocabulary is as accurate and copious as that of any author of a Book of Sport.

Shakespeare never troubled himself about this language, or how it might be learned, any more than about the vulgar tongue in which he was brought up. But Ben Jonson's mind was exercised on the subject. In a *Speech according to Horace*, he thus formulates the creed of the old nobility :—

> Why are we rich or great, except to show
> All licence in our lives ? What need we know
> More than to praise a dog or horse ? Or speak
> The hawking language ?

The speech that came naturally to the Beauchamps and Nevills, Cliffords, Audleys bold, was painfully acquired by the

> Hodges and those newer men
> As Stiles, Dike, Ditchfield, Millar, Crips, and Fen,

whose accession to the rank of gentry he attributes curiously enough to the use of guns in lieu of the older and more gentleman-like methods of warfare ; reminding us of the ' certain lord, neat and trimly dressed,' who so excited the wrath of Harry Hotspur, and who told him that ' but for these vile guns he would himself have been a soldier.' (1 *Hen. IV.* ii. 3. 63.)

' If he can hunt and hawk ; ' thus Burton begins his enumeration of the qualities of the would-be gentleman of the day. ' Nothing now so frequent,' he tells us, as hawking ; ' a great art, and many bookes written of it ' (*Anatomy of Melancholy*) ; and Bishop Earle says of his Upstart Knight, ' a hawke hee esteemes the true burden of Nobilitie.' (*Micro-cosmographie.*)

How to acquire this great art, and to learn this gentle language, Ben Jonson tells us by the lips of Master Stephen :—

Stephen. Uncle, afore I go in, can you tell me an we have e'er a book of the sciences of hawking and hunting, I would fain borrow it.

Knowell. Why, I hope you will not a hawking now, will you ?

Step. No, wusse ; but I'll practise against next year, uncle. I have bought me a hawk and a hood and bells, and all ; I lack nothing but a book to keep it by.

Know. O most ridiculous !

Step. Nay, look you, now you are angry, uncle : why you know an a man have not skill in the hawking and hunting languages nowadays, I'll not give a rush for him ; they are more studied than the Greek or the Latin. He is for no gallants company without them.

(Every Man in his Humour, i. 1.)

The earliest attempt to supply this want, and teach the hawking and hunting languages to those to whom they do not come by nature, is to be found in the *Boke of St. Albans.* The schoolmaster printer, in his prologue to the *Booke of Hawkyng,* included in the same volume with the curious old metrical treatise on hunting attributed to Dame Juliana Barnes, or Berners, addresses himself not only to ' gentill men,' but to ' honest persones,' and attributes to them a desire to ' know the gentill termys in communing of theyr hawkys ; ' a condescension to the vulgar, to which I believe Dame Juliana, had she been then living, would have been no party. The greater your accuracy in the use of this language, ' the moore Worshyp may ye have among all menne.' Between the publication of the *Boke of St. Albans* in 1486, and Shakespeare's death in 1616, it was reprinted in whole or in part, more or less altered, no fewer than twenty-two times. Meanwhile that most industrious bookmaker, Gervase Markham, had published in 1611 his *Country Contentments,* which ran through fourteen editions before the close of the century. The oldest English treatise on Falconry bears the significant title of *The Institution of a Gentleman* (1555, 2nd Ed. 1568). ' There is a saying among hunters,' says the author, ' that he cannot be a gentleman whyche loveth not hawkyng and hunting.' The same idea suggested the title, *A Iewell for Gentrie* (1614).

When Shakespeare was a boy, George Turbervile, a gentleman by birth, and a poet, wrote, or rather edited, *The Booke of Faulconrie* (1575, 2nd Ed. 1611), which became the standard work on the subject, although Symon Latham's *Falconry, or The Falcon's Lure and Cure* (1615), and Edmund Bert's *Approved treatise of Hawkes and Hawking* (published in 1619, but written many years earlier) deservedly enjoyed a high reputation. *The Noble Arte of Venerie or Hunting* was published and bound with Turbervile's *Booke of Faulconrie.* The author's name is not given, and the verses which it contains on various subjects connected with the chase were contributed by George Gascoigne, best known as the author of a satirical poem called *The Steel Glas* (1576). A great part of this work is a translation from the French of du Foulloux ; but there are many extracts from other authors, and some original matter.

Notwithstanding the fact that *The Noble Arte of Venerie* is attributed to Turbervile by Gervase Markham and by Nicholas Cox, I am disposed from the style of the work, from the publisher's preface, and from the calling in aid of Gascoigne's literary skill when it is deemed necessary to drop into poetry, to judge it to be the work of some hack scribe, inferior in literary skill as well as in social position to Turbervile, whose spirited verses on Falconry prefixed to *The Booke of Faulconrie* are, in my opinion, superior to the task-work of George Gascoigne.

The first book on fishing published in England was Dame Juliana Berners' *Treatyse of fysshinge wyth an angle*, printed by Wynkyn de Worde in 1496. It was followed by Leonard Mascall's *Booke of Fishing with Hooke and Line* (1590) ; Taverner's *Certaine experiments concerning Fish and Fruite*, 1600 ; and *The Secrets of Angling*, by J. D. [John Dennys].

Meanwhile the horse had come in for a full share of attention. I extract from Mr. Huth's *Index to works on Horses and Equitation*, the dates of works published during the lifetime of Shakespeare. *The fowre chiefyst offices belongyng to Horsemanshippe*, by Thomas Blundevill (1565, 1580, 1597, 1609) ; *A plaine and easie way to remedie a Horse that is foundered in his feete*, by Nicholas Malbie (1576, 1583, 1594) ; *Remedies for Dyseases in Horses*, by the same author (1576, 1583, 1594) ; *The Art of Riding*, by John Astley (1584) ; *The Schoole of Horsemanship*, by Christopher Clifford (1585) ; *De procreandis, eligendis, frænandis et tractandis Equis* (a curious work), by Richard Sadler (1587) ; *A Discourse of Horsemanshippe*, by Gervase Markham (1593) ; *How to chuse, ride, traine and dyet both hunting and running horses*, by Gervase Markham (1596, 1599, 1606) ; *Cavalerice, or the English Horseman*, by Gervase Markham (1607, 1616) ; and by the same author, *A Cure for all diseases in Horses* (1610, 1616), *Country Contentments* (including a Treatise on horses) (1611), and Markham's *Maistre-Peece*, a treatise on farriery, published in 1615, which went through many editions, the tenth being dated 1688 ; *The Perfection of Horsemanship*, by Nicholas Morgan (1609) ; *A very perfect discourse (on the horse)*, by L. W. C. (1610).

No wonder that Burton exclaims at the 'world of bookes,' not alone on arts and sciences, but on 'riding of horses, fencing, swimming, gardening, planting, great tomes of husbandry, cookery, faulconry, hunting, fishing, fowling, and with exquisite pictures of all sports, games, and what not?'

The truth is that these old books of sport as a rule deserved the estimation in which they were held, in so far as (unlike the philosophical works of the day) they were founded, not on theory and authority, but upon fact, and upon an honest and thorough, if unscientific interrogation of nature. Francis Bacon could have taught observers of the hare, of the falcon, and of the hound, little beyond the names of the processes which they were unconsciously applying. And so this part of their work is as fresh and useful now as on the day when it was written ; birds and beasts having changed their nature even less than mankind since the days of Elizabeth.

Then came Puritanism, Civil War, and the Commonwealth, and if the Book of Sport was mentioned, the name suggested sabbatarianism rather than field sport. After the Restoration, the would-be gentleman was no longer a sham sportsman, but a real blackguard, and he needed no book to teach him how to live up to his profession. Nor did field sports during any part of the eighteenth century attract the attention of any section of the book-buying public. Peter Beckford published his celebrated *Thoughts on Hunting* in 1781, in which he expresses his surprise at the lack of books on his favourite sport, at a time when the press teemed with works of all sorts and kinds. But the Will Wimbles and Squire Westerns of the eighteenth century would have scorned the aid of books, and as to men of letters and their readers, their ignorance of the hunting and hawking language may be gauged by the fact that the author of *Spectator* No. 116 makes Sir Roger de Coverley hunt the hare with 'stop-hounds' in the month of July.

And so from the death of Shakespeare until the beginning of the present century but few books were printed on sporting subjects, and those few were, for the most part, reproductions of older books, either altogether or in substance ; as were the compilations of Nicholas Cox (1674) and Richard Blome (1686). Izaak Walton's immortal *Compleat Angler*, and Somerville's *Chase*, belong rather to literature than to sport, and Beckford's *Thoughts on Hunting* is probably the only Book of Sport, of the first rank, published during this period, extending over nearly two centuries.

Had Peter Beckford lived now, he would have no reason to complain of either the quantity or the quality of the sporting literature of the day. But I have already travelled wide enough from William Silence and his diary, and I must not be led so far afield as to discuss the sporting literature of the nineteenth century, even if it were possible in the compass of a note to do justice to the painstaking labour, scientific observation of nature, enthusiasm, and literary skill by which it is distinguished.

NOTE III
SHAKESPEARE ON ANGLING

The fishing near Stratford is thus described in the truthful pages of the *Angler's Diary*: 'On Avon, pike, bream, roach, perch, chub, dace, carp.' Some distance off, 'running through Charlecote Park, Dene joins on left bank.' This, however, was the 'peculiar river' of Sir Thomas Lucy, and if the youth of Stratford would take trout from its waters, they must needs resort to less noble methods than honest angling. These irregular methods of taking trout—in which Shakespeare shows some interest—must exercise a strange fascination over minds of the higher order of creative genius. For John Bunyan, apologising for giving to the world a production which his graver advisers condemned to the flames, betrays his familiarity with them when he writes :

> Yet Fish there be, that neither Hook nor Line
> Nor Snare nor Net, nor Engine can make thine ;
> They must be grop't for, and be tickled too,
> Or they will not be catch't what e're you do.

The Rev. Henry N. Ellacombe, author of *The Plant-lore and Garden-craft of Shakespeare*, collected allusions to angling, rivers and fish in articles entitled *Shakespeare as an Angler*. (*Antiquary*, vol. iv., 1881. See also the *Gentleman's Magazine*, Jan. 1895.) The references to angling collected in these interesting papers seem to me to be of an ordinary kind (see *ante*, p. 170), and to present none of the features of the distinctively Shakespearian allusion ; as when Claudio says: 'Bait the hook well; this fish will bite,' and Hamlet (with many others) uses the words 'angle' and 'bait' in a metaphorical sense. I have no doubt that Shakespeare understood angling, according to the use of anglers of his day, as he understood everything else appertaining to country life by which he was surrounded. But if he had been a true lover of the sport, his frequent references to rivers and fish would surely have betrayed him. It has been noticed that Izaak Walton, whose *Compleat Angler* (1653) is full of quotations from English poets, never mentions Shakespeare. It may be that he opened the Folio of 1623, and his eye lighting on the sentiment quoted from *Twelfth Night* (at p. 71), he could read no further.

NOTE IV
THE BEAR-GARDEN

Foreigners have remarked on the fondness of the English people for bear-baiting and kindred pursuits, and attributed it to the inborn ferocity of the race. Erasmus noted the 'many herds of bears maintained in this country for the purpose of baiting' (*Adagia*). Hentzner (1598) writes of the bear-garden at Bankside as 'another place, built in the form of a Theatre, which serves for the baiting of Bulls and Bears. They are fastened behind, and then worried by great English bull-dogs, but not without great risk to the dogs from the horns of the one and the teeth of the other, and it sometimes happens they are killed upon the spot; fresh ones are immediately supplied in the places of those that are wounded or tired.' He adds a description of the favourite sport of whipping a blinded bear, which the reader may well be spared. Sunday was the favourite day for such sports.

> And yet every Sunday
>   They surely will spend
> One penny or two
>   The bearward's living to mend.—CROWLEY.

Nor was the taste for these amusements confined to the base and unlettered rabble. Sir John Davies in his *Epigrams* tells us how

> Publius student at the Common Law
> Oft leaves his books, and for his recreation
> To Paris Garden doth himself withdraw,
> Where he is ravished with such delectation
> As down among the bears and dogs he goes.

Thirteen bears were provided for a great baiting before the Queen in 1575, of which Laneham says, 'it was a sport very pleasant to see the bear, with his pink eyes, tearing after his enemies' approach; the nimbleness and wait of the dog to take his advantage, and the force and experience of the bear again to avoid his assaults; if he were bitten in one place how he would pinch in another to get free; that if he were taken once, then by what shift with biting, with clawing, with roaring, with tossing and tumbling he would work and wind himself from them; and when he was loose to shake his ears twice or thrice with the blood and the slaver hanging about his physiognomy.'

Bear-baiting and kindred sports survived—as Sir Hudibras found—the assaults of Puritanism, and so lately as 1709 Steele wrote in the *Tatler* (No. 134): 'Some French writers have represented this diversion of the common people much to our disadvantage, and imputed it to a natural fierceness and cruelty of temper, as they do some other entertainments peculiar to our nation. I mean those elegant diversions of bull-baiting and prize-fighting, with the like ingenious recreation of the bear-garden. I wish I knew how to answer this reproach which is cast upon us, and excuse the death of so many innocent cocks, bulls, dogs, as have been set together by the ears or died an untimely death, only to make us sport.'

NOTE V
SIR THOMAS MORE ON FIELD SPORTS

The Utopians condemned both hunting and hawking, relegating the former to butchers, as the lowest, vilest, and most abject part of a craft to which they were used to appoint their bondsmen. But the Thomas More of every-day life was no Utopian. He was a strange compound of consistency and inconsistency. Rather than desert his principles at the bidding of a bloody and ungrateful tyrant, he cheerfully laid down on the block the wisest and wittiest head in Christendom. But neither the principles for which he died, nor the practice in which he lived, had aught in common with the universal religious toleration of the Utopians, of whom, indeed, the most and the wisest part are represented as pure Theists, worshipping as God and Father of all a certain unknown power, diffused throughout the whole world, everlasting, incomprehensible, inexplicable, and above the reach of the wit of man. 'At multo maxima pars, eademque longe prudentior nihil horum, sed unum quoddam numen putant, incognitum, æternum, immensum, inexplicabile, quod supra mentis humanæ captum sit, per mundum hunc universum, virtute, non mole diffusum ; hunc parentem vocant.' I know no sadder picture of human nature, even in men 'quibus arte benigna E meliore luto finxit præcordia Titan,' than is presented by More the Chancellor, in contrast with More the author of *Utopia* ; and in the face of his graver inconsistencies, I find it easy to imagine the author of *Utopia* bestriding his lusty steed, and cheering on his hounds : not the less easy because I learn from his life by his great-grandson that there was a tradition in the family connecting it somehow with the Irish race of More. It may be fanciful to call in aid of this tradition of Celtic origin certain qualities of More, such as his light-heartedness in face of the gravest events ; but I do not feel bound altogether to discredit it. There are some traditions the existence of which can best be accounted for by the hypothesis of their truth, and among these may fairly be included the Irish descent of an English Lord Chancellor.

Erasmus, whose remarks on the breaking-up of the hart are quoted at page 63, was, during his stay in England, the friend and companion of More, to whom he dedicated *Moriæ Encomium*, the title of which embodies a play upon the name More. He thus writes to his friend Faustus Anderlin at Paris, giving a description of some of his English experiences (I quote from Mr. Froude's *Life and Letters of Erasmus*) : ' Your friend Erasmus gets on well in England. He can make a show in the hunting field. He is a fair horseman, and understands how to make his way ' (Ep. lxv).

NOTE VI
ROGUES AND VAGABONDS

Those who desire information as to this curious phrase of six-teenth-century life will find a full account of the vagrant fraternities and their different orders in the books by Awdeley and Harman quoted above, the reprinting of which, with excellent notes, is one of the many services rendered to students of the Shakespearian age by the New Shakspere Society. The subject of vagabondage is also dealt with by Harrison in the chapter of his *Description of England*, entitled *Of Provision made for the Poore* (1577), (also re-printed by the New Shakspere Society), but most of his informa-tion is derived from Harman. An account of the ' strict statutes and most biting laws,' directed against this social evil, is given by Mr. Froude (*History of England*, ch. i.) in order to dissipate what he calls a foolish dream—the sentimental opinion that the increase of poverty, and the consequent enactment of the Poor Laws, was the result of the suppression of the religious houses. Sturdy vagrancy certainly co-existed with these establishments, not only in England but on the continent. In the *Liber Vagatorum*, written about 1509, and reprinted with a preface by Martin Luther in 1528, more than twenty different ways are pointed out whereby men are cheated and fooled by vagabonds of various kinds. The records of the trials at Basle in 1475, and the description of beggars in *The Ship of Fools* (1500), tell the same tale. The number of vagrants certainly increased greatly between the reign of Henry VIII. and the establishment of the poor law. This fact is variously accounted for. The ' huge nomber of Beggers and Vacaboundes ' in England is attributed in Robert Hitchcok's *Pollitique Platt* (1580) to ' the pouerty that is and doth remane in the shire tounes and market tounes.' Harrison (book 2, chap. 11) appears to think that the laws against vagrants and rogues might be better executed, although ' there is not one yeare commonlie wherein three hundred or foure hundred of them are not devoured and eaten up by the gallowes in one place and other.' I do not find this increase of vagrancy anywhere attributed by contemporary opinion to the suppression of the religious houses. Mr. Ribton Turner's *History of Vagrants and Vagrancy*, and the valuable and interesting work edited by Mr. H. D. Traill, entitled *Social England* (vol. iii.), contain much information in regard to this matter.

NOTE VII
SHAKESPEARE AND GLOUCESTERSHIRE

A considerable body of evidence has been collected bearing upon the question of Shakespeare's connection with Gloucestershire. In a note to Mr. Huntley's *Glossary of the Cotswold Dialect* may be found the statement (which I submitted to a practical test), that Woodmancote is still known to the common people as Womcot or Woncot, and Stinchcombe Hill as ' the Hill.' From this note, and from Mr. Blunt (*Dursley and its Neighbourhood*) we learn that a family named Shakespeare formerly lived in the neighbourhood, and that parish registers have been searched with success. James Shakespeare was buried at Bisley on March 13, 1570. Edward, son of John and Margery Shakespeare, was baptized at Beverston on September 19, 1619. The parish register of Dursley records that Thomas Shakespeare, weaver, was married to Joan Turner on March 3, 1677–8, and contains entries of the baptism of their children. It appears from the Churchwardens' Register that there was in Dursley in 1704 a mason, named John Shakespeare, a Thomas Shakespeare in 1747, and that Betty Shakespeare received poor's money from 1747 to 1754. Some of this family, Mr. Huntley tells us, ' still (1848) exist as small freeholders in the adjoining parish of Newington Bagpath, and claim kindred with the poet.' A physician, he adds, named Dr. Burnett, who died at an advanced age, had a vivid remembrance of the tradition that Shakespeare once dwelt in Dursley, and of a spot in a neighbouring wood called ' Shakespeare's walk.' He thus concludes : ' The portion of Shakespeare's life which has always been involved in obscurity is the interval between his removal from Warwickshire and his arrival in London, and this period, we think, was probably spent in a retreat among his kindred at Dursley in Gloucestershire.'

Mr. P. W. Phillimore, in an article entitled ' Shakespeare and Gloucestershire ' (*The Antiquary*, vol. iv.), mentions, as the result of similar researches, that a branch of the Hathaway family was also settled in Gloucestershire. He suggests that Shakespeare's ' marriage in 1582 with Anne Hathaway, who was so much his senior, may have offended his Stratford friends, and compelled him to take refuge with his, and his wife's kindred in Gloucestershire, some time between that date and his removal to London.'

Shakespeare has given evidence of his familiarity not only with the games, but with the husbandry of Cotswold. We read in Marshall's *Rural Economy of Cotswold* (1796), that the wheat grown in Cotswold ' is principally red lammas.' In some districts it was usual ' to begin sowing the first wet weather in August.' It is there noted that ' the Cotswold Hills are in a manner proverbial for the early sowing of wheat. August and September are the principal months.' ' Shall we sow the headland with wheat ? ' asks Davy of Justice Shallow, who replies, ' With red wheat, Davy.' (2 *Hen. IV.* v. i. 15.) This was said at a season of the year when the interval between supper and bedtime might best be spent in the orchard, which could scarcely be later than the month of August.

The connection of the families of Vizard, or Vizor, with Woncot, and of Perkes, or Purchas, with the Hill, is noted in the text. (*ante*, p. 86.) ' Clement Perkes, filius Johannis de Fladbury,' whose birth in 1568 is recorded in the register of the parish of Fladbury (*Dursley and its Neighbourhood*), was a native of the same county, and may have had a kinsman and namesake on the Hill. ' On Stinchcombe Hill there is the site of a house wherein a family named "Purchase" or "Perkis" once lived, and it is reasonable to conclude that Perkis of Stinchcombe Hill is identical with " Clement Perkes of the Hill." ' (*Dursley and its Neighbourhood.*) The connection of the Perkses with the Hill, as of the Visors with Woncot, continued up to the present century. A contributor to *Notes and Queries* (Fifth Series, vol. xii. p. 159) mentions that the following notice appeared in the obituary of the *Gentleman's Magazine* (vol. ii. 1812) : ' At Margate in his 75th year, J. Purchas, Esq. of Stinchcombe Hill, near Dursley, Gloucestershire.'

A curious note appeared in the same periodical (*Notes and*

Queries, Fourth Series, vol. iv. p. 359), the writer of which professes to have found mention of ' Squeal of Cotsall ' among some manuscript entries in a folio copy of Sir Walter Raleigh's *History of the World* (1614) ' containing many *marginalia* of a most miscellaneous character.' The authenticity of this entry is more than doubtful. The name Squele is of the same order as Shallow, Slender, and Silence. If such a name had been actually in use in Gloucestershire, the fact could hardly have escaped notice.

Mr. Phillimore, in the article already quoted, writes : ' All who are acquainted with the glorious view from the top of Stihchcombe Hill will acknowledge that Shakespeare's allusion to " the castle " is an accurate one, even at the present day.' I have already quoted a description of the castle, which I received from a horseman on the Hill; some mute inglorious Shakespeare, for aught I know (p. 87, *n.*).

Mr. Blunt (*Dursley and its Neighbourhood*) illustrates the progress of puritanism in Dursley by extracts from the Churchwarden's Register. In 1566 there were paid ' to a man of Sadburie for xiij Sacks of Lyme to whyt lyme the church iiij^s viij^d,' and in the same year twelve more sacks were procured from the ' Lyme brener of Sadburie ' ' at xiij a sack.' The large expenditure on ' glassing ' suggests that the painted glass windows in the fine old church had been broken, and white glass ones substituted. The Rev. George Savage, Rector of Dursley from 1575 to 1602, was a man of some note. According to Mr. Blunt he was ' a member of the High Court of Commissioners, and in 1580 was appointed Commissary for his metropolitan visitation by Archbishop Whitgift.' From the large sums paid by the churchwardens for the destruction of foxes, I conclude that no inhabitant of Gloucestershire who happened to meet a fox would ' stand on quillets how to slay him.' (See *ante*, p. 178.)

NOTE VIII
THE LANGUAGE OF FALCONRY

Many traces of the hawking language, in addition to those explained and illustrated in the foregoing pages, may be found scattered through the works of Shakespeare.

(1) When Hamlet (iii. 4. 92) speaks of an ' enseamed bed ' he used a term of art. ' Ensayme of an hawke is the grece,' says the *Boke of St. Albans*.

(2) The falconer purges his hawk from this grease by what were known as castings—fur or feathers given to her together

with her food—a process to which reference is made when Isabella, huddling hawking metaphor on metaphor with impossible conveyance, says of Angelo,

> This outward-sainted deputy,
> Whose settled visage and deliberate word
> Nips youth i' the head and follies doth enmew
> As falcon doth the fowl, is yet a devil;
> His filth within being cast, he would appear
> A pond as deep as hell.

The meaning of the word-' enmew' has been already explained (p. 201).

(3) Professor Baynes, writing in an article in the *Edinburgh Review*, October, 1872, reprinted with other essays, under the title *Shakespeare Studies*, suggested that Gloucester, when he said to the Bishop of Winchester,

> I'll canvass thee in thy broad cardinal's hat,
> If thou proceed in this thy insolence,
>
> 1 *Hen. VI.* i. 3. 36,

had in his mind the mode then in use of capturing wild hawks by means of a net thrown as a canvas. He quotes from the *Mirrour for Magistrates*;

> That restless I, much like the hunted hare,
> Or as the canvist kite, doth fear the snare;

and explains the passage as expressive of Gloucester's ' determination to trap and seize the arrogant churchman if he persisted in his violent courses.' But the use of this word by Mistress Tearsheet (2 *Hen. IV.* ii. 4. 243), where she says to Falstaff, ' I'll canvass thee between a pair of sheets,' read in connection with the passage cited by Steevens from *The Cruel Brother* (1630), ' I'll sift and winnow him in an old hat,' suggests a different meaning as being at least equally probable.

(4) Mr. Dyce, in his *Glossary*, explains the expression, ' Mail'd up in shame,' applied to herself by the Duchess of Gloucester (2 *Hen. VI.* ii. 4. 31) as meaning wrapped up in shame, as a hawk is in a cloth : quoting from R. Holmes, *Academy of Armory and Blazon*, ' Mail a hawk is to wrap her up in a handkerchief or other cloth, that she may not be able to stir her wings or to struggle.' The expression ' Mail you like a hawk' occurs in Beaumont and Fletcher's *Philaster* (Act v. s. 4).

(5) Professor Baynes, in the article already quoted, notices the use of the word ' gouts' in the dagger scene in *Macbeth*.

> I see thee still,
> And on thy blade and dudgeon gouts of blood,
> Which was not so before. *Macbeth*, ii. 1. 45.

'Gout' is a technical term in falconry, applied to the little knob-like swellings or indurated drops, which (Turbervile tells us) rise up at diverse times upon the feet of hawks. It is more probable, however, that the word is here used in its original meaning.

(6) When Henry IV. thus addressed his son, he probably borrowed a phrase from the hawking language :

> God pardon thee ! yet let me wonder, Harry,
> At thy affections, which do hold a wing
> Quite from the flight of all thy ancestors.
>
> 1 *Hen. IV.* iii. 2. 29.

(7) So did Katherine in the following wit-combat :

> *Pet.* Should be ! should—buzz !
> *Kath.*　　　　　Well ta'en, and like a buzzard.
> *Pet.* O slow-winged turtle ! shall a buzzard take thee ?
>
> *Tam. of Shrew*, ii. 1. 206.

And Lear, when he exclaimed, ' O, well-flown bird ! ' (iv. 6. 32).

(8) Iago thus spoke of Roderigo :

> Thus do I ever make my fool my purse ;
> For I my own gain'd knowledge should profane,
> If I would time expend with such a snipe,
> But for my sport and profit. *Othello*, i. 3. 389.

The full significance of these words becomes apparent on reading a passage in Colonel T. Thornton's *Sporting Tour* (recently edited by Sir Herbert Maxwell), in which he gives an account of the time expended in an effort to take a single snipe, with a tercel and a falcon ; his bag, for the day, comprising twenty-two moor-game and one snipe. Iago's expression was possibly a proverbial one, expressive of expenditure of time and labour, with a disproportionate result.

(9) The phrase ' to check' signified, in falconry, the action of the hawk when she ' forsakes her proper game to fly at pies, crows, or the like, crossing her in her flight' (*Gentleman's Recreations*, N. Cox). Metaphorically, it was applied to casual, random, or intermittent action, as distinguished from a sustained and deliberate effort. Thus in the passage from *Twelfth Night*, quoted in the text (*ante*, p. 149), Olivia contrasts ' a wise man's art ' with the ' kind of wit ' displayed by the random jester, who must needs,

like the untrained hawk, 'check at every feather that comes before his eye,' instead of selecting a legitimate object of pursuit, and steadily following it to the end.

Dr. Johnson suggested 'not like the haggard,' instead of the reading of the Folio. The change is slight, and it is supported by high authority. I think, however, that the Cambridge editors have rightly excluded it from the number of necessary corrections. For the rapid change of subjects implied by the use of the word 'check' does not seem to be inconsistent with the observation of persons, moods and times, inculcated on him who would successfully play the fool.

This idea, borrowed from falconry, was present to the mind of the King when he said of Hamlet:

> If he be now return'd
> As checking at his voyage, and that he means
> No more to undertake it, I will work, him
> To an exploit now ripe in my device,
> Under the which he cannot choose but fall.
>
> *Hamlet*, iv. 7. 61.

The readings of the Quartos afford a good illustration of the treatment which such-like phrases meet with at the hands of the copyists, three of them reading 'as liking not his voyage.'

(10) The difficulty of acquiring a knowledge of the hawking language by study of even the best modern authorities is well illustrated by the following exposition of the term 'falcon-gentle,' extracted from that vast storehouse of information—usually accurate—the *Oxford Dictionary of the English Language*. 'Falcon-gentle, a name applied to the female and young of the goshawk, 1393, Gower, *Conf.* iii. 147. As a gentil-falcon soreth. 1486, *Bk. St. Albans*. There is a hawken gentill and a tercell gentell.' The reader of the foregoing pages will have learned that the falcon-gentle is the female of the peregrine, not of the goshawk (which latter does not soar, as Gower well knew), and that her male is the tercel-gentle, as set forth in the *Boke of St. Albans*.

(11) The following is the passage from Fletcher's sequel to *The Taming of the Shrew* (referred to *ante*, p. 155), in which Maria avenges her sex by taming the tamer.

> Hang these tame-hearted eyasses that no sooner
> See the lure out, and hear their husband's holla,
> But cry like kites upon 'em. The free haggard
> (Which is that woman that hath wing, and knows it
> Spirit and plume), will make a hundred checks

To shew her freedom, sail in every air,
And look out every pleasure, not regarding
Lure nor quarry till her pitch command
What she desires ; making her founder'd keeper
Be glad to fling out trains, and golden ones,
To take her down again.   (Act i. s. 2.)

This lavish display of the hawking language naturally calls forth the remark :—' You're learned, sister.' ' The Comedy,' Mr. Weber observes, is ' avowedly an imitation and continuation of Shakspeare's *Taming of a Shrew* (*sic*).' It is significant of the taste of the age that Shakespeare's comedy was acted at court (1633), before the King and Queen and ' likt,' while ' Fletcher's sequel was presented two days after and " very well likt " by the royal spectators.' Thus Mr. Weber, in his edition of Beaumont and Fletcher. According to Mr. Fleay (*Chronicle of the English Drama*) Shakespeare's play was ' not liked.'

(12) According to the strict grammatical construction of the following passage, the pronoun ' his ' is referable to the noun ' falcon ' :

This said, he shakes aloft his Roman blade,
Which, like a falcon towering in the skies,
Coucheth the fowl below with his wing's shade,
Whose crooked beak threats if he mount he dies :
So under his insulting falchion lies
    Harmless Lucretia, marking what he tells
    With trembling fear, as fowl hears falcon's bells.

                            Lucrece, 505.

I have already referred to Mr. Abbott's *Shakespearian Grammar* as evidence of the truth that Shakespeare's grammar is not our grammar. Tarquin is the idea present to the writer's mind, and all pronouns suggested by this idea are masculine. It seems therefore unnecessary to read ' her ' for ' his ' in the third line.

INDEX

OF

Words and Phrases relating to Field Sports, Horses, or Horsemanship, used by Shakespeare and explained or illustrated in the foregoing pages.

WOODCRAFT

FALCONRY

HORSES AND HORSEMANSHIP

COURSING, ANGLING, FOWLING, &c.

INDEX OF SUBJECTS